DEADWOOD'S JEWISH PIONEERS

A GOLD RUSH ODYSSEY

Deadwood's Jewish Pioneers
A Gold Rush Odyssey

Ann Haber Stanton

Design by James W. Parker

Copyright © 2019 by Ann Haber Stanton

All rights reserved under International and Pan-American Copyright Conventions

Published in the United States by Prairie Hills Publishing

Design by James W. Parker

Photographs used by permission, courtesy of:

The Adams Museum
Deadwood History, Inc.
Centennial Archives, Deadwood Public Library
Homestake Adams Research and Cultural Center
Leland Case Collection, Black Hills State University
Minnilusa Historical Association
Historic Deadwood When
Lawrence County Historical Society
Library of Congress
Who's Who in South Dakota
How to Enjoy the Black Hills.com
Rootsweb.com

Stanford Adelstein
Marc Aldrich
Al Alschuler
Jerry Bryant
Richard Dunwiddie
Faye Gitter
Charlotte Hattenbach
Esther Hattenbach
Florence Hawki
John Hirsch
Ruth Sinykin Kozberg
Rick Mills
Michael and Joyce Niederman
Steve Norquist
Etta Fay Kozberg Orkin
Charles Rambow
Sihaya Reed
Diane Sinykin Small
David Strain
Don Toms

ISBN 978-1-7333767-1-6

Library of Congress Control Number: 2019910747

FIRST EDITION

Lovingly dedicated to my dear parents, Joseph Joshua Haber and Cecelia Minkoff Haber. My Yiddishe Mama showed us the beauty of our culture; my precious father could fix anything, even a broken heart. And to my beautiful sister, Diana Haber Hirsch, who always stood by me, and is with me even now. They are all of precious memory. May their names and their memory be a blessing.

TABLE OF CONTENTS

INTRO	1
PROLOGUE	3
PART ONE—WHERE IT ALL BEGAN	**11**
WESTWARD BOUND	12
DISCOVERY	13
TREASURE HUNT	19
EARLY SETTLEMENT DAYS	23
POPULATION BOOM	25
BIRTH OF A TOWN	25
GOVERNMENT BY THE PEOPLE	30
OPEN FOR BUSINESS	33
DEVELOPMENT STARTS WITH COMMUNICATION	36
WEATHERING THE STORMS	40
RELIGION	43
ANTISEMITISM—OLD EVIL IN NEW CLOTHING	50
JEWISH NEIGHBORS	55
SOCIETY, POLITE AND OTHERWISE	56
CHINATOWN	60
GETTING FROM HERE TO THERE	61
PART TWO—LIVES AND TIMES	**71**
HARRIS FRANKLIN	**73**
CATTLE	74
DIVERSE BUSINESS INTERESTS	75
TRAVEL	78
BANKING	79
POLITICS	80
HOTEL	81
HOME	83
HEALTH	86
NATHAN FRANKLIN	**91**
YOUTH	91
AUTOMOBILES	94
AIRPLANES	95
MOTION PICTURES	96
POLITICS	97
NATHAN RETIRES FROM BANKING	99
MILDRED	102
THE FRANKLIN LEGACY	103
WERTHEIMER	**105**
JACOB AND HENRIETTA WERTHEIMER	105
M.J. (MAX) AND LOUIS WERTHEIMER	105
MERCHANTS HOTEL	105
WERTHEIMER BROTHERS STORE	108
WERTHEIMER HALL	111
RELIGION	112
POLITICS	113
HENRY WERTHEIMER	115
MISFORTUNE STRIKES	116
ENDINGS	119
GOLDBERG	**120**
FEEDING THE POPULATION	122
ADVERTISING	126
CHARITABLE, COMMERCIAL, & FRATERNAL ENDEAVORS	126
JACOB AND LENA	127
CIVIC ACTIVITIES	132
REWMAN	**134**
COMMUNICATIONS	134
ELECTRIC POWER	136
FAMILY	137
COLMAN	**139**
NATHAN, AMALIA & FAMILY	139
RABBI COLMAN	143
PUBLIC SERVICE	144
BUSINESSMAN	145
ANNE COLMAN NIEDERMAN	148
BLANCHE COLMAN	150
THERESA COLMAN	153
BAER	**156**
BUSINESSMAN	156
FAMILY	159
HORSES	160
GOVERNMENT	161
MINING	161
LEGACY	161
SCHWARZWALD	**162**
NATHAN, LOWENTHAL, SILVER, ALDRICH	162
SCHWARZWALD BUSINESSMAN	162
NATHAN AND LOWENTHAL	163
SILVER	166
PARTNERSHIPS	167
ALDRICH	168
STAR	**170**
STAR AND BULLOCK PARTNERSHIP	170
POSTMASTER	173
STAR & BULLOCK HARDWARE	178
AGRICULTURE—S&B RANCH	183
DEADWOOD FLOURING MILL	185
FIRE PREVENTION	187
GOVERNMENT	188
LEADERSHIP	189
DEVELOPMENT	194
LAW AND ORDER	195
MINING	197

- HEALTH 197
- EVENTS 200
- FRATERNITIES 201
- JUDAISM 201
- SOCIAL LIFE 202
- BULLOCK HOTEL 204
- TRAIL'S END 204

LEVINSON 208
BLOOM 211
JACOBS 213
- BLUMENTHAL, SALINSKY, AND MARGOLIN 213
- CLOTHING BUSINESS 213
- DEADWOOD TORAH 214
- BLUMENTHAL FAMILY 215
- SIDNEY JACOBS AND FAMILY 217

HATTENBACH 222
- GODFREY AND FRANCES HATTENBACH 224
- NATHAN AND DENA HATTENBACH 225
- JOSEPH AND JENNIE ROSENTHAL HATTENBACH 233
- LUDWIG AND EMMA HATTENBACH 236
- ADELIA HATTENBACH MAGEE AND DAVID MAGEE 237
- AARON AND BELLE HATTENBACH 238
- MITCHELL HATTENBACH 241
- DAVID HATTENBACH 242
- HATTENBACH LEGACY 242

FINK 244
- JOSEPH FINK 244
- WOLFF FINK 247

STROOL 250
- FOUNDING A TOWN 250
- REIZEL STEPS IN 252

BOBER 254
- INSPIRED BY A SEED 254
- ROSE STOLAR BOBER 255
- JEWISH AGRICULTURAL MOVEMENT 256
- HOMESTEADERS 258
- SEEDSMAN 259

SINYKIN AND KOZBERG 261
- HARRY DAVID SINYKIN AND ETTA FANNY KOVAL SINYKIN 261
- KOZBERG 263
- LOUIS SINYKIN 265

BAILEY COHEN MARTINSKY 267
POZNANSKY 273
- FELIX POZNANSKY 273
- JOSEPH POZNANSKY 277
- BENJAMIN POZNANSKY 279
- MARCUS (MOX) POZNANSKY 279
- JULIA POZNANSKY 280

MORRIS 282

PART THREE—WHAT REMAINS 285
- THE JEW PEDDLER TRAIL 286
- DEADWOOD'S SYNAGOGUE 289
- JEWISH CEMETERIES 289
- SYNAGOGUE OF THE HILLS 291
- WHERE DID ALL THE JEWS GO? 292
- SOME BLACK HILLS JEWISH PIONEERS 293

EPILOGUE 301
BIBLIOGRAPHY 305
- ABOUT THE AUTHOR 310

Deadwood from Mount Moriah, 1888
Photograph J. C. H. Grabill, Library of Congress

Jacob Goldberg
Photo courtesy Adams Museum

Calamity Jane/ Martha Jane Cannary
Photo courtesy Historic Deadwood When

"His name became a synonym for integrity and square dealing, and he built up an extensive business on the same lot on which he originally started."

— **John S. McClintock**

Did killer Jack McCall make his getaway through Goldberg's grocery store's back door?

Deadwood's Main Street in 1877
Photo courtesy Adams Museum

"On the 2nd of August, while setting at a gambling table in the Bell (Bella) Union saloon, in Deadwood, he (Wild Bill Hickok) was shot in the back of the head by the notorious Jack McCall, a desperado. I was in Deadwood at the time and, on hearing of the killing, made my way at once to the scene of the shooting and found that my friend had been killed by McCall. I at once started to look for the assassin and found him at Shurdy's (Shoudy's) butcher shop and grabbed a meat cleaver and made him throw up his hands; through the excitement on hearing of Bill's death, having left my weapons on the post of my bed. He was then taken to a log cabin and locked up, well secured as every one thought, but he got away and was afterwards caught at Fagan's ranch on Horse Creek, on the old Cheyenne road and was then taken to Yankton, Dak., where he was tried, sentenced and hung."

— **Life and Adventures of Calamity Jane (in her own words)**

Now you ask me, darling? Do you know how long it's been? Almost 60 years, but I still remember because it made such a big impression. What year was it? It was 1959. That I remember very clearly. What I don't remember, I can find in my notes. They're here somewhere. You know I was a journalist. I majored in Journalism at the College of the City of New York—a very good school. I got my first job after graduation working for the New York Lantern, a monthly Jewish magazine. That made your great-grandparents very proud, you know.

I was so young. I'd only been working there for six months, but maybe the editors thought I was up to a big assignment. Besides, none of the other reporters would touch this job. Mama and Papa weren't so sure this was a good idea, either.

But it was 1959, I was excited to apply this newly-minted education, and brimming with curiosity. My bosses had said, we want you to go to the Black Hills of South Dakota. There are rumors of Jewish people living out there in the middle of nowhere. In fact, a man named Nathan Franklin, supposedly from Deadwood in the Black Hills, died here in New York City at Mount Sinai Hospital about 30 years ago. He'd been some kind of a celebrity out there. It was a wild and wooly place during the Gold Rush days—and there were Jews there! All we ever hear about Deadwood is about some *umglik* (person surrounded by bad luck) named Calamity Jane, and a *gonif* (crook) named Wild Bill Hickok. Don't worry, you'll take a plane, we'll pay your expenses. There were newspapers out there from the very beginning, and they printed everything! Send us the details. Get to know the place. Find out who these people were, how they made a living, how they got their supplies, how they fit in. Did they have a synagogue or a *Torah*? Are any of them still there? Follow the newspapers and make sure you include citations. Get us background, dates, events, facts, take pictures, take notes. Just tell the unbiased truth. Even if it takes a month, bring us back a good story.

My sense of adventure was in high gear and I must tell you I could hardly wait to get started. It was late May, an exciting journey lay ahead of me, and I was packed and ready within a week. It was all arranged. As I stood in the terminal at LaGuardia Airport, surrounded by family, and buoyed by the confidence of colleagues from the New York Lantern, no-one or nothing could have stopped me from boarding that 6 a.m. Denver-bound TWA flight.

Although my bosses back at the Lantern had never asked whether I'd flown before, this was my first airplane trip. It was completely exhilarating. I loved flying over the countryside speckled with small towns, looking down at fields and rivers, marveling at the clouds, thrilled at the wonder of hurtling through the air in this big metal bird.

The bus took me from the metropolis of Denver, within sight of the front range of the Rocky Mountains, and on into Rapid City. Along the way, I chatted with the bus driver, who appeared to be well versed in western history. He filled me in on a little background, and told me we were following a route close to the old stagecoach trail. Rapid City was somewhat less of a metropolis; it was somewhere between a large town and a very small city. It had a population of about 40,000, but it appeared to have an active downtown. The most prominent building was the city's tall, half-timbered Alex Johnson Hotel, originally built in 1927 to accommodate railroad executives and wealthier travelers. Across the street from the hotel was

Duhamel's, a saddlery specializing in ranching gear. To the west, the silhouette of the Black Hills appeared through a gap in the ridge of low hills that bisected the city.

The last leg of the trip through the Hills northwest of Rapid City was inspiring. Under the expanse of clearest blue sky rose rocky cliffs, pine-covered hills and canyons, stunning vistas of verdant terrain.

It was growing late and I was happy to finally arrive at my destination. It had been a long trip, but certainly not as long, or arduous, or perilous as trips by mule, wagon, or stagecoach in the 1800s. Here I was in the northern Black Hills, in Deadwood, South Dakota, heart of the 1876 Gold Rush, famous for being infamous. If this place had once been the center of commerce, as I'd been told, compared to Rapid City, this was definitely a very small town. The people shopping and browsing along Main Street looked remarkably like shoppers and browsers anywhere, and nary a gunslinger in sight.

The Lantern had made a reservation at the Franklin Hotel, Deadwood's foremost hostel of the day. The bus let me off at the stone front steps of the Franklin where I was greeted by some old-timers relaxing in large red rocking chairs, taking in the early evening breezes on the porch. The hotel entry, surprisingly, was colonnaded, the lobby lavish with marble floors, crystal chandeliers, and richly polished woodwork. The most ornately chiseled mahogany credenza I'd ever laid eyes on occupied the length of the wall to the left. Luxury was clearly the intention here.

I'd need a convenient base from which to pursue my research, but little had I expected such splendor. However, the Adams Museum, city hall, and the public library, all essential to my assignment, were within easy walking distance. In fact, the entire town appeared to be within walking distance.

The desk clerk welcomed me warmly, offered me a guidebook and some colorful brochures, and handed me the key to my room on the third floor. He directed me to a little lift in the lobby with a folding gate for a door. The elevator operator, handsomely attired in a braided uniform and white gloves, delivered me to the third floor where a maid waited to show me to my room and help me get settled. Strangely, I noticed two tiny nail holes in the door frame, positioned on the diagonal, almost as if there had once been a mezuzah affixed to that spot on the frame. Could that be, I wondered?

The room was small and neat, the décor decidedly flowery. The bathroom, with black-and-white checked tile walls and floor, claw-foot bathtub, and sink with individual faucets labeled "hot" and "cold" reminded me of old apartments in New York. The windows overlooked Main Street, with a view of passersby and traffic up and down the hilly side streets. But, the bed beckoned, and I was ready for a nap before dinner.

Refreshed by a little rest, I bypassed the lift, choosing to glide grandly down the creaky old wooden staircase and into the elegant dining room. The curved walls wrapped in flocked green covering spoke of an opulent past. I was ushered to a table set with sparkling silverware; a candle flickered in the floral centerpiece. The menu was comparable to that of any good restaurant in New York, the wait staff courteous and helpful. Familiar melodies issued softly from a grand piano at one end of the room. A fine dinner in a first-class hotel, excellent service. Not a bad place to spend a month, I thought.

The next morning, after breakfast, I took the first of many walks down Main Street. Here was a picturesque, bustling little town, with narrow, cobblestone streets hemmed by precipitous slopes. Streets along the hillsides were dotted with neat residences, but the buildings along Main Street showed their antiquity. There were shops, small cafes and an abundance of saloons, but there were also gas stations and even a little department store. I browsed in a few shop windows, bought a newspaper, and kept an eye out for familiar names.

Deadwood was thoroughly steeped in history and legend; it was impossible to tell where legend left off and history began. Wild Bill Hickok appeared to have been shot in just about every saloon on Main St. The man was either a hero or a villain, but the story went that he'd been shot in the head on August 2, 1876, as he sat at a poker table in Saloon #10 with his back to the door. Legend had mutated into superstition: I was told that folks did not like to sit with their back to a door. They also got just a bit nervous if they happened to draw Hickok's last hand, a pair of black aces and eights, the "Dead Man's Hand." The shooter was Jack McCall, the shooting allegedly in revenge for the killing of McCall's brother, an event routinely re-enacted for tourists in the summer.

And then there was Calamity Jane, right there beside Hickok, or so it went, not just in the oddly unconvincing romantic story, but according to the guidebook, in her grave beside his in Mount Moriah Cemetery. I could easily picture her in life— buckskinned, squinty-eyed, foul-mouthed, jauntily blowing smoke off the end of her six-shooter. She was reputed to have been a hard-drinking professional scout, an Indian-fighter, a roughshod whore, as well as kind nurturer of victims of typhoid fever, in an unrequited love affair with Wild Bill. This was a tough frontierswoman with quite a strange and complex history.

I hadn't gone two blocks before I found what I'd come looking for. There before me, clearly lettered on the storefront window was a sign reading "Goldberg's Grocery"! I hurried excitedly into the dimly lit interior, approached the clerk, and asked to speak to Mr. Goldberg. She looked up from the cash register and smiled indulgently. "Jacob Goldberg has been dead for at least 60 years." It seemed absurd that a man with the clearly Jewish name of Jacob Goldberg might have been within elbow-rubbing distance of the scandalous Calamity Jane and notorious Wild Bill Hickok who once roved these streets. And that was where it all began.

Goldberg's Grocery ca 1959
Photo courtesy Deadwood History, Inc.

As I continued down Main Street, other unmistakably familiar Jewish names on storefronts and inscribed on buildings caught my eye: Levinson, Jacobs, Schwarzwald. I learned that my new home-away-from-home, the Franklin Hotel, was actually named for a man named Harris Finkelstein. There was even said to be a sanctified Jewish section called "Hebrew Hill," in the cemetery, high above the city, where Franklin was buried.

The names I was finding were almost all reflections of a bygone Jewish presence. There were a few noteworthy exceptions. Blanche Colman, daughter of Deadwood's first lay Rabbi, and likely the first Jewish child born in Deadwood, was well into her 90s. This charming, elderly font of information was also my neighbor at the Franklin Hotel. The extant Schwarzwald's furniture store was still a thriving concern with a significant line of descendants. The New York Store was still operated by the Jacobs family, and although the parents were still active in the business, their sons had moved, appropriately enough, to New York City. Levinson, a jeweler, also among the earliest of the settlers, had a son who had moved their jewelry business to Rapid City. The few Jews left were only a minute remnant of a much larger earlier population. The Jacobses told me of local family history, showed me scrapbooks and photographic treasures, and told me to go and check out the cemetery.

I was panting as I reached Historic Mount Moriah Cemetery, high on a hill overlooking Deadwood. Just as the guidebook had said, the graves of Calamity Jane and Wild Bill Hickok were center stage. I turned the corner to climb Jerusalem Avenue to the Jewish section, Mount Zion, or Hebrew Hill. At the summit I tried to imagine a horse-drawn dray bearing a coffin in a funeral procession up that steep incline. Cemetery records provided by Deadwood historian, David Akrop, told of 86 Jewish burials. Those 86 burials represented only a small part of the story...

I had to know who these mavericks were. On one of the last of the American frontiers to be explored and settled, who were these Jews who had chosen opportunity and risk over the comparative safety of the settled American city? Where did they come from? When and how did they get here? What did they do here? How long did their community last? Who were their leaders? How did they maintain their Jewish identity? What did they contribute? Did they cooperate? How did they fit into the larger community? What did they bring to the Black Hills, and what did they leave behind? There were so many questions.

I found myself in archives and libraries, and hours sped by as the research drew me ever deeper. Why weren't any of their stories in books about American Jewish history? There was a bit written in contemporary sources about Jews of the American West, but nothing beyond brief references to Sol Star, the Franklins and the Colman family. Only scraps of information could be extracted from scattered brittle old books, archives and microfilmed newspapers. Tantalizing tidbits, a thousand little trails to follow. I kept searching for names, dates, events, articles, advertisements, and photographs. Every answer led to another question, every question to another trail. Every person with a memory or an interest became a precious resource— and a new friend. Surprise after surprise unfolded as Deadwood's past, and its Jewish history in particular, came into view.

Names, many more than I'd anticipated, began to appear. There were names in the cemetery. Some names came from newspaper advertisements. Some were found in announcements of business and social associations, religious holiday observances, and funerals. Weddings were especially fruitful sources of Jewish names. Many came from visits with descendants. So far I could identify over 300 names. This was a real community, with many of the families being intertwined. Sometimes only a last name was revealed, but in some instances there was a full name. Spellings varied. Women's and children's names were rarely given, which made any accurate assessment impossible. Sometimes bits of information held erroneous and conflicting details. I would have to verify information wherever possible, but now at least there was a starting point.

Clearly, there was a serious gap in the historical record. There had to have been many the newspapers never wrote about, or for whom there was no documentation available. For the most part, articles springing from the Black Hills Daily Times and other sources also referred to many other citizens who were not Jews, but this study was specifically focusing on those who were Jewish. In order to fulfill the scope of my assignment, this report would be confined to those individuals who were identifiable as Jews without intending to deny or diminish the efforts or contributions of the many other players in this scene.

I reminded the editors of the Lantern that despite all efforts to substantiate information, some particulars would always remain in question. This was compounded by the fact that there were valuable original documents lost in the Great Fire of September of 1879 that almost destroyed Deadwood together with the Lawrence County Courthouse and all its records. Also, due to lack of standardization and gaps or errors in record-keeping, variable spellings, and dates would occasionally conflict. The classic journalistic "who, what, when, where, why, and how" questions provided a useful framework. We already knew the answer as to "why," and that was *opportunity*.

Whose stories to write about, of course, would depend on what my findings revealed. There were "hundreds of Jews," according to Blanche, but most of them were just folks living their lives, hoping to grab the gold ring like everyone else. I would have to focus on a few personalities, probably the high-fliers, those who made the newspapers most often, or maybe just those for whom the most information was available. Most of these people had left footprints on Deadwood or Lead's main streets. They had also left their mark in Spearfish and Sturgis and Rapid City. The tiny towns of Keystone and Custer and Buffalo Gap were in this picture, and there was evidence of Jewish people establishing homes and businesses, farms and ranches, in even more far-flung outposts.

As to "when," there would have to be some parameters limiting this singular moment in time. It seemed reasonable to settle on the years of most heated activity, 1876 to 1926, following the onset of the Black Hills Gold Rush, but there would inevitably be spillover. Blanche Colman, the last of Deadwood's original Jewish pioneering population, still very much alive in 1959, had a wonderful story to tell.

Then there was the question of how to present it. I would start at the palatial Franklin Hotel and let the ghosts of the past lead me down Main Street to the neighborhood called the Badlands, (not to be confused with the geographic Badlands to the east). This place, so-named for its scandalous reputation during its heyday, would lead me past some of the more notorious theaters and dens of iniquity, Chinatown, and also a few legitimate Jewish businesses. I'd cross to the opposite side of the cobblestone street where Sol Star started his hardware business, and follow Main Street to the Masonic Temple where most religious services were held. From there I would cross over to Sherman Street, and then up to Van Buren Street, where the Franklins' home stood in the Ingleside area, also known as the Presidential District. I would climb the hill leading up to the Historic Mount Moriah Cemetery, where some of those earliest Jews were buried. I already knew that those gravestones held stories.

But what of those Jews of Rapid City, and the others who'd settled in the more out-of-the-way places? I'd heard about these places, and I had to find them.

Yes, I'd found the editors of the New York Lantern a story. In fact, I found them quite a few stories. And I knew that if the stories weren't told, they would vanish into the ether.

These people had lived in such risky, challenging, fascinating times. Could we allow all these lives and their accomplishments to be forgotten?

What an adventure for a young easterner to follow this trail through western history!

At the end of the first month, I telephoned my editor; I was finding enough material for a book. Indeed, a rather hefty book. This was a bigger story than I'd bargained for. I would need another month, maybe two.

The Wide Missouri
Photo by Ann Haber Stanton

WESTWARD BOUND

Beyond the main span that bridges east and west, vistas past the Missouri River bluffs open out onto vast landscapes. Where bluff rises to meet prairie, an undulating, windswept ocean of grass punctuated by valleys of brush reaches into the western horizon. Open panoramas unfold before the voyager, shifting with the mood of season and sky, shades of green and yellow under radiant light. These are the high plains of Dakotaland.

As we cross the prairie, let your imagination take over. This is now Dakota Territory of the late 1870s and a great westward migration is taking place in the United States. You blink away the roadside signs, wipe away the fences. No muscular trucks, smoothly paved highways, or speeding automobiles; only a train of wagons in a slowly-moving, canvas-covered caravan. Now only the dull thud of plodding hooves, the evil crack of whip, the creak of wooden wagon wheels. For the next 200 miles there is little except prairie and sky. The sense of isolation is inescapable.

Idyllic landscapes of grassland roll out and away into the distance; carpets of buffalo grass, grama grass, prickly cactus. A herd of massive buffalo grazes indifferently. Disturbed now, they snort and bolt, stampeding away at breakneck speed. This land is alive. A crow shrieks at a magpie, a meadowlark calls from the tip of a yucca stalk. Prairie dog towns are everywhere—a wary little head pokes up from a burrow, sniffs the air, chatters at a neighbor, dips out of sight. You soon learn the difference between rattling wings of a grasshopper and the menacing buzz of a prairie rattlesnake. High overhead a red-tailed hawk soars in wide circles.

Every 40 miles or so you may notice a sod shack, children playing in a small farmyard, a woman milking a cow, a man on horseback. Homesteading began here in 1862. This was free land offered by the U.S. government, but the elements exact a toll. These people draw a defiant living from the soil, bulwarked by a determination to persist, humbled by a profound appreciation for the forces of nature. Here and there a dusty wagon trail or planted windbreak of scrub trees resists the blowing dust of merciless summers and drifting snow of bitter winters. The prairie wind is unrelenting. Livestock outnumber people, and tiny clusters of human settlement are separated by grass and more grass.

You have paid $75 for the privilege of traveling with this wagon train for some very sound reasons: the guide knows the way as he navigates the prairie from butte to prominent butte, and the wagon train affords some measure of protection. The wagons travel at 15 miles per day, weather and Indians permitting. You walk beside the wagon; precious space is needed in the wagon for your possessions.

Your traveling companions are a disparate group, prepared to stake their futures on some daring gamble. A family of Scandinavian homesteaders; a prospector, convinced that his fortune gleams through the icy waters of a mountain stream; a couple of Jewish merchants with their supply of dry goods. One wagon brims with young women, unfortunate souls, duped into believing that they're headed for legitimate jobs as "actresses" in Deadwood. There are civil war veterans and unemployed lawyers, con men, and doctors, each a gambler in his own right, There are as many reasons and as many possibilities as there are bodies. This undertaking will test their mettle. The only ones who anticipate easy money are those who thrive on a roll of the dice.

The wagon train lumbers slowly westward. After many days, an interminable 125 miles, it reaches terrain of stark beauty, Les Mauvais Terres, the Badlands, so-named by the French explorers for their dense impenetrability. As the wagon carefully traces sheer cliffs beside the steep Badlands wall, the unfolding scenery reveals sandstone spires and pipes, deep canyons, a striking, layered watercolor moonscape of sculpted pastel pinks and ochres, pale greens and deep reds, ever-changing with light and time. Here the earth erodes with nature's artistry, chiseled by wind and water. This was once the floor of a primeval sea, home to great reptiles, and later, as the sea subsided, to primitive mammals. Fossilized bones and shells of prehistoric life, caches long hidden, lie bleaching in the sun, telling of the land's past.

A distant dark line emerges from the western horizon. Another 50 miles or more, and a blurred contour, the silhouetted peaks and crags of the Black Hills appear.

Badlands Skyline
Photo by Ann Haber Stanton

Prized by the fur trapper, El Dorado to the prospector, sacred winter refuge to the Indians, this remote outpost now lures those with visions of adventure and prosperity. You are among this undaunted company. You happen to be Jewish, so there may be a few complications.

DISCOVERY

"Far out of the ordinary lines of plains travel, surrounded on all sides by the arid wastes of the 'Bad Lands'..., the 'Black Hills' loomed up in silent majesty, mysterious, unknown. More than 200 miles east of north of the Laramie Range, in the midst of a desert of dreary alkaline plains, rises a magnificent mass of mountains, covering a country almost as large as the State of Vermont, and closely embraced within the two principal branches of the Cheyenne River. To this country all the tribes of the great Dakota or Sioux Nation give the name Paha-sapa," which liberally interpreted, is black hill, Pa-hill, sapa-black..."

Excerpt from report of Lieut. Col. Richard L. Dodge, military commander, Jenney-Newton exploratory expedition to the Black Hills, 1875.

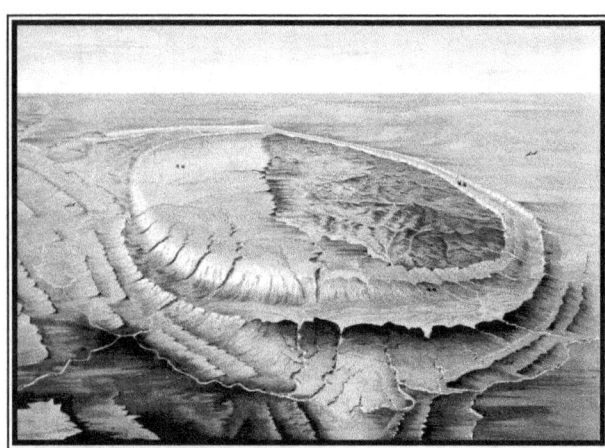

Early Geologic Map of the Black Hills
Photo courtesy Library of Congress

In 1804, reports about the Black Hills were included in the journals of Lewis and Clark on their Voyage of Discovery; however, under President Thomas Jefferson's directive, their expedition passed to the north of the Hills in its quest for the fabled Northwest Passage. Subsequent westward migrations of white men also circumvented the Black Hills, keeping to the south by following the Platte River. Except what was reported by French fur trappers, little was known of the island of mountains that emerged from the plain.

From as early as 1833, according to the much-debated Thoen Stone, it was alleged that gold could be found in the Black Hills. That stone tablet, housed at Deadwood's Adams Museum, was found at Lookout Mountain near Spearfish. Named for its finder, Louis Thoen, it bears a message describing the bleak fate of a gold-seeking party. Scratched into the surface of the stone is a sort of desperate farewell signed by Ezra Kind, and represents a bit of controversial Black Hills lore.

"Came to these Hills in 1833, 7 of us,
De LaCompt – Ezra Kind - G. W. Wood -T. Brown
-R. Kent - William King - Indian Crow - all dead
but me, Ezra Kind, killed by Indians beyond
the high hill, got our gold June 1834."

On the reverse side is inscribed:

"Got all the gold we could carry, our ponies all got by the Indians. I have lost my gun and nothing to eat, and Indians hunting me."

It is known that missionary Father Joseph DeSmet, an early Jesuit priest, was aware of gold in the Hills, but had cautioned the Indians to whom he ministered not to reveal information about the shiny metal to the white man, probably recognizing that the resulting stampede would change the Indians' way of life forever. One might wonder why he advised the Indians to keep this secret, when, in fact, he himself did finally report the presence of gold in the Black Hills when he returned to the East.

Earlier bonanzas in California and in Montana piqued interest in the prospect of gold in the streams of the Black Hills. The 1849 California Gold Rush inspired many an adventurous youth to follow Horace Greeley's advice and look to the West for his future. Overland and by ocean steamer, defying the hazards of Cape Horn, they flocked to the California gold fields. Merchants provided the necessary goods and services to the gold-seekers. Some found their fortunes in the streams and the rocks, but more often, fortunes were made by those like Levi Strauss, Jewish inventor of blue jeans, the world's most enduring pair of pants.

In the spring of 1868 a conference was held at Fort Laramie, in early-day Wyoming, which resulted in a treaty with the Sioux, in order to bring peace with the whites. In the treaty, the Sioux agreed to settle within the Black Hills reservation in Dakota Territory.

The likelihood of gold in the Black Hills was still strongly suspected, but hostility of the natives was initially a deterrent—not for all, and not for long. Gold has a strong magnetism. Ignoring the Fort Laramie Treaty, President U.S. Grant's administration decided it was time to know the facts. In 1874 Brevet General George Armstrong Custer and his Seventh Cavalry received instructions from Washington, D.C., to lead a reconnaissance southward from Fort Abraham Lincoln near Bismarck, Dakota Territory, to explore the Black Hills, in order to find a suitable location for a fort, and to verify rumors of gold. Custer mounted a grand expeditionary caravan, and an entire band of musicians under the direction of Italian-American bandmaster Felix Vinatieri accompanied their ostentatious departure from Fort Abraham Lincoln.

On July 24th, 1874, Custer's party entered the Black Hills. The party was well equipped with provisions for two months, as well as reporters and scientists. In a train of 110 wagons, there was a photographer with his own darkroom wagon, a herd of cattle for meat, experienced miners, at least one geologist, Indian scouts, ambulances, and one wagon specifically for alcoholic beverages. They brought the Seventh Cavalry to defend the flanks, and artillery for the vanguard. With Custer leading the way, there were at least 1,000 men and one indomitable freed slave, Custer's personal Black cook, a woman named Sarah Campbell, popularly known as Aunt Sally. They traveled southwest, proceeding in somewhat of a figure-of-eight pattern, circling around at the southern Black Hills.

Custer Expedition – 1874
Photo courtesy Adams Museum

While advancing into the high elevations of the central Hills, the expedition marched down Castle Creek where they found themselves in a beautiful, flower-carpeted valley. In high spirits, the soldiers fashioned garlands of wildflowers for the necks of their horses. When they reached French Creek in the vicinity of what is now the town of Custer in the southern Hills, free gold in the stream confirmed what they had hoped for. In a letter dated August 15, 1874, addressed to the Assistant Adjutant General of Dakota, Custer wrote, "There is no doubt as to the existence of various metals throughout the hills. As this subject has received the special attention of experts who accompanied the expedition, and will be reported upon in detail, I will only mention the fact that iron and plumbago have been found and beds of gypsum of apparently inexhaustible extent. I referred in a former dispatch to the discovery of gold. Subsequent examinations at numerous points confirm and strengthen the fact of the existence of gold in the Black Hills." In two months, the expedition of over 1,000 men, cattle, and horses, advancing at only 4-5 miles per day, had covered close to 900 miles, and sealed the fate of the Black Hills forever.

Although these reports seemed to play down the deposits of gold they found on French Creek and Castle Creek, the artifice fooled no-one, and instead caused considerable attention. Everyone was sure there were mineral and timber resources waiting to be exploited. In spite of the illegality of such enterprises, maverick expeditions formed, with hopes of establishing colonies and outposts in the Black Hills. The first, and one of the more diverse of the maverick civilian expeditions, was the Gordon party, named for its leader and guide, John Gordon. Originating in Sioux City, Iowa, in 1874, members of the party included everything from adventurous novices to experienced frontiersmen. Each eagerly paid Gordon $300 to outfit and lead him into the Black Hills. The lone female member, a schoolteacher named Annie Tallent, is credited with being the first white woman to enter the Black Hills.

Annie Tallent
Photo courtesy Adams Museum

According to Annie Tallent's memoir, among the array of intrepid souls in the Gordon party was a young Jew named Moses Aarons. Aarons was noted to be one of the more "cheerful and uncomplaining" of the outfit. More is known about Aarons' death than his life. Annie Tallent wrote that driven by intense thirst while crossing the parched Badlands region, Aarons drank impotable water, a fatal error. He succumbed on November 27, 1874, following a brief, painful illness. Other members of the beleaguered party were similarly afflicted, but Aarons was the only one who never made it to the Hills. A kindhearted member of the party, J.J. Williams, fashioned a wooden coffin joined with wooden pins, and the Odd Fellows burial ritual was recited. Aarons was buried in a grave overlooking the Bad River. As a final act of kindness, and possibly in an effort to ward off desecration of his resting place, the grave was marked with a cross despite his comrades' awareness that he was a Jew. No sign of Moses Aarons' grave remains, but Williams Street in Deadwood is named for the kindly Mr. Williams.

Williams Street circa 1900
Photo courtesy Adams Museum

With perseverance, making every effort to avoid discovery by either the Indians or the U.S. Army's 7th Cavalry, the Gordon Party made it into the Black Hills. In the deep winter of 1875 they built a sturdy, 80-foot-square stockade on the site of the old Custer Camp on French Creek. The army, charged with upholding the Fort Laramie Treaty with the Lakota Sioux nation by keeping unwelcome white invaders out, eventually discovered and surrounded the camp. The inhabitants were given two days in which to pack up and leave. The party agreed to the order, and gave the appearance of leaving, but when the cavalry was well out of sight, they returned to claim that for which they had come.

Gordon Stockade
Photo courtesy Centennial Archives, Deadwood Public Library

Gold fever held a stronger hook than the government could combat. Like water through a sieve, prospectors found their way into the Hills through the gullies and gulches. Some of the very soldiers sent to prevent the miners from entering, deserted and went prospecting themselves. It didn't take long before President U.S. Grant conceded to reality in the face of increasing desertions, and withdrew the Army. The government had no way of administering justice in this unruly setting, and what little there was of law and order simply disappeared.

The local newspapers of Iowa and Nebraska competed, outdoing one another with excessive claims supporting their own towns, all in rivalry for the business of outfitting expeditions headed for the Hills. The government sent out other exploratory expeditions, one of which, the Jenney-Newton expedition of 1875, was guided by California Joe Milner, and attended by one Martha "Calamity Jane" Cannary disguised as a man. The Jenney-Newton party was officially authorized as a geological exploratory party under the protection of the U.S. Army. Although it never received the publicity of the Custer exploratory expedition, in its five months in the Black Hills the Jenney-Newton expedition conducted studies of the topography, geology, botany, hydrology, soils, timber, and climate, and was highly successful in gathering scientific information. Their group named the most prominent Black Hills peaks for outstanding military leaders of the time, including Warren, Terry, Crook, Harney, and Custer. Dr. Valentine Trant McGillycuddy, the party's brilliant young surgeon and scientist, was called upon to survey the topography, and was the first white man to ascend to the top of Harney Peak, at 7,244 feet, the highest point between the Black Hills and the Pyrenees. McGillycuddy became a strong influence in early western South Dakota history. Among his many accomplishments,

McGillycuddy became mayor of Rapid City. For a time he was agent on the Pine Ridge Reservation, where he was known as a friend to the Indian. He also was a friend of Mark Twain, and noted historian, Dr. Watson Parker, recounted Mark Twain's sardonic comment regarding the white man's treatment of the Indian.

"They were good, God-fearing people and when they landed that day on Plymouth Rock from off the Mayflower, they fell upon their knees and thanked Almighty God for the many blessings He had vouchsafed them that day, in enabling them to reach a land of liberty and free thought. Later on, they fell upon the aborigines."

White infiltration of the Hills proceeded inexorably, enraging the Sioux, and setting the stage for the Great Sioux War, a series of battles and negotiations of 1876 to 1877 between the Lakota Sioux and Northern Cheyenne Indians, and the government of the United States. In June of 1876 Custer and his 7th Cavalry injudiciously attacked an Indian camp in Montana. To Custer's astonishment, he was seriously outnumbered by the Sioux, and the attack resulted in their massacre by Sitting Bull, Crazy Horse, and Gall, at the Little Big Horn, called Greasy Grass by the Indians. Emboldened by their victory over Custer, the Sioux became ever more audacious in their attacks against the invaders, fighting back against the certainty that their nomadic existence was swiftly drawing to a close.

Custer's utter defeat did nothing to prevent the whites from gradually acquiring more and more Indian land, including the gold-lined Black Hills. The government started discussions with the Sioux for cession of this section of the reservation. There was still danger from Indians at the outskirts of the Hills. The Sioux raided outposts, stole cattle and horses, and were very likely to kill those they encountered. In the smaller settlements where the whites could be overcome by large numbers, the settlers organized for self-protection.

Black Hills Daily Times, Jul 25, 1877
The news of murders committed by the Indians in our immediate vicinity of Spearfish, Yellow Creek, Crook, and Crow, call for immediate action of our people.

In 1877, a new treaty was enacted in which the U.S. government took a 50-mile-wide strip of land along the western border of Dakota Territory, plus all land west of the Cheyenne and Belle Fourche Rivers, including all of the Black Hills, from the Indians. The Sioux were to be confined within their new boundary lines of the Sioux Reservation. The government declared that any Lakota or Cheyenne not on the reservation would be considered hostile. Indian attacks began to diminish, although travel was still risky.

Black Hills Daily Times, Aug 29, 1879
Star & Bullock. Letter from Evans at Belle Fourche tells of Indians.

Meanwhile, events in American history had conspired to prepare the country for another Gold Rush. When Robert E. Lee, commanding General of the Army of Northern Virginia, surrendered to Union General Ulysses S. Grant at Appomattox Courthouse on April 9, 1865, the country's troubles were by no means over. In 1874 the United States was still recovering from the devastating experience of the Civil War. Jobs were scarce, bankruptcies all too common, crime was rampant, and the country was undergoing a serious economic depression. Widely publicized by the newspapers, there was growing demand for exploration for gold in the Black Hills among legislators. Commercial interests recognized the potential and were eager to open up the area to prospecting and expansion.

In 1875, with economic hardship, unemployment and drought plaguing the rest of the country, desperation and gold proved a strong impetus. At first Custer City on French Creek in the southern hills, site of the initial gold discovery, was the main magnet for prospectors. Later that year, a miner named John B. Pearson discovered far richer deposits in Deadwood Gulch, a narrow canyon in the northern Black Hills named for the many dead trees that lined the canyon walls. Within days of the word getting out, Custer City emptied out as the mad scramble for the richer placer fields in the northern Hills took over. J.J. Williams, among the lucky ones to have reached Deadwood at the start of the Gold Rush, was well rewarded for his beneficence toward Moses Aarons. He took $40,000 in gold from his placer claim, #22 below Discovery, from streams that converged in Deadwood—a great fortune in 1875.

TREASURE HUNT

Good luck and prosperity walked hand-in-hand in the Black Hills. Golden dreams of great nuggets and overnight riches cast the Hills into the spotlight of the mining world. Even if relatively few actually succeeded, if a person were gritty, enterprising, and hard-working, there was a chance to cash in on a bonanza. Those who prospected earliest found that free gold in placer deposits was comparatively easy mining. Prospectors nosed through every nook and cranny and stream of the Hills for placer gold. Some of the best placer grounds were found in Deadwood Gulch. Inspection of a land office map of any of the many mining districts reveals thousands of mining claims abutting one another and, unfortunately, in a few cases, overlapping. Claim-jumping was a serious problem, sometimes ending up in a miner's court, but occasionally with more immediate and disastrous results.

One unsettling story is recorded in a confusing newspaper reference in 1879 to "Murder of Jewish citizen, shot while working on his mining claim by one of four men employed by Homestake." A young Jewish man named Alex Frankenberg, an employee of the Lewis, Cohen and Johnston Company, was shot in a mining dispute at the Homestake Mill by Sam McMasters, foreman of the Homestake Mine. Frankenberg, wounded in the face by buckshot, died from his wounds. The Times referred to the victim as "a man named Cohen." Lewis, Cohen and Johnson claimed the disputed prospect hole on Homestake's new mill site, but the victim's name was Frankenberg. Thereafter, McMasters was warned to stay out of Lead and deputies were placed to guard the Homestake Mill.

Black Hills Daily Times, Jan 17, 1879

Sam McMasters, Foreman at Homestake Mill, shot a man named Cohen.

Placer mining was the original method of recovering free gold. It is also the most ancient. There are a variety of placer mining techniques. Included among these is the most familiar— panning from a stream. Here, small amounts of gravel are dipped from the stream in a special pan. By swirling the contents in stream water, washing off the lighter materials reveals "colors," that much-sought-after glitter of heavy gold flecks at the bottom. There is also the rocker, the small, portable, cradle-shaped box where gravel is added at the top and the box is rocked, again using water to wash off the lighter material and slats to grab the gold before it leaves the box. There is the sluice box, a trough with a series of riffles at the bottom; and there is also the Long Tom, a longer sluice that requires several men to operate. These are among the least destructive to the land.

One method of placer mining, however, involves heavy equipment and leaves permanent scars on the landscape. Hydraulic mining employs high-pressure streams of water to wash out large areas of gravel from streambeds. This type of gold mining utilizes a barge or raft to float machinery over the gravel, leaving small mountains of tailings alongside the streams. In the first three years alone after discovery, placer gold operations produced about 4.5 million dollars.

Real pay-dirt was struck in the spring of 1876 when some of the more determined among the prospectors explored the hard rock deposits that were believed to be the motherlode, the origin of gold found in the streams. On April 9, 1876, two Canadian brothers, Fred and Moses Manuel, whom some believe to be Jewish, and their partners, Alex Engh and Hank Harney discovered an outcropping, a "ledge", or lead (pronounced leed) of gold near what would later become the city of Lead. The lead was indeed the mother lode from which originated free gold in the streams running down Deadwood Gulch. They named their find the Homestake Mine. Little did they realize that they had actually found one of the richest mineral resources on earth. The ore deposits were actually quite low grade, but the extent of the ore body was massive! In 1877, the Manuel brothers and their partners sold their share to George Hearst, San Francisco newspaper magnate and father of William Randolph Hearst, for the bargain basement price of $70,000. The brothers collected their "home stake" and headed back home to Canada.

Fred Manuel
Photo courtesy Centennial Archives,
Deadwood Public Library

Moses Manuel
Photo courtesy Centennial Archives,
Deadwood Public Library

In October of that year Hearst arrived to take active control of the mine. The gold ore was "refractory," chemically bound to rock and difficult to extract. Hearst had an 80-stamp mill brought in by wagon from the nearest railhead at Sidney, Nebraska, to crush the rock with heavy stamps by means of gravity. The ore would then be exposed to mercury in order to release the gold chemically. Hearst listed the Homestake Mine on the New York Stock

Exchange in 1879. It would eventually produce billions of dollars and one-tenth of the world's gold. Hearst's prize would in time descend to 8,000 feet below the city of Lead and make Homestake the longest-lasting gold mine in the US. Hearst was not Jewish, but almost every businessman in the Black Hills, regardless of faith or national origin, owned a stake in the business of mining.

George Hearst, "Father of Homestake"
Courtesy Adams Museum

Black Hills Daily Times, Nov 6, 1879
Homestake Mining Company. Four fat gold bricks worth $120,000, deposited.

According to Cleophas C. O'Harra, professor of mineralogy and geology, and president of the South Dakota State School of Mines at Rapid City in 1929, in a little more than fifty years of settlement, the Black Hills produced approximately one-eighth of all the gold that was ever mined in the history of the world. Gold was so prevalent that it even turned up in building materials.

Black Hills Daily Times, Feb 24, 1888
... free gold found in Syndicate Building stone.

The Black Hills was once called the richest hundred square miles on earth. There probably was no place on earth where such a small area held such quantities of mineralized gold, silver, copper, tin, columbite-tantalite, antimony, lead, bismuth, beryl, feldspar, mica, lithium, tungsten, vanadium, iron, uranium, and industrial and decorative minerals such as limestone, sand, rose quartz, granite, talc, graphite, fireclay, Fuller's earth and coal. In an effort to stimulate development, the newspapers editorialized with confident assertions.

Rapid City Daily Journal, May 21, 1891
The tin deposits of the Black Hills are now attracting worldwide attention, and with good reason, as they give promise of being made the basis of mammoth industries in the production of this valuable and necessary metal. Several thousand claims have been taken up already, and the English and American companies will be producing and shipping the metal here before the close of the present year. At present the United States imports strictly from England $7 million in tin, and $20 million in tin plate annually, both of which items will be ultimately cut off from our list of imports by the development of our tin mines here.

Nearby Carbonate Camp was a town built almost entirely around silver. The town of Galena was built around galena, a mineral that frequently occurs with silver, cleaves smoothly into cubes, and is the main ore of the mineral lead. Gold, however, was the primary engine that drove the Black Hills economy, and the highest concentration of gold was mainly found around the community of Lead. The Homestake, Father DeSmet, Golden Reward, Gilt Edge, and hundreds of other mines were located in this vicinity.

By 1880 the major share of the rush for placer gold was over and underground hard rock mining was well established. Hearst and Homestake were raking in vast fortunes. Rampant unemployment was abroad in the rest of the country, but the mines were booming. The Black Hills was one place in the United States where a man was sure to find a job. Willing workmen, many of them immigrants from Italy, Ireland, the Slavic countries, and Scandinavia, swarmed in by the hundreds. Many settled in Lead, forming their own little ethnic neighborhoods. Despite the clear danger, difficult working conditions, heavy work, and the serious toll on health, the tide of human capital increased. Hard rock mining, challenging and hazardous as it was, was a well-paying, steady job.

Black Hills Daily Times, Dec 28, 1879
Peter Deconevich, Death, killed by belated explosion at Homestake Mine.

Black Hills Daily Times, Mar 26, 1880
Homestake Mining Company. One rope, weighing 4 tons, carried on 14 mule wagon.

Black Hills Daily Times, Jun 20, 1880
Ed Marone, Miner at Homestake injured by rock falling on hip.

Black Hills Daily Times, Sep 1, 1880
Homestake Mining Company. Lumbermen kept busy 7 days a week to supply mills.

Black Hills Daily Times, Sep 14, 1880
Homestake Mine: Rasmussin fell in mine, died from fractured skull.

Black Hills Daily Times, Nov 20, 1880
Homestake Miner Herman Veets, falls to death in mine.

Black Hills Daily Times, Nov 19, 1880
Homestake Miner O'Neal taken to hospital, hit on head by a rock.

Black Hills Daily Times, Dec 10, 1880
Homestake Miner had head badly bruised by cage in descent.

Black Hills Daily Times, Jul 1, 1884
Homestake north stope caves in. Last fall and winter the Homestake company opened a stope north of the Star hoisting works, and about 100 feet from the surface. This was done that in case the mine should fill with water in the spring, ore enough could be taken from this stope to run part of the mills. About four days ago this place commenced settling down on the timbers, and a day or two later shots were put in to break the timbers, and yesterday morning about 4 o'clock the whole business caved in, opening a hole about 100 feet deep by as many feet in width.

Homestake's Open Cut, Lead
Photo courtesy Centennial Archives, Deadwood Public Library

Black Hills Daily Times, Jan 1, 1880
Homestake Mill incorporates an 80-stamp and a 120-stamp mill.

Black Hills Daily Times, Jun 12, 1880
Mining companies of Black Hills organize under California laws.

Black Hills Daily Times, Sep 15, 1880
Homestake Mining Company Using all their water supply, digging another ditch.

Black Hills Daily Times, Nov 11, 1880

Homestake Mine, Californians own most of the water rights in hills.

Black Hills Daily Times, Dec 19, 1880

Homestake Mill, Five bricks taken from mill aggregating $160,000. Homestake Co. erecting new hoisting works on mine.

Black Hills Daily Times, Dec 28, 1880

Homestake Mining Company, Paid out 28 dividends in past year, total: $840,000.

Black Hills Daily Times, Dec 30, 1880

Homestake Mine. Will soon employ thousands instead of hundreds.

Shipments of gold bullion leaving the Hills, tempting prey to stage robbers, required some serious protection. Heavily armed guards were hired to ride with specially constructed "treasure coaches" to defend against holdups.

Guarding gold bullion en route to U.S. Mint
Photo courtesy Centennial Archives, Deadwood Public Library

Black Hills Daily Times, Mar 14, 1880

Bullion robbery represented nearly every mine here: Homestake Mine; Rhoderick Dhu Mine; Highland Mine; Golden Terra Mine; Father DeSmet Mine; Esmeralda Mine; Durango Mine; Deadwood Mine; Caledonia Mine.

Black Hills Daily Times, Apr 8, 1880

Express agent at Sidney arrested in bullion robbery.

Black Hills Daily Times Jun 4, 1880

Sat astride Homestake bullion with 2 Gatling guns.

With an annual output exceeding $3 million, by 1891 the enormous sum of $34 million had been produced in gold alone.

EARLY SETTLEMENT DAYS

Microfilmed historical newspapers, photographs, yellowed history books, and interviews, odd fragments, form an unanticipated pre-settlement picture that includes Jewish people. Before Moses Aarons, a soldier named Goldstein had served at the military station at Cheyenne River Indian agency in 1874, the year of Custer's expedition into the Black Hills. A Jewish hospital steward named Oscar Pollack was found dead among the Indians after the Wounded Knee massacre in 1890. These men met disastrous fates, and recorded documentation ascertained that they were Jews.

There were Jewish homesteaders on the prairie in the years before statehood. While Dakota was still a Territory, Jews from Eastern Europe had formed settlements, developed farms and ranches, even built towns and agricultural colonies. They fought fire and flood, insect, disease, and harsh weather. They faced the wrath of understandably irate Indians. There were Jewish cattlemen and farmers, bankers, watchmakers and innkeepers, purveyors of cigars and whiskey and confections, and suppliers of hardware, stationery, bread and boots. They were mayors and judges, firemen and miners. Those who came for the gold needed provisions of every kind. What they couldn't produce themselves had to be freighted in by wagon trains pulled by mules or oxen. These people filled gaps in all corners of society.

At the very beginning of settlement there was neither law nor law books, which made for a chaotic picture. Of the deluge who came for the golden prize, more failed than succeeded. There was also a small bit of real estate on Boot Hill for the ill-fated among them. Frontier justice was swift. But amid this untamed scene, there was a small population of Jews who settled in and participated in laying the foundations for a real civilization. They came for the commercial prospects, but along with their mercantile spirit, they helped bring a sense of durable community and stability.

The Deadwood Pioneer, one of the first and most long-lasting of Deadwood's newspapers, wrote an article on October 21, 1877, stating three reasons for discouraging the thoughtless discharge of firearms upon the city streets: First, it is placing the lives of our people in jeopardy. Second, residents would get so accustomed to the sound of gunshots they might go unwarned in case of an actual attack by Indians. And third, the money wasted on cartridges could better be used for civil and charitable causes.

These Jews straddled two worlds, the old distinguished by limits, oppression, and other languages; the new one as unfettered, freedom-loving, flag-waving Americans with the *chutzpah* (audacity) to participate in the great adventure that was the Black Hills Gold Rush.

Early structures on Main Street
Photo courtesy Adams Museum

Black Hills Daily Times, Jul 1, 1888

Proclamation from Deadwood Mayor (Sol Star); holiday garb unparalleled for Fourth of July celebrations for the metropolis of the Hills; Brett, champion hose-coupler of the world, to run with the Deadwoods.

Black Hills Daily Times, Jul 4, 1888

Sol Star. The day of days to every patriot and every lover of highest liberty — how it will be observed in the metropolis of the Hills.

Black Hills Daily Times, May 28, 1892

Sol Star, Mayor's proclamation. To commemorate the fidelity of the defenders of our country, I hereby assignate May 30th as day to pay respects to the dead.

POPULATION BOOM

As early as 1860 in the Dakotas, there had been a small settlement of Russian Jews in what is now northeastern North Dakota. In the wave of immigration that occurred during the 1870s and 1880s, most immigrants came from northern Europe, Germany, Ireland, and England, and among them were Jews. This group mainly settled in the cities of the northeastern U.S. There were also those who found their way further west, attracted by prospects of jobs, business opportunities, land, and adventure. The railroads advertised far and wide, even distributing flyers and posters in Germany and other northern European countries, hoping to attract newcomers who would establish communities at intervals along their routes. There, the steam-driven locomotives would stop to take on water. The little towns that sprouted up along the railroad tracks in Iowa and South Dakota frequently had Jewish-owned grocery or dry goods stores. In 1878 the first national Jewish census, conducted under the auspices of the Board of Delegates of American Israelites and the Union of American Hebrew Congregations, revealed that there were 230,257 Jews nationwide. The report found that at least 21,465 of these lived in 11 western states and territories. This count did not include many towns, settlements, and outposts. Furthermore, they had only primitive methods of reporting, and there may simply have been some failures to respond. The true numbers have to be considered far greater.

In 1862, the Homestead Act was passed by Congress, and signed into law by President Abraham Lincoln, encouraging western migration by providing settlers with free land. If you were a United States citizen, at least 21 years of age, all that was required was to stake a claim to a tract of this federal land, pay a filing fee of $10, and prove up on the land. "Proving up" meant residing on the homestead for at least five years, developing it by building fences and a structure, even a sod house, in which to live. You would confront the danger, overcome the isolation, hardship, toil and disease, persevere in the continuous struggle against the unforgiving elements, occupy and cultivate your lands, and perhaps, in some cases, even keep a Kosher home. By the end of the Civil War, 15,000 homestead claims had been established, and more followed in the postwar years. By 1900, homesteaders had filed 600,000 claims for 80 million acres. Needless to say, the Indian inhabitants were not pleased.

By 1880 there were pioneer Jews living throughout the far western United States, including Dakota Territory. There were well over 100 Jewish adults, many with growing families, living in and around Deadwood. According to the South Dakota State University Census Data Center at Brookings, South Dakota, the general overall population of Lawrence County had expanded to over 13,000, close to 4,000 alone in Deadwood, and about 1,500 in Lead. By comparison, Rapid City had a population of about 300, which would surprise South Dakotans of 1959, who knew Rapid City as a growing community of well over 40,000, and Deadwood with the comparatively small number of 2,000. In Gold Rush days, Terraville, Canyon City, Rochford, Carbonate, Gayville, and many other small mining settlements throughout the Hills all claimed relatively sizable populations, with schools, basic housing, shops and local newspapers.

BIRTH OF A TOWN

The main Black Hills towns were established in Lead, Deadwood, Sturgis and Rapid City, and among them were a few Jews. They set up shops and had merchandise shipped in by ox train. The numbers grew, and they built business houses and residences. The boldest brought their families, intending to turn their lawless environment into fit places to live. Deadwood and Lead had become home to a small but relatively significant Jewish population.

Deadwood sits high in a remote northern section of the Black Hills, cradled in a narrow gulch between tinder-dry, pine-covered bluffs in a rocky valley cut through by small waterways. At first Deadwood was a series of mining camps that sprang to life along Deadwood and Whitewood Creeks with names like Gold Run, Pluma, Ingleside, Cleveland, City Creek, Whoop Up, South Deadwood, North Deadwood, Chinatown, Fountain City, Elizabethtown, and Montana City. They were a chaotic, male-populated collection of tents and shanties built around mining claims, some right in the middle of the street, as photographs show. An aspiring millionaire might spend wary days and nights, firearm at the ready, protecting his precious assets against would-be claim-jumpers.

Stampede into Deadwood in 1876
Photo courtesy Adams Museum

Elizabethtown and Fountain City to the north, and Cleveland, South Deadwood, and Ingleside to the south, surrounding Deadwood City itself, did have a certain limited amount of organization, but it was lawless. With no law books, makeshift "miners' courts" comprised the earliest legal system. Just as the mining camps of California, Colorado, and Montana employed miner's meetings to provide the first crude forms of local government, so too every gold camp in the Black Hills was ruled by miner's meetings. At an initial mass miner's meeting, boundaries of a mining district were laid out and a temporary chairman and committee were appointed to draw up a code governing mining claims for the area. The code provided a procedure for locating, defining and recording claims, as well as establishing machinery for settling disputes through mass meetings or action by a special committee.

For the first 2-1/2 years after gold was discovered in the Black Hills, the area remained a part of the Great Sioux Reservation and not subject to direct control by the Territorial government in Yankton. The whole system of miner's meetings was regarded as a temporary expedient until official institutions could be organized.

By some very liberal estimates, at least one murder per day in Deadwood was committed in 1876. By far the most notorious murder trial in the Black Hills gold camps took place during the first week of August 1876. Jack McCall was set free after shooting James Butler (Wild Bill) Hickok. Public protest was reflected in a newspaper editorial wherein the Black Hills Pioneer proclaimed: "Should it ever be our misfortune to kill a man, which we pray God it may not, we would simply ask that our trial might take place in some of the mining camps of the Black Hills."

During July and August of 1876 several killings took place in the northern gulches which gave the mining camps of that region, and Deadwood in particular, the reputation of being entirely devoid of justice. On July 8, a prospector named Hinch was murdered in Gayville. His killer was tried by a miner's court, but set free after a verdict of "guilty, but not proven." Nine days later a thug named Shannon was shot to death during an argument over money. The miner's court again returned a verdict of not guilty, with the jury foreman later explaining that the "killing was done according to Hoyle, and what he says goes in that town." A short time later, one Gayville jury finally brought in a "guilty" verdict in a homicide case, although the crime was defined as assault and battery rather than murder.

Black Hills Daily Times, Aug 27, 1877
Post Office near area of shooting by stage robbers.

Black Hills Journal, May 4, 1878
Deadwood is livening up as spring opens; only three shooting cases last week, and all fatal.

Deadwood's Main St., ca. 1878
Photo courtesy Adams Museum

Ox team resting in Sturgis
Photo courtesy Adams Museum

Main Street, Deadwood's principal commercial thoroughfare, snakes down the ravine cut by Whitewood and Deadwood Creeks. Overlooking it are the residential neighborhoods of Forest Hill on the west and Ingleside on the east. Crowning the eastern slope is Historic Mount Moriah Cemetery where Wild Bill Hickok and his pal Martha Jane Cannary Burke, or Calamity Jane, rest —we can only hope— in peace.

Deadwood's Main St., ca. 1879
Photo courtesy Adams Museum

It was estimated that stampeders flooded in at the rate of 100 per day. After a brief period of being a collection of tents, the first log structure was a little cabin built in April by Paul Rewman, an English Jew, and located on the site of what would later become the first telephone building. The first frame building was erected near the log cabin and became the first grocery store, which would be owned by Jacob Goldberg. Other rudimentary structures quickly followed, providing goods and services for those with a poke (pouch) of gold dust in their pockets. Food could not come in fast enough to supply the need, and beds were rented out by the hour. Fortunately, there were those on hand with a camera and the foresight to record the tumultuous scene.

Early Deadwood
Photo courtesy Adams Museum

Early Deadwood was no-one's idea of an attractive settlement. Newly arrived entrepreneurs wasted no time in slapping up false-fronted shacks, the traditional method of making a 1-roomer appear to be a taller building. Wooden planks served as sidewalks. Deliveries of merchandise loaded onto long wagon trains pulled by pack animals streamed into the Gulch from Cheyenne, Bismarck, Sidney, and Fort Pierre. The mucky main thoroughfares could be blocked for hours by freight wagons.

Black Hills Daily Times, Jul 19, 1877
Mail has to stay in stage. Deadwood streets blocked.

One merchant received 150,000 pounds of freight in one day. The bull trains made their deliveries, turned around at upper Main Street, and headed back down Sherman Street while the bullwhackers (teamsters) cussed their unfortunate beasts in earthy language. By mid-October of 1876 the population of Deadwood was 3,000, with 173 businesses in town. While Lead was the main center of mining, space in Deadwood was at a premium. Supplies piled up on the porches of the Big Horn grocery and other stores along Main Street. Lawless, dirty, and thirsty, the prospectors were spending freely. One of the first businesses to open in any camp or town was the saloon. Gold towns like Deadwood, Central City and Lead, and silver towns like Carbonate and Galena, and some towns that never saw a population of 100, all had to have a saloon—it was simply a requirement of the times. By 1877 there were an astounding nine breweries and 258 liquor dealers in the Black Hills. In 1878 Deadwood alone supported approximately 100 liquor establishments.

The chaotic mix of weather-hardened prospectors, experienced miners and ordinary laborers, swindlers, gamblers and dance-hall girls, all attracted by the excitement and prospects, made for a turbulent atmosphere. In the midst of this roiling stewpot, the merchant Jewish pioneers carried on their lives.

There was plentiful competition between the Black Hills towns, particularly Rapid City and Deadwood, some of it tough, much of it good-natured. An amusing article published in a Rapid City newspaper takes a jab at the whiskey being served in Deadwood.

Black Hills Journal, Feb 15, 1879
"This is the way the Chicago Tribune tells it: The bar keeper hurriedly mixed some alcohol (kept for cleaning the mirror), and spirits of turpentine, and Jamaican ginger, and Perry Davis' pain killer, and when the Black Hills man said yes in reply to his question whether he'd like to some bitters in it, shook half a gill of pepper sauce into a tumbler and

pushed the bottle toward him. The Black Hiller filled a heaping tumbler full and passed it off; and when he had recovered his breath, said to the bar keeper: "young man, that's whiskey. I haven't tasted nothing like that since I left Custer City, two weeks ago today. That's real genuine liquor; kinder a cross between a circular saw and a wild cat. That takes hold quick and holds on long. Just you go to Deadwood and open a saloon with that whiskey and you might charge an ounce (of gold dust) a glass for it and the boys would not kick."

Renowned for its paucity of sanitation, Deadwood was also the butt of the occasional jibe from Rapid City's pioneer journalists.

Black Hills Journal, Feb 15, 1879

We have not yet seen the full text of the penitentiary bill; but suppose the Black Hills will not have a penitentiary of its own. Should they, however, be accorded an institution of the kind it ought to go to Deadwood—unless the reformation of the convicts should be a leading consideration, in which case Rapid City would be the most fitting selection. A due regard for sanitary conditions also is on the side of Rapid City by a large majority.

Black Hills Journal, Jul 26, 1879

A mixture of fluid quick silver and the white of an egg is said to be a dead shot on bed bugs. A house can soon be cleared of them by its use. We published this for the benefit of Deadwood; bed bugs are terrible bad there, it is said.

By April of 1876 large numbers of prospectors had drifted into the Black Hills and placer mining had begun in earnest. Along with this increase in population came wagon-loads of supplies which had to be lowered down to Deadwood's diggings, roads having not yet penetrated into Deadwood Gulch. On April 26, the town of Deadwood was platted and streets cut through the timber. The influx of population quickly exhausted the available ground and nearby gulches with a result that newcomers threatened to relocate or jump some of the more prosperous 300-foot claims already staked out.

On August 5th the Pioneer announced that local improvements had reached a value of $50,000 but noted that nearly all the buildings were log and frame structures. It deplored the miners' habit of building campfires wherever convenient and urged that steps be taken to protect the town against fire and regulate the location of streets, alleys, and sidewalks. In response to this editorial leadership, a public meeting was held favoring an organized government. A committee was appointed to draft the necessary resolutions. While the committee was engaged in its task, an incident took place which hastened the creation of a provisional government for Deadwood. A gambler, newly arrived from Cheyenne, learned that the skin affliction he brought with him into Deadwood was not poison ivy as originally diagnosed, but smallpox. Though of a mild type, the disease was contagious, and several other cases were soon reported. On August 14th, a second public meeting was held in Saloon #10 to hear the recommendations of the committee on organization and how to deal with the smallpox outbreak. The gathering resulted in the creation of a five-man "Board of Health and Street Commissioners," the first public body of any permanency and authority to exist in the gold camps of the northern Black Hills. The board was authorized to assume virtual control of Deadwood for as long as the threat of smallpox existed, and to take whatever steps necessary to put a stop to the jumping or diverting of cross streets and alleys into town lots. Assurances were given to the Board that any orders they issued would be backed up by the general populace—with firearms if need be. One member of the five-man board was Seth Bullock. With its guarantee of public support, the board was to take immediate steps to deal with the smallpox problem. A public subscription was taken to pay for the construction of a "pest house" where victims of the disease would be confined. Acquiring a satisfactory site was the first priority, but acquiring a building fund proved as difficult. One location on the outskirts of town had to be abandoned when the inhabitants, living in brush huts and rude shacks, suddenly named the area "South Deadwood" and refused to have a smallpox hospital disturb their suburban lifestyle. Another otherwise adequate site was found to be on the banks of the stream that supplied water for one of the local breweries, and all agreed that this was more than adequate reason for locating the building elsewhere.

An indication of the public stature the Board had gained can be seen in the role it played following Deadwood's second recorded homicide, which took place in late August 1876. Immediately after committing the crime, the killer surrendered voluntarily to members of the Board of Health. Trial had been arranged for the following day, with one of their number serving as sheriff to round up the necessary jury. The jury deliberated three and half hours. This unusual amount of thoughtful deliberation can be credited to the stabilizing influence the Board was exercising in the community.

The Pioneer hailed the establishment of the Board of Health and Street Commission as a step in the right direction, but argued against public apathy, which failed to see beyond the immediate problems of contagious diseases, the threat of fire, and the proper location of public thoroughfares. Charles V. Gardner, businessman and financial backer of the Pioneer, continued to press for election of a city council and justice of the peace to create and administer local ordinances.

The final public service performed by Deadwood's Board of Health and Street Commissioners took place during the first week in September, when they called a public meeting to take positive steps toward the organization of a city government. After extensive discussion it was agreed to hold a general election on September 11th to decide the question. At the same time the citizens would be given the opportunity to select the mayor (who also served as justice of the peace), a City Marshal, and six councilmen, two from each of Deadwood's three subdivisions. In this election Deadwood got its first mayor, grocer G. B. Farnum. Solomon Star, a Jewish hardware merchant, was among those elected to the post of City Councilman.

GOVERNMENT BY THE PEOPLE

Deadwood City first began to take shape in April 1876 when the town was platted with the aid of a compass and lariat. The effort was not so much to formally organize a town, but rather to gain federal recognition in order to sell town lots, the goal being legitimacy and civil autonomy.

Among its duties, the city council was to create a police force; draft fire regulations; issue licenses; lay out, improve and vacate streets and alleys; levy taxes; and impose penalties for violation of ordinances. The mayor received $100 a month, the Clerk-Treasurer $75, the Town Marshal $150 and fees, and the councilmen served without salary.

At its first meeting following organization, the council passed ordinances to meet the most pressing needs facing the community: raising revenue and the establishment of building, fire, and sanitation codes, in that order. Subsequently, they created the office of community health officer and provided for the regulation of street peddlers. The license fee for this occupation was set at $25 per quarter, an amount equaled only by that paid by bankers, express drivers, and sawmill operators. The council exhibited a definite protectionist attitude and concern for local agriculture, by exempting from fees all residents of surrounding Lawrence County who came to Deadwood to sell berries, vegetables and other produce grown in the county. They probably made an effort to encourage the improvement of menus at public eating places by means of the ordinance which permitted "all street vendors of cakes, pies, and fruits" to operate without any regulations.

Jewish citizens were active in civic affairs from the earliest days. They ran for office, joined city councils, ran for county commissioner. Sol Star helped persuade Harris Franklin, another Jew, to run for city council. Harris's main interest was always in business rather than politics, but he participated, if only briefly. In September, Jacob Wertheimer, another Jew, ran for city council. Economic, civic and social stability would be necessary if they were to secure those benefits that arose from good governance. Jewish citizens were among those needed to establish law and order, and lay down an infrastructure. One of the council's duties was to establish a means of providing for the health of the citizenry, no small task in a mining camp lacking running water, animal control, or a means of maintaining sanitation. They would join forces with other solid citizens to lay down the streets, build the bridges, provide for water, health, sanitation, power, communications, schools, a library, a jail, fire protection, and animal control for their growing towns.

Black Hills Daily Pioneer, Sep 16, 1876
Jacob Wertheimer runs for council in Deadwood 1876.

Black Hills Daily Pioneer, Oct 28, 1876
Sol Star is member of city council. Deadwood, City Council not entitled to salary.

Year by year improvements were made. Streets were surveyed and lots platted, water and sanitation were put in place, as were fire and police protection, animal control, licensing, and taxation to support local government. From the barest fundamentals to the need for territorial representation at the legislature in Yankton, there was opportunity for every able-bodied citizen to assume some role in shaping the town in its infancy.

Black Hills Daily Pioneer, Dec 22, 1878
Gottstein & Idelman, Petition signed for opening thoroughfare of Main St.

Black Hills Daily Times, Sep 11, 1879
Matthiessen and Goldberg. At no time has there been so much building.

Black Hills Daily Times, Aug 11, 1881
Franklin & Gottstein. (Ox) Train blocks sidewalk while they unload goods

In 1881 an organized system of city government was recognized when House Bill No. 59 was introduced into the 14th session of the Dakota Territory Legislative Assembly, calling for the incorporation of the six main camps into the City of Deadwood. The bill provided for the creation of the position of mayor, and Daniel McLaughlin was appointed to fill that office until the first municipal election could be held in 1882. On March 15, 1881, Mayor McLaughlin called his first meeting of the Deadwood City Council to order. For the first few years, mayoral elections were held annually, and eventually the mayoral term was extended to two years.

Black Hills Daily Times, Mar 30, 1880
Plank crossing being laid down next to Wertheimer's Dry Goods store.

Black Hills Daily Times, Aug 26, 1881
Suggested city council adopt water ordinance.

Black Hills Daily Times, Nov 15, 1881
City council to buy fire bell, open Sherman St.

Black Hills Daily Times, Jun 3, 1883
Harris Franklin, Contributions for construction of Deadwood St bridge.

Black Hills Daily Times, Feb 21, 1884
City hall, on Lee Street, is now complete. The first floor contains rooms for the Hooks and Homestake Hose Company, with parlors for each. Upstairs there is a large hall for the city council, and two private rooms in the rear end for the city justice and clerk. The upstairs is lathed and plastered, as are also the two parlors downstairs. The rooms for the apparatus are ceiled with seasoned lumber. The building, although erected in the winter time, is a creditable job for the contractors.

In 1884 Deadwood was still far from a safe or tidy town. In wet weather Main Street was a morass of churned up mud and animal excrement; in dry weather the air was filled with a choking cloud of fetid dust. In an effort to control the dust and cool the air in summer, each side of Main Street had a water ditch, and each business establishment was equipped with a basin at the end of a long pole used to sprinkle down the streets. Sister city Lead was foul with smoke from the smelters; the hills echoed with a continual din from pounding of the stamp mills ceaselessly crushing ore.

Black Hills Daily Times, Oct 22, 1885
The people's movement. Petitions or calls were circulated and numerously signed for a citizen's meeting, Re: management of county affairs — the undersigned request people to meet Oct. 22 to discuss the situation. Franklin and Baer, S. Koenigsberger, Max Fishel and Brother, M Leibmann, L Reuben, J. Hattenbach, M.J. Wertheimer, Sol Rosenthal, Sol Star, Louis Epstein.

Black Hills Daily Times, Oct 24, 1885
Lawrence County. Committee of safety meeting. Meeting of the committee of 15 held last evening. Sol Star, Ben Baer, Harris Franklin.

Black Hills Daily Times, Apr 20, 1886
City council meeting April 19. Regular meeting of council to allow bills, discuss school finances, drummer's license, railroad right of way; Forest Avenue and Main Street paving.

Black Hills Daily Times, May 26, 1886
City council authorizes contract for immediate macadamizing of Main street. Solomon Star, Harris Franklin, J. Fink, Koenigsberger brothers, D.Holzman, M. Liebmann, Max and Henriette Wertheimer, Jacob Goldberg, Ben Baer, Louis Reuben

Black Hills Daily Times, Nov 16, 1886
City council meeting discussion on embankment obstructing Main street; Van Buren street matter; appeal for increase of appropriation for purchase of new fire truck. Solomon Star, Harris Franklin, Paul Rewman.

Black Hills Daily Times, Dec 7, 1886
Deadwood City council meeting. Regular meeting of city council hears quarterly report; calaboose plans; bills reported. Solomon Star, Harris Franklin

Black Hills Daily Times, Jan 4, 1887
Lawrence County Commissioners met yesterday with new commissioners sworn into office. Harris Franklin, Ben Baer.

Black Hills Daily Times, Jan 20, 1887
Fire department, The new truck arrived at dusk last evening and without blemish so far as could be discovered. Formal presentation to the company by council will occur Saturday evening.

Black Hills Daily Times, Jan 20, 1887
Deadwood City Council, Solomon Star. Marshal Dunn distributes notice among saloons and public resorts calling attention to ordinance No. 81, prohibiting the admission of minors.

Black Hills Daily Times, Apr 20, 1887

Election proclamation. Deadwood General city election to be held first Tuesday in May. Solomon Star, Harris Franklin, Nathan Colman, Louis Reuben.

Black Hills Daily Times, Dec 5, 1889

Petition completed and forwarded to Washington for post office location in new city hall.

Even after the railroad's arrival in 1890, an event that signaled the end of both the stagecoach and the ox train, which did much to clear the air, the dusty town streets were still hard on clothing, and, of course, breathing.

Black Hills Daily Times, Aug 9, 1891

One of most noticeable needs of Deadwood is daily sprinkling of the streets. Not a lady or gentleman can appear but their clothes are more or less ruined by whirling flying dust.

When agitation for statehood began to intensify, in 1888 the Republican party adopted the statehood movement as a campaign issue, and Sol Star was sent to Pierre as the Republican representative to the territorial legislature. In 1889 the U.S. Congress passed an enabling act, and the Dakotas were separated north from south. Dakota Territory became the states of North and South Dakota on November 2, 1889. South Dakota had finally achieved statehood. Although Yankton was a strong contender, centrally located Pierre was named South Dakota's capitol.

Throughout its history, Jewish leadership was a force for stability in the region. They participated in the political and legal process, assuming leadership roles as mayors, state legislators, judges, justices of the peace, city councilmen, postmasters, county auditors, and county commissioners. Deadwood's first Jewish mayor, Sol Star, competent and popular, led a life dedicated to public service. Star served six terms, or 14 years, as mayor, in addition to acting as city councilman and as postmaster. Nathan Franklin, son of Harris Franklin, served two mayoral terms, from 1914 through 1918. Their combined service accounted for 18 of the first 50 years of Deadwood's mayoral leadership. In later years, Jewish mayors would include Art Welf, manager of the Black Hills Mercantile; Sam Margolin of the New York Store; and Abe Blumenthal, one of Deadwood's most esteemed businessmen and member of an enduring Black Hills family.

Jews were involved in trade, technology and transportation, local and state government, and social and fraternal organizations. It was not uncommon for a business enterprise that originated in Deadwood, to branch out to neighboring towns or states. Buffalo Gap, a remote, but centrally located small town to the south, was considered a potential area for commercial development.

OPEN FOR BUSINESS

At some point in Deadwood's early history, fully one-third of all downtown business establishments were either owned, operated, or occupied by Jewish merchants. While most of those businesses were related to clothing, dry goods or groceries, there were also such fundamentals as utilities, hotels and banks, and such necessities as Sol Star's Deadwood Flouring Mill. Whether the thousands of hopefuls found wealth or disappointment, they all needed provisions, goods and services. As mines sprang up throughout the Hills, Deadwood, Central City, and Lead came to be known as the "Triangle of Trade." Most of the general population, which topped over 10,000 at the height of the Gold Rush, was located around Deadwood and Lead in Lawrence County. Central City, Terraville, Whitewood, Crook City and many other mining camps scattered throughout the Hills soon had busy populations needing newspapers, groceries, hotels, banks, and the ever-present saloon. The Jews started hotels, and businesses in clothing, dry goods, groceries, furniture, hardware, stationery, tobacco, equipment, and provisions of all kinds. Liquor was no exception, and they traded in alcohol, wholesale and retail.

Black Hills Daily Times, Nov 12, 1879

Gottstein & Franklin. Wagon load after wagon load was unloaded at fireproof (warehouse).

In 1876 Deadwood, gold dust was the coin of the realm. Not yet part of the United States or subject to its regulations, the major businessmen of Deadwood met to decide on the value of their legal tender. Contracts that had been agreed upon before July 2, 1877, would be honored at the earlier-agreed-upon rate of $20 an ounce of gold dust. Transactions subsequent to that would be valued at $18 an ounce. With the advent of greenbacks and silver, the leather poke, the pouch with its currency of free-flowing gold dust, faded from the scene.

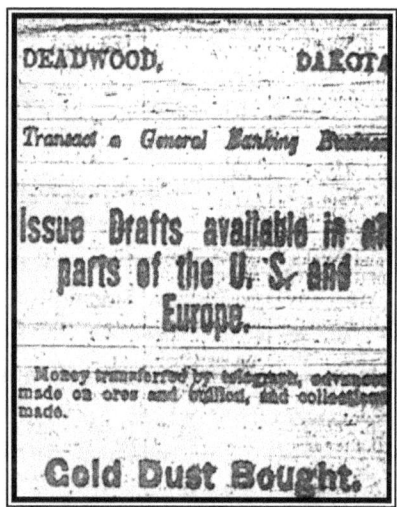

Courtesy Centennial Archives, Deadwood Public Library

Black Hills Daily Times, Jul 2, 1877

Max Fishel signs gold dust agreement.

Black Hills Champion, Jul 9, 1877

Citizens to keep value of gold at $18 per ounce.

Black Hills Daily Times, Feb 1, 1878

Gold dust currency, almost all businesses signed.

Revenue was needed to fund this newly founded city. By 1879 Deadwood's established merchants found it necessary to shield themselves against the growing number of outside peddlers and independent traveling salesmen. Fearing encroachment, taxation by way of heavy licensing fees was one means of protecting their home territory. A general licensing ordinance produced the greatest amount of grumbling in Deadwood. Lawyers and butchers demanded that their fees ($10 per quarter) be reduced, while prohibitionists argued that the saloon fee, also $10, was not high enough. The council took the frontiersmen's practical view of the situation and refused to make any changes. The saloon license, they decided, was deliberately kept at a low figure because the Black Hills were still part of the Sioux Reservation, and the liquor dealers were therefore engaged in a hazardous occupation and subject to federal arrest and expensive legal fees.

Black Hills Daily Times, Nov 25, 1879

Matthiessen and Goldberg. Patronize home institutions, don't buy from salesmen.

Black Hills Daily Times Mar 5, 1884

To the editor of the Times from Custer: The prospects for a busy spring in Custer and vicinity are growing daily more flattering. Oscar Silver, of Lead City, is now east buying a stock of clothing and dry goods, and as soon as they arrive will open up in his old stand.

Black Hills Daily Times, Jan 29, 1886

Harris Franklin returned yesterday from Buffalo Gap and Rapid. The Gap, he says, is rather quiet, notwithstanding the fact that the camp contains twenty-six saloons.

Black Hills Daily Times, Jan 22, 1887

First step for organization of Deadwood Stock Exchange taken last evening.

Black Hills Daily Times, Jan 27, 1887

Stock exchange meeting; No change on stock market; Homestake dividend, the Monitor, Iron Hill Mining Company, Hotspur Mining Company, Horseshoe Mining Company, Homestake Mining Company, Deadwood-Terra Mining Company, Father DeSmet Mining Company, Caledonia Mining Company, Monitor Mining Company, High Lode Mine, Spanish R. Mine, Monarch Mine.

Partnerships played a major role in business practices. Although partnerships could be created and dissolved, re-shaped with new partners, even engaging in several active partnerships simultaneously, the Jewish businessmen often formed business affiliations with other Jewish people. The trust engendered by their commonality also appears when one of them needs a friend to step in and mind the store for a while.

Black Hills Daily Times, Sep 15, 1882

Aaron Hattenbach in charge of Big Horn store while Goldberg gone.

Black Hills Daily Times, Jan 6, 1884

Two large wholesale liquor firms unite to form Franklin and Baer. They will occupy both buildings, but hold office in the former Franklin and Gottstein building.

Black Hills Daily Times, Oct 9, 1884

Deadwood Flouring Mill Company formed. A new organization completed by election of officers. Sol Star, Harris Franklin, Ben Baer.

Black Hills Daily Times, Sep 15, 1885

Deadwood merchants in Chadron. Chadron Journal reports Felix Poznansky in with large stock of goods to take immediate possession of new building purchased of Ben Lowenthal. Gottstein and Owens will soon be ready for business.

Rapid City businesses of Hyman Levy, Felix Poznansky, Harris Franklin and Ben Baer
Photo courtesy David Strain

To be sure, there were many notable exceptions to this, such as the enduring, if sometimes conflicted, partnership of Seth Bullock (a gentile) and Sol Star (a Jew), among the brightest constellations in Deadwood's economic firmament. Between Star's efforts in government leadership, and Bullock's effectiveness in maintaining law and order, they sought to bring Deadwood from an unruly mining camp to an orderly community.

Stock certificates still in existence testify to the mining interests of Ben Baer, Sol Star, Sam Goldberg, and others. The newspapers reported updates about the mines. Jake Goldberg, Max Wertheimer, the Hattenbach brothers, Harris Franklin and Sol Star were mentioned regularly, as were Fishel, Bloom, Reubens and Gottstein.

Some, like Nathan Colman, in addition to dealing in tobacco, coal, marble, and other goods, services, and civic affairs, were active prospectors. To whatever degree, mineral wealth was flowing, and they were using their fortunes not only to accumulate private holdings, but also to improve the region.

In 1887 Sol Star, Ben Baer, and Harris Franklin, joined with other major players in the burgeoning economy to organize a stock exchange suitable for accommodating the large number of mines in the area.

Homestake Mining Co. stock certificate of Sam M. Goldberg
Photo by Ann Haber Stanton

But financial success can breed resentment. In 1894 and 1895, disputes over wages and compensation led to labor strife in Lawrence County. A handbill, undoubtedly printed by members of a local miner's union in conflict with the South Dakota Mining Company, calls on "organized laborers and their friends" to boycott a large number of Deadwood businesses that labor leaders saw as unsympathetic to their cause.

DEVELOPMENT STARTS WITH COMMUNICATION

The first stagecoach brought U.S. mail into Deadwood on September 25, 1876, but 1876 was also a landmark year in the outside world. Across the Atlantic, Queen Victoria still ruled over the British Empire, as she would until 1901 but the United States of America was celebrating the 100th anniversary of its independence from the English crown. It was also the year that brought a flood of migration into the Black Hills, and the most advanced of modern technology was needed for the mining industry. Inventions thus far only seen in the major cities of the East were now becoming reality in faraway Deadwood. Toward the end of that momentous year, on December 2, 1876, the telegraph arrived. Deadwood, no longer isolated, was in instantaneous, if limited, contact with the outside world. On that day a crowd gathered around the telegraph office to listen to the clack of the new instrument. A celebratory bonfire was lit, and 39 salutes were fired in honor of the occasion. A grand ball was held at the Grand Central Hotel to crown the festivities, largely attended by the elite of the city. The elegantly attired guests enjoyed the event until the "wee small hours." An eventful year, indeed.

When Alexander Graham Bell invented the telephone in 1876, growth of this revolutionary technology exploded. Paul Rewman, who bore the rare distinction of being an English Jew in a community where most Jews were either German, Polish, or Russian, organized the Deadwood Telephone Company in 1878. At the beginning there were 100 connections and soon there would be a demand for 50 more lines. The modern home of Harris and Anna Franklin would be the first private residence to have a telephone. The Franklin Hotel now would be equipped with in-house telephone service.

The mines required self-sufficiency in order to operate continuously and efficiently. If a piece of equipment broke down, the operators had to be prepared to repair or replace it. Prosperity led to a demand for the newest and choicest fruits of technology of the time. Because of the treasure discovered here, within 10 years the Black Hills went from an untamed region with no development of consequence, to the most important developing area of the entire United States.

By 1882 Deadwood's streets and public buildings were lit with electric lights. Three of the four officers on the first Board of Directors of Black Hills Electric Light Co. were Jewish: Paul Rewman, Sol Star, and Harris Franklin. Prosperity grew from more than personal wealth; it also came from a commitment to making their community grow.

Black Hills Daily Times, Dec 11, 1884

The electric light was introduced at Lead City, Tuesday night, when three lamps — two in the Hearst store, and one in Martin's saloon were turned on.

In 1887 a building boom was well underway throughout the Hills, and the merchants of Lead and Deadwood were bringing in wagon trains full of merchandise for their branch stores. Deadwood was thriving and seeing real progress.

Black Hills Daily Times, Jul 28, 1887

Raising property values in Deadwood. The assessed valuation of Deadwood increased over $40,000. Sol Rosenthal, M. Liebmann, Jacob Goldberg, Abraham Hoffman, David Holzman, Sol Star, Henrietta Wertheimer.

Black Hills Daily Times, Jun 21, 1890

Black Hills Electric Light Company elects officers. Harris Franklin, Solomon Star.

Liebmann's Bazaar
Photo courtesy Centennial Archives,
Deadwood Public Library

Newspapers served a vital function by keeping the population informed of local, national and international events. The Pioneer, which claimed to be Deadwood's first newspaper, printed its first edition on June 8, 1876. The Daily Times made similar claims to the position of being first, but in time there were at least 15 newspapers throughout Gold Rush country. Even the smallest camps had their own papers from the start because newspapers were essential in order to publish legal notices, including those of mining claims. Their place in the context of Black Hills society and where they fit into the bigger picture of the world of their times was reflected in the press.

Black Hills Daily Times, Apr 4, 1879

On Monday, the seventh, the Daily Times entered upon its third volume, the first issue having been made on the seventh day of April, 1877. The Daily Times was the first daily paper published in the Black Hills and the second in the Territory. Upon beginning the second volume in April 1878, we promised our readers an enlargement of the paper which we made within two weeks after that time, by the addition in its size of fully one-third. We find ourselves in the same predicament as we were a year ago, viz: that while we had made the necessary arrangements to enlarge upon the commencement of volume 3 by fully one-third, the delay in the transportation of our material compels the postponement of our improvements which we shall have to defer until near the first of May. Upon this next enlargement the paper will be something over twice the size of the daily we published the first year ending...

Black Hills Daily Times, Oct 10, 1884

A recent number of the London World contains a letter from Mr. Henry M. Stanley upon the Nile expedition. He eloquently eulogized his General Lord Wolsley and ridiculed the absurd exaggerations which have been circulated regarding the difficulty of an expedition to the river by means of boats. Mr. Stanley says there are no obstacles in the river or on its banks which can daunt men of Wolsley's stamp.

Black Hills Daily Times, May 16, 1915

First Cargo of Freight to Pass through (Panama) Canal. Waterborne freight will begin passing through the canal at noon Monday, when five barges of miscellaneous cargo will be towed from Balboa to Cristobal. Just when the first steamer will pass through the canal Gov. Goethals was unable to say tonight.

Heirs to those pioneer newspapers, the Black Hills Pioneer and Rapid City Journal, endure to this day.

One of Deadwood's first newspaper offices
Photo Courtesy Centennial Archives,
Deadwood Public Library

While many newspapers and developers were encouraging as much immigration and development as Deadwood could hold, not all early visitors were convinced that Deadwood could ever become a success. One such opinion was expressed in florid detail in an article by Leander P. Richardson in 1877 entitled, "A Trip to the Black Hills." Clearly shocked at the scene around him, Richardson colors the picture of the Black Hills gold boom, vividly describing its character, with emphasis on its many shortcomings, and certainty of its ultimate failure.

"Buildings, known as 'ranches' abound along the lines of all the stage and freight roads in the Black Hills, forming a peculiar phase of frontier life. They are hotels, bar-rooms, and stores for general merchandise, all combined in one, and the whole business is usually transacted in a single room. In fact, but few of them can boast of more than one apartment. At any of these places, a traveler can purchase almost anything, from a glass of whisky to a four-horse team, but the former article is usually the staple of demand.

Down the side of a steep hill the road wound its way into the lower end of Deadwood Gulch. The gulch is about ten miles long, and very winding in its course. Through its bottom stretches a long line of shanties and tents, forming in all, four towns. At the lower end is Montana City, then come Elizabeth Town, Deadwood City, and Gayeville (or Gaye City). Our train finally halted in Deadwood City, and we were immediately surrounded by a crowd of miners, gamblers and other citizens, all anxious to hear from the outer world. It was Sunday afternoon, and all the miners in the surrounding neighborhoods were spending the day in town. The long street was crowded with men in every conceivable garb. Taken as a whole, I never in my life saw so many hardened and brutal-looking men together, although of course there were a few better faces among them. Every alternate house was a gambling saloon, and each of them was carrying on a brisk business. In the middle of the street a little knot of men had gathered, and were holding a prayer-meeting, which showed in sharp contrast to the bustling activity of wickedness surrounding it...

My stay in the Deadwood region was of five days' duration. The mines now in operation are all gulch, or sluice mines, although prospecting for quartz mining is constantly going on. Five or six, possibly ten, mines in the whole region pay from $200 to $2,000 per day. The largest amount I saw taken from any one excavation in a single day was $1,085, which was the result of the work of seven men employed by the owner. The average Deadwood gulch mine will just about pay "grub," and those that pay good living wages are rare. Seven out of every ten men in the whole region have no money and no means of getting any. The Deadwood ground is all taken up, and men do not dare to go out prospecting away from the main body, on account of the Indians. Summed up briefly, the condition of mining affairs is this: placer mines all taken up; quartz mines the only resource left. In order to work these, capital, machinery and mills for the crushing of ore must be introduced. Men of wealth will hesitate about sending capital into a country so far from a railroad communication, and about which so little is definitely known. Most of the men now in the Black Hills are laboring men, inexperienced as miners. Their chances for employment in the mines, then, are small, and their prospects in quartz mining are even poorer. The mineral riches of the Black Hills cannot be developed for fully twenty-five years to come. So far no great success has followed the best efforts; what future work will bring forth is a matter of uncertainty, of course, but there seems little reason for prophesying anything remarkable.

Farming there is out of the question. Throughout a great part of the district heavy frosts begin in September; snow-storms did not cease last spring until the eleventh day of June. Every farmer will see that a country where winter reigns from September to June cannot support its inhabitants upon its agricultural products. It follows, then, that the necessaries of life must always be imported at immense cost. There is to be considered the collateral fact that during a greater part of this long season of ice and snow, placer-miners cannot work. Can a man earn enough money in two months of labor to subsist with profit through ten months of idleness? It is asserted by miners and engineers, grown gray in experience, that a region where mining cannot be carried on at least seven months out of every twelve, can never be of any permanent value to its operators.

I have no hesitation in saying that I think the Black Hills will eventually prove a failure. The trip thence would be a severe trial for most men, even if the danger of being murdered were removed. At present the journey is exceedingly dangerous, and if by good fortune the gold-hunter succeeds in surviving his hardships and getting through alive, his chances for success are few and his expenses necessarily will be large."

Two years later, with a distinctly contrasting outlook, the Daily Times registered its own unflinchingly positive opinion.

Black Hills Daily Times, Mar 8, 1879

HOW WE'RE BOOMING: The Black Hills are not only growing richer every day with new development of mineral, but their material wealth is being greatly augmented by the almost daily introduction of trainloads of machinery. The several routes leading into the metropolis, it is said, are lined with wagons heavily freighted with boilers, engines, stamps, rock crushers, and so forth. In addition to this permanent source of wealth, we would add that the character of the immigration is vastly different from that which over-ran the country two years ago. Instead of being composed of poverty-stricken tramps... it is made up of millionaires and well-to-do businessmen who bring the requisite means for the development of the rich mineral leads hidden in the mountains, and for the cultivation of our extensive agricultural valleys. The present outlook for this country could not be better, even could we fix it with a wish.

Black Hills Daily Times, Aug 14, 1884

Medora Cow Boy writer compliments Deadwood. A.T.Packard, Medora Cow Boy, writes of his recent Black Hills trip, complimenting Deadwood: From the narrowness of the gulch, Deadwood can never become a beautiful city, but it would be a monument to the ability of any person; Deadwood now contains about 4,000 inhabitants.

Black Hills Daily Times, Apr 4, 1890

Real estate filed for record; market is booming.

Black Hills Daily Times, Jul 20, 1890

A very metropolitan appearance. Mayor Star received from the east, shields, batons and lanterns for the police force.

By the late 1800s and early 1900s, Lawrence County, particularly the area around Deadwood and Lead, had become the richest and most populous region of South Dakota. Mineral and timber resources were producing riches... for the lucky few. Despite the risks and setbacks, by 1903 some of those pioneers who had started in cabins and shacks, now had handsome residences in Forest Hills and Ingleside, and were among the most prominent businessmen of their various communities. The Deadwood Business Club, ever the city's main advocate, published a pamphlet describing Deadwood as a "city of comfortable homes, cultured people, refined society- a business city that has a population of 7,000 souls – that has two national and one state bank – the finest hotel in all the northwest – elegant stores occupying large handsome business blocks of brick and stone – a fine water and sewer system, and with complete fire protection – electric light and gas works – seven churches thoroughly supported – the best public schools in the west – a $60,000 Masonic Temple – two daily and three weekly newspapers, machine shops, foundries and carriage works – a $50,000 City Hall. The United States government is erecting a $200,000 federal building – it is the termini of two great railways, the Burlington and the Northwestern, of four narrow-gauge systems – has an electric interurban line, and in its gold reduction works has a smelter, a stamp and amalgamation works, and several large cyanide plants, as well as a complete ore testing and sampling works, and U.S. government assay office."

WEATHERING THE STORMS

The state of medicine was primitive and abysmal. No-one was safe when epidemic struck. Disease could spread like wildfire and was especially hard on young families. It was not uncommon to lose several family members during a single epidemic. They died much too young, and much too often. The Colmans lost four of their seven children to childhood diseases. The large number of tiny burials in Mount Moriah Cemetery, and all Black Hills cemeteries, speaks to the ravages of typhoid, scarlet fever, measles, diphtheria and other scourges.

All pioneers face similar challenges as they literally build their livelihoods and their communities from the ground up. What you toiled so hard to create today could be gone tomorrow. In Deadwood, safety was a daily issue, fire and flood were commonplace. As fire denuded the hillsides of vegetation, the ground, unable to absorb the run-off of spring rains, became the vehicle for devastating floods. The fire threat was compounded by the natural backdrop of narrow, heavily timbered hillsides flanking normally dry, windswept gulches, a veritable funnel of tinder ready to ignite. Wildfire could be ignited by lightning or an incompletely doused campfire, and spread swiftly with the wind. Standing dead pine timber, dry grass and brush were the ideal fuel. In an age when most structures were built of wood and lit with oil lamps, when explosives and flammables were stored in wooden buildings, and heating and cooking were accomplished with wood stoves, protection against fire was acutely important.

Black Hills Daily Times, Nov 29, 1878
Fire from overturned Student lamp

Black Hills Daily Times, Dec 7, 1878
Gottstein & Idelman, Businessmen signing petition for 2 night watchmen for fire protection.

Black Hills Daily Times, Sep 12, 1879
Gottstein & Franklin. Merchants that have contributed to fire fund, $50.

Deadwood's most disastrous fires occurred in 1879 and 1881, but the Great Fire of September 26, 1879, went down in history as the most catastrophic of all. This fire started in Mrs. Ellsner's Empire Bakery on Sherman Street, and spread to a nearby hardware store where it blew up eight kegs of gunpowder. The resultant explosion and conflagration involved the entire town, destroying 300 buildings in a 1/2- x 1/4-mile area, leaving 2,000 people homeless and causing property losses estimated at $3 million, an enormous amount in 1879. The Deadwood business district was decimated. Some historians mark this as the beginning of the end of the early Gold Rush.

Black Hills Daily Times, Sep 30, 1879
Marking Sept 26, 1879, the Great Fire, a day to remember.

Before the Great Fire of 1879
Photo courtesy Centennial Archives,
Deadwood Public Library

After the Great Fire
Photo courtesy Centennial Archives,
Deadwood Public Library

Yom Kippur is a day on which Jews take stock of their souls, repent for the past year's transgressions, and are reminded of the fragility of human existence. How very close to obliteration by inferno they must have felt on that fateful day in September when most of Deadwood Gulch was consumed in flames. That Deadwood's Great Fire of Sept. 27th, 1879, occurred one day after Yom Kippur, the holiest day of the Jewish calendar, must have exacted an enormous emotional toll on the Jewish community.

Undaunted, Deadwood literally rose to the challenge. Sifting gold dust from the ashes of bank vaults, within six months, Deadwood became a new city of fireproof warehouses and brick Victorian buildings. Each successive rebuilding in brick and stone added another level of security, quality, and protection. Indeed, the brick buildings themselves were called "fireproofs," and fireproof safes and vaults became more prevalent in the attempt to protect valuables. Likewise, the people who built them had become a little stronger and more resilient. One building that rose from the ashes was named the Phoenix Building, in later years occupied by the Jacobs family's New York Store. The Phoenix building, especially valued for having withstood the flames, still stands in tribute to man's persistence. Fire, always the nemesis, also decreed that Deadwood would remain in a continual state of renewal.

The populace did everything within its power to protect life and property from the fire and flood cycle. Each immediate loss was a personal disaster, but with the exception of human injuries, the net long-term effect was a benefit. The city council took what measures it could, passing ordinances to minimize the potential for blazes.

Black Hills Daily Times, Jul 22, 1884
City council under Mayor Star met last evening. Ordinance passed limiting the quantity of coal fuel oil to be stored in the city limits.

Deadwood was not alone in this test.

Black Hills Daily Times, Oct 12, 1886
Spearfish in ashes. One of the principal business blocks of Spearfish burned; 10 business houses and contents, including the hotel, destroyed; as many more buildings damaged to a greater or less extent involving a loss of $70,000. Zoellner Brothers, M.J. Wertheimer, Sol Bloom

Black Hills Daily Times, Apr 27, 1888
The Black Hills has another Phoenix in Central City; the shovel, saw and hammer in the work of transformation; plucky men undismayed by their misfortune; fireproofs survive. Barney Franklin, David Lowenthal, David Goldbloom, Harris Franklin

Black Hills Daily Times, Dec 27, 1892
Two blocks of buildings and several stocks of goods destroyed by fire at Custer.

Most of Deadwood's business and civic leaders had some degree of involvement with the fire hose companies. The citizens held balls, competitions, and other fundraisers to support the hose companies, which continually sought donations to maintain and improve their equipment. Volunteer fire companies became an important part of the social life of the community.

Black Hills Daily Times, May 19, 1886
Red-letter day for South Deadwood Hose. Pomp and circumstance laud arrival of new hose cart. Herman Bischoff thanks Deadwood band for their services.

Black Hills Daily Times, Apr 30, 1890
South Deadwood Hose Elects Officers. South Deadwood hose company elected Nathan Colman foreman.

Fires that left the hillsides bare made them vulnerable to flooding. The bare hillsides were defenseless against subsequent mid-winter snow melts and spring rains. Flooding was the next danger. A major flood in the spring of 1883 resulted in losses equal to some of the fires.

Black Hills Daily Times, May 18, 1883
Found "female seminary" turned 1/4 around & floating.

Black Hills Daily Times, May 20, 1883
Statement of losses by Deadwood citizens from flood.

Black Hills Daily Times, Jun 7, 1890
Flood aftermath. Whitewood creek. Rapid subsidence of water, extent of damage.

After the flood of 1883
Photo courtesy Centennial Archives,
Deadwood Public Library

Black Hills Daily Times May 18, 1883
Harris Franklin, Stable arose and sailed away upon the floodwaters

Black Hills Daily Times Nov 2, 1883
Nobles, the toll road man, owns the ground from Kiemer Hall up the gulch to a point above Pine Street. He has a man at work who has turned in the pulp from Deadwood Gulch, and will soon have the entire ground filled up to a grade. It is a cheap and effective manner of repairing the damage occasioned by the flood last May.

Black Hills Daily Times, Mar 25, 1886
Mayor Star met with Supt. Grier, Homestake, and secured a promise to restore water main from John Farley and Co. to the former site of Joseph Fink's pawn shop, washed out by the flood.

The populace learned to cope, and Deadwood was forced to continually reinvent itself while trying to maintain a positive spirit.

RELIGION

This heart of the Black Hills Gold Rush marked its place in South Dakota history as having an organized Jewish congregation before statehood was granted in 1889. Like all nascent Jewish communities, one of their first acts was to organize the Hebrew Benevolent Society in 1879, responsible for purchasing cemetery land and for preparing the deceased for burial. In time they had a Torah and the benefit of skilled lay rabbinical leadership.

Newspaper articles reported of *b'rit milahs* (circumcisions). Felix Poznansky, who started a clothing business in Deadwood and later established himself and his family in Rapid City, was referred to as "Rabbi" in the newspapers. As the Black Hills' only *mohel,* Felix traveled from Rapid City when called upon to perform the infrequent but religiously necessary ritual circumcision, sometimes of more than one child at a time.

Black Hills Daily Times, Aug 19, 1888
Felix Poznansky of Rapid is in the city and today will celebrate the Jewish rite of circumcision on the infants of Nathan Colman, Wolff Fink and Barney Franklin.

Black Hills Daily Times, Feb 9, 1892
Felix Poznansky, rabbi, was in Lead and circumcised the infant son of Mr. and Mrs. Joe Chamison.

There were announcements of business closings for the High Holidays, the more observant among the proprietors posting notices on the doors of their shops informing customers of these annual events.

Necessity dictated early on that Deadwood establish a burial ground. In 1877 the hillside in Whitewood Gulch was selected as the location for a "Boot Hill," the first cemetery. An area of Ingleside became the temporary resting place for such notables as Wild Bill Hickok and Preacher Henry Weston Smith. Soon, the newly formed Lawrence County Board of Commissioners determined that Deadwood should find a more stable location, one less likely to be developed. In 1878 a site higher up the hill was selected, an access road built, and a plateau cleared. In 1879 the Ingleside graves were exhumed and relocated, and the cemetery was moved to its present location and named Mount Moriah Cemetery.

The Jewish community organized a Jewish burial society, a *Chevreh Kaddishe* (holy society), charged with performing the required functions of Jewish burial ritual. The *Chevreh* prepares the body of the deceased and oversees the burial in accordance with Jewish custom. In April of 1879 the Hebrew Benevolent Society, Deadwood's *Chevreh Kaddishe*, was organized under the leadership of a small group of devout Jewish men. Judge Ed Whitehead was elected president and Nathan Colman was elected secretary.

Black Hills Daily Times, Apr 11, 1879
"NOTICE TO ISRAELITES: there will be a meeting at Munter and Lilienthal's store on Sunday at 3 PM for the purpose of organizing a Benevolent society. All are cordially invited to attend.

Black Hills Daily Times, Apr 16, 1879
Officers elected to Hebrew Benevolent Society

Black Hills Daily Times, Jul 14, 1883
Mrs Cohen, Remains temporarily interred in Jewish cemetery

In August of 1896 a section of land was formally purchased by the Hebrew Cemetery Association, the first organized group to purchase burial ground. It was formally consecrated and named Mount Zion. The road leading up to the Jewish section was named Jerusalem Avenue. The Mount Zion section holds at least 20 gravestones dating back to before 1896. One of the earliest graves, sadly enough, includes the burial site of the infant son, first child of the Holzmans, the first Jewish couple to have been married in Deadwood. The Jews of Lead who wished to be buried in a Jewish cemetery were buried in Mount Moriah's section 4, the Mount Zion section. Cemetery records indicate 86 burials; however, the small number of burials does not reflect the true size of the area's Jewish population, which according to Blanche Colman, numbered in the "hundreds."

The earliest newspaper notices of Jewish holiday observances appear in the Black Hills Daily Times in September of 1877. Life in Deadwood and Lead was anything but dull, and much of what happened was written up in the newspapers. There were the everyday holdups and shootings, but there also were weddings and grand balls and glittering receptions, and many firsts. For the Jewish population, there were special life-cycle events and holidays to observe. Hills towns joined Deadwood for worship services, holidays, and other occasions.

Black Hills Daily Times, Sep 6, 1877
Jewish New Year, Rosh Hashonah, will be celebrated. Munter and Lilienthal will close for Jewish holy day.

Black Hills Daily Times, Sep 25, 1878
Services of Hebrew New Year will commence Thursday.

Black Hills Daily Times, Oct 6, 1878
Atonement, Jewish holiday celebrated by Hebrews.

Black Hills Daily Times, Sep 17, 1879
Jewish New Year starts this evening.

Black Hills Daily Times, Sep 16, 1880

All believers met for prayer, end of Yom Kippur.

Black Hills Daily Times, Apr 14, 1881

Feast of the Passover has commenced.

Black Hills Daily Times, Sep 13, 1882

Celebration of 5643 New Years Day, Rosh Hashonah.

Black Hills Daily Times, Oct 3, 1883

Devout Jews celebrating Jewish New Year.

Black Hills Daily Times, Sep 9, 1885

The Jewish New Year commences tomorrow at 6 PM. Lowenthal Brothers and others of upper camps will close their stores at above time.

Black Hills Daily Times, Oct 1, 1886

Jewish New Year terminated at sundown today. This season was only partially observed in Deadwood, no divine service being held, and few mercantile houses closing.

Black Hills Daily Times, Sep 20, 1887

Yesterday being the Jewish New Year, all the Jews of our Belt cities celebrated the day appropriately.

Lead Evening Call, Oct 8, 1894

"Wednesday is the Jewish holiday known as Yom Kippur or the day of atonement. It is the most important of all Hebrew holidays, as they abstain from food and drink for 24 hours, fasting from sundown on Tuesday evening to sundown Wednesday evening. The business houses of Wolff Fink; Oscar Silver; Cohen, Gumbiner & Company; and M. Jacobs will be closed during this time."

Jews were observant to varying degrees, more or less liberal or strict in their adherence to religious rules and rites, but here their "one roof" had to accommodate all degrees of Jewish observance. Despite the fact that they held organized services almost from the start, Deadwood's Jewish community never built a permanent synagogue structure. Occasionally, services were held at City Hall, Elks Hall, or at a private residence. Seders could be held at the Franklin Hotel, but the Masonic Temple was of ample size to accommodate the larger numbers of High Holy Days worshippers or it could readily be scaled back for weekly Sabbath services. Why they never built a synagogue is open for speculation. The Masonic Temple probably provided a comfortable setting in which to hold services since so many of the Jews were Freemasons, and the tenets of Masonry were in accord with those of Judaism. This was not an uncommon practice in small towns throughout the country. Sol Star, who achieved the rank of Grand Master both in Helena, Montana, and in Deadwood, was no doubt most at ease with services at the Masonic Lodge.

Black Hills Daily Times, Sep 30, 1881

Devout to hold Yom Kippur services at Masonic Hall.

Black Hills Daily Times, Sep 14, 1882

Owing to absence of place to worship, Jews meet at Masonic Temple.

Deadwood primarily drew from its own pool of talent for rabbinical leadership. Nathan Colman, the scholarly and well-regarded lay Rabbi, held this position throughout his years in Deadwood. Called Judge Colman, a title warranted by his longtime position as Justice of the Peace, Colman presided over most religious services, funerals and weddings for 30 years. His untimely death at the age of 56 left the community with a void.

Sidney B. Jacobs, also learned in Hebrew liturgy, followed Judge Colman in assuming the position of lay Rabbi in 1906. In later years the Jewish community occasionally invited visiting clergy to lead High Holidays services or cantors to sing the liturgy.

Although much of the meaning of certain Jewish practices was misunderstood by the press, the newspapers valiantly attempted to report on these occasions, even when news was scarce. Jewish holidays were interpreted by the newspapers in relatable terms. Such innocent blunders as construing the High Holidays as the "Jewish Christmas", and Passover as the "Jewish Easter," were common. Nevertheless, the Vienna Bakery on Lee Street was said to produce "the best mazzos" for the Passover holiday.

Black Hills Daily Times, Sep 5, 1880
Jewish church meeting at Masonic Hall, Wall and Main.

Black Hills Daily Times, Sep 7, 1880
Rosh Hashonah, dear to Jews as Christmas is to Christians.

Black Hills Daily Times, Sep 28, 1887
Today is Jewish Christmas, and all the Jews of our Belt cities will fast and enjoy themselves. Yom Kippur, that means today until sundown, the Hebrew Day of Atonement, the anniversary of the day on which Moses handed down the law to his people on Mt. Zion.

Black Hills Daily Times, March 27, 1888
Yesterday was the first of the Jewish Easter, and was celebrated by several families on the Belt.

Certainly there were those who could read Hebrew, including Sol Star, who read the Hebrew prayers at the funeral of Anna Franklin, and M.J. Wertheimer, who could translate Yiddish written in Hebrew characters. While schooled in Hebrew, the Russian-Polish Jews were also comfortable with vernacular Yiddish, which was not necessarily the case with the German Jews, although Sol Star, a German Jew, was a Yiddish-speaker.

Black Hills Daily Times, Jun 28, 1882
Mike Gottstein, Letter from father in Russia, in Hebraic character. Jacob Wertheimer translated Gottstein's letter in Hebrew language.

Black Hills Daily Times, Jul 28, 1885
Mayor Star passes Sabbath in town.

Because most of them were merchants and had businesses in Deadwood, many of the Jews of the northern Hills made their homes in Deadwood. There were some Jewish homes and businesses in Central City, such as that of Barney Franklin, and in Lead, such as Oscar Silver's. The merchants' homes were most conveniently located near their business places, with some, such as the Blumenthals, Jacobses and the Goldbergs located on the hillsides of Forest Hill and those of the Franklins and Sol Star located in Ingleside, within a short ride or walking distance of the Masonic Temple, the main place of congregation.

Lead Daily Call, Oct 19, 1906
This evening at sundown the Jewish New Year begins and will be celebrated until sundown tomorrow evening by all of the orthodox faith. This is time for

rejoicing, of pleasantry and good fellowship. This is in the Jewish calendar, the year 5667.

Lead Daily Call, Oct 21, 1906

At sundown last evening the Jewish New Year ended. During the day there were gatherings of a social nature and in the afternoon services conducted by I. Shane were attended by all of the orthodox. Contrary to general belief, the day was not one of fasting, but rather in the nature of a feast. It ushered in the ten days' penitential period which an old belief allows Jews to atone for their sins.

Lead Daily Call, Oct 28, 1906

At sundown this evening the Jewish feast of Yom Kippur or Day of Atonement commences and most of the Jewish stores in the city will close that hour and remain closed until the same hour tomorrow when the feast is over.

When neither Nathan Colman nor Sidney Jacobs was able to conduct services, at various times local men were asked to fill in for them. Occasionally a visiting rabbi would conduct High Holidays services. In 1915, a Rabbi Cohen from Lincoln, Nebraska, was brought to Deadwood.

Lead Daily Call, Sep 9, 1915

Jewish New Year. Will be observed Wednesday evening and Thursday this week. The Jewish new year, being the year 5676 in the Hebrew calendar, commences Wednesday evening, September 8, and will be observed that evening and the following day. This festival is the oldest of all festivals celebrated in the civilized world, and is unique for its significance as well as for its antiquity. This day is placed, by a tradition, at the beginning of August, when men enter upon their enterprises and obligations with zest and zeal, when they are thought to be in need of a right interpretation of life and a true measure of its value. It is a time for serious thought on the meaning of life and its function is to establish a moral judgment in life and experience. The orthodox Jews observe two days with religious rites, but among the reformed one day is observed. The Lead and Deadwood congregations will have services in the Masonic temple in Deadwood, Wednesday evening, commencing at 7:00, and also on the following day. These services will be conducted both in Hebrew and in English. On the 16th of the present month, Yom Kippur, the Day of Atonement, will be observed. This is the most holy day in the Hebrew calendar and all Jews, orthodox and reformed, close their places of business and devote the entire date to solemn services. Inasmuch as there is no rabbi in either Lead or Deadwood, Rabbi Cohen has arrived from Lincoln for the purpose of conducting the Hebrew Services here.

Lead Daily Call, Sep 16, 1915

Jews to observe Saturday. Regarded as the most sacred date in their religion. From Friday evening at 6:00 PM to Saturday evening at the same time, the Jewish people of Lead will observe the most sacred day in their religion, the Jewish Day of Atonement. During the 24 hours, it is the custom for adults, and the younger folks who have reached the age of 13 years, to abstain from all food and drink. Should such a day fall during the week, children are absent from the schools and all elders refrain from all manner of work, devoting the time to prayer and penitence. In Lead a number of men employed in the mines will observe the day, and places of business conducted by Mrs. L.D. Jacobs, Wolff Fink, Jake Kozberg, I.J. Krainson, and J.J. Levinson, will be closed during the prescribed period.

There were glowing descriptions of Jewish weddings. The first Jewish wedding in Deadwood was a splendid affair. The ceremony was presided over by Louis Reubens, father of the bride, and legally sanctioned by Justice of the Peace, Judge Nathan Colman. In a practice which might be considered indelicate by contemporary standards, gifts and their bestowers were noted in the article. The announcement does help color the otherwise black-and-white picture of frontier life among the Deadwood Jewish merchant class. The guest list reads like a Who's Who of the Black Hills's most prominent citizens.

The First Hebrew Wedding in the Hills
Black Hills Daily Times November 4, 1879

The first Hebrew marriage ever celebrated in the Black Hills occurred in Deadwood Sunday evening [November 2, 1879], and in addition to this important historical fact it was one of the most prominent social events since the settlement of the country. Upon the occasion referred to, Mr. David Holzman, one of our business clothing dealers, and Miss Rebecca Reubens, the beautiful and accomplished daughter of Mr. Louis Reubens were joined in the holy bonds of wedlock. The interesting ceremony took place at the residence of the bride's parents in Ingleside in the presence of at least sixty ladies and gentlemen of our best Hebrew society and of other nationalities. At 5 o'clock the bride and groom entered the parlor, looking a little timid but happy as a garden of roses in June, when the Hebrew marriage ceremony was performed by the bride's father, which was subsequently sanctioned, or legalized according to our laws, by Judge Coleman, after which the newly married couple adjourned to the banquet room and received the congratulations of the assembled guests. The festivities continued until about 1 o'clock yesterday morning, at which time the joyous company began to disperse and before the dial band marked another hour of the couple's wedded life all were gone, leaving them to peaceful slumbers and blissful dreams. The presents presented to the bride and groom were altogether the most elegant bridal gifts ever seen in the Hills. They were as follows:

Mr. and Mrs. Ed Whitehead, a large silver water pitcher and fruit boat; Jacob Behrman, an elegant silver cake basket and spoon holder; J. Goldberg, a handsome silver jewel case; J.A. Schiller, a large and handsome silver water pitcher and goblet; P. Cohn, silver butter dish and knife; Leo Rosenthal, silver mounted glass pickle dish and fork; Wm. Munter, a large silver caster; Louis Epstein, a jewel box mounted with a cut glass cologne bottle; Moses Liverman, a beautiful rosewood jewel box; Jake Wertheimer, large table lamp; Mr. and Mrs. G.M. Gillette, a neat little clock; Wm. Brown, silver spoons and case; Ed Cohn, silver caster; Joseph Mitchell, two beautiful silver goblets; Mr. and Mrs. C.H. McKinnis, a handsome perfumery bottle; Ben Baer, a pair of very nice cut glass in a silver frame for pickles, etc.; Mr. and Mrs. Judge Colman, a silver call bell; Mr. and Mrs. O.P. Grantz, an elegant silver cake basket; Mr. and Mrs. Seth Bullock, a full set of silver knives and forks and case; Mr. and Mrs. Goldbloom, silver card receiver; M.J. Wertheimer, napkin rings and case; Mr. and Mrs. Liebmann, a handsome silver card receiver; W.W. Baird, pin cushion and jewel case, a very neat affair; Mr. and Mrs. H.B. Beaman, a cigar ash receiver, which is not particularly rich nor elegant but unique; Mr. and Mrs. M.H., silver door bell, Mr. and Mrs. J.B. Graves, large silver pudding knife and fork.

Many young Jews who made their home in Deadwood found their matches on the outside.

Black Hills Daily Times, Jan 30, 1882

Silver-Lowenthal betrothal party was Jewish custom.

Black Hills Daily Times, Oct. 4, 1889

Joseph Hattenbach returns accompanied by his bride, nee Jennie Rosenthal, niece of Sol Rosenthal.

In 1904, Judge Nathan Colman, officiated at the wedding of his eldest daughter, Anne, to Maurice Neiderman of Chicago. The joyous event took place in the Green Room of the new Franklin Hotel.

Charitable and social gatherings were often a matter of Jewish community participation.

Black Hills Daily Times, Jan 16, 1879

Hebrew Benevolent Society to give masquerade ball at Welch House Hotel. To engage two bands for the Hebrew masquerade ball.

Black Hills Daily Times, Jan 19, 1883

Young Hebrew men of city gave annual ball, unsurpassed.

Black Hills Daily Times, Jan 1, 1893

Jolly sleighing party. Mr. and Mrs. Joseph Hattenbach, Miss Laura Rosenthal, Clara L. Fishel and Miss Friedlander constituted a jolly sleighing party around the belt yesterday.

Deadwood Pioneer Times, Jan 1, 1914

"I wish all my friends a happy and prosperous (secular) new year, signed Sidney B. Jacobs."

An obligation to help those in need, *tzedakah* (charity), is a deeply-rooted Jewish value. Not only were charitable events newsworthy as early as 1878, but names of contributors often became a matter of public record. The lists of donors demonstrated solidarity with the plight of those who were suffering, whether under the weight of oppression, illness, or some other misfortune.

Black Hills Daily Times, Jun 1, 1878

Oscar Silver, Charity Ball for the Benefit of Sisters' Hospital.

Black Hills Daily Pioneer, Sep 11, 1878

Ben Baer gives money for Yellow fever victims in South.

Black Hills Daily Pioneer, Sep 15, 1878

Charity Ball for Yellow Fever Sufferers.

Black Hills Daily Times, Oct 25, 1881

Israelite Relief Association formed in Deadwood

Black Hills Daily Times, Nov 29, 1881

Collection taken up to help Hebrews, Donated money to help Jews. Zoellner Brothers, M.J. Wertheimer, Strass & Kohorn, M. Stern, Sol Star, Oscar Silver, Sol Rosenthal, M. Rosengarden, Louis Minzer, M. Lowenthal, L. Liebmann, M. Jacobs, David Holzman, A. Hoffman, Hattenbach Bros., Gottstein & Franklin, J. Goldbloom, J. Goldberg, M. Fishel, J. Fink, P. Cohn, J. Chamison, Sol Bloom, Ben Baer.

Black Hills Daily Times, Nov 6, 1888

Polish Jews suffering. Letter requests aid for crop failure among Polish Jews of Ramsey county.

In 1893, in keeping with the spirit of the Jewish principle of performing good deeds, a chapter of B'nai B'rith was instituted. B'nai B'rith, an international organization founded in 1843, is one of the oldest and largest global Jewish humanitarian organizations. Members established hospitals, orphanages, libraries, and other public service initiatives. The Deadwood chapter, Columbian Lodge #431, started with 24 charter members and 11 board members, and many of Deadwood's Jewish leaders: Israel Cowan, Nathan Colman, Jacob Goldberg, Morris Stern, Gus Cohen, Louis Minzer, Ben Blumenthal, Joseph Hattenbach, Aaron Hattenbach, Jonas Zoellner, and M.J. Wertheimer. Although well-intentioned, it lasted only briefly.

Black Hills Daily Times, Jun 27, 1893

B'nai B'rith instituted. 11 officers

Order of B'nai B'rith instituted with 24 charter members; the 11 elected officers were

Israel Cohen, Nathan Colman, Jacob Goldberg, M. Stern, Gus Cohen, Louis Minzer, Joseph Hattenbach, Ben Blumenthal, Aaron Hattenbach, Jonas Zoellner, M.J. Wertheimer

Lead Daily Call, Jun 6, 1903

The Jewish Relief Fund. The following parties have donated for the relief of the thousands of destitute Jews of Kischineff, Russia. The soliciting committee will furnish the names and amounts given from time to time and advise the public of the entire proceeding when completed:

Oscar Silver	$10.00
Wolff Fink	10.00
Wm. Feiler	10.00
Jos. Chamison	10.00
Nathan Jacobs	5.00
Paul Chamison	5.00
I. Shane	5.00
Jas. Cotton	5.00
Chas. M. Levy	2.00
Jas. Halloran	2.00
H. Maillard	2.00
John Walsh Jr.	2.00
J. L. Marcoux	1.00
J.W. Curran	5.00
P.A. Gushurst	5.00

F.W. Brown	1.00
Clark & Lyon	1.00
John Esterbrooks	1.00
A.J. Johnson	2.50
Morris Cohen	.50
Rathbone Sisters	5.00
Wm. M. Walter	.25
P.L Kricboom	1.00
Jacob Hansen	.25

The Jews were on the whole a positive influence, but these were real people, subject to human frailty, and their stories are by no means all about great successes. There were shootings and scandals and disappointments. There are also strange stories, such as the one about infamous Bummer Dan Baum who may, or may not, have been a Jew. This involves one of the most bizarre barroom shootings in Deadwood's history. Bummer Dan (mavens of South Dakota history will be stunned at this revelation), was the victim of either a setup or a lethal prank. Bummer Dan (his real name was Meyer Baum), became one of the first occupants of a grave on Boot Hill. His remains were later exhumed and moved to the Jewish section, but his gravesite is unmarked. Meyer Baum is listed among other Jewish burials in the Mount Zion section. Deadwood could be a deadly place.

ANTISEMITISM— OLD EVIL IN NEW CLOTHING

In the 1700s there were great numbers of Jews living in Russia. In 1742, Russian Empress Elizabeth personally issued a general order expelling the Jews, and few were left behind. Many of those who survived the forced expulsion found their way into other European countries, including Poland. However, the first partition of Poland in 1772 meant the compulsory return of Jews into Russia, where they were, of course, unwelcome by the traditionally anti-Semitic czarist regime. The advent of Nicholai I (1825-1855), brought about a systematic plan to rid Russia of its Jews, and schemes evolved according to the whim of the czar. Through taxation, mandatory military conscription, curtailed education, and—worst of all—violent pogroms, the Jews were cast out or otherwise eliminated. Also, the blood libel, the wicked medieval superstition that the blood of Christian children was part of Passover ritual, surfaced once again. Jews were forced into slum-like ghettos, limited as to how they could earn a living, where and when they might move about, and how they could educate their children. In the 1860s, in the impoverished, crowded ghettos and *shtetls* (little villages), with pogrom after pogrom, appalling persecution was rampant. By 1881 the great diaspora from Russia came into full force. While state-sponsored antisemitism was the rule in Europe, America was seen as the land of freedom and opportunity.

The *"Goldene Medina"* (Golden Land) could also present threats, and an attempt at institutionalized antisemitism was not unheard of in American history. In December of 1862, Union Army General Ulysses S. Grant issued General Orders No. 11, otherwise known as "The Jewish Exclusion Act", expelling Jewish settlers from Union camps in the Mississippi Valley. The orders read:

"The Jews, as a class violating every regulation of trade established by the Treasury Department and also department orders, are hereby expelled from the department within twenty-four hours from the receipt of this order. Post commanders will see that all of this class of people be furnished passes and required to leave, and any one returning after such notification will be arrested and held in confinement until an opportunity occurs of sending them out as prisoners, unless furnished with permit from headquarters. No passes will be given

these people to visit headquarters for the purpose of making personal application for trade permits.

By order of Maj. Gen. U.S. Grant:
JNO. A. RAWLINS,
Assistant Adjutant-General"

Official Records of the War of the Rebellion, Series I, Vol. 17, Part II, p. 424.

This was met with an immediate response. Outraged, an indignant letter was drafted and signed by some of the offended Jewish citizens, and sent to President Abraham Lincoln, explaining that this order violated their constitutional rights.

PADUCAH, KY.,
December 29, 1862.

Hon. ABRAHAM LINCOLN,
President of the United States:

General Orders, No. 11, issued by General Grant at Oxford, Miss., December the 17th, commands all post commanders to expel all Jews, without distinction, within twenty-four hours, from his entire department. The undersigned, good and loyal citizens of the United States and residents of this town for many years, engaged in legitimate business as merchants, feel greatly insulted and outraged by this inhuman order, the carrying out of which would be the grossest violation of the Constitution and our rights as good citizens under it, and would place us, besides a large number of other Jewish families of this town, as outlaws before the whole world. We respectfully ask your immediate attention to this enormous outrage on all law and humanity, and pray for your effectual and immediate interposition. We would respectfully refer you to the post commander and post adjutant as to our loyalty, and to all respectable citizens of this community as to our standing as citizens and merchants. We respectfully ask for immediate instructions to be sent to the commander of this post.

D. WOLFF & BROS.
C. F. KASKELL.
J. W. KASKELL.

President Lincoln, obviously struck by the infringement on these people's rights as citizens, issued a counter-order resulting in the immediate revocation of Grant's General Orders No. 11.

WAR DEPARTMENT,
Washington, January 4, 1863.
Major-General GRANT,
Holly Springs, Miss.:

A paper purporting to be General Orders, No. 11, issued by you December 17, has been presented here. By its terms it expels all Jews from your department. If such an order has been issued, it will be immediately revoked.

H. W. HALLECK,
General-in-Chief.

HDQRS. 13TH ARMY CORPS, DEPT. OF THE TENN.,
Holly Springs, Miss., January 7, 1863.

By direction of General-in-Chief of the Army, at Washington, the general order from these headquarters expelling Jews from the department is hereby revoked.

By order of Maj. Gen. U.S. Grant:

JNO. A. RAWLINS,
Assistant Adjutant-General.

Official Records of the War of the Rebellion, Series I, Vol. 17, Part II, p. 506.

Yet, when General Grant's death was announced in July of 1885, the newspapers expressed the Black Hills' mourning for their former President, including the Jewish community. From the perspective of time, it is hard to fathom such a seemingly sincere outpouring of sympathy from the Jews of Deadwood, especially under mayor Sol Star, other than to assume that either time eased their wounds, or the need for civility and patriotism overrode their anger.

Black Hills Daily Times, Jul 24, 1885
Deadwood mourns. No event, local or national, since the assassination of Garfield, has so visibly affected this entire community as the death of General Ulysses S Grant. Merchants hotel.

Black Hills Daily Times, Aug 5, 1885
Mayor's proclamation on Ulysses S. Grant. It is but fitting that citizens of Deadwood commemorate Gen. U.S. Grant's services by observing the day with appropriate ceremonies. Mayor Star requests that business be suspended from 1-3 p.m. and bells be tolled from 1-2 and proper emblems of mourning be displayed Aug. 8.

In looking for overt antisemitism in newspaper accounts of early Deadwood, with a few striking exceptions, one is hard-pressed to find any serious instances of this blight. One issue did arise concerning the name "Hebrew Hill." Section 4, the Jewish section of Mount Moriah Cemetery, was named Mount Zion by the Jewish citizenry, and they found the Hebrew Hill label insulting. Despite their protestations, the label stuck.

Black Hills Daily Times, Apr 2, 1879
Hebrew Hill. Some of our Hebrews said to be offended by name.

Black Hills Daily Times, Feb 27, 1883
Mt Moriah commonly known as Hebrew Hill.

Another questionable instance involved an incident that took place on the street in 1877 involving a peddler named David Goldstone and a fair damsel of the demimonde. Goldstone, characterized in the newspaper by the distasteful label of "Jew Peddler," chose an unseemly place, Main Street, to attempt collection of an unpaid debt from one of Deadwood's "upstairs girls". Not only did the lady in question refuse to pay, but she physically attacked the foolish chap, knocking him out cold.

Black Hills Daily Times, Sep 18, 1877
David Goldstone "Jew Peddler," lady knocks him out.

To make matters worse, the police were summoned and Goldstone was arrested, the presumption being that he, not the lady, was to blame for the ruckus. The newspaper fairly salivated over the story, repeatedly referring to Goldstone simply as the "Jew Peddler." The following day Goldstone was cleared of the charges, but he'd spent a night in the hoosegow pondering his predicament. Goldstone objected to the newspaper's rush to judgment, and the paper, surprisingly, published his complaint.

Black Hills Daily Times, Sep 19, 1877
David Goldstone, Times does injustice to him.

The Black Hills Daily Times printed a retraction, but continued to refer to Goldstone as the "Jew Peddler." Whether the editors appreciated the effrontery of the label was never apparent. In general, cultural sensitivity was not a major concern in the world at large at the time, nor was it in early Deadwood.

Occasionally, a Jew would find the means to overcome the obstacle that was deliberately placed in his path, as in the case of Baron de Hirsch. Baron Maurice de Hirsch was a German-Jewish financier/philanthropist who dedicated his wealth to assisting Russian-Jewish victims of European pogroms by planned resettlement in agricultural colonies throughout the New World. Colonies were established from Argentina to Canada. Two such colonies were established briefly in eastern South Dakota near Mitchell. Another just east of Rapid City in an area known as Rapid Valley was entertained. A wryly amusing news item illustrating de Hirsch's unique method of exacting retribution appears in the Rapid City Daily Journal in 1891.

Rapid City Daily Journal, May 5, 1891

Baron de Hirsch will fit out the mansion in Paris which he bought over the heads of the club that blackballed him, and will throw it open to any friends who may visit him in the French capital.

Deadwood was well aware of the significance of its Jewish neighbors. The Jewish population, with its inherent values of social justice and responsibility was usually the object of respect. Sol Star, Deadwood's long-time Jewish civil servant, was appreciated for his lack of discriminatory behavior. In support of Star's application for the position of Lawrence County Clerk of Courts, the Times suggests that not only were the Jews considered a valued segment of the establishment, but that the community relied on them for fairness, regardless of the nationality of the person with whom they were dealing.

Black Hills Pioneer Times, Oct 21, 1906

With such a man as Sol Star, the able clerk of courts, numbered among its candidates, strength is conceded to the Republican ticket. Name over the list of old-timers, and find if you can the man without a host of friends to swear by him, and then add to this the friends gained through a career of impartial, judicious, and liberal treatment to all and you have Sol Star. One of Mr. Star's strongest endorsements for re-election is the known fact that he handles every phase of his work with a precision that shows he has it at his fingertips and that no matter what the nationality of anyone with business at the clerk of courts office, he invariably goes away satisfied.

Black Hills Daily Times, Jan 11, 1879

"A most important portion of our population"

The Black Hills Daily Times published in its entirety the Bar Mitzvah speech of Jacob Goldberg's younger brother back in New York City.

Another lengthy article published in 1885 contained the eulogy for Sir Moses Montefiore, wealthy Jewish humanitarian and philanthropist, Sheriff of London, a dedicated believer in *Eretz Israel* (the Land of Israel), knighted by Queen Victoria for his efforts on behalf of his fellow Jews.

But hatred needs no excuse or explanation. In the 1920s, America's unique brand of bigotry, the KKK, Ku Klux Klan, which had been suppressed in earlier years following emancipation, once again reared its ugly, white-sheeted head. There were "klaverns" all across South Dakota. A traveler might encounter a roadside sign advertising 'The Hub for Suits,' a Jewish-owned establishment in Deadwood, with KKK painted across it as a warning. Klan parades were a form of public entertainment. The Black Hills towns of Sturgis and Belle Fourche were particularly noted for Klan activity, including night-ridings and cross-burnings. In 1925 the annual Fourth of July Tri-State Rodeo, held at Belle Fourche, included convening a "Konclave" of the Klan. There was a substantial turnout, though not as sizable as the women of the Klan anticipated. They had prepared deviled eggs by the hundreds for lunch, and set them out for the crowd. Afterward, the surplus eggs made ammunition for a splendid food fight among the youngsters.

The KKK posted a notice just outside of Sturgis, admonishing Jews, Negroes and foreigners to be out of the vicinity of the northern Black Hills by sunset. Rallies were held where they could be most effective. One cross-burning in Rapid City involved three crosses, the center cross being the tallest, with two smaller ones on either side. The crosses were wrapped in oil-soaked cloth and set afire.

Klan Initiates on Parade in front of Duhamel Building in Rapid City in the 1920s.
Photo courtesy Charles Rambow

Klansmen on Horseback at a Nighttime Konklave
Photo courtesy Charles Rambow

Prominent members of the community and local government could and did succumb to its allure, and many became aligned with the Klan. Klansmen carried miniature Christian bibles, and identified one another in civilian clothing by wearing badges with the embroidered KIGY (Klansman I Greet You) insignia. With their forbidding white robes and fiery crosses, part of the Klan's intent was to inspire fear and create an atmosphere of supernatural power. A hooded Klansman, particularly one on horseback, was a fearsome-looking creature. In true vigilante style, the Klan actually tarred-and-feathered two women in Farmingdale whom they singled out as being "loose." In small communities, membership was hard to remain a secret, but they tried, even to the point of disguising their horses behind formidable white garments. However, certain individuals, some of whom held respected positions of leadership, could be identified by their shoes or boots.

The Fourth of July was a favored time for the Klan to hold rallies. The diary of William A. Remer, paymaster at Homestake Mine and sheriff of Lawrence County, told of a rally on July 4th, 1925. He notes there was a large crowd assembled at a place they called "Nigger Flat" to hear the Klansmen speak and watch the parade. He writes of 80 horsemen and about 700 on foot. Despite the obviously imposing size of the throngs, Remer saw the absurdity of this entire gathering, and called it "a joke." It was not a joke to President Woodrow Wilson, credited with saying, "If it had not been for the Klan, the South and the United States would not have survived."

The Klan used violence and intimidation to achieve their purposes, namely to ensure their warped idea of "good American values" throughout the land. There were Klaverns in all the main towns around the Black Hills, carrying out bullying and acts of violence against Negroes, Jews, Orientals, and "foreigners." They were especially opposed to Roman Catholics, seeing the papacy as a threat. On October 26, 1921, a Roman Catholic priest from Lead, Father Arthur Belknap, was shot and killed. Although all signs pointed to the Klan, the killer was never brought to justice, probably because some of the law enforcement officers were also Klansmen.

At its peak there were roughly 3,000 members statewide, mostly "good old boys." Although it tried to give the superficial appearance of a benevolent social organization, at its heart the KKK was thoroughly evil and dangerous. For all its secrecy, the KKK still exists, occasionally emerging from the shadows.

JEWISH NEIGHBORS

Much of the earliest commerce in the northern Hills was based in Lead, Deadwood's sister city and site of the Homestake Mine. Jewish businesses ran the gamut of goods and services; everything from Jake Kozberg's saloon to Wolff Fink's fine jewelry manufacturing establishment. Jacobs' Bazaar, run by Mr. and Mrs. L.D. Jacobs, was an unpretentious mom-and-pop establishment, with a bare wood floor and modest fixtures. It had a soda fountain where one might enjoy a Coca-Cola or other confection, and plain display cases which held an array of cigars (with a convenient spittoon on the floor nearby). Their shelves were stacked with boxes containing musical instruments, stationery and toys. They advertised the Bazaar as a "general news depot."

Interior of Jacobs' Bazaar
Photo courtesy Don Toms

In sharp contrast to Jacobs' Bazaar, Wolff Fink's luxuriously appointed jewelry store was carpeted and mirrored, with costly fixtures and handsome glass cases, emblematic of the prosperity that the Homestake and other mines brought. As Fink's business flourished, he added a jewelry-making factory, providing many jobs to the region.

Scattered settlements appeared. There were a few Jewish ranchers and farmers in the outlying areas, At the tiny town of Camp Crook in the northern Black Hills, Isaac and Jennie Roet, émigrés from Kiev in the Ukraine, worked their farm, while Isaac also kept a blacksmith and harness shop. There was a community on the high prairie east of the Hills known as Jew Flats, complete with cowboys and a rabbi and an icy stream that served as a *mikveh* (ritual bath). A fearless Jewish grandmother homesteaded in the remote area of the Badlands (the geographic variety), and adhered to the rules of keeping a *kosher* home. Black Hills communities that grew up around the mining industry had Jewish entrepreneurs, and in some cases Jewish miners. Many arrived with limited capital, but an enterprising spirit, hard work, good investments, and good luck paid off. Star and Bullock had branches of their hardware store in Deadwood, Belle Fourche, Sturgis, Spearfish, Sundance and Carbonate. Franklin and Baer had a branch in Rapid City as did Jake Goldberg. Wertheimer branched out into Spearfish. Sol Bloom, Joe Poznansky, and the Zoellner brothers opened stores in Sturgis and Spearfish, and Fishel opened in Sturgis. The town of Strool, in remote Harding County, named for its Jewish founder, Benjamin Strool, once a optimistic little community, faded away to just a notation on aerial navigation maps, until even that vanished.

SOCIETY, POLITE AND OTHERWISE

Black Hills Daily Times, April 9, 1879
Deadwood City, Dakota Territory

THE CHARACTER OF OUR IMMIGRANTS: According to the extract we published yesterday from the Press and Dakotian, there is now large immigration pouring into the eastern section of the Territory. "The tide of immigration has been turned across the eastern borders and thousands of people are planting their homes upon the prairies, while other thousands are coming on from the East," in the way that paper expresses it. The immigration to this section of the Territory bids fair to be on a scale that will compare favorably with that in the eastern section. Those that come this year are hardy pioneers, who will aid in re-claiming our territorial empire, and in planting and nurturing herein a young and giant Commonwealth; men who will cause the desert to bud and bloom and the mountain to yield up its treasures. They will build homes within sight of the wigwam and scalping knife; and today will embark fortunes in developing the resources and increasing the industries of the country; add wealth to the nation, increase its revenues, add to its income, and multiply its power. They embrace the best hearts and brains of the land. The bravest and most enterprising of the pioneer classes of the country always lead in immigration. In America immigration robs the old states of the very cream of their producers- takes from them the most sagacious and ambitious. And then, having settled in their new field, surrounded by rich undeveloped resources, they have incentives to attain what they never had before. The new environment leads to broadened liberality and expanded thought. Means and objects are at once planned and accomplished on a large scale. The same man who would be content with a little street-grading contract in any eastern village can give his attention to nothing of less importance after coming West, than building and owning an extensive full road, and if his ambition before immigration was limited to teaching a country school, he now, as a pioneer, aspires to a seat in the territorial legislature. There is inspiration in our mountain air which quickens every faculty, and dignifies and ennobles. This has been noticed and admitted by all keen observers who have traveled through the far West. "

Except for a few outstanding oddities, it's safe to say that the Jewish people of Deadwood and western South Dakota were well regarded in the early days of settlement. Some joined school boards and set up libraries. Some organized charities and benefits for the needy. In a culture of disturbingly heartless treatment of animals, Nathan Franklin's special fondness for animals moved him to help launch a humane society, where he served as president.

Ox team in Rapid City.
Photo courtesy David Strain

Black Hills Daily Times, Mar 20, 1887

Nothing could be done for poor dumb brutes. More than one person had sympathy for starved bull outfit struggling with monster load.

Black Hills Daily Times, May 16, 1890

Washington Hughes, Spearfish, arrested on charge of cruelty to animals, allegedly beating his horse to death.

By the 1880s, Deadwood's establishment was taking on some legitimacy. As families became more affluent, there arose a need for domestic help. Jewish families advertised in the eastern papers for Jewish women to provide such help. Fortunately for the young women, these were valid advertisements, as opposed to some other calls for young women to work as domestics which were sometimes a ploy to recruit girls for ill-intentioned purposes. Jacob Goldberg's family hired a young servant woman named Tillia to help with the family chores.

Black Hills Daily Times, Jul 21, 1882

Jewish women could come to the Hills as domestics.

The Jews engaged in altruistic fraternal and charitable organizations such as Masons, Elks, Odd Fellows, and the Knights of Pythias, which held among their lofty principles that the organization would tend to make men better, more friendly, charitable, benevolent and patriotic, and promote the highest and best interests of mankind.

Black Hills Daily Times, Dec 14, 1887

Black Hills encampment, I.O.O.F., elects officers. J. Hattenbach.

"The Fraternal Order of Knights of Pythias and its members are dedicated to the cause of universal peace. Pythians are pledged to the promotion of understanding among men of good will as the surest means of attaining Universal Peace. We believe that men, meeting in a spirit of goodwill, in an honest effort of understanding, can live together on this earth in peace and harmony."

Jewish people helped run the county fairs and local festivals, and participated in charitable church fairs. They freely acknowledged the blessings of being American, and were fiercely patriotic, preparing weeks in advance for Fourth of July celebrations, complete with decorated streets, brass bands and fireworks.

Black Hills Daily Times, Feb 15, 1885

Full-blooded pig race eventuated, but pig manifested more sense than his would-be human persecutors — he just stood still. Sol Star, Paul Rewman.

Black Hills Daily Times, Jul 11, 1886

Fair committees appointed. Deadwood Fair Association directors appoint committees for September exposition. Paul Rewman, Ben Baer, Harris Franklin.

Black Hills Daily Times, Dec 1, 1891

Mrs Harris Franklin. Catholic Church fair an unqualified social and financial success.

By 1885 Deadwood had gone from a collection of tents to a businesslike town in the center of a thriving population, and there was a need for legitimate theater, music, and other forms of cultural enrichment as well as recreation. Although burlesque and bawdy performances served as entertainment for most frequenters of the Badlands, hunger for culture prevailed even among the rough, tough prospectors and others associated with the mines. Dr. Watson Parker wrote that a performance of The Mikado by Gilbert and Sullivan took place in Deadwood on December 20th, 1886. It ran for 130 days, although probably not to packed houses.

The Deadwood Opera House opened to grand fanfare in 1906, the ladies in their finest evening gowns and jewelry, gentlemen in black tie and tails. It operated for half a century, with theatrical and musical performances. A San

Francisco summer stock company played a long engagement, the Minneapolis symphony orchestra performed, and a big event was the appearance of the Christy Minstrels.

With the advent of moving pictures, the opera house was converted into a motion picture theater which showed the latest productions, and Charlie Klein managed the theater in Deadwood. Fire destroyed the building in 1952, and it was never rebuilt. Hilda Klein, Charlie's widow, lived out her retirement years in an apartment in the Franklin Hotel directly across the street, with a view of the theater from her arched window.

Deadwood Opera House Interior
Photo Courtesy Adams Museum

Other cultural facilities were built in Lead and Spearfish. Mrs. Phoebe Apperson Hearst, wife of George Hearst, owner of the Homestake Mine, gifted the elaborate Homestake Opera House to the city of Lead in 1914. The Hearsts were not Jews, but Mrs. Hearst believed money should be used for the good of mankind. The earliest performances included a New York grand opera company, a 3-piece orchestra, vaudeville shows, and silent movies. The opera house was intended as part of a recreational center. Besides the theater, it also featured a bowling alley, library, social rooms, a billiards room, and a tiled swimming pool in the basement. Mrs. Hearst also established a free kindergarten for the town's children.

Homestake Opera House, Lead
Photo courtesy Adams Museum

The beautiful Matthews Opera House in Spearfish was another example of a response to the need for arts and culture.

Matthews Opera House, Spearfish
Photo courtesy Adams Museum

County fairs were the ideal places to demonstrate public spirit, and the Jewish merchants participated freely, entering contests and donating prizes. Star and Bullock became perennial exhibitors, displaying outstanding livestock and high-quality corn and wheat grown at their

Belle Fourche ranch. Picnics were popular summertime activities along with baseball games. Baseball clubs were organized, church socials and church fairs were mounted. Roller-skating became a fashionable leisure activity, and in winters, sleigh rides and ice-skating were pleasant pastimes.

Black Hills Daily Times, Dec 31, 1884

Rollerskating prize to most graceful lady. The attraction at the rink last evening—prizes for the most graceful lady skating. Awarded by Sol Star, et al.

Horse racing was also a popular sport. Sol Star's herd at the Star and Bullock Ranch in Belle Fourche included some of the country's finest racehorses.

Black Hills Daily Times, Jul 23, 1879

Horse racing fever is what is the matter with camp.

Black Hills Daily Times, Sep 10, 1887

Bicycle received by Sol Star is to be operated on the race track during fair time; will be drawn by a thoroughbred trotter and be known as a trotting sulky.

Black Hills Daily Times, Sep 1, 1888

Seth Bullock wired Sol Star that Stanley made a mile in 2:17 and How made a quarter of a mile in 31 seconds, each of the colts pacing.

And then there was the shady side of life in the mining camp. It was said that in 1876 about 90% of Deadwood's females were prostitutes, most of whom inhabited the Badlands (as distinguished from the geologic Badlands some 50 miles to the southeast). Besides offering a bit of fleeting female companionship, Deadwood's Badlands were notoriously awash in cheap liquor, abounding in saloons and theaters such as the Bella Union, the Gem, the Langrische, the Park, and a multitude of other establishments offering musical and theatrical entertainment of many kinds.

Gem Theater
Photo courtesy Adams Museum

Black Hills Daily Times, Aug 27, 1879

Sweet sounds of song issue from such a b-a-d place.

In 1878 the Bella Union advertised a "Great Parisian Can Can." Performers like Ella LaRue, Oscar Willis, The Vincents, Edith Valentine and such comedians as Georgie Morrell who "kept the audience in convulsions at every scene," entertained the mining population. The theater managers engaged clog and jig dancers, actors, singers, living statuary, adult contortionists and child acrobats. "Hottentots," Negro minstrels, and comedians were all the rage.

Black Hills Daily Times, Jan 10, 1880

Billy Mack, in his Ethiopian songs and sketches was simply immense.

Black Hills Daily Times, Nov 20, 1879

Voice of charcoal man singing "char-co-a-al."

A bad case of vertigo brought on by the double trapeze act of sisters Lola and Jeannette Parchal at the Bella Union in 1878 was said to have been cured by the caresses of said young ladies. Little Pearly Duval, feted by the Black Hills Pioneer as "simply wonderful for a child her age," performed on the trapeze, demonstrating amazing feats of contortion, at one point winning the heart of a certain attorney, and being rewarded with his shirt stud. Little regard was paid to the dangers inherent in the child's situation. There were sister acts and brother acts and family acts, some so popular that they were brought back year after year for return engagements.

1878: Boisset Family of Six, Acrobats and Musical Artists, Trapeze, Song, Dance with Banjo,

1879 – 1880: Edith Valentine and Georgie Morrell, Serio-comedic Vocalist, Song and Dance,

1877 and 1879: Ella LaRue, Female Banjoist and Cornet Soloist,

1879 – 1880: Oscar Willis, A Clever Ethiopian Comedian,

1879 - 1880, 1892 – 1893: Billy Mack, Deadwood's Favorite Comedian,

1879 – 1880: Trixy and Vernie Vernon, "marvels of beauty and way up as queens of song",

1880: Inez Sexton, Queen of Operatic and Ballad Song,

1880: M'lle Blanche, "Too much praise cannot be given her as a danseuse",

1884 Park Theater. Formerly Stone's Opera House. Lower Main Street, Deadwood. J.C. Burns, sole proprietor. Harry Butler, director of amusements. Professor Upwald, musical director. J.A. Upwald, leader of brass band. The only first-class place of amusement in the city. Crowded houses nightly. Everything new and spicy. Admission 25 cents. Private boxes 50 cents.

Green Front Theater
Photo courtesy Centennial Archives, Deadwood Public Library

Suicides were not at all uncommon among the young women caught up in this life of sordid amusements. Many women sealed their fates as they fell into the clutches of addiction. Suicide was sometimes the only escape.

Black Hills Pioneer, Dec 26, 1890
Former Gem belle commits suicide. "Edith Valentine committed suicide recently at Seattle by shooting herself thro' the head. She was formerly a belle of the variety artists at the Gem, in this city."

CHINATOWN

Hundreds of Chinese, sometimes referred to as "celestials," sought work in the Black Hills. Most of them settled in Deadwood, where they were needed in laundries, restaurants, and stores. By the end of the 1880s, Deadwood had its own Chinatown at the northern end of Main Street. It was a struggle, but the Chinese managed to establish their own community with stores, a fire department, and a separate Masonic temple into which few Caucasians were permitted. A rare exception to that rule was Sol Star, who was a recognized friend of the otherwise badly treated Chinese population. Although they strove for recognition in the dominant white society, they were often subject to suspicion and hostility.

Black Hills Daily Times Nov 6, 1879
Sol Star, Attended Chinese funeral as an invited guest.

Black Hills Daily Times Mar 27, 1881
Sol Star, Wing Tom & Quong Soon ask him to interpret in court.

Black Hills Daily Times, Jul 15, 1885
Hi Kee makes good on promise of payment to fire department from last winter's Chinatown fire. Sol Star.

GETTING FROM HERE TO THERE

The first of the pioneers to flood into Deadwood in the earliest days of the Stampede arrived either by shank's mare, horseback, or atop a mule, as did Nathan Colman in 1876. After February 1877, the Black Hills of Dakota was no longer judged Indian Territory, and United States citizens could travel there under government protection. The railroads terminated at Cheyenne, Pierre, Bismarck and Sidney, and any public transportation or freight into the Hills beyond those points was limited to freight wagons and stage lines. The stagecoaches began running into the Hills almost immediately, carrying passengers, goods, and mail. The freight companies with their bull trains could haul in heavy equipment, but these were extremely slow. Development depended heavily upon both communication and transportation.

A unique designation, "stagecoach aristocracy," was conferred upon those who entered the Black Hills during the Gold Rush. It was deemed that you left your past behind to begin a new life when you came to the Hills, and you were entitled to this special brand of frontier nobility. Among the anointed were the Bennetts and the Bullocks, as well as their Jewish counterparts Sol Star, the Franklins, the Jacobses, the Schwarzwalds, the Wertheimers, the Fishels, and those pioneers who arrived in the initial Stampede of 1876. The restriction was expanded in later years, enough so that the Colmans were entitled to the distinction.

Stagecoach Aristocracy
Photo courtesy Adams Museum

There was a certain amount of theater attached to stagecoach arrivals into Deadwood. A practice of the stagecoach lines was to halt a few miles outside of town to exchange the dusty, road-worn coach and team for fresh horses and a shiny, splendid Concord, queen of stagecoaches, and finally make a grand entry. The Concords were drawn by spirited horses who sashayed into Deadwood with a flourish, bringing with them a hint of the possibilities that lay beyond the secluded hill town.

Estelline Bennett, daughter of pioneers, recalled with eloquence what the stagecoach meant to Deadwood:

"Deadwood was the most important town in the world to the stagecoach. It was the only one on the long stage trail that saw it dressed up in its six horses, nickel-plated trappings, and spectacular manners... The stagecoach came into Deadwood and

went out dashing, prancing, rolling, and glittering. Its canvas curtains might be shabby and dirty, its wheels ragged with the gumbo out of the Badlands, but it was always a romantic, valiant courier to and from the outside world. Days that the stage did not arrive were days of harrowing suspense in this isolated island of mountains in a sea of flat Indian reservations. We were lost if it failed us, and sometimes men were sent out on horseback to search for it."

In her memoir, "Old Deadwood Days," Estelline recalled watching from the window of Goldberg's Big Horn Grocery store where she had been sent on an errand for some sugar. From the safety of the window, she watched as a bull-whacker gave an exhibition of his expertise with his long whip, a "graceful but explosive lash," being cracked in the direction of the Merchant's Hotel, the Northwestern Stagelines stop at Wertheimer's establishment, next door to the Big Horn.

Board sidewalks, dusty streets, and cold baths.
Photo courtesy Centennial Archives, Deadwood Public Library

Deadwood's Main Street
Photo courtesy Adams Museum

Black Hills Daily Times, Sep 10, 1879

Passengers going east will bear in mind that via Sidney and Union Pacific Railroad is the old roundabout route to the East. The new and short route is via Bismarck. The Northern Pacific Railroad now runs daily trains, and passengers by this line save 300 miles travel, get one good night's rest, and yet make 17 hours off their time to St. Paul, and the same time to Chicago by way of Sidney.

Black Hills Daily Times, Sep 13, 1879

D. Goldberg, The clothier returned by the Bismarck coach.

Black Hills Daily Times, Jun 26, 1880

D. & J. Goldberg, Incoming freight from Bismarck.

Black Hills Daily Times, May 11, 1887

Best man is a woman. The most industrious man in Dakota is a woman bull whackeress who engineered the outfit through the city with ability, unloaded with alacrity and retired with dexterity.

Even after Indian attack ceased to threaten travelers, masked road agents made every trip a hazard and every road another danger point. Despite the primitive and risky nature of transportation, traffic was brisk. Traveling to railroad depots by stagecoach was Deadwood's main passage to the world outside the Hills. Passengers were aware of the threats, and they relied on the drivers for protection. Stagecoach drivers like John T. McClintock were hired for their qualities of character and sturdiness, and were heroes of their day. They were tough, dependable and accountable, good with a gun, prepared to defend the coach, its passengers and their property, and the U.S. mail.

Black Hills Daily Pioneer, Aug 23, 1878

Cheyenne Coach robbed 4 miles South of Cheyenne River, J.Gottstein relieved of valuables, shaken but unharmed.

With so many travelers booking passage, the stagecoaches were active and overcrowded. A familiar sight was the stagecoach with passengers clinging to the outside or riding on the top. The only scheduled pauses were to eat and change horses at the stagecoach stops. The coaches, at least those that traveled without impediment, usually made surprisingly good time despite the rutted trails.

Black Hills Daily Times, Apr 27, 1881

Pierre coach made it here in 36 hours from railroad.

Black Hills Weekly Times, Jul 19, 1884

Stagecoach Loaded to Overflowing. A Sidney coach arrived at 6 o'clock last evening loaded to overflowing with passengers, four finding seats on the outside. The popularity of the Sidney route is constantly increasing since the change of superintendents. Coaches are making excellent and regular time, and many reforms have been introduced.

Stagecoach entering Deadwood
Photo courtesy Steve Norquist

Black Hills Daily Times, Jul 8, 1885

Woman Crashed Through Stagecoach Floor. Spearfish coach loading a woman whose avoirdupois forfeited her claim to a "sylph-like being," entered the vehicle and passed through the floor.

Black Hills Daily Times, Sep 5, 1885

Stagecoach loaded to utmost capacity. A Northwestern coach arrived at 7 o'clock last evening, loaded to its utmost capacity with passengers, mail and express.

Black Hills Daily Times, Dec 1, 1885

Stagecoach connects at Buffalo Gap. Northwestern coaches now connect with the cars at the (Buffalo) Gap, making the run in about 19 hours. The road will be turned over to the railway company in about 10 days.

Arrivals and departures were noteworthy events. The newspapers published passenger lists, and Jewish businesspeople frequently seemed to be either coming or going.

Black Hills Daily Times, Mar 25, 1882

On incoming coach, M. Hattenbach, Ben Lowenthal.

Black Hills Daily Times, Feb 26, 1884

Jake Wertheimer, fine host of the Merchants Hotel, leaves by this morning's Pierre coach for the east on a trip for pleasure and rest from business. Mr. W. will stop a few days in Chicago, thence to Washington and New York, and in from four to six weeks, return.

Black Hills Daily Times, Jun 9, 1886

Arrivals and departures via Northwestern; incoming Rapid passengers, Oscar Silver, Sol Rosenthal.

Black Hills Daily Times, May 27, 1887

Arrivals and departures via Northwestern. S. Poznansky, M. Gottstein.

Black Hills Daily Times, Oct 14, 1887

Arrivals and departures via Northwestern. Aaron Hattenbach, Mrs. Hattenbach.

Black Hills Daily Times, Mar 21, 1888

Arrivals and Departures via Northwestern Stagelines. J. Schwartz, M. Lowenstein, Max Fishel.

The stagecoach companies did their best to glamorize their form of transportation, but travel was at best grimy and uncomfortable, risky, rarely according to schedule, and at very worst life-threatening. An arrival could be delayed by days if the stagecoach happened to run into muddy roads, especially coming through the Badlands.

Stagecoach stop in Rapid City. Dirt streets and telegraph poles.
Photo courtesy Minnilusa Historical Association

Horses were a ubiquitous and essential part of the scenery in the Black Hills. Almost everyone rode. Children learned to ride, some even learned to manage a team of horses, at an early age. Harris Franklin, Sol Star and Ben Baer, raised their own horse herds. Horse theft was considered among the worst of crimes—leaving a man without a horse rendered him helpless. The crime was potentially punishable by lynching. A horse thief took his own chances and justice was likely to be applied swiftly and on the spot.

One such renowned incident left the town of Rapid City with lingering infamy. It involved the hanging of three accused horse thieves, one of whom, a mere teenager who gave his name as James Hall, was caught up in a crime of which he was most likely innocent. The lynch mob acted with more haste than expertise, bungling their efforts to carry out the execution. Legend has it that the victims gradually strangled to death while dangling from a tree high on Hangman's Hill, the hogback ridge later known as Skyline Drive, that defined the town's western border. The alleged "hanging tree" was a dismal monument, a relic of Black Hills early vigilante days that earned early Rapid City the dubious nickname of "Strangler City."

Black Hills Daily Times, May 27, 1883

Horse thief found hanging from tree at Sun Dance.

Black Hills Daily Times, Mar 18, 1884

On Saturday night last some fiend incarnate went in the Homestake stable at Lead City, saddled up and rode away the horse that is used by the water ditch man, and has not been heard from since. The horse is 8 year old, and has the government brand I C S on him.

Black Hills Daily Times, Jun 6, 1884

James Lindsay was laid to rest at Mount Moriah cemetery after being killed in Sturgis in the process of stealing a horse and tack along with "Brigham" Andy Brown.

Injury or loss of a horse or its wagon was the equivalent of today's automobile accident and was likely to be reported in the newspapers.

Black Hills Daily Times, Aug 7, 1879

Gottstein, Horse pretty badly cut and bruised in fall over hill.

Black Hills Daily Times, Mar 28, 1883

Lost; dark bay horse, 15 hands high, liberal reward, Harris Franklin,

Black Hills Daily Times, Jul 23, 1885

Runaway carriage. Mrs. Harris Franklin and Miss Nettie Holstein enjoyed a carriage ride until crowded by empty wood wagon driver, causing carriage to overturn and team to run away. Ladies escaped with slight bruises.

Black Hills Daily Times, Nov 22, 1885

Al Howarth, messenger accompanying the Northwestern coach that upset south of Rapid, arrived to report on accident. Jacob Goldberg among passengers.

What Deadwood most wanted and needed was a railroad to secure its future. It took years of politicking and negotiating on the part of Deadwood's most effective and influential citizens to finally bring a railroad to Deadwood. There were already smaller railroads in place, like the one that serviced the Homestake. Planning for the local horseless commuter railroad, the Deadwood Central Railroad, a commuter line to carry passengers from Deadwood up to Lead, began in 1877, finally materialized in 1889, and was ultimately sold in 1893. That little local line was 12 years in the planning, but operated for only 4 years.

Black Hills Daily Times, Sep 25, 1877

Deadwood Railway Company to build narrow-gauge R.R.

Black Hills Daily Times, Mar 30, 1880

Deadwood to Central R.R. won't be a horse railroad.

The Deadwood Central was of most benefit to the "smelter men", the well-to-do gentlemen with offices in Deadwood who had made fortunes, primarily in mines to the north and east, such as the Iron Hill Mine at Carbonate. Carbonate, a town grown from a mining camp that began as an apple orchard planted in the hills northeast of Deadwood, was the site of the second major silver discovery in the Black Hills, the other being Galena. The smelter built there by the Hattenbachs served to smelt ore from their own Far West Mine as well as others, including the Iron Hill Mine. Carbonate's Iron Hill Mine had undergone its own mining stock boom which made great fortunes for its stockholders, many of whom built their homes on Deadwood's hillsides in Ingleside and Forest Hill. Almost everyone who lived in "Iron Hill Row," or on Forest Avenue in the terraced residential neighborhood of Forest Hill, owned stock in Carbonate and reaped the benefits of the Hattenbach smelter—when it was working.

Many of Deadwood's Jewish businessmen, including the Hattenbachs, Harris Franklin, Jacob Goldberg, and the Lowenthals, had invested in the Iron Hill Mine at Carbonate. Convenient as it was, at 45 cents a ride, the sprightly little Deadwood Central Railroad suffered a succession of unfortunate accidents.

Black Hills Daily Times, Sep 11, 1889
Train fire spreading rapidly. Herald reports brush fire on mouth of Gold Run again set fire by sparks from D.C. locomotive and fire is spreading rapidly.

Black Hills Daily Times, Oct 30, 1889
The Deadwood Central Railroad locomotive is equipped with a new chime whistle. It is a very melodious whistle.

Black Hills Daily Times, May 10, 1890
Boulder strikes locomotive. D.C. train narrowly escapes serious accident when immense boulder strikes locomotive just behind the pilot. Rock completely demolished, else the train would have gone into the ditch. No one hurt and engine escaped injury.

Black Hills Daily Times, Jun 7, 1890
Flood aftermath. Rapid subsidence of water, extent of damage (of Deadwood Central) reported by Solomon Star.

Black Hills Daily Times, Dec 28, 1892
Wreck on the Deadwood Central. Train breaks and cars damaged.

Residents supposed the train gave the city a certain metropolitan air, but after four star-crossed years, the Deadwood Central Railroad was purchased by the Burlington Railroad, and ceased to operate. Deadwood still lacked railroad connections to the rest of the country.

On July 5, 1886, 10 years after Rapid City's founding, the Elkhorn railroad reached Deadwood's neighboring town 50 miles to the south, and was welcomed with much fanfare, as such a momentous event warranted. A symbolic race from Sidney, Nebraska, to Rapid City, South Dakota, was held between the Sidney-Deadwood stagecoach and the first train. The train won, arriving at the Rapid City station slightly ahead of the coach. Rapid City turned out in grand style, including its most outstanding citizens, among them luminaries Dr. and Mrs. Valentine McGillycuddy, friends of Sol Star.

Black Hills Daily Times, Jul 7, 1886
Rapid jubilee. Interesting exercises upon arrival of the first through train; hose race replete with disaster; incidents of the day. Valentine T. McGillycuddy.

First train into the Badlands
Photo courtesy Rick Mills

But the railroad had yet to come the whole way to Deadwood. Years of expectation marked the coming of a railroad from the outside. From the earliest times the newspapers tracked the approaching railroad with alternating anticipation and frustration. Deadwood knew it would need the railroad if it were to succeed as the major center of Black Hills commerce. The town applied all the prestige and pressure it could summon up to that end. Regular reports of progress were framed in cautiously optimistic language throughout the years as the railroads approached Deadwood.

Black Hills Daily Pioneer, Jan 6, 1877
Pennsylvania Railroad manager may look at Deadwood.

Black Hills Daily Times, Sep 26, 1877
Railroad moving toward the hills.

Black Hills Daily Times, Oct 18, 1877
Northern Pacific Co. to begin work west of Missouri.

Black Hills Daily Times, Nov 1, 1877
Northern Pacific R.R. built to within 150 miles of Black Hills.

Black Hills Daily Time, Mar 4, 1878
Jay Gould determined to build railroad in Hills.

Black Hills Daily Pioneer, Apr 9, 1878
Black Hills Railroad Notes, contractors on way.

Black Hills Daily Times, Jun 4, 1878
Spearfish Townsite has fenced in 160 acres for railroad company.

Black Hills Daily Times, Sep 30, 1878
Agent for railroad in town to survey.

Black Hills Daily Times, Jul 17, 1879
We now have two surveyors in town for two railroads.

Black Hills Daily Times, Jul 23, 1880
Railroad building being pushed as never before.

Black Hills Daily Times, Aug 6, 1880
Report of dirt flying in earnest for railroad.

Black Hills Daily Times, Jan 12, 1881
Dakota leads the country in railroad growth.

Black Hills Daily Times, Jan 30, 1881
Says money will build railroad, not 'wind'.

Black Hills Daily Times, Sep 27, 1881
Deadwood will be trade center when railroad comes through.

Black Hills Daily Times Dec 6. 1881
Deadwood's development hampered without railroad. Will be crippled until we have railroad.

Black Hills Daily Times, Feb 7, 1882
Railroad committee to meet at Phoenix hall.

Black Hills Daily Times, Feb 9, 1882
Would build Deadwood-Pierre railroad for $500,000 bonds.

Black Hills Daily Times, Feb 17, 1882
Ben Baer on Committee on arrangements for railroad delegates.

Black Hills Daily Times, Feb 20, 1882
Jacob Goldberg. At board of trade's railroad banquet.

Black Hills Daily Times, May 4, 1882
Give us railroad & we will show "land of promise."

Black Hills Daily Times, Sep 4, 1883
Citizens meeting held with railroad representative.

Black Hills Daily Times, Jul 26, 1884
Another promised railroad.

By 1885 there were 40,000 people already in the Hills, and more on the way. The stagecoach lines couldn't possibly keep up with the demand for transportation. As the railroad gradually approached, officials of the Northwestern Stage Company rightly deduced they were about to have some competition. In 1886 the coaches suddenly became quite handsomely upholstered, more efficient in carrying mail, freight, and passengers, and with more horses per team. The trains reached Sturgis and Whitewood two years before they arrived in Deadwood.

Black Hills Daily Times, Jul 18, 1885
Harris Franklin holds to the opinion the Sioux City and Pacific extension will be completed across the Cheyenne by the 1st of November.

Black Hills Daily Times, Jul 19, 1885

Sidney drivers report that the railroad reached Chadron on Thursday.

Black Hills Daily Times, Oct 20, 1885

Railroad through Rapid City. Deals being made for railroad to pass through Rapid City via St. Joe Street, to Parkhurst's brewery, thence over to Box Elder and, hugging the Hills, continue on to Bear Butte and Whitewood.

Freight wagons gathered in Rapid City, end of the Fremont, Elkhorn and Missouri Valley Railroad, 1886
Photo courtesy Steve Norquist

Black Hills Daily Times, Jul 8, 1886

Railroad progressing at two miles per day. H.L. Hall, connected with the Burlington and Missouri arrived from the south last evening, and assures us that his company is making for the Hills at the rate of two miles a day.

Black Hills Daily Times, Mar 26, 1887

Railroad work to begin this summer. Mr. Warner came out from Chicago with Contractor Treat, who says work will begin on the Black Hills extension about July 1 and be pushed as far as possible this year.

Black Hills Daily Times, Oct 13, 1887

Railroad only five miles from Sturgis. End of track at a point one mile this side of Bull Dog last evening, leaving only five miles to complete to Sturgis.

Black Hills Daily Times, Oct 15, 1887

Track to reach Sturgis tomorrow. Railroad track to reach Sturgis tomorrow — immediate extension to Whitewood.

Black Hills Daily Times, Oct 25, 1887

Railroad news... on to Whitewood.

Black Hills Daily Times, Jan 12, 1888

Passenger agent arrives from railroad. Chris Jensen, passenger agent for the Northwestern between Sturgis and Rapid, arrived from the railroad last evening.

Black Hills Daily Times, Oct 29, 1889

City takes initiative on railroad. An important move: City Council takes initiative to encourage railroad building; representative citizens take the matter into their own hands and will wait on Burlington officials with a generous offer. Harris Franklin, Solomon Star, Sol Bloom, Louis Reubens

Black Hills Daily Times, Jan 1, 1890

...with particular reference to mines and mills and the ore and bullion output of Lawrence County respectfully submitted to railroad companies pointing lines in this direction; businessmen pledge to aid and support railroad line. Max Fishel, Sol Star, Harris Franklin, Ben Baer, W. E. Lowe and Company, M. Liebmann, Sol Rosenthal, Zoeckler Brothers, A. Hoffman and Brother, Blumenthal, and Jacobs, J. Hattenbach and Bro., L. Reuben, Franklin and Baer, Sol Bloom, M. J Wertheimer and Brother, Nathan Colman, H. Stein.

The arrival in December of 1890 of the through train changed Deadwood entirely and forever. The Fremont, Elkhorn and Missouri Valley train, otherwise known as the Elkhorn, followed shortly thereafter by the Burlington Railroad, signaled an end to the frontier, an end to the world of travel by stagecoach and freighting by bull train, and essentially tamed Deadwood. With the Deadwood band playing and flags flying, the entire population of the gulch turned out to welcome the Elkhorn, the first through train from Chicago, which finally connected Deadwood with the rest of the world.

The Elkhorn, the first standard gauge railway, heads for Deadwood
Photo courtesy Centennial Archives,
Deadwood Public Library

While conceding the benefits that derived from the advent of the railroad, Estelline Bennett wrote:

> "The essential qualities that made Deadwood a flaming frontier town went out with the old stagecoach or were ground to dust under the wheels of the incoming train."

As much as the Elkhorn had arrived in Deadwood, Deadwood had arrived in the world. The real estate market was already booming. Deliveries and shipments to and from the east would be expedited. Travel by train, although with no guarantee of safety, would be more comfortable and convenient, the mail more secure.

Black Hills Daily Times, Sep 29, 1877

James boys may have robbed Union Pacific Railroad.

Black Hills Daily Times, Dec 20, 1890

Railroad arrives in Deadwood. Yesterday was an historical one for Deadwood, when there came upon the Elkhorn line two of the locomotives driving a construction train and a gang of track layers before them, into our city limits.

Black Hills Daily Times, Jan 1, 1891

The days of freighting by wagon, and of passenger travel by stage have passed, never to return to Deadwood.

On January 24, 1891, the Burlington Railroad steamed northward into Deadwood from Lincoln/Edgemont. The Burlington also extended from Edgemont on into northeastern Wyoming Territory. Deadwood now had passenger and freighting service from two lines.

Black Hills Daily Times, Mar 28, 1891

Railroad accident. Fifty tons of rock and frozen earth suddenly gave way at a point behind Star & Bullock's Hardware store. Two graders had narrow escapes from burial.

Rapid City Daily Journal, May 5, 1891

The mining districts above Deadwood are becoming a veritable hive of industry. Railroads are extending their lines, not only into the districts, but practically to the workings of every prominent mining. By means of these facilities of transportation much ore will be handled and worked at a profit that was heretofore of no practical value.

Black Hills Daily Times, Aug 4, 1891

Harris Franklin shipped 11 carloads of cattle to market over the Elkhorn road. He will ship this season market between 3,000-4,000 steers.

Coal and timber companies laid track even in the highest reaches of the Hills. The Chicago and Northwestern with lines into Lead and Terry, maintained one of the most extensive rail systems in South Dakota. The Black Hills became pitted with mines and crisscrossed with rails, trails and roads. The image of a violent, lawless Black Hills frontier was to be perpetuated and romanticized by the likes of Annie Oakley and Buffalo Bill's Wild West Shows, artists like Charles Remington, dime novels, and moving pictures.

Strolling the streets of Deadwood made time melt away. I found some of the people and some of their places that helped make this town come to pass. From my new home-away-from-home, the Historic Franklin Hotel, I made my way along upper Main Street, from the "high-rent" district where the principal hotels and shops once flourished, down to the tumultuous "Badlands". It soon became apparent that during the first 50 years of Deadwood's existence, fully one-third of buildings along the way were either owned, operated or occupied by Jewish merchants and businesses. As I gleaned their stories, the significance of keeping a solid historical record became ever more evident. Some of the stories were more complete than others, some little more than scraps of information. With the help of a remarkably astute elderly lady, Blanche Colman, my neighbor at the Franklin Hotel, I would try to fill in the historical gap about the first 50 years of Jewish settlement in the Black Hills and western South Dakota.

Walking southward toward Wall Street, the beginning of the "Badlands," so named for the neighborhood's shady reputation, where no respectable lady would have ventured unaccompanied in Gold Rush days without a very good reason, the pictures began to develop. Despite the unwholesome character of this neighborhood, a few Jewish merchants had maintained successful businesses here. Ben Baer started his wholesale liquor business here. Sam Schwarzwald had his furniture business two doors down.

Across Main Street stood the Bullock Hotel, where Sol Star and Seth Bullock had started their hardware store. Mayor Solomon Star's leadership was so highly valued that he was elected for seven terms, each term of 2 years, for a total of 14 years. Their adjoining lot was purchased from the partnership of Henry Beaman and Sam Schwarzwald in April of 1877.

Moving northward along Main St., I noted the Levinson name engraved in the cornice of a building. On Sherman Street I found the sturdy brownstone Hattenbach Building, formerly their grocery business, also with the owner's name inscribed in the cornice. On Jefferson Street stood the elegant Franklin mansion, built as a family home by Harris Franklin, known as the wealthiest man in Deadwood, whose rags-to-riches story could have been the embodiment of the American dream. Now it was in use as a Bed and Breakfast hostel. And I climbed the hill to Mount Moriah and visited the Mount Zion section, known as Hebrew Hill, at the top of Jerusalem Avenue, where the tombstones, some beautifully inscribed in Hebrew, spoke of origins far across the Atlantic and ties unforgotten.

Later I would venture further up the mountain to Lead, where the mile-deep underground Homestake Mine, source of the mother lode of precious gold that made many, especially the Hearst family, fabulously wealthy. But there were other mines in the Hills, some owned and maintained by Jewish families, which deserved recognition. The Black Hills were mineral-rich and timber-rich, and those who could afford to do so, invested in the resources.

Ghost towns told stories, remote communities and trails where Jews had left a footprint held memories. I followed the Jew Peddler Trail where Harry Hyman Marks plied his solitary trade as a pack peddler. Jews had founded towns, they started communities. They weren't all millionaires or wealthy businessmen; some were farmers and ranchers and blacksmiths and hard-working miners.

I must admit I found certain place names objectionable, but my job as a journalist demanded nothing less than the truth. There were stories in all these places, but I would start on the streets of Deadwood and follow their path wherever it led.

HARRIS FRANKLIN

FRANKLIN HOTEL – 700 MAIN ST.

Harris Franklin
Photo courtesy Adams Museum

Harris Franklin was the primary investor in the Franklin Hotel, the most elegant lodging-place of its time. His story may be the quintessential American-Jewish success story. Early Deadwood and Lead owe much of their prosperity to the Franklins, who provided leadership, development, and jobs to the region. Harris and his son, Nathan, were foremost among Deadwood's early Jewish movers and shakers. The man for whom the Franklin Hotel was named was certainly one of the most powerful influencers in all the history of Deadwood. With his energy and involvement in a wide range of commercial, social and civic enterprises, boundlessly energetic, Harris Franklin never seemed to indulge in an idle moment.

Although few today are aware of the wealthy man's humble beginnings, Harris Franklin's name is legendary in Deadwood history. Franklin and his family were among the cream of Deadwood society and the darlings of the newspapers. Nearly everywhere they went and almost everything they did drew notice from the press. This European immigrant with the given surname of Finkelstein, grew up to become Harris Franklin, American multimillionaire, someone who affected not only the business, but the cultural climate of the Black Hills. His visionary leadership helped shape Deadwood's future from the very first. In a life filled with daring, extraordinary opportunity, equally astonishing good luck, and endless vitality, Harris Franklin is remembered for his generosity as well as for being a banker who never foreclosed on a mortgage.

Franklin Hotel under construction
Photo courtesy Centennial Archives,
Deadwood Public Library

Harris Finkelstein was born to Z. and Ellen Finkelstein on March 18th, 1849. His European origin was the shtetl (little town) of Pilvisok in Russian Poland. He lost his mother in early infancy and was raised by his father, a dealer in flaxseeds. His father left for America in 1864, leaving Harris in the care of an uncle, and the boy had a meager education.

In 1866 Harris, his brother Bernard (Barney), and a brother-in-law Wolf Frank, followed the elder Franklin, leaving Europe behind for a better life in America, and settling in Syracuse, New York. At the age of 15, like so many young Jewish men starting out in business, Harris picked up a peddler's pack and proceeded to conduct a small traveling enterprise throughout western New York State for the next two years.

At the age of 21, Harris moved on, and in Burlington, Iowa, managed to fulfill the dream of every pack peddler by opening a profitable little store. Finkelstein's name became Americanized to Franklin, and the young peddler with a good head for business was now a successful entrepreneur.

In 1870 Harris met Anna Steiner. Anna was born in Hanover, Germany, in March of 1848. When Anna was one year old the Steiners immigrated to the U.S.A., also settling in New York State, where Anna was raised and educated. Like Harris, the family eventually moved to Burlington, Iowa, where Anna and Harris met. There they married on January 1, 1870, and on December 15th, 1870, Anna gave birth to a son, their only child, Nathan E. Franklin.

Harris continued with his business in Iowa until 1871, when he sold out and moved his young family to Nebraska City, Nebraska, where he engaged in a wholesale and retail liquor business, building up a flourishing trade as one of its traveling salesmen. In 1873, however, times were hard and he lost all he had. He found a job working on the road for a cigar company out of Council Bluffs, Iowa, which continued for two more years. He decided to move to Laramie, Wyoming, where he again went into the wholesale liquor trade, this time so successfully that in 1877 he opened a branch store in Cheyenne. The Black Hills Gold Rush next attracted his interest, and Franklin traveled to Deadwood speculatively, carefully assessing business conditions in that camp.

Black Hills Daily Times, Aug 9, 1877
Hotel arrivals: Harris Franklin of Cheyenne at Grand Central Hotel.

Harris concluded that the liquor business in Deadwood was bound for success. In this wild, wide-open gold boom town, the mostly male population was all too ready to exchange a pinch of gold dust for a shot of whiskey. Based on his conclusions about the prospects of the Black Hills, in 1877 Harris sold his interests in Wyoming, opened a new branch of his liquor business in Deadwood, and moved his wife Anna and their seven-year-old son Nathan to their new home in the Black Hills.

CATTLE

In May of 1885 Harris went into a second business. With Ben Baer as his silent partner, Harris and Ben bought a herd of 600 head of beef cattle which they ran on Alkali Creek near Belle Fourche. In the brutal Dakota winter of 1886-1887, despite suffering severe losses of his own livestock, they took a huge gamble. When cattlemen in the area, owners of 23 brands, feared their herds would not survive the winter on the open range, the partners bought up their remaining livestock. The weather and good luck were on their side— most of the cattle made it through that winter. Beginning with his herd in the Belle Fourche Valley, the firm of Franklin Cattle Company built up one of the largest businesses in the state. Franklin and Baer found themselves the owners of an enormous herd. Franklin took an active part in supervising and managing their cattle business. These were free-range days, before barbed wire fences obstructed the movement of cattle. With summer pastures in Saskatchewan and Eastern Alberta, to winters in Texas, their cattle company prospered, absorbing both the huge Hash Knife and Turkey Track outfits as well as others adjoining. With a large number of horses, and annual shipments of some 10,000 cattle from a herd of at least 45,000 head, the Franklin Cattle

Company contributed greatly to Belle Fourche's reputation as a cow town.

Black Hills Daily Times, Apr 13, 1886

Large calf crop. Harris Franklin is advised that a bunch of 136 cows on his range has dropped over 100 calves.

Black Hills Daily Times, Apr 1, 1887

Franklin brand, Belle Fourche range. Brand 7S, also L S left side, Y S left side, S Y right side, 9 (inverted) T left side and triple bar 7 B on either side. Harris Franklin, Will pay reward for information for any strayed or stolen.

Black Hills Daily Times, Apr 13, 1887

Harris Franklin, Admitted to Wyoming Stock Growers' Association.

Black Hills Daily Times, Jul 23, 1887

Harris Franklin returned yesterday from a visit at his Alkali cattle ranch and the range. Round-up shows loss of 50 percent.

Black Hills Daily Times, Jul 28, 1887

Franklin purchases Cross S brand. That all cowmen are not disheartened by reverses of the season, was indicated yesterday by the purchase by Harris Franklin of the Cross S brand owned by Mahan & Baird; E6—Dorr Clark —brand sold to the Hash Knife

Black Hills Daily Times, Sep 13, 1887

Harris Franklin in from three days at XS ranch. Cattle looking fine on the range.

Black Hills Daily Times, Aug 4, 1891

Harris Franklin shipped 11 carloads of cattle to market over the Elkhorn (rail)road. He will this season market between 3,000-4,000 steers.

Black Hills Daily Times Sep 30, 1891

Harris Franklin returned from Belle Fourche where he superintended loading of 600 head of cattle he is shipping to Chicago market.

Black Hills Daily Times, May 1, 1892

Charlie King, Sturgis, states he has closed out his cattle interests to Harris Franklin.

As his profits from liquor had grown, he reinvested the assets in livestock and agriculture. By 1885 free-range days were drawing to a close. Homesteaders were claiming land, setting up their tar paper shacks and sod houses, and developing their acreages. The invention of barbed wire in 1783 had changed the way livestock would be raised, and now settlers plowed the land and fenced in pastures. Franklin started to invest more in agriculture, planting crops on 80 acres in the fertile Centennial Valley near Spearfish.

Black Hills Daily Times, Sept 24, 1885

Harris Franklin nets $800 from the crop of 80 acres of Centennial land, all work with hired help.

In 1905 Harris sold off half his cattle. In 1907 he sold the remainder of his cattle to the American Livestock and Loan Co. in Denver, and effectively left the livestock business.

DIVERSE BUSINESS INTERESTS

Meanwhile, Harris had continued to diversify. In 1884 he promoted the Deadwood Flouring Mill, the first flour mill of Deadwood, entering into this venture with Sol Star, Ben Baer, and Daniel McLaughlin. It had a capacity of 200 barrels of flour per day and operated successfully for 16 years. In 1897 the mill burned and was not rebuilt.

Black Hills Daily Times, Oct 9, 1884

Deadwood Flouring Mill Company formed. A new organization completed by election of officers for the Deadwood Flouring Mill Company. Harris Franklin, Sol Star, Ben Baer, Daniel McLaughlin.

Franklin developed a wide range of business interests. Deadwood needed electricity for mining operations, public and private use. In 1883 Paul Rewman had organized Black Hills Electric Light Company, forerunner of the present-day Black Hills Power and Light Company. The company struggled at first. In 1887 Harris Franklin came forward with others, bought the plant and put it on a permanent and successful basis with modern methods. Consolidated Power and Light Company of South Dakota was formed, the result of a merger of the Lead and Deadwood power and light companies, with the principal office in Deadwood. Harris, one of nine directors, was elected president. The company enlarged the new Pluma power plant to 3,500 kilowatts and distribution lines were built to Lead and Deadwood at 2,300 volts. Power for the rapidly growing gold mining operations was served at 11,000 volts in the Bald Mountain and Galena districts.

Electrically lit signs for advertising became a favorite of the business community. Star and Bullock were said to have a sign that could be seen from a great distance, and the modern lighting system became an object of city pride, impressing visitors with Deadwood's up-to-the-minute technology, the first community of the Black Hills to have electric power.

Black Hills Daily Times, Jan 1, 1892
Black Hills Electric Light Company organized in 1883 and is a credit to any city in the country. Harris Franklin, Sol Star, Paul Rewman, Consolidated Power and Light Company of Deadwood and Lead, now one of the largest power and light companies in the west, furnished light and power to all of the mining companies in the locality and to a number of small cities, including Whitewood, Sturgis, Belle Fourche, Portland, Terry, and Central City.

Black Hills Daily Times, Dec 2, 1881
Harris Franklin on board of directors, Deadwood Smelting Co.

Franklin's Golden Reward Mining Company spent four years attempting to develop a process of extracting precious metals from refractory ore at a profit, a technology that required research, expertise, and equipment. It also demanded substantial capital. Their eventual discovery of a successful chlorination process made the work much more profitable, finally making it pay. In 1890 his chlorination process was put into full operation, making it the first successful chlorination plant in practical use in the world.

Black Hills Daily Times, Jan 1, 1891
Chlorination works. What the Golden Reward has accomplished at its plant; a great industry built by coinage, enterprise and good management.

South Dakota's Governor Mellette addressed the state legislature in 1893 and declared that the advance in the gold industry had been phenomenal. The previous two years had shown marvelous mining developments and evolutions. The successful treatment of refractory ores was the single greatest advance. As the Governor stated, "the refractory ores had long baffled the genius of invention and the skill of science in an effort to extract the metal with profit. The profitable treatment of these ores, which were numerous in extent, marks the beginning of a new and most important era in the development of the mineral resources of the state and has increased by 33.5 per cent the shipment of gold bullion from the Hills"

By 1894, the Black Hills had produced $56 million in gold. By 1896 the Black Hills gold output surpassed that of Leadville, and was second only to Cripple Creek, Colorado.

Harris Franklin's influence eventually extended eastward to include the vast financial resources of New York State. In 1896 Franklin sold most of his interests in mining to New York capitalists, turning the presidency of the Golden Reward over to partner E.W. Harriman, who was among many eastern financiers jockeying for the investment opportunity. Late in 1897 the company was reorganized as the Golden Reward Consolidated Gold Mining and Milling Company. At that time the property contained more than 440 patented claims, or about 3,400 acres of land. Early in 1895, the Golden Reward Mining Company showed as the product of six days' work a flat brick worth $17,000. By 1901 it was estimated that $8 million dollars' worth of gold had been taken out of the Black Hills region. The Golden Reward was behind Homestake with $1.2 million, lower than the $4.3 million of the Homestake. This standing continued until high costs as a result of World War I caused the Golden Reward to close. By the time the Golden Reward closed in 1918 it had produced approximately $21 million or 371,000 ounces in gold. The Golden Reward never produced spectacular gold specimens, rich veins, or headline stories, but as a result of its innovative recovery techniques its production figures were enormous.

When Anna died, Harris moved to New York City, leaving his son to succeed him on the board of Consolidated Power and Light. Nathan expanded Consolidated's reach in June of 1910 when the company purchased the assets of Black Hills Traction Company and the stock of Black Hills Water Power Company. The company's assets included a canal that ran water from Crow Creek and Redwater Creek via a wooden flume to a power house where the water turned two 1000-horse-power turbines connected to a 500-kW, 3-phase, 60-cycle Westinghouse generator.

Awaiting the Treasure Coach
Photo courtesy Adams Museum

Franklin took an active part in most of the major economic developments of the day. Franklin, Ben Baer, Paul Rewman, and Sol Star were in large part responsible for the existence of such financial underpinnings as the Deadwood Stock Exchange in 1887 and the Board of Trade which was organized in 1891.

Black Hills Daily Times, Jan 22, 1887

First step for organization of Deadwood Stock Exchange, taken last evening. Charter obtained last summer, but nothing done towards organization. Sol Star, Ben Baer, Harris Franklin.

Black Hills Daily Times, May 7, 1891

Board of trade organized at last. A board of trade brought into existence last night. Ben Baer, Seth Bullock, Paul Rewman, Harris Franklin.

Black Hills Daily Times, May 10, 1891

Board of Trade earnestly at work; delegates to Yankton and Denver; hotel committee.

TRAVEL

Harris Franklin traveled extensively and tirelessly following his business pursuits and family affairs. He would no sooner come back from one trip, but there would be another reason to be off on the next. Deadwood was a long way from the nearest railroad depot until 1890. In a day when travel required either scheduled trips by way of stagecoach or unscheduled trips by horseback, or horse and buggy over very rough, dangerous, and undependable roads, Harris was unfazed. He traveled to Chicago for his cattle business and to New York for his mining interests. He traveled more locally to evaluate potential investments in property in up-and-coming Buffalo Gap and Chadron. He took his family to Indiana where his son, Nathan, attended pharmacy school at Notre Dame University. He traveled to Seattle to visit old friends. Little trips to Belle Fourche and Sturgis and Rapid City and Hot Springs were all part of the weekly schedule. Small wonder Harris Franklin was determined to bring the railroad to Deadwood.

Black Hills Daily Times Feb 6, 1884

Mr. Franklin has returned from Sturgis where he was attending to business.

Black Hills Daily Times Jul 4, 1884

Harris Franklin returned last evening from an extended eastern and southern purchasing tour.

Black Hills Daily Times, Jan 27, 1885

Harris Franklin, wife and Nathan, leave this morning for Chicago and New Orleans, to be absent two or three months.

Black Hills Daily Times, Jul 16, 1885

Harris Franklin reached Rapid yesterday on his return from Chadron. He will not arrive home for a day or two.

Black Hills Daily Times, Nov 25, 1885

Postmaster Carney and Harris Franklin leave by coach this morning for Buffalo Gap, to attend the sale of town lots on Friday.

Black Hills Daily Times, Dec 6, 1885

Harris Franklin returned yesterday from a speculative trip to the Gap and Chadron. He says that Chadron is the liveliest and prettiest town for its age in the West.

Black Hills Daily Times, Dec 29, 1885

Harris Franklin was at Rapid last evening.

Black Hills Daily Times, May 14, 1886

Harris Franklin arrived at Rapid from the East by private conveyance last evening, and will return to Deadwood tomorrow.

Black Hills Daily Times, May 14, 1886

The Coeur d'Alene Record announces the arrival of Harris Franklin en route to the Pacific coast. Harris evidently has a double in the northern country.

Black Hills Daily Times, May 15, 1886

Harris Franklin returned last evening from a circuitous trip of 4,064 miles. Ostensibly the jaunt was undertaken to buy cattle, but practically in search of stock of an entirely different character.

Black Hills Daily Times, May 25, 1886

Harris Franklin went out to the round-up yesterday, finding it about three miles below Fort Meade, making very satisfactory progress.

Black Hills Daily Times, Sep 12, 1886

Mrs. Harris Franklin meets her husband at the end of the track this morning, and thence they proceed to Chicago.

Black Hills Daily Times, Oct 15, 1886

Mrs. Harris Franklin returned from Chicago last evening. Mr. Franklin was re-called to the Gap, and will be up today.

Black Hills Daily Times, Oct 17, 1886

Harris Franklin reached home from Chicago last evening.

Black Hills Daily Times, Nov 5, 1886

Harris Franklin went down to Rapid yesterday

Black Hills Daily Times, Oct 7, 1887

Harris Franklin leaves this morning for Chicago with a train load of beef cattle.

Black Hills Daily Times, Oct 29, 1887

Where's Harris Franklin? The wire freely resorted to in an endeavor to locate Harris Franklin. When last heard from he was at New York.

Black Hills Daily Times, Jul 3, 1888

Harris Franklin returned from his eastern trip yesterday.

Black Hills Daily Times, Nov 4, 1888

Harris and Mrs. Franklin returned from the east, where Mr. Franklin gave the political situation much study.

Black Hills Daily Times, (undated)

" Looking the picture of health and happiness, Harris Franklin came in on yesterday's Northwestern after a three months' trip through the West and South. He left Mrs. Franklin in excellent health with her mother in St. Louis for short visit, after which she will join him here. The Franklins had a splendid trip. They went all over the Western Coast and then down through the south to Hot Springs, Arkansas, where they rested up a little. Mr. Franklin declares that Seattle is the best City in the northwest and is booming with three railroads building in. It presents, according to Mr. Franklin, the best outlook for a man that he has seen. At Seattle he found M. Gottstein, his former partner, who left here 10 years ago and got rich in Seattle. In Los Angeles he found Selbie, Dr. Dickenson, Will Dickenson, Hattenbach, and others, all of whom are doing nicely. He will be here now for some time.

BANKING

First National Bank: 666 Main St.
Photo courtesy Adams Museum

In the spring of 1877, the First National Bank building, a two-story wood frame building located at 666 Main St., the corner of Main and Lee Streets, was originally organized as the Bank of Stebbins, Post & Company. It was destroyed along with so much of the town in the Great Fire of 1879. Despite the loss, the bank rebuilt. In August of 1910, it underwent extensive exterior and interior remodeling. This included total reconstruction of the first floor, relocation of the main entrance, and a 25-foot addition on the back of the building.

In 1895 Harris had used his financial skills to organize the American National Bank of Deadwood with a capital stock of $50,000. This bank flourished, and in 1902 he bought a controlling interest in the First National Bank in partnership with Ben Baer. Along with Franklin and Baer, among the roll call of stockholders and directors was Jacob Goldberg. The two banks consolidated, together holding capital of $100,000 and a surplus of $90,000. Harris Franklin assumed the position of bank president, and brought his son, Nathan, a recent graduate of Notre Dame Pharmacy School, who was already operating the Palace Pharmacy, into the bank as cashier. Nathan disposed of the

Palace Pharmacy, and continued on as cashier at the bank for the next three years. The young man showed considerable executive and administrative talent and Nathan was named president of that institution. Harris remained one of the directors and active managers, although management of the bank was in the hands of Nathan from 1905 until his resignation in 1917.

POLITICS

Although Harris Franklin kept an eye on the political situation, it was an area in which he dabbled only briefly. He managed to stay independent of party control. His various business interests occupied his attention, and he showed little taste or time for political life. Harris never sought or desired public office, but in 1885 a group petitioned to have him run for City Council, to which he agreed. Baer and many of his fellow Jewish citizens, including Charles Posner, Max Fishel, B.H. Kohorn, S. Koenigsberger, Louis Reubens, Joseph Reubens, Ben Holstein, and William Rosenbaum, were among those who urged him to run. The ticket was supported by the Black Hills Daily Times, which jubilated when their nominee won.

Black Hills Daily Times, Apr 21, 1885
Citizens petition Franklin for councilman, Residents and taxpayers of Fourth ward petition Harris Franklin to become candidate for councilman. Seth Bullock, Ben Baer, S. Koenigsberger, B. H. Kohorn, Zoeckler Brothers, Charles Posner, Max Fishel, L. Reubens, J. Reubens, Ben Holstein, William Rosenbaum, L. Gross.

Black Hills Daily Times, Apr 25, 1885
A.J. Plowman's votes as candidate for district attorney in 1892 should settle the question of personal influence and popularity. Harris Franklin is the people's choice.

Black Hills Daily Times, Apr 30, 1885
Harris Franklin, popular candidate from the Fourth ward, has built 125 feet of new sidewalk at his own expense.

Black Hills Daily Times, Jun 16, 1885
Deadwood city council meeting. Common council met at the usual hour with petitions for a street; a sewer; repairing sidewalk; and water mains.

Franklin believed his main public service resided in his skills with economic development. During his tenure he supported street repairs, the installation of water mains and other civic issues, but Franklin's support for Deadwood was brought to bear mainly in his activities in the private sector. He was earnestly interested in the advancement and general welfare of his community, and spared no effort in promoting them. Once having served his term as city councilman, Harris Franklin withdrew from government service and never ran for office again, but his interest and influence helped bring the railroad to Deadwood, a major achievement.

Black Hills Daily Times Sep 4, 1883
Harris Franklin, Citizens meeting held with railroad representative.

Black Hills Daily Times, Jul 18, 1885
Harris Franklin holds to the opinion the Sioux City and Pacific extension will be completed across the Cheyenne by the 1st of November.

Black Hills Daily Times, Nov 29, 1885
Railroad news includes announcement of tin spike driven at Buffalo Gap.

Black Hills Daily Times, Jan 29, 1886
Harris Franklin informed by Contractor Treat that track laying would resume Feb.1.

HOTEL

In 1891 Deadwood businessmen recognized that if their city were to sustain its central role in the Black Hills, one major, indispensable element was missing: Deadwood needed a modern, luxurious hotel where it could welcome visitors in style.

Black Hills Daily Times, Feb 7 1891

Deadwood Club committee on yesterday began canvass for subscriptions toward purchase of site for mammoth hotel, Mr. Casey agrees to build.

The Deadwood Business Club was formed in 1892 and comprised 250 of the city's elite and most successful businessmen. For the membership price of $100 a gentleman could find a refuge where he might relax, dine in comfort, discuss business or socialize in a refined atmosphere. One of the primary objectives of the Deadwood Business Club was to promote Deadwood as the commercial and tourism capital of the Black Hills; the luxurious Franklin Hotel was a major part of the plan. Included among the roster of charter members were such outstanding Jewish citizens as Ben Baer, Harris Franklin, Jacob Goldberg, Max Fishel, and Sol Star

In 1892 Harris sold off some of his cattle and used the proceeds to begin construction of the hotel. Forty thousand dollars was expended in purchasing the site and laying the foundation. Owing to the general depression of business in the country, the enterprise languished for about nine years. By 1902 Franklin's finances were nearly exhausted and the hotel was still not complete. For a token $1, Harris sold his share of the hotel to his son, Nathan, who together with the Deadwood Business Club, raised money and subscriptions totaling $150,000 to complete the four-story brick and stone hotel.

The magnificent Historic Franklin Hotel, grand dame of Deadwood hospitality, first opened its doors on June 4th, 1903. This enduring showplace was welcomed with an elaborate reception and ball.

At a time when only 14% of the homes in the U.S. had a bathtub, and only 8% had a telephone, the Franklin Hotel offered the height of luxury while it cultivated a sense of hearth and home in the untamed West. The grand opening in June of 1903 was described in the newspapers in exquisite detail.

Daily Pioneer-Times, Jun 5, 1903

GRAND INAUGURAL OF THE FRANKLIN HOTEL,

Hotel Opened to Public in Extravagant Ceremonies, A Model Structure in Every Respect

"The Franklin, Deadwood's magnificent new hotel, built at a cost of a tenth of a million and named after one of the most enterprising citizens of the town, Harris Franklin, was inaugurated last night, Thursday, June 4th, 1903, with an elaborate reception and ball.

The interior of the handsome new building was ablaze with a great number of electric lights, which shown as artistic decorations about the large rooms. Guests entered through the spacious lobby and were ushered to the cloak rooms, and were free to dance or become spectators of the concert.

The general dining room was used for dancing purposes with the musicians occupying a platform in the southwest corner of the room, where they were all but obscured by a bank of palms and other plants, and draperies. The orchestra in the dancing hall consisted of seven pieces.

The concert was given on the balcony of the second floor. Some very pretty music was heard. The first number was a march, composed by G. B. Beere, leader of the orchestra, especially for the occasion and named 'The Franklin'. This was followed by nearly a dozen popular pieces, including 'The Ram',

'Fortune Teller', 'I've Got My Eyes on You' (medley), selection from the catchy opera 'Floradora', selection from 'Chimes of Normandy', and also from the Opera 'Prince of Pilsen'.

The balcony over the principal entrance was a brilliant spectacle. All around the ballustrude evergreens were placed, and festoons of Chinese lanterns swung a little above the heads of the people. The balcony was set with round tables and chairs, and groups of people partook of refreshments throughout the evening.

The new hotel is one of the most sightly structures in the west and would be fitting in a city of 100,000 inhabitants. Its interior appointments are entirely in keeping with its classic exterior.

The exterior walls are of White Burke stone for the first story and of St. Louis hydraulic press brick of the remaining three stories, with White Burke stone trimmings.

The entrance is of pure Greek in style, constructed of golden oak, finished natural, with French art glass transoms, and trimmed in antique copper. The loads above the entrance are supported by four massive Greek pilasters of White Burke stone, cut and carved with Greek tracery.

Immediately over the entrance is a Greek portico with balcony above for outdoor use. The balcony is floored for dancing and other open-air amusements. All around the balcony is a ramp ballustrude. The portico is supported by heavy Greek columns resting on stone bases.

The main entrance opens into a lobby with a classic brick fireplace which has specially molded bases and cornices, manufactured at St. Louis after a special design detailed by the architect. The lobby is floored with ceramic mosaic tile; the side walls are burlapped terra cotta, and wainscoted four feet high in golden oak; the ceiling a steel, Greek design, finished in the old ivory white and highlighted in fire bronze. The main stairway and elevator communicate with the lobby and off the lobby is the library and waiting room. The lobby has a public entrance and a private entrance for ladies.

The general dining room, with rounded corners, is finished in golden oak, with classic Greek ceilings, finished in old ivory white and highlighted in gold bronze. The side walls are maroon burlap stenciled in old gold, and wainscoted with golden oak.

On the second floor over the lobby are two ladies parlors, communicating with the balcony; one of these parlors is public and the other for private use, with sliding doors between. In the public parlor, which is the larger of the two, is a classic fireplace. Both parlors are finished in golden oak, with green burlap side walls.

The main stairway from the lobby forms a rotunda clear to the roof, lighted by a large skylight above. The corridors are in a line and well lighted.

The rooms are arranged for use in suites, capable of being thrown into from two to five rooms to the suite. There are 30 private baths and three public baths in the building. All inside baths are provided with duct ventilators. They all have modern plumbing, the bathtubs and lavatories being of enameled cast iron.

All the best rooms are wired for the inter-communicating Bell Telephone System. A telephone instrument will be placed in each room, and guests may talk with the clerk or with the other rooms of the house. This system may be still further extended if an arrangement is entered into with one of the telephone companies, so as to give the guest the benefit of the general outside telephone system over the city and county from his room.

The building is richly furnished throughout. The dining room furniture consists of antique oak tables and chairs; the draperies in the main dining room are Oriental surrah and the floors are laid with Wilton carpet runners between tables. A private dining room is draped with silk damask and colored applique lace curtains.

The main bedrooms, including the bridal chamber, corner and some of the front rooms, are furnished with brass beds, and the other rooms with fancy *iron beds all made on special order. There are hair box springs and hair mattresses throughout. The floors are laid with Wilton rugs. There are caches in all the larger rooms, old dressers and wash stands, leather covered rockers, fancy small chairs, and lace curtains.*

According to the hotel's brochure, the "Franklin Hotel was the scene of one of the most elegant dinners ever served (in Deadwood), that cooked for President Taft on October 21, 1911, by Franklin Chef Arthur E. Bailey. "

Menu

Consomme
Black Hills celery
Salted almonds
Rainbow trout
Swansdown rolls
Frog saddle au gratin
Mountain sheep
Stuffed baked potatoes
Domestic green peas
Native pheasant on toast
Fruit salad
Cantaloupe a la mode
Roquefort cheese
Coffee
Wafers
Mineral water from
White Rock
&
Minnekahta Springs

Using some imagination, a procession of celebrity ghosts files through the elegant lobby and ascends the grand staircase to survey the view from the second-floor veranda. The Green Room leading to the veranda, with its tile fireplace and velvet fainting couch, was the setting for some of the more fashionable events and weddings of their time.

Through the years, the Franklin Hotel hosted a long list of celebrity guests, some of whom had rooms and suites named for them. Such notables as Pearl S. Buck, President Theodore Roosevelt, William Howard Taft, Buffalo Bill, Babe Ruth, and John Wayne were hosted here. The Franklin also became the retirement residence for some of the well-to-do of Deadwood's own citizenry, including Blanche and Theresa Colman. Blanche was honored with suite number 201, which bore her name and where she had her office for 12 years. Mrs. Charlie Klein, widow of the owner of Deadwood's earliest movie theater, also made her residence on the third floor, with a sweeping view of Main Street.

HOME

22 VAN BUREN ST.

The Franklins' first residence in Deadwood was a small cottage, but the needs of their lifestyle and social status soon outgrew their first house. As the Franklins' position in society grew, it demanded a fine home in which to reside as well as entertain. In 1892, two years following the arrival of the railroad, they began planning for a change. Anna had paid $1,175 between 1883 and 1890 for lots she'd purchased in the stylish Ingleside neighborhood in anticipation of their wish to relocate.

Black Hills Daily Times, Mar 22, 1892

Mr. and Mrs. Harris Franklin will commence erection of an elegant residence upon their choice lots on Ingleside. First story will be of Buffalo Gap red granite, second of metallic shingles; plate glass windows, tile and hardwood floors and antique oak inside finish.

Black Hills Daily Times, May 18, 1892

Austin Mabbs commenced moving Harris Franklin cottage to lot opposite freight depot. The other house will be moved right away and work on elegant new residence will be pushed rapidly.

Black Hills Daily Times, May 22, 1892

Small residence building owned by Harris Franklin moved to lot on east side of Lincoln Avenue.

In 1891 Franklin engaged renowned Chicago synagogue architect, Simeon Eisendrath, of the Chicago firm of Adler & Sullivan, to design their new home on Van Buren St. Eisendrath's portfolio included some of the premier buildings of the East, including Hebrew Union College/Jewish Institute of Religion in New York City near Central Park West; the Brooklyn Hebrew Home for the Aged; Shaari Zedek Synagogue in Brooklyn, New York; and the Jewish Orphan Asylum in Chicago. Eisendrath designed an elegant Queen Anne-style home for the Franklins on Anna's four parcels of land on Van Buren St. in the Ingleside section below Mt. Moriah. All the design was done from his Chicago office; Eisendrath never came to Deadwood, never saw the finished home. Local contractors Tuplin and Johnston began work in 1892.

The stately Franklin mansion was the town showplace. The opening of their home symbolized a new age of wealth and social status for Deadwood. The home was remarkably modern and elaborate, and thanks to the arrival of the railroad in 1890, Franklin was able to import the latest in modern furnishings and fixtures from the east. The Franklin mansion was the first in Deadwood to have modern electricity, plumbing and telephone. In typical Queen Anne style, the house had contrasting building materials, a turret, stained glass windows, a balcony, and a wraparound porch. The granite for the foundation came from Buffalo Gap. Similar houses in urban centers at the time cost approximately $5,000-$6,000. Within a year they had built a home that was variously called the finest residence in Deadwood, the finest residence in the Black Hills, and the finest residence west of the Mississippi. Once the Franklins took residence, they entertained extensively in their new home.

Franklin family at home
Photo courtesy Adams Museum

Black Hills Daily Times, Jun 2, 1893

Palatial home of Mr. and Mrs. H. Franklin all finished except a little painting

In the summer of 1893 a pioneer reporter was invited to the house to enjoy "a pleasant hour looking through the elegant new home of Mr. and Mrs. Harris Franklin of the Ingleside." His report paints a rich picture of the splendid new residence, a scene hardly imaginable a little over one decade before.

Built principally of the handsome red granite of this section, of their dimensions and moderate design, it presents an external appearance very much in harmony with the spacious apartments and sumptuous furnishings within. The four principal rooms of the first floor are the reception room, parlor, library, and dining room. These four large rooms and a broad hall can all be thrown into practically one apartment for receptions and other social occasions. The finishing is all in hardwood and the stairway based on the first landing with an elegant ornamental panel of Persian workmanship, is in harmony with the general elegance of the furnishings. The parlor, which forms one of the three large rooms in the circular northwest corner, has a rose tinted moquet carpet, and yields furniture upholstered in soft tinted satin and silk. The curtain drapings, which are very rich and beautiful, are, as with all the other draping and carpet work, the work of an expert sent here from Chicago for that purpose. The mantle front of this elegant room is of onyx.

The library is carpeted in green and mahogany furniture upholstered in dark leather. It is one of the most comfortable rooms in the house, and will be Mr. Franklin's den. The dining room is carpeted in a soft tinted drab with curtains to match and rosewood furniture upholstered in harmonious shades. The dining room floor is finished in oil and covered with rich rugs, and flanked on one side by a very large mirror and on the opposite side by an elegant side board. The conservatory flanks the dining room on the South and will be the home of some of the most choice plants grown. The china closet is perhaps one of the most richly furnished in china and elegant cut glassware while the pantry, kitchen and other appointments are as complete as money can furnish.

On the second floor are four large apartments, a sitting room and three sleeping rooms, besides the servants' apartments. This sitting room is carpeted in a soft shaded moquet with pink tinted curtains and rosewood furniture upholstered in crimson silk plush. The sleeping room of Mr. and Mrs. Franklin has a rich pink-flower carpet and heavy rosewood furniture, light drab draperies and a general air of modest elegance. Mr. Nathan Franklin's room is carpeted in Chinese flooring and covered with loose rugs. The furniture is black walnut and the apartment one of the most comfortable in the house.

The guest chamber is an elegant apartment, carpeted in a soft drab moquet with rich draperies. The canopied brass bedstead with elegant finishing of satin and silk complete the equipment of this lovely apartment. The bathroom is tiled on the floor and side walls clear to the ceiling. In the ceiling handsomely ornamental and the fittings are of the finest. On the third floor is a pretty card room which is furnished throughout with red moquet, and altogether one of the richest and most complete apartments of the kind we have yet seen.

The entire house is equipped with electric lights and call bells, heated by a Bolton self-regulating hot water heater. The plumbing is all exposed work, nickel, and throughout the entire residence there pervades a delightful air of rich but modest elegance such as is truly refreshing today. It is one of the most sumptuous homes west of Chicago and in which we hope Mr. Franklin and his excellent family may find many happy years."

When the Franklins decided to redecorate in 1896, again they turned to Chicago for professional help, enlisting the firm of Mitchell and Halbach to paint delicate friezes on the parlor and bedroom walls.

Gracious living made the house the scene of some of the most elaborate dinners ever seen in Deadwood. The teas and society gatherings were reported in generous detail in the newspapers. One early edition of the Deadwood Pioneer-Times refers to a sumptuous banquet consisting of oysters, grouse, Philips dates, turkey, French peas, chicken salad, plum pudding with brandy sauce, and five kinds of cake. An invitation to one of their luncheons or soirees was highly prized.

Black Hills Daily Times, Sep 5, 1891

A pleasant party at Franklin residence. Ladies fortunate enough to have enjoyed Mrs. Harris Franklin's hospitality all agree the tea and euchre party one of the most agreeable of the season.

Black Hills Daily Times, Jul 23, 1894

Mrs. Franklin last evening entertained about 5 chosen lady friends at 6 o'clock tea and cards, in honor of her guest, Mrs. Sol Bennett, of Peoria, Illinois. The spread was delicious and consisted of many of the daintiest dishes. The evening was progressive and was pleasantly passed. Mrs. Bennett won the gent's prize, Mrs. Charles won the lady's prize, and Mrs. Doctor Howe the grand prize, and Mrs. Kate Madden won the booby.

Now it is designated as the Adams House Museum. The home that Harris Franklin built was declared a National Historical Landmark. and was opened to visitors as the Adams House Museum in 2000. In 2007 a historic interpretive plaque explaining the origins of Franklin's home was installed in the side yard by Jerry Klinger of the Jewish American Society for Historic Preservation.

HEALTH

The life of the Franklin family was of interest to the people of Deadwood, and as public figures the Franklins were constantly in the spotlight. Whether they traveled, or had cause for sorrow or celebration, it all made the news.

Black Hills Daily Times, May 3, 1890

Mrs. Franklin recovering. Mrs. Harris Franklin was downtown yesterday for the first time in four months, or since she was first taken ill.

Black Hills Daily Times, Jun 25, 1890

M. Liebmann returns from Hot Springs, reporting J.J. Groff, Mrs. Harris Franklin and Mrs. A. Needham all greatly benefitted by the water. John Hunter and wife and Harris Franklin returned. Franklin says the plunge bath the best feature, even if he did mash a toe therein.

Black Hills Daily Times, Mar 21, 1890

Harris Franklin continues much of a sufferer with rheumatism. He goes to Hot Springs today in search of relief.

Black Hills Daily Times, Mar 29, 1890

Two out of three benefit from springs. Harris Franklin, Mayor Star and Jack Gray return from Hot Springs, Mayor Star very little if any benefited.

No ordinary travelers, when Anna's health began to fail and she felt in need of a vacation on the Pacific Coast, Anna, Nathan, Ada, and Mildred, accompanied by a nurse and Doctor W.W. Torrence (and his own private physician), were provided the private railroad car of A.G. Bert, president of the Union Pacific Railroad Company. The newspapers noted that Mrs. Harris Franklin had been having poor health for some time, and she deemed it best to provide for anything that might occur en route. Dr. Torrence had not been feeling well himself for some time, and he considered this a good time to take a vacation.

Anna's health continued to fail. When she died in Chicago on January 10, 1902, her remains were returned to Deadwood for burial in the Franklin family burial plot high in the Mount Zion section of Mount Moriah Cemetery. Sol Star recited the liturgy.

Following his wife's death, the house was too big for Harris. He sold the family's mansion to their son, Nathan, for $1, and left Deadwood for New York City. Still an energetic and zestful man, Harris found new life with a new woman. Mrs. Sadie Rohr, a young widow to whom he had been introduced in Atlantic City, New Jersey, would become the newest object of Deadwood's affection. Harris returned to Deadwood from a trip to the east beaming with pride, looking "10 years younger" and eager to set rumors of his approaching wedding day to rest as his friends hurried to congratulate him.

The papers were delighted to report each detail of Harris's happy new engagement.

Black Hills Daily Times, (undated)
WEDDING DATE IS NOT SET

Mr. Franklin is as jubilant in manner as his voice indicates and he appears to be 10 years younger than when he went East. He talked of his engagement with the frankness of a boy. "Indeed, I am entitled to congratulations", he replied to a query "for I am engaged to one of the sweetest women who is as attractive as she looks." Here he paused long enough to draw from his pocket the portrait of a good-looking young woman of some 30-odd years. "Yes", he continued "she is a most noble woman and I am very happy. While all that was printed was not true, I think it must have been a case of love at first sight for we were mutually attracted. She is gracious, charming, and has a rare amount of good sense."

"I met her (Mrs. Sadie Rohr) through her sister who is a good friend of mine at Atlantic City, NJ. She is a widow and comes from an excellent old family and is a very congenial woman. She is a good housekeeper and talented in more ways than one."

"Married? Oh, that is some time off yet and we have not yet set a date. We are happy as it is and there is time enough. We will make our home in Deadwood for I could never go back on this place although we will take a European trip and be away sometime after I get my business affairs straightened out." Mr. Franklin will be here for about three weeks before going East where he will probably be married. He is a wealthy man and known throughout the country.

Sadie and Harris Franklin were married in St. Louis in the latter part of October, honeymooning in Washington, New York, and other cities and resorts, returning by way of Indiana and Chicago. Their stop in Deadwood was part of their travel plan which also included continuing on to the Pacific Coast. Immediately upon their return to Deadwood on the Northwestern, the couple became the center of society interest, and the newspapers, once again, waxed eloquent.

Black Hills Daily Times, (undated)

... (The Franklins) are at the Franklin Hotel where they will remain a few weeks while Mr. Franklin looks after some business matters and then they will continue thereafter to the Pacific Coast, spending the winter near Los Angeles and in the City of Mexico, returning as far north as Hot Springs, Arkansas, in March. Mr. Franklin is in the peak of health and his bride has impressed the large numbers of Mr. Franklin's friends who have called upon her as being all that his fancy painted her. Kindness and good will beam from every line of her features, and lends an irresistible charm to a face made handsome by nature. A number of social functions will be given in her honor during their short stay in the city and all who meet her will respect and admire her.

Black Hills Daily Times, 1905 (otherwise undated)
MANY GREET MRS. FRANKLIN

Elaborate Reception by Mrs. Goldberg at Hotel well attended- Bride Warmly Welcomed

The first entertainment given in honor of Mrs. Harris Franklin was a large reception yesterday afternoon at the Franklin Hotel, tendered by Mrs. J. Goldberg. Arrangements had been carefully made under the watchful eye of manager Harold Hamilton and no detail that could add to the attractiveness of the occasion was overlooked. The handsome parlors were beautifully decorated. Smilax was hung around the windows and draped the small flower tables on which stood clusters of American Beauties and pink tea roses. Everything about the rooms breathed exquisite taste and harmony.

Mrs. Goldberg was assisted in receiving by Mrs. Norman T. Mason. The reception was from 2 until 3, during which time, Miss Bessie Stewart rendered some choice music and Mrs. Ayers favored the guests with a song. Dainty refreshments were served in the ante-room.

Mrs. Franklin wore a magnificent gown of Paris importation. It was an Irish crocheted Princess of white, the entire gown being embroidered in flowers to match the crocheting with white satin slippers. On her bosom she wore a diamond heart, two inches in diameter, diamond butterflies in her hair, a diamond ring and other jewels of value.

Mrs. Goldberg was gowned in a champagne colored silk crepe trimmed with rare Cluny lace and touched over the bodice and shoulders with pale blue satin. Half hidden in the bodice was a diamond star.

Mrs. Mason was a Symphony in old rose, the gown being silk crepe graced with a diamond neck ornament. She wore slippers to match.

Despite his strong affection and generous disposition toward Deadwood, Harris and Sadie moved to Chicago where they made their home before moving on to New York City. Nathan, Ada, their daughter Mildred, a housekeeper and a coachman, continued on in the house, which they remodeled in 1904. The decorative scheme on the first floor, and the reconfigured entryway and sitting room, were the result of this work. The second Mrs. Harris Franklin also suffered a health crisis but she survived.

Black Hills Daily Times, (undated)
MRS. HARRIS FRANKLIN TAKEN SERIOUSLY ILL.

Yesterday Mayor Franklin received a telegram from New York, telling him of the serious illness of Mrs. Harris Franklin, his stepmother. The telegram said that Mrs. Franklin's life was in despair. Mrs. N. E. Franklin will leave this evening for New York City to be near the invalid. From what can be learned of Mrs. Franklin's illness, it appears that a week ago she had visited a hair dressing parlor and submitted to the manipulation of one of its attendants. During the process of dressing her hair her scalp must have received a slight scratch, for it was not noticed at the time, and the wound, slight as it was, became infected. From the infection erysipelas has set in, and from her head has extended to her body. The telegram said that Mrs. Franklin was suffering greatly, and that her condition was considered very serious. Mrs. N. E. Franklin will remain in New York City during the illness of the patient, and hopes that upon her arrival she will find that her condition has improved and then she has passed the danger point.

Harris Franklin's life was more than one of pursuit of wealth and accomplishment. In his business life his legacy included his reputation for never foreclosing on a mortgage. He was known for his generosity, always ready to contribute to one of the many charities that sought his support. A sad fact of life in an age before the inception of Social Security or many of the public safety nets of the 20th and 21st centuries, the county poor farm was the last refuge for the indigent. These unfortunate people included the battered or abandoned wife, with or without her children; the mentally ill for whom there was no room at the Dakota Hospital for the Insane at Yankton; or those overwhelmed by debt due to illness or the plethora of issues that can lead to penury. Although this was the last stop on the trail of degradation, and to be living within its borders was to be avoided if at all possible, without the county poor farm there was no refuge, only utter homelessness for those without the strength or means to survive. Perhaps recalling his own humble origins, on April 8, 1898, Harris Franklin purchased 80 acres north of Sturgis which he donated to Meade County, the land to be used specifically for a refuge for the poor. The land was later incorporated into neighboring Lawrence County and was thereafter known as the Lawrence County Poor Farm.

Black Hills Daily Times, Jul 1, 1884
An insane wanderer. V.P. Shoun and others came upon an individual whose attire, antics and conversation indicated insanity.

In 1923, Harris Franklin died in New York City at the age of 75. His remains were returned to

Deadwood for burial beside his first wife, Anna, in an imposing gravesite in the Jewish section of Mount Moriah Cemetery. Acknowledgment of his passing was noted from New York to Deadwood, and appreciations of his life were written by eminent South Dakota historians.

New York Times, Apr 17, 1923

Harris Franklin, banker, ranch man, and mine owner, and one-time partner of E. H. Harriman, died yesterday at the Savoy Hotel in his 75th year... He then removed to Wyoming and when gold was discovered in the Black Hills in South Dakota he went with the rush to that place. Until fifteen years ago when he retired and moved to Chicago to live, Mr. Franklin was engaged in stock-raising on a large scale in South Dakota and still kept up his affiliations with large mining and banking interests. For the last seven years he had lived in New York. He is survived by his widow and one son, Nathan E. Franklin of this city.

Harris was reputed to have been worth more than $5 million when he died in 1923. His estate was divided into four parts: 33 percent to wife, Sadie A. Franklin; 33 percent to granddaughter Annie (Mildred) Traitel; 12 percent to nieces and nephews "who may be living"; and the residue in the equal parts to brother, Bernard (Barney) Franklin, and sister, Dora Blalsky.

George W. Kingsbury in his History of South Dakota said of Harris Franklin:

"... (He was an) effective builder and the now famous principal advocate of the Black Hills and has been the most stalwart worker in the interest of Deadwood and its people. He was one of the earliest to enter business here and there has not been a move calculated to advance the welfare of the city or community by his staying as not being identified with it. He was the founder of the Golden Reward mining company which occupies a place next to that of the famous Homestake among the mining companies of South Dakota. He established the American National Bank.

He is a man of unusual public spirit and was always willing to give of his ability and money to assist in any project that would promote the advancement of Deadwood and its vicinity. His generosity is well known and no worthy cause ever sought his assistance in vain. Although he did so much for the public good outside of the political field, he always refused to hold office.

Mr. Franklin has contributed liberally to other enterprises for the improvement of the town and the advantage of its people, and has probably done more than any other person for the development and progress of the whole Black Hills region."

Doane Robinson, (1856-1946), South Dakota State Historian, in his History of South Dakota, said of Harris Franklin:

"... it is the men of action who move the world forward in its destined course, especially in this intensely practical age. Where such men hail from, and the circumstances of their birth and breeding, are usually matters of little moment. Nature has no favored spots for the creation of her choice products. According to her needs and occasions she is all Athens, all Stratford-on-Avon, all Wall Street. When a man is required for any specific purpose, she produces him apparently without regard to circumstances and fearlessly flings him into the crisis. She knows her brood, and those she singles out for great events never disappoint her. Sometimes she even proves them in the alembic of stern adversity, and then they come forth from the trial only purified and strengthened for the work before them.

Harris Franklin, of Deadwood, is essentially and notably a man of this character—clear in perception, resolute in pursuit, quick and firm in decision. These qualities have given him force and leadership among men, and wrought out for him a record in commercial and industrial life creditable alike to himself and to the people in whose service it has been made...

In all the relations of life and in every field of labor in which he has engaged he has exemplified in a signal degree the best attributes of American citizenship, and he has the satisfaction of not only seeing the results of his energy and public spirit blooming and fructifying around him but of being securely established in the lasting regard and good will of his fellow men wherever he is known."

NATHAN FRANKLIN
YOUTH

Nathan Franklin
Photo courtesy Adams Museum

Harris and Anna Franklin's only child, Nathan E. Franklin, grew up to become Deadwood's second Jewish mayor. He was born in Burlington, Iowa, on December 15th, 1870, and the Franklins moved to Deadwood when Nathan was seven years old. Unlike his father, who had little education and in youth struggled for a living, Nathan grew up in a world of wealth and privilege. His father was arguably the richest man in all the Black Hills, but advantage and opportunity did not seem to impair the character of his son. The Franklins were always in the public eye, and Deadwood appeared to enjoy watching Nathan grow into young manhood, even his shenanigans. The appreciation was mutual; Nathan's fondness for Deadwood was apparent from the time he was a teenager.

Black Hills Daily Times, Sep 7, 1879

List of scholars attending public school, age 8, Nathan E. Franklin.

Black Hills Daily Times, Mar 19, 1881

Ten-year-old Nathan Franklin recites poem at school.

Black Hills Daily Times, Sep 14, 1884

Mrs. Harris Franklin and Nathan have returned from Hot Springs, in the best of health. Nathan has grown, apparently, a foot during the last month, and will soon outweigh the old man.

Black Hills Daily Times, Dec 16, 1884

Intimate friends of Harris Franklin celebrate 15th birthday of their son Nathan.

Black Hills Daily Times Apr 3, 1884

Grandest juvenile party ever given in this city came off last evening at the residence of Harris Franklin, in Ingleside. Party was given by Mrs. Harris Franklin to her son Nathan.

Black Hills Daily Times, May 13, 1885

Nathan Franklin the proud possessor of the toniest cart ever sent west of the Missouri, is being too hykanobious (sic) for our limited flow of language.

Black Hills Daily Times, May 24, 1885

Nathan Franklin and his nobby little turnout attract much attention on the streets. He acquired the cart in Chicago after finessing the purchase out of his father.

Black Hills Daily Times, Jun 4, 1885

Nathan Franklin carries an arm in a sling, the result of too much sportiveness on the part of his pony.

Nathan Franklin and friends
Photo courtesy Adams Museum

In 1887, at age 17, while working with the McDonald Fire Hose company, young Nathan experienced a rather serious accident that left him temporarily incapacitated. Obliged to spend most of the summer recuperating, he missed his graduation ceremony from Deadwood High School.

Preparing their son for higher education, the family traveled to Indiana to take Nathan to Notre Dame University. There he studied at the school of pharmacology, graduating in 1890.

Black Hills Daily Times, Oct 30, 1887
Harris & Anna & Nathan E Franklin returned from Chicago, New York, Kentucky and Notre Dame

Black Hills Daily Times, Nov 29, 1887
Nathan sound as a dollar. Harris Franklin met his son Nathan in Chicago. The latter has entirely recovered from his injury.

Black Hills Daily Times, Jan 27, 1888
Telegram informs that Nathan Franklin is ill at Notre Dame. Mrs. Franklin leaves for the school this morning.

Black Hills Daily Times, Feb 18, 1888
Mrs. Harris Franklin returned last evening from Notre Dame, with Nathan, who we understand, has recovered from a one time alarming illness.

Showing signs of homesickness at first, summer recesses from pharmacy school at Notre Dame were opportunities for Nathan to return to Deadwood and spend time with friends. In the summer of 1887, Nathan served an apprenticeship in the drugstore of Kirk G. Phillips. By the summer of 1888 Nathan was fully recovered from his injury and back at his post as one of the officers of the McDonald Hose Company of the Deadwood Fire Department.

Black Hills Daily Times, Jul 14, 1888
George Cushman, Stewart Fox, John Russell, Herman Clark, Ed Ford, Albert Miller, Nathan Franklin and their young lady friends went to Spearfish yesterday for a picnic.

In 1890 Phillips employed Nathan as a clerk in his drug store during breaks from college. After graduation from Notre Dame, Dr. Nathan Franklin returned to Deadwood to resume his active participation in the life of his hometown. Nathan and Dr. James A. Paddock formed a brief partnership and opened the Palace Pharmacy at 649 Main St. At the age of 20, fresh out of pharmacy school, Nathan found himself treating patients, much as a medical doctor would.

Black Hills Daily Times, Jan 3, 1891

Dr. Nathan Franklin… had his first patient when Warren Hastie sustained severe injuries by running his hand sled into a tree box.

Black Hills Daily Times, Dec 16, 1891

Nathan Franklin celebrated his 21st birthday yesterday.

Black Hills Daily Times, Mar 11, 1892

Wednesday Dr. Nathan Franklin pulled two teeth for Dr. Paddock, and yesterday the latter was unable to leave his home, and "hasn't done anything since."

Black Hills Daily Times, May 2, 1893

Nathan E. Franklin and James A. Paddock dissolve partnership.

Friends at Nathan Franklin's Palace Pharmacy
Photo courtesy Centennial Archives,
Deadwood Public Library

The Palace Pharmacy operated under Nathan's proprietorship from 1891 until 1902. The pharmacy had a close call in 1893 when someone stepped on a match and started a fire. Fortunately, it was promptly extinguished with buckets of water.

Harris had had little time for politics, but Nathan demonstrated an interest in politics at a young age. He had a broad range of interests, and was always ready to explore new avenues of opportunity.

Black Hills Daily Times, Feb 3, 1892

Nathan E. Franklin and a number of prominent young men organize Deadwood Baseball Club.

Black Hills Daily Times, Feb 25, 1892

Nathan Franklin has taken agency for an eastern florist and will hereafter furnish floral designs and cut flowers to order and deliver them quickly.

Black Hills Daily Times, May 31, 1892

Chilly atmosphere and black clouds filled with moisture did not prevent the ball game between east side and west side of Main Street.

Black Hills Daily Times, Jun 3, 1892

Young Men's Democratic Club met and effected a permanent organization.

Black Hills Daily Times, Dec 6, 1893

Will Whealen and Nathan Franklin making arrangements to attend Antwerp expo: Whealen to make balloon ascensions and parachute jumps and Franklin to work ossified man racket.

These years were also a time for the more enjoyable pastimes. The Kellers were not Jewish, but Nathan courted Ada F. Keller, a Deadwood girl and graduate of Deadwood High School, daughter of Frank and Minnie Keller of Cheyenne, Wyoming.

Black Hills Daily Times, Jun 9, 1888

Programme of reading contest to be held this evening at the Congregational church. Ada Keller.

Black Hills Daily Times, Mar 4, 1892

Franklin and Keller ride to Belle. Nathan Franklin and Miss Ada Keller took a pleasure ride to Belle Fourche yesterday, returning in the afternoon.

Nathan and Ada Keller were married on September 14, 1893, a marriage that would last for Ada's lifetime. Ada was well liked in the community, and took part in all of city's social and charitable affairs.

Ada Keller Franklin
Photo courtesy Adams Museum

Ada loved the Franklin mansion, and they both enjoyed entertaining there.

Black Hills Daily Times, Jun 10, 1910
Mrs. N.E. Franklin was the hostess yesterday in the handsome Franklin mansion to a number of her women friends at a card party. Eleven tables were set. Delicate refreshments were served after a very enjoyable afternoon.

AUTOMOBILES

With the turn of the century, technology brought significant changes to Deadwood. Transportation still included the pack mule and the horse and buggy, but the railroad had arrived, the horseless carriage had rattled into the picture, and aviation was in its infancy. Modern marvels of the industrial age captured Nathan's imagination. Among his extensive interests were the automobile, the airplane, and motion pictures, all of which he brought to Deadwood.

In 1904 there were only 8,000 cars in all the United States, and only 144 miles of paved roads, but Nathan had the means and the enthusiasm to enjoy automobiles at their earliest appearance. In 1905 he and Ada purchased a model F Cadillac on a trip to the east. Arrangements were made to have it shipped from the factory in Detroit, to arrive in Deadwood the first of May of 1905. Even though the maximum speed limit in most cities at that time was 10 mph, the model F was especially recommended for the Black Hills owing to its great power, its hill-climbing abilities, as well as its speed possibilities. The car arrived on May 23, 1905, the first modern automobile to reach the city, and immediately became the talk of the town. It was a first class machine, attractive in appearance, and although designed as a 2-seater, it was large enough to accommodate three people comfortably. Besides the oil lamps, special features included the 60-candle-power acetylene headlights.

Black Hills Daily Times, May 25, 1905

CADILLAC TOURING CAR HERE
14 horsepower machine arrives: N.E. Franklin, cashier of the American National Bank of Deadwood, has received his new automobile, and was directing it about town yesterday. It is a Cadillac touring car, manufactured at Detroit, Michigan, having 10 horse energy normally, but in reality about 14 high and low speed and capable of taking a 20 percent grade.

Black Hills Daily Times (undated):

Yesterday there were delivered in the city two new cars, both Whites, four cylinder and 45 horsepower machines. One was for Charles P. Wasmer and the other for N.E. Franklin. Both are beauties and the latest word in automobiles and attracted much attention from those who know what a good machine is. In the car that brought the machines to the city was a big White truck for the Adams Co., one of the best that has been in commission in the Hills, and it too, attracted much attention from many. It will have a capacity of three tons, and will go any place that a horse and wagon can go.

Black Hills Daily Times (undated)

HAD GOOD TRIP ON VERY POOR ROADS
When you have the time and inclination for an automobile outing, a trip to Hot Springs from Deadwood may be enjoyed if the proper methods are employed, but from the present condition of the roads to that resort, speed records are not likely to be created this year. Mr. and Mrs. N.E. Franklin and Miss Mildred return on the Northwestern from the Springs yesterday. They left here last week accompanied by the Schlichtings in the Franklin touring car. Mr. Franklin declares that the rockiness and seeming impassibility of the roads are indescribable, but nevertheless the party enjoyed the trip down. They went leisurely and also they lost their way below Rapid and met many inconveniences and disparagements, the weather was good and the air invigorating. At one point the men were obliged to build their own bridge across a small creek that contained some mud like quicksand and Mr. Franklin says he wonders how the machine withstood the roads as well as it did. Mr. and Mrs. Schlichting remained over another day and will return on tomorrow's Northwestern.

At the end of July 1909, Deadwood's citizens were amazed by the ascent of two automobiles up Mt. Moriah's steep slope to the Brown Rocks area.

AIRPLANES

Not only was Nathan captivated by up-to-the-minute machines, but his objectives, like his father's, were directed toward promoting Deadwood, and he could combine the two interests successfully. In the summer of 1912, the Deadwood Business Club, major promoters of Deadwood commerce, sponsored the first airplane flight in the state of South Dakota. Seventeen-year-old Art Smith from Fort Wayne, Indiana, had contracted with the Deadwood Business Club for six flights of ten minutes each. The contract was to earn him $1,250, a sum he intended to use to finish paying off the new motor and moving on to his next engagement. Smith's machine arrived crated in a railroad boxcar. As the young man was completing assembly of the flying machine on what is now the Days of '76 rodeo grounds, he realized that the field was completely surrounded by mountains and he would have to refuse the offer. With only $1.90 in his pocket, Smith explained the situation to Nathan Franklin, then president of the Deadwood Business Club. Nathan considered it and then offered the young man another option.

Franklin woke young Smith before daylight the following morning, and they drove through the moonlight over mountain roads to a location three miles outside of Deadwood on Boulder Canyon Rd. Franklin showed Smith a field half a mile long and fairly level; on all sides the ground fell away to depths of hundreds of feet. If Smith could get the flying machine into the air before it raced over the edge, there would be room to turn before he struck a mountain. Smith declared the site acceptable and decided he would fly there. Smith made aviation history that afternoon by flying the airplane despite turbulent air that almost caused the flimsy craft to crash. Onlookers thrilled and cheered from the mountainsides, and although Art Smith only made three of the six flights for which he contracted, he was paid the full $1,250.

Photo courtesy Lawrence County Historical Society

MOTION PICTURES

Motion pictures were invented by Eadweard Muybridge in 1877, but didn't reach Deadwood until Nathan Franklin took an interest in them in 1913. Nathan himself was seen in the "Pathé Weekly Review of Events," a type of newsreel movie, which was shown at the Early Grand Theater in Deadwood. It depicted the meeting of the executive council of the American Bankers Association at Briarcliff, New York, where Nathan, president of the First National Bank of Deadwood was featured prominently.

By 1918 Deadwood had many automobiles. Nathan engaged film-makers from New York to come to Deadwood to make a motion picture, the object being to promote Deadwood as a tourism destination. The cameras were set up at one o'clock in the afternoon for optimal lighting, on a corner of Main Street. They were to shoot a procession of 25 or more open-topped automobiles as they came up from lower Main Street, past the Elks Building, and toward the Franklin Hotel. The townspeople were invited to participate, and the streets became abuzz with well-dressed "extras." The procession of automobiles, with Nathan's daughter, Mildred, and some of her girlfriends in the lead car, was a grand sight.

Pioneer, Sep 6, 1918
Operator Predicts Pictures Will Be Good.

Faidley and Hackett, the motion picture operators who have engaged with the Deadwood Business Club and City Council to put Deadwood on the motion picture circuit made their first step in this direction yesterday afternoon. The people were prepared for them and made the various streets in which the motion pictures were taken scenes of life and color while the camera was in action. The first picture was taken shortly after one o'clock under good light conditions at the First National Bank corner. The sidewalks and streets were crowded with people and the line of 25 or more autos moved past to get into the first 100 feet of film run through. The procession was headed by the Franklin auto carrying Miss Mildred Franklin, Lucille Craft, Helen and Dorothy Hyde, Mary Thornby and Sarah Moffitt. The second picture was taken further up the street, above the Elks building and the third taken at the Franklin Hotel and Deadwood Theatre. The camera was then moved to Sherman Street, where the federal building, the county building, and the auditorium were gotten into the picture.

This afternoon at 3 o'clock a stretch of the new Spearfish Road will be taken and the auto owners are requested to assemble near the Spindler ranch for the occasion. Monday afternoon the camera will be turned loose in the United States assay mill and will also catch the Homestake slime plant and a train carrying ore from Bald Mountain to the Golden Reward Mill. Tuesday several views in Spearfish Canyon will be added to the reel. Thus far, the operators have used 300 feet of film and 700 feet more will be used before the reel is complete. Immediately after the return from Spearfish Canyon Tuesday the film will be sent east for development and on its return here in about ten days will be exhibited at the Deadwood Theatre. A small strip of the film used yesterday was developed and showed that a good picture may be expected.

That remarkable footage has been carefully restored and preserved by Wayne Paananen of Historical Footprints, Inc., Lead, SD.

POLITICS

Although both Franklin men were deeply committed to advancing Deadwood, their approaches differed. Nathan included politics as part of his contribution to Deadwood's progress, serving two terms as mayor of Deadwood, one from 1914 to 1916, and in another term from 1916 through 1918. In his first mayoral race Nathan Franklin opposed incumbent William E. (W.E.) Adams, popular pioneer grocer and merchant. The campaign was contentious, but Franklin had the popular vote as well as the support of the newspapers. As a Republican and under the Citizens Ticket, Nathan swept into office with 4/5 of the vote, the largest majority ever given in a municipal contest in Deadwood up until that time.

The strong vote in support of Franklin was seen as a pointed rebuke to those who allowed themselves to be misled into believing in the sincerity of E.L.Senn, editor of the Daily Telegram, publisher of several other newspapers, and supporter of W.E. Adams. Senn was a rabid prohibitionist whose fanatical rantings against Deadwood in general and Franklin in particular embarrassed and outraged the community. His newspapers had pursued a policy of crusading against Deadwood.

Nathan's attitude toward alcohol was more sanguine and practical than had been that of Sol Star, his Jewish predecessor in the office of mayor. Senn's hyperbole was dismissed as excessive, and Nathan's solid, common-sense policies in pursuit of a prosperity-producing city government prevailed.

The strength of the vote was viewed as a compliment to Franklin and positive assurance of the people's confidence in their new mayor.

Black Hills Daily Times, Apr 22, 1914

Nathan E. Franklin won a sweeping victory in the municipal elections for Mayor, recognized as a distinct and emphatic expression of confidence on the part of four-fifths of the voters of this community in the ability and integrity of the man they have selected to administer public affairs for the next two years. Mr. Franklin's majority and almost 500 in a total vote of 849, is a splendid compliment to him and a positive assurance on the part of the people of their confidence in his intention and ability to conduct a prosperity-breeding administration and to continue in the pursuit of the business— which the present incumbent of the mayoral the office, W.E. Adams, has so faithfully followed.

In his mayoral acceptance speech Franklin outlined the goals of his administration. In addition to expressing his appreciation for his predecessor, W.E. Adams, Nathan promised to carry out his projects of continuing to pave and light the streets, and look after the widows, orphans and mentally infirm. He vowed to make every effort to beautify the city, ensure a plentiful supply of good water, and increase the efficiency of the fire department. He had served as fire chief, and now would actively work to install a modern fire alarm system that would locate and announce fires, noting that every encouragement and assistance should be extended to the volunteer firemen. A practical businessman, he acknowledged that better firefighting efficiency would mean lower fire insurance rates.

Although the Franklin family was not especially religious, Nathan's care for animals reflected an important Jewish value relating to their proper treatment. His sense of protectiveness was demonstrated in his activities on behalf of the local Humane Society, where he acted as president. In his mayoral acceptance speech, Franklin referred to the one law covering both city and state regarding cruelty to animals, insisting that this be rigidly enforced.

He entreated the press not to work against Deadwood, but to join with neighboring cities to forget past differences and think of their future in this, the "Richest 100 Miles Square on Earth." He encouraged the people of neighboring cities to come to Deadwood where they would be well treated. Nathan vowed that his term of office would cast aside past differences and jealousies, and create a "sentiment of friendship and cooperation" for the mutual benefit of the Black Hills community.

Mayor Nathan Franklin Making a Speech
Photo courtesy Centennial Archives,
Deadwood Public Library

Franklin's administration was considered vigorous and clean. In 1916, with the endorsement of the Deadwood Pioneer-Times, Nathan was returned to office for a second 2-year term. The members of the city council clearly showed their intention to stand united for the welfare of the community and to work as one body.

Nathan was a member of the Benevolent Protective Order of Elks, and attained the thirty-second degree in the Masonic order. He maintained a strong commitment to the Deadwood Business Club, acting as director for eight years, and as president for three years. Under his direction the organization was credited with accomplishing much good for the city.

Deadwood Pioneer-Times, Apr 18, 1916
He is energetic, progressive, and today at the polls is entitled to every bit of support that the voters of Deadwood can give him.

Freedom to travel by automobile changed the face of tourism in the Hills. Tourism was beginning to take hold in the country and Deadwood was already attracting a large number of tourists and visitors. Mt. Moriah was drawing eastern visitors who came to view the graves of Wild Bill Hickok, Calamity Jane, and other notable characters. South Dakota needed some innovative thinking to encourage the tourist trade and promote Deadwood's historical assets.

In 1914 the Deadwood Business Men's Club, sometimes known as the Deadwood Business Club, joined forces with the Mount Moriah Cemetery Association to develop a pamphlet that visitors might carry away with them. The pamphlet was deemed important because the Cemetery Association acknowledged their responsibility to preserve an accurate history.

Another project of the Deadwood Business Club was the Annual Automobile Exposition at the Deadwood Auditorium, inviting motorcar dealers to showcase their ideas and merchandise. The Expo attracted thousands of automobile enthusiasts and brought increasing revenue to the city. The Club made every effort to promote Deadwood as a tourist destination.

NATHAN RETIRES FROM BANKING

In 1916, having completed his first term as mayor of Deadwood, Nathan decided it was time to resign his post at the bank. Upon the Board of Directors' reluctant acceptance of Nathan's resignation on August 8, 1916, the board issued a statement declaring that "by his ability and by his sound methods, and his acquaintance with conditions, (Nathan Franklin) made that bank one of the soundest financial institutions in the West."

During his tenure as president of the First National Bank, he had represented the State of South Dakota on the executive council of the American Bankers Association, and was vice president of the South Dakota State Bankers Association.

Black Hills Daily Times, Dec 27, 1916
GAVE A LITTLE SUPPER TO N.E. FRANKLIN.

Saturday evening the employees and officials of the First National Bank gave a little supper at the Franklin Hotel in honor of N.E. Franklin, president of the First National Bank of Deadwood, who will retire from that position after the first of the coming year. (Mr. Franklin) as head of that institution had been on terms of the closest intimacy with its employees, and maintained relations with them of closest friendship, in fact the line of demarcation between friend and employee was so finely drawn as to be scarcely discernible. The supper had been arranged for the purpose of expressing in a happy way the appreciation of the employees for their employer and it was one of the happiest of gatherings. During the course of the evening, M.M. Wheeler on behalf of the officials and employees of the bank presented Mr. Franklin with a token of their esteem, which was in the shape of a full dress set of studs and sleeve buttons, worked out in white gold and pearl, a beautiful gift. Mr. Wheeler made the presentation in a little speech, and in his response Mr. Franklin expressed himself as surprised and more than pleased with the gift, not for its intrinsic value, but the sentiment which prompted it, and declared that he would always prize it and cherish it always. Only the bank force and the gentleman in whose honor the supper had been arranged were present.

In 1922 the Black Hills Daily Times (undated) wrote of the record of the banks:

The First National Bank of Deadwood was established 27 years ago. The American National Bank was established January 1, 1895. Both the American National and the First National have experienced large volumes of business and have carried enormous deposits. Its deposits aggregate in the two banks $1,181,700; with the capital of $150,000, and a surplus of $150,000, may make the reorganized First National approximately a million and a half bank.

The American National Bank has had a remarkable record. Its stock at first paid dividends of 8 percent, then 10 percent, and finally 15 percent per annum, and from its par value, and which it was subscribed to when the bank was started it has risen to $500 per share. In other words, the stockholders have witnessed an increase in their belongings of 400 percent in addition to the dividends they have received.

Franklin stated that he would still maintain his interest in the Bear Butte Valley Bank of Sturgis, of which he was president, and would give it more of his attention in the future. In 1915 the Bear Butte Valley Bank had paid 158%, or $237,000 on its capital stock in the shape of dividends to its shareholders. That bank had shown a greater increase in the percentage of deposits than any other bank in the Black Hills.

So much of Nathan Franklin's business life was given over to his work with the First National Bank of Deadwood, that the tribute offered upon his resignation from that institution serves to point up his appreciation by the town where he grew up.

Black Hills Daily Times, Jan 9, 1917
Nathan E. Franklin's Resignation as President of First National Effective.

At a meeting of the Board of Directors of the First National Bank Deadwood, held at the bank offices yesterday afternoon, the resignation of Nathan E. Franklin as president of the bank and as a member of its Board of Directors was reluctantly accepted by the board. Mr. Franklin, on Aug. 8, 1916, tendered his resignation as president of the bank to the Board of Directors, but at the earnest solicitation of the members of the board, he acceded to their wish that the resignation not be made effective until the first meeting in January 1917 of the board. After the acceptance of Mr. Franklin's resignation the board adopted the following resolutions: "Whereas, Mr. N.E. Franklin, who has been a director and president of this bank for the past 11-1/2 years has tendered his resignation which now has been accepted, therefore, be it resolved that the remaining members of the Board of Directors on this, the occasion of the separation of his official relations with the bank, hereby place on record its high appreciation of his undying devotion to the interests of the bank for such a long period. He brought to bear on the affairs of the bank the same business acumen and clear judgment as has distinguished him in the conduct of his own business. As a citizen and public official he has added to his laurels by a broad and comprehensive administration of the affairs of the community. The board desires also to place on record the high regard in which they hold Mr. Franklin personally, as well as his noble wife and family, and to convey the wishes, although we will be separated from him officially, we will continue to enjoy their presence in the community in which they have so long acted a prominent part. Mr. Franklin began his career in the banking business on May 1, 1902, when he accepted the position as cashier of the American National Bank of Deadwood, and during his connection with that bank, by his ability and by his sound business methods, and his acquaintance with conditions, made that bank one of the soundest financial institutions in the West. On July 1, 1906, the business of the American National Bank was consolidated with that of the First National Bank and the combined institutions continued to be known as and to do business as the First National Bank of Deadwood. With consolidation of the two banks Mr. Franklin became president of the consolidated banks and had held that position until his resignation was accepted yesterday afternoon. That he brought to the bank and assets which have proved a great value in its affairs and which assisted in gaining the position which it now holds, as one of the strongest and one of the safest financial institutions in the northwest. During the 11 years that he has been president, the bank has increased its business, grown in public favor and is looked upon as one of the solid institutions of the state, and today that First National Bank of Deadwood is probably better known throughout the middle West, the northwest, and money centers of the East than any bank of the smaller cities of the United States. That this is the case is due to the personality of Mr. Franklin, his energy at and untiring efforts in the interests of the community in which the First National Bank does its greater business. He has an acquaintance with almost every financier of prominence in the country, and that his character is known and held in high regard was evidenced when the fact of his intention to sever his connection with First National was first made public. At the time this fact was noted by the Wall Street Journal and other financial papers, whose comment on Mr. Franklin would have been gratifying to any businessman, and while many of these papers declared that the First National was losing one of its big assets, they asserted that an opportunity was now presented for many big businesses to secure a much-needed man to be the head of their affairs.

News of Nathan's retirement from the bank in Deadwood was noted in the Wall Street Journal and other eastern financial journals. The papers observed that an opportunity was now presented for many big businesses to secure a much-needed man to be head of their affairs. It was noted that he had several tempting offers, was considering two or three of them, but was waiting to make a decision. However, Franklin's term of office as mayor would not expire until May 1918, and he announced his intention to remain and give his best attentions to his duties as the city's chief executive.

When his second term as mayor expired in May of 1918, Nathan sold the Franklin family home to W.E. and Alice Adams for $8,500. His decision came as a surprise to many, considering the divisive nature of the 1914 mayoral race. On August 13th, 1919, his term of office completed, Nathan and Ada followed father Harris Franklin and their daughter Mildred eastward to settle in New York City where Nathan had decided to engage in the investment business. After living in New York for 6 years, Ada took ill shortly after her 55th birthday on January 25th, 1925. She passed away in New York on May 14th, 1925; her daughter Mildred was with her at the time of her death. Funeral services were held in New York City, and her body was returned to Deadwood for burial in Mt. Moriah.

Deadwood Pioneer May 15, 1925
Mrs. N. E. Franklin Passed Away Yesterday

Yesterday a telegram was received from N.E. Franklin, dated that morning in New York City, telling of the death at her home of his wife, Mrs. Ada Franklin. This news will be received with regret by many people in Deadwood and the Hills, where Mrs. Franklin grew to childhood and to beautiful womanhood, was married and had endeared herself to scores of friends, all of whom will take her death as a personal loss, for she had grown in their affections by her womanly virtues, kindness and willing friendship.

Besides her husband, Nathan E. Franklin, a former mayor of Deadwood, cashier of the First National Bank, chief of the fire department and prominent in this city's business affairs during his residence here, she leaves a daughter, Mildred, who was with her at the time of her death, and her father and mother, Mr. and Mrs. Frank Keller of this city, and to them the sympathy of many friends is unstintingly given.

Mrs. Franklin had been ill about a year, her serious illness occurring shortly after her birthday last January. She recovered from that attack and apparently was on the road to health, when about a week ago she was again taken with another attack of illness, which resulted in her death yesterday morning.

Mrs. Franklin, who at the time of her death was in her 55th year, was born in Cheyenne, Wyoming, coming to Hills and Deadwood with her parents in the early days of this city, where she grew up, attended this city schools and took a prominent part in later years in all of its social and charitable affairs. After funeral services, to be held at the home in New York City, the body will be placed in a vault and later be bought brought back to Deadwood, the old home which Mrs. Franklin loved so well, and laid to rest in the cemetery on Mt. Moriah. Announcements will be made later of the arrangements for her burial.

There is a brief reference to Nathan having remarried a woman named Caroline in New

York. Little is known about this marriage, except that there were no children. They resided at 227 East 57th Street, a five-story Italianate Upper East Side brownstone off Park Avenue. He also had another Upper East Side address in Manhattan, today a chic hotel known as 1871 House.

In 1940, at 69, the man who had loved Deadwood so well, but had found another life in New York, chose to end it. Apparently despondent, apprehensive about impending surgery, Nathan leaped from a window of his hospital room at Mt. Sinai Hospital in New York City. A passing taxi driver witnessed the tragedy and notified the police, who listed the death as a suicide.

Black Hills Pioneer, 1940 (otherwise undated)

Patient Dies in Leap. Facing an Operation, He Ends Life at Hospital. Nathan E. Franklin, retired businessman, jumped to his death about 7 o'clock last night from the second floor of Mount Sinai Hospital, 2nd Avenue and 98th Street. The body landed on a basement grating three stories below. He was 69 years old.

Mr. Franklin was admitted to the hospital last Tuesday and was to have undergone an operation Monday. The police listed the case as a suicide and said that a passing taxi driver had seen Mr. Franklin leap. They said that he had apparently been apprehensive about the operation. He lived with his family at 227 East 57th Street.

In 1915 George W. Kingsbury in his History of South Dakota said of Nathan Franklin:

"A community owes much to those men who direct and control its financial institutions and Nathan E. Franklin as president of the First National Bank of Deadwood has done a great deal to further the development of the city and its vicinity, making the bank of which he is the executive head of great service to the community. The first care of the institution has been the safety of the deposits, but it has been so wisely directed that this end has been attained and worthy business enterprises have also been fostered through the judicious extension of credit...

Although he has business interests which occupy much of his time and attention, he has been prominent in public affairs and is the present mayor of Deadwood. He has been a director of the Deadwood Business Club for eight years and its president for three years and under his direction the organization has accomplished much good for the city. "

MILDRED

The younger Franklins had one living child. In 1894 Ada gave birth to a daughter. Named for her grandmother Anna, Anna Mildred, or Mildred, as they called her, was raised in the beautiful Franklin home on Van Buren Street.

Mildred Franklin and handsome young gentleman.
Photo courtesy Adams Museum

Mildred, center, kids on ponies, Franklin Hotel
Photo courtesy Centennial Archives,
Deadwood Public Library

A second child was born in 1903, but only survived one day and was buried in Mount Moriah Cemetery. Mildred grew up the apple of her parents' and her grandparents' eyes, with many of the advantages her grandfather Harris lacked in his youth. The adoring grandfather customarily gave Mildred $10 for every year on her birthday. By the time she reached her 13th birthday, the gift amounted to $130, a considerable sum for a young lady in those days.

Nathan and Ada's only child found her mate on the East Coast. In 1913, much to the surprise, and perhaps chagrin, of family and friends, Mildred eloped and married David Traitel of New York City, a 24-year-old marble importer and building contractor. The Traitel Marble Company of Long Island was well known to the trade. The wedding took place in Washington, D.C., where Mildred had been visiting friends.

Washington Post (Washington, D.C.), Nov 8, 1913

ELOPING BRIDE AN HEIRESS.......DAKOTA BANKER'S DAUGHTER AND NEW YORKER MARRIED IN THIS CITY......... Anna Mildred Franklin, daughter of N. E. Franklin, president of the First National Bank of Deadwood, S. Dak., and granddaughter of Harris Franklin, a capitalist, of New York City, was married here Wednesday to David Salisbury Traitel, son of Benjamin D. Traitel, a New York contractor. Both admitted their appearance in Washington might be called an elopement. Her parents had objected to her marriage because of her health. It was said she would receive their blessing. The bride, who is 19, is heiress to a large fortune. The ceremony was performed by Judge C. S. Bundy, of the municipal court. Harris Franklin is a director in the Nevada Smelting and Mines Corporation, and lives at 65 West Seventy-first Street New York. While the marriage was not completely unexpected by those close to the couple, most people had anticipated that they would wait longer.

Nevertheless, Mr. Traitel was acclaimed in Deadwood newspaper reports as being a "young man of sterling qualities." Mildred left Deadwood to make her home with David in New York, but the couple would return for visits to Deadwood where David had also made friends. Mildred was popular in her home town, and the newspapers described lavish parties arranged in her honor during visits with her parents and old friends, with sad goodbyes at the Northwestern station at the end of those visits.

THE FRANKLIN LEGACY

After W. E. Adams died, his second wife, Mary Mastrovich, closed the house the Franklins had built and where she had resided with W. E., but Adams' widow specified that the contents remain exactly as they were left. The house remained as per Mary's directives, occasionally serving as a bed-and-breakfast, but remaining astoundingly intact for many years, a living piece of history.

Under Nathan Franklin's leadership, the Deadwood Business Club was commissioned by the Deadwood City Council to communicate with other city governments in order to promote a special first-class road from Chicago to

Yellowstone by way of the Black Hills. The Black and Yellow Trail Association, based in Huron, South Dakota, had been conceived to build a road diverting traffic to the cities along its line from the Black Hills to Yellowstone Park, hence the designation "Black and Yellow." Highway 14 would be known as the Black and Yellow Highway, intended to pass right through the Badlands and the Black Hills, its distinguishing black and yellow signposts marking the route. In a speech to the Black and Yellow Trail Association on January 22, 1924, State Historian Doane Robinson revealed his inspired proposal. Robinson envisioned giant statues of western figures such as Brevet General George Armstrong Custer, Buffalo Bill Cody, Lewis and Clark, and legendary Sioux warriors, carved into the Needles, great granite spires of the Black Hills. Robinson believed that a massive mountain memorial carved from stone would put South Dakota on the map as a tourist attraction. His concept would prove him right, but the characters and location of the rocks would be slightly different.

Mount Rushmore, a monument memorializing four great presidential figures, Washington, Jefferson, Lincoln, and Roosevelt in stone, would serve as an eternal reminder of the birth, growth, preservation, and development of a nation dedicated to democracy and the pursuit of individual liberty. The project was begun in 1927 and not completed until 1941. Unfortunately, neither Nathan Franklin, who died in 1940, nor sculptor Gutzon Borglum, who died in 1941, ever lived to see the completed project, but the success of Mount Rushmore National Monument exceeded either their or Doane Robinson's wildest expectations.

Mount Rushmore under construction
Photo courtesy Steve Norquist

Mount Rushmore
Photo courtesy James W. Parker

WERTHEIMER

JACOB AND HENRIETTA WERTHEIMER

MERCHANTS HOTEL - 688 MAIN ST., ELK'S BUILDING, AND 692 MAIN ST.

M.J. (MAX) AND LOUIS WERTHEIMER

WERTHEIMER CLOTHING 653 MAIN ST.

MERCHANTS HOTEL

The Wertheimer family of Baden, Germany, were among the earliest Jewish pioneers to come to Deadwood in 1876, and they are represented on both sides of Main St. The Wertheimer Brothers clothing store at 653 Main St. was built by Max (M.J.) and Louis Wertheimer, and the Merchants Hotel at 688 Main Street, was built by Jacob and his wife, Henrietta.

When Jacob arrived in Deadwood in 1876, he was 33 years old. Together with Henrietta and their son, Henry, a boy of 7 years, to whom this must have seemed a great adventure, Jacob and his family plainly meant to stay and make a life in the frontier town. For a young boy in a rough gold-mining camp setting, every day must have brought an exciting new experience. Weekend excursions to places like Bear Butte Camp would be a special thrill for Henry.

Black Hills Daily Times, Jul 15, 1878
Group that visited Bear Butte camp on Sunday. Mrs Wertheimer.

Deadwood needed lodging spaces, and starting a hotel was an excellent opportunity for an entrepreneur willing to work hard, deal with the public, and compete with challengers. It was also a very expensive undertaking. Jacob and Henrietta's first venture into the hotel business was a little boardinghouse which they started in 1878. Their business managed to survive an attempted takeover in November of 1878 by T.M. More. The boardinghouse did well, and the couple decided to use that same lot to build a hotel. Both an eyesore and a hazard while under construction, their boardinghouse was finally replaced with the Merchants, a full-fledged hotel.

Black Hills Daily Times, Mar 7, 1878
Jake Wertheimer, T.M. More to take control of boarding house.

Black Hills Daily Times, Jul 18, 1878
Break neck piece of walk in front of boarding house.

Black Hills Daily Times, Oct 14, 1878
Boarding house presents rather an awkward appearance.

Black Hills Daily Pioneer, Nov 1, 1878
Grand jury occupying upper portion of building

Black Hills Daily Times, Nov 8, 1878
Three story house on upper Main very imposing.

Black Hills Daily Times, Nov 21, 1878
Remodeling boarding house, accident for boarder.

Black Hills Daily Times, Dec 2, 1878
Mrs Liebmann sustained injuries falling from walk.

Black Hills Daily Times, Dec 31, 1878
Wertheimer to open house as a hotel called the Merchants tomorrow.

Deadwood, June 15, 1876
Courtesy Adams Museum

During the earliest Gold Rush days of the 1870s a bachelor could manage in a tent or dugout on $3 to $5 a week. As reported by eminent historian Dr. Watson Parker, a week's room and board at a boardinghouse could cost $8 to $10. Room and board at a good hotel could run from $10 to $20 a week. On New Year's Day of 1879, Jacob and Henrietta Wertheimer opened the Merchants Hotel, a 24 x 75-foot, three-story building on Main St. The Merchants Hotel became one of Deadwood's largest wood-frame commercial structures, and most important landmarks. A menu shows that an everyday dinner at the Merchants could be quite extensive and appealing, reflecting the appetites of the times. A holiday menu could be even more elaborate.

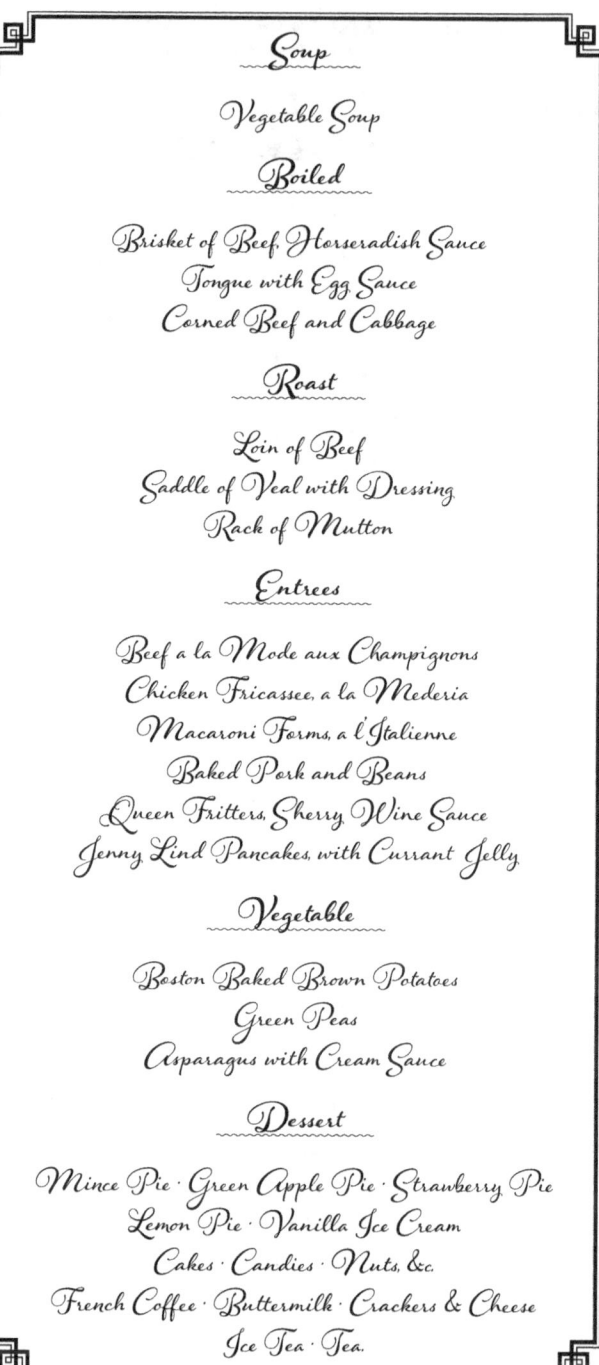

Soup
Vegetable Soup

Boiled
Brisket of Beef, Horseradish Sauce
Tongue with Egg Sauce
Corned Beef and Cabbage

Roast
Loin of Beef
Saddle of Veal with Dressing
Rack of Mutton

Entrees
Beef a la Mode aux Champignons
Chicken Fricassee, a la Mederia
Macaroni Forms, a l'Italienne
Baked Pork and Beans
Queen Fritters, Sherry Wine Sauce
Jenny Lind Pancakes, with Currant Jelly

Vegetable
Boston Baked Brown Potatoes
Green Peas
Asparagus with Cream Sauce

Dessert
Mince Pie · Green Apple Pie · Strawberry Pie
Lemon Pie · Vanilla Ice Cream
Cakes · Candies · Nuts, &c.
French Coffee · Buttermilk · Crackers & Cheese
Ice Tea · Tea.

Henrietta was particularly noteworthy for her prominent role in the family's hotel and for her hardiness in the face of personal tragedy. She was every bit as involved in managing the business as her husband.

The Wertheimers traveled east to Chicago to purchase the furnishings which then had to be delivered to Deadwood via ox train. The hotel contained 45 guest rooms, a billiards parlor, and sample rooms for salesmen. The bar furniture, costing $750, was described as "the handsomest set of bar fixtures to be seen in this or any other country." The main floor was occupied by several businesses, including the Black Hills and Sidney Stage Company. Arrivals and departures from the Merchants were regularly reported in the paper and it was a favorite stopover place for travelers and salesmen.

Black Hills Daily Times, Oct 7, 1879

Sargeant's Hotel to unite with the Wertheimer Hotel.

Black Hills Daily Times, Oct 14, 1879

Mrs Wertheimer, Has purchased furniture in east for new hotel.

Black Hills Daily Times, Dec 13, 1879

Merchants Hotel Grand opening next Sunday, Wertheimer block.

Notices appearing in the Black Hills Daily Times in 1880 and 1881 tell of improvements at the Merchants Hotel. They bought a new organ for the ladies' sitting room. They also installed a new porch light, which pleased Jacob so much that he would sit out at night, enjoying the cool July evening air.

Black Hills Daily Times, Jul 17, 1880

Has placed a new organ in ladies' sitting room

Black Hills Daily Times, May 4, 1881

Jakey Wertheimer, Has put up awning in front of the Merchants Hotel.

Black Hills Daily Times, May 07 1881

Jakey Wertheimer, Will run the Merchants for another year.

Black Hills Daily Times, May 27, 1881

Reduced the price of day board at Merchants Hotel.

Another attempted takeover of the hotel happened in October of 1881, when Wertheimer had to take Major Langdon to court in order to regain possession of his hotel. The hotel re-opened in November, still under Wertheimer's management.

Black Hills Daily Times, Oct 5, 1881

Wertheimer has Major Langdon arrested to get hotel back.

Black Hills Daily Times, Oct 13, 1881

Wertheimer vs. Langdon, for possession of hotel.

Black Hills Daily Times, Oct 17, 1881

Wants to get rid of former hotel landlord.

Black Hills Daily Times, Nov 2, 1881

Will re-open the Merchants Hotel. Oliver B Stout, To manage Merchants Hotel for Wertheimer again.

The hotel continued to expand and make progress. In 1884 they annexed the old Denee residence as an addition. They built a large room in the rear of his billiard parlor, "to be furnished and used for private parties in consultation, etc." It was considered to be a great improvement.

Black Hills Daily Times, Jul 2, 1884

Jake Wertheimer is decorating the Merchants Hotel in an elaborate manner for the Fourth. It is the most eligible place in the city to view the parade, the tournament and the fireworks

Black Hills Daily Times, Jul 31, 1884

Col. Wertheimer to open a new register at the Merchants tomorrow; first page highly embellished by artist W.V. Herancourt.

Black Hills Daily Times, Nov 26, 1884

Northwestern (ox) train delivered handsomest set of bar fixtures to be seen for the Merchants Hotel.

Black Hills Daily Times, Nov 27, 1884

Free lunch at Wertheimer's sample room opening. Colonel Wertheimer's opening of his magnificent sample room drew a large crowd.

Another service was added in July of 1885, when George King, superintendent of the Welcome Mine, also an excellent boot polisher— when adequately compensated— opened at the Merchants.

Dealing in liquor was considered a respectable business on the wide-open frontier, provided you were willing to conform to the prevalent blue laws and close your store on Sunday. Liquor offered an unqualified prospect for success. The Wertheimer brothers started their Deadwood enterprises almost immediately, laying the groundwork for their various business concerns, forming partnerships and purchasing property. The first newspaper notice referring to the Wertheimers appears in the Black Hills Daily Pioneer in 1876.

Black Hills Daily Pioneer, Aug 5, 1876

J. Wertheimer & Co. are liquor dealers.

Black Hills Daily Pioneer, Oct 28, 1876

Jacob Wertheimer, & Ranahan create partnership.

Black Hills Daily Pioneer, Nov 11, 1876

Jacob Wertheimer, corporator of New Chicago partnership.

Black Hills Daily Pioneer, Jun 21, 1878

Wertheimer & Co. Closing on Sunday, agree to close business.

WERTHEIMER BROTHERS STORE
653 MAIN ST., DEADWOOD

In June of 1877 Jacob's brothers, M.J. and Louis, started their Wertheimer Brothers clothing, dry goods, and men's furnishings store on the opposite side of Deadwood's Main St. Other Jewish business establishments on or near that same location were those of Adolf and his brother Jonas Fishel, and Charles Zoellner.

Deadwood Daily Pioneer-Times, Feb 15, 1917, ad.

The Wertheimer brothers began taking buying trips to the east, making voluminous purchases that were freighted in by ox train from shipping centers such as Fort Pierre, Bismarck, North Dakota, and Sidney, Nebraska. From the more mundane items, such as underwear and hosiery, to the more luxurious like carpeting, lavish silks and velvets, and even Paris originals, Wertheimers' merchandise helped provide for the clothing and home furnishings needs of the community.

Typhoid fever, among other infectious diseases, was a prevalent killer. Among Louis Wertheimer's earliest experiences in Deadwood was the unwelcome attack of such a visitor.

Black Hills Daily Times, Mar 1, 1878

His brother in bed with attack of typhoid fever.

Louis survived, and their business prospered. The brothers continued to increase their stock and improve the building while trying to protect their property against fire. For a time in 1878, Gottstein and Idelman leased space in one half of the Wertheimers' new fireproof building. Whether man-made or as a result of natural causes, fire was Deadwood's persistent challenge.

Black Hills Daily Times, May 22, 1878
Variety of sun umbrellas & parasols very cheap.

Black Hills Daily Times, Jun 3, 1878
M.J Wertheimer, Donations to pay for the fire engine en route

Black Hills Daily Times, Sep 11, 1878
Stone masons are engaged on foundation of storeroom.

Black Hills Daily Times, Sep 18, 1878
Immense iron doors for new fire proof warehouse.

Black Hills Daily Times, Sep 28, 1878
M.J. Wertheimer, Fire proof completed, one of the finest in city.

Black Hills Daily Times, Oct 29, 1878
New fire-proof filled with Gottstein, Idelman & Co.

Black Hills Daily Pioneer, Nov 19, 1878
Fanciful railing being constructed around the porch.

Black Hills Daily Times, Nov 29, 1878
Wertheimer fire from overturned student lamp.

Black Hills Daily Times Dec 7, 1878
M.J. Wertheimer, Businessmen signing petition for two night watchmen for fire protection.

The year 1879 started out with high expectations. In January the Wertheimer Brothers store ran advertisements offering dry goods, suits, cloaks, carpets as well as furs and more luxurious fashions. In February they added fire-proof steel doors to the basement level of their storehouse, manufactured especially for their storehouse by Star and Bullock. In April they brought merchandise in from Sidney, Nebraska, and in June they started planning for a second story. They were seeing progress.

Black Hills Daily Times, Mar 11, 1879
M.J Wertheimer, Will return soon from eastern markets buying trip.

Black Hills Daily Times, Mar 18, 1879
Has been east purchasing his spring stock of goods.

Black Hills Daily Times, Mar 26, 1879
Has two Paris originals in his store window.

Black Hills Daily Times, Apr 24. 1879
To keep buyers in Eastern markets for latest fashions.

Black Hills Daily Times, Jun 1, 1879
Thanking our patrons for past favors, ad

Black Hills Daily Times, Jul 17, 1879
Went out yesterday on his annual purchasing tour.

M.J. went east on a buying trip, returning to Deadwood on September 5th with a sizable amount of stock. Perhaps he had a premonition, or perhaps conditions were ripe for fire, but on September 11th, 1879, Wertheimer made a donation to the fire department for a new fire hose. Two weeks later, with the Jewish High Holidays approaching, announcements of their business's closing for Yom Kippur appeared in the Deadwood newspapers and were posted in the doorway.

Black Hills Daily Times, Sep 26, 1879
M.J. Wertheimer, Closing business for Atonement Day, the 26th.

On September 27th 1879, one day after Yom Kippur — a date on which an observant Jew acknowledges the fragility of existence— disaster struck. The one common enemy against which everyone fought, blazed through Deadwood Gulch, demolishing the Wertheimers' first store. Losses were calculated at $4,000, but their family was safe.

Black Hills Daily Times, Sep 27, 1879

M.J. Wertheimer, Losses in the big fire of September 27, $4,000.

Black Hills Daily Times, Oct 1, 1879

Wertheimer & Co. Fireproof succumbed to flames, contents destroyed.

Not to be deterred, the Wertheimers accepted their losses, made their decisions, and set to work. They hired a large construction crew and began rebuilding, laying the foundation for a new building at 653 Main St. By October 1st, the public was already being invited to the grand opening of their "elegant" new headquarters, a 25- x 47-foot brick building. Amazingly enough, by November they had moved a stock of merchandise into their new store. M.J., the main force behind the Wertheimer Brothers company, was reportedly very happy in his new store.

Black Hills Daily Times, Sep 30, 1879

Has a large force of men working on a building. Has a large foundation laid for new building.

Black Hills Daily Times, Oct 1, 1879

M.J Wertheimer, Public invited to our grand opening, ad

Black Hills Daily Times, Oct 2, 1879

Wertheimer & Co. Putting in foundation for 25x47' brick building.

Black Hills Daily Times, Nov 8, 1879

Moved stock of goods into new brick building yesterday.

Black Hills Daily Times, Dec 11, 1879

Incoming Freight from Sidney.

The brothers continued to improve their store, dressing it up with iron shutters, laying plank sidewalks in front, and purchasing extensive amounts of merchandise. Shipment after shipment was brought in by ox train from Bismarck to the north and Sidney to the south.

Black Hills Daily Times, Jan 1, 1880

Furs of all kinds for ladies & children, ad.

Black Hills Daily Times, Jan 27, 1880

Goes out on an eastern purchasing tour, gone 30 days.

Black Hills Daily Times, Feb 7, 1880

Front of store being dressed up with iron shutters.

Black Hills Daily Times, Mar 2, 1880

Silks, cashmeres, French novelties, ad.

Black Hills Daily Times, Mar 9, 1880

Purchased more extensively this time than before.

Black Hills Daily Times, Mar 30, 1880

Plank crossing being laid down next to store.

Black Hills Daily Times, Sep 15, 1880

Returned from protracted purchasing tour in east.

Black Hills Daily Times, Nov 2, 1880

M.J Wertheimer, All shades of colored silks, cashmeres, ad

Black Hills Daily Times, Dec 1, 1880

Fall silks & dress goods, broquet & striped velvet.

Black Hills Daily Times, Dec 1, 1880

Silks, cashmeres & velvets at greatly reduced prices.

Ironically, the Wertheimers Brothers' new building also served as a temporary location for the Lawrence County Courthouse. Part of the tragedy of the Great Fire of 1879 was that it demolished whatever records were stored in the original courthouse, obliterating much of Deadwood's earliest historical accounts.

Another fire on January 19 of 1881 brought further setbacks. Their building suffered a burned roof and water damage, and considerable damage to their stock. They estimated over $1,400 in damages. In March they were still selling damaged dry goods and by April they were working night and day to excavate the rear of their store for a new office. Business was excellent and merchandise continued to flow into Deadwood by ox team and mule train. To keep up with demands of the region, the Wertheimers purchased a lot and built a branch store in Sturgis in 1883.

Black Hills Daily Times, Jan 26, 1881
M.J.Wertheimer, Hooks thank him for liberal & timely donation of $25 donation to Homestake Hose Company.

Black Hills Daily Times, Apr 1, 1881
Selling dry goods damaged by water, ad.

Black Hills Daily Times, Jun 15, 1881
M.J.Wertheimer, Mentioned as treasurer for fire department. Elected 2nd assistant of fire department.

Black Hills Daily Times, Sep 30, 1881
Received bulk of dry goods brought in by ox train.

Black Hills Daily Times, May 31, 1883
Mule train came in loaded with goods for merchants.

Black Hills Daily Times, Jun 1, 1883
M.J Wertheimer, Large engraving of Brooklyn Bridge on window.

Black Hills Daily Times, Jul 13, 1883
M.J.Wertheimer, Purchased lot at Sturgis, opening branch store.

M.J. traveled widely, his buying trips taking him everywhere from New York to Europe.

Black Hills Daily Times, Aug 10, 1882
M.J.Wertheimer, Registered at Sherman House, Chicago, on 6th.

Black Hills Daily Times, Jan 11, 1883
Popular dry goods merchant leaves on Sidney stage.

Black Hills Daily Times, Aug 30, 1885
M.J. Wertheimer is in New York buying a new stock of goods, and the clerks say that he will astonish the public with bargains the next season.

Black Hills Daily Times, Mar 28, 1886
M.J. Wertheimer safely arrived on the other side of the Big Pond. Says he intends to buy extensively while abroad.

Another fire damaged their store 1888, and once again they rebuilt, this time adding on a second story. The only path to success was forward.

WERTHEIMER HALL

The Fourth of July was celebrated in all its glory in Deadwood. Henrietta, who was on the 1878 Fourth of July committee, may have had something to do with the decision, when in 1879 Jacob offered to build the town a 35 x 85-foot concert hall in which to hold their Fourth of July celebrations. That summer, Jacob went to Fort Meade to arrange to have the 7th Cavalry Band come to Deadwood to perform a promenade concert at the hall.

Black Hills Daily Pioneer, Jun 15, 1878
Mrs Wertheimer, Fourth of July Celebration committee.

Black Hills Daily Times, Apr 2, 1879
Jacob Wertheimer, Committee on Altitude for the Do Goods Club.

Black Hills Daily Times, Jun 12, 1879
Jacob Wertheimer, Offered to build 35 X 85 hall for 4th celebration.

Black Hills Daily Times, Jul 6, 1879
J Wertheimer, One of the millionaires in procession on July 4th.

Black Hills Daily Times, Jul 27, 1879
Promenade concert to be held at Wertheimer Hall.

Black Hills Daily Times, Jul 29, 1879

Jacob Wertheimer, Went to base to arrange for band at concert.

Black Hills Daily Times, Aug 26, 1879

At Ft Meade to arrange for promenade concert.

Black Hills Daily Times, Sep 16, 1879

Jacob Wertheimer, Proposal to make Wertheimer Hall into a theatre.

Wertheimer Hall became a venue for a variety of events, partly due to Jacob's personal charisma and his talent for attracting clientele. The hall periodically metamorphosed from concert hall into theater or into skating rink, depending on the needs of the times. To the delight of Deadwood's citizens, on Christmas Day of 1879, Wertheimer Hall was transformed into the town's first skating rink, a place for one of the favorite pastimes of the day. The next year Wertheimer's once again became a concert hall and theater.

Black Hills Daily Times, Dec 25, 1879

Opening a skating rink at Wertheimer Hall.

Black Hills Daily Times, May 30, 1880

On committee of arrangements for July 4th celebration.

Black Hills Daily Times, Jul 2, 1880

Prince of magicians & fire king, Martel Mazarto, at Wertheimer Hall.

Black Hills Daily Times, Dec 11, 1880

Wertheimer Hall. To be reconstructed to be used as a theatre.

Black Hills Daily Times, Dec 22, 1880

Sawtelle completely metamorphosed Wertheimer Hall.

Black Hills Daily Times, Feb 18, 1881

Wertheimer Theater. Change of management promises change of style.

RELIGION

The Wertheimers were observant Jews who closed their businesses for the High Holidays. Jacob Wertheimer never forgot the mother tongue, the language of his youthful Hebrew education. In 1882 Jacob was called upon to act as translator when a letter arrived from Russia written in Hebrew characters, addressed to Mike Gottstein, a fellow merchant and partner of Harris Franklin. The Daily Times reported, more with amusement than accuracy, that in the face of an impending weather crisis, Jakey could pray in seven languages.

Black Hills Daily Times, Jun 8, 1881

Jakey Wertheimer, Prayed in 7 different languages in fear of cyclone.

Like most Deadwood Jews of German origin, Jacob's English and that of his brothers was tinged with a persistent German accent. In Deadwood, where everyone came from somewhere else and so many were immigrants, foreign accents were not unusual. The sad news of the death of the Wertheimers' father back in Germany arrived in April of 1883, a profound reminder of their distance from the old country and family ties.

They followed the Jewish precept of giving charity, and the Wertheimers' generosity took many forms, from sending donations to help Jews in Europe, to helping victims of yellow fever in the South, to providing breakfasts for the local firemen, to helping out with church raffles. Through their activities in various fraternal associations, such as the Masons, they helped organize charity balls and raise funds to help the local needy. When roomers at the Merchants Hotel appeared to be in need, Mrs. Wertheimer set about finding ways to help her boarders.

Black Hills Daily Times, Jun 26, 1878

Members of organization known as buttermilk brigade.

Black Hills Daily Pioneer, Sep 13, 1878

Masons to take contributions for Yellow fever victims Masonic Aid, to yellow fever sufferers of the south.

Black Hills Daily Times, Feb 8, 1881

Mrs. Wertheimer Raised funds for boarders of Merchants hotel.

Black Hills Daily Times, Jun 8, 1881

Collected funds for victims of cyclone.

Black Hills Daily Times, Sep 16 1883

Donated satin to dress a doll, silk handkerchief to raffle Catholic Fair.

Black Hills Daily Times, Aug 19, 1884

Col. Wertheimer entertained an entire family of immigrants, strangers, gratuitously, Saturday night.

Black Hills Daily Times, Jun 13, 1884

A sad case. German family burned out, receiving injuries. He expired near Forest City. Jacob Wertheimer and citizens raise money for family and burial.

In 1893 a chapter of B'nai B'rith, an organization dedicated to advocating for Jewish causes, promoting the Jewish heritage, and turning ideals into deeds of service, was founded in Deadwood. Of the 24 charter members, M.J. Wertheimer was one of the elected officers.

Black Hills Daily Times, Jun 27, 1893

Wertheimer, M.J. Order of B'nai B'rith instituted with 24 charter members; officers elected.

Jakey Wertheimer, with his Cupid-like appearance, was given to practical jokes. April 1st was his yearly opportunity to act on his inclinations and for his friends and neighbors to respond in kind. Their April Fool's jokes were passed around liberally. More than once was Mike Gottstein, early partner of Harris Franklin, the object of Jacob's April Fool's Day entertainment. He obligingly returned the favor.

Black Hills Daily Times, Apr 2, 1880

Werthy Jakeheimer's hall rent of $800 is paid.

Black Hills Daily Times, Nov 17, 1880

Cupid on cigar box bears resemblance to Jakey Wertheimer.

Black Hills Daily Times, Apr 2, 1881

Mike Gottstein plays April Fool's joke on Wertheimer.

POLITICS

The Wertheimers had good reason to support law and order. Personal assaults and gunfights were rampant in wide-open Deadwood; one shooting actually took place right in front of the Wertheimer Brothers' establishment, almost hitting their partner, Mr. Neumann. Confidence games, prostitution, and criminal activity of all sorts proliferated. Proficiency in self-defense as well as acumen in business were basic necessities; M.J. Wertheimer could hold his own in both.

Black Hills Daily Pioneer, Aug 19, 1876

Storms & Barnes have gun fight. Mr. Neumann, partner of Mr. Wertheimer almost hit.

Black Hills Daily Times, Aug 5, 1879

Thomas Pearce, A painter of Lead, attacked Wertheimer as he walked on the street with Smiley. Pearce attacked Jake in a somewhat cowardly way.

Black Hills Daily Times, Sep 5, 1880

Dutchman lit into him thinking he couldn't defend himself.

Jacob demonstrated his willingness to help stabilize the wild town by announcing a run for city council. He was also called to participate in county government, and in 1878 he was elected to the board of Lawrence County Commissioners. In 1881 he was once again elected to public office, and gave a dinner at the Merchants Hotel to celebrate his election.

Black Hills Daily Pioneer, Sep 16, 1876
J. Wertheimer runs for council in Deadwood.

Black Hills Daily Times, Apr 27, 1877
Jacob Wertheimer, testified in Obrodovich murder trial.

Black Hills Daily Pioneer, Apr 02, 1878
Jacob Wertheimer, County Commissioners hold meeting.

Black Hills Daily Pioneer, Dec 12, 1878
Special session of the board of county commissioners.

Black Hills Daily Times, Feb 11, 1879
M.J Wertheimer, Bills allowed by new board of county commissioners.

Black Hills Daily Times, Dec 16, 1880
County commissioners in session.

Black Hills Daily Times, May 20, 1881
Jakey Wertheimer, Only man in the city with a true political spirit

In 1881 the Dakota Territorial Legislature passed a bill to provide for erection of a normal school (teacher's college) in Spearfish, Dakota Territory. As one of the Lawrence County Commissioners, Jake Wertheimer supported the bill and with the commissioners tried to convince the people of Spearfish to provide the necessary 40 acres for the school as provided by law. Spearfish let the opportunity slip by, however, and within six months the law expired. A few citizens realized that this was an opportunity missed, and they went to work to get the law reinstated. In 1883 they managed to raise close to $800 and 40 acres, and the school that has since become Black Hills State University became a reality.

Black Hills Daily Times, Feb 24, 1881
Jakey Wertheimer, Bill for erection of Dakota College.

Black Hills Daily Times, May 19, 1881
Jakey Wertheimer, 3rd ward citizens to run him for council.

Black Hills Daily Times, May 22, 1881
Jake S. Anthony, Beat Wertheimer in third ward vote.

Black Hills Daily Times, Jun 15, 1881
Wertheimer to give dinner Merchants Hotel in honor of his election.

Although his political career had its ups and downs, Jacob Wertheimer remained active in territorial, city, and county government throughout his time in Deadwood. In June of 1881 Jake celebrated his election to the city council by giving a dinner at the Merchants Hotel.

Black Hills Daily Times, Oct 10, 1882
Jacob Wertheimer, Voting places established & judges appointed.

Black Hills Daily Times, Sep 10, 1884
Republican county committee meets, sets convention Oct. 4.

Black Hills Daily Times, Sep 13, 1884
Colonel Jacob Wertheimer leaves this morning as delegate to Territorial republican convention.

In 1884 Jacob Wertheimer brought a complaint against Albert E. Swearingen's Gem Theatre, asserting that it should be recognized for what it was— a den of prostitution in the guise of a dance hall. His voice was heard, but the practice of prostitution was too deeply rooted in Deadwood to be blocked. The ancient practice would continue so for the next hundred years.

Black Hills Daily Times, Sep 5, 1884
Jacob Wertheimer, Albert E. Swearingen's Gem Theatre a den of prostitution under the guise of a dance hall; stocked with unsuspecting and innocent girls. Alice Maguire, Maria Marron, Mollie Chappel.

By 1885 Deadwood had a well-established legal system, and disputes could be settled reasonably in court. One conflict involved Louis Wertheimer and two other Jewish merchants, Sol Rosenthal and Adolph Fishel. Rosenthal, who was having some financial difficulties at the time, sued Louis to recover $50 which he had deposited with Louis as stakeholder in a bet he had made with Fishel. The amount would be considered petty by today's standards, but this case took two days to decide, with the court ultimately ruling in favor of the defendant, Louis Wertheimer.

Black Hills Daily Times, Sep 11, 1885
Case of Sol Rosenthal vs. Louis Wertheimer, to recover $50 deposited as stakeholder in a bet with Adolph Fishel, was called yesterday. Adjournment taken until this morning.

Black Hills Daily Times, Sep 12, 1885
Case of Sol Rosenthal vs. Louis Wertheimer, to recover $50 deposited in a bet, ruled in favor of defendant.

As with most of Deadwood's merchants, Jacob Wertheimer had interests in the mining sector. Besides serving on the executive committee for one of Harris Franklin's mining concerns, Jacob actually had his own gold mine, the Little Nettie mine. Legends grew up around the names of these mines, which frequently took their name from a female particularly significant to the owner. Possibly Little Nettie was a young lady dear to Jacob and his family. It was said that the Holy Terror Mine, one of the Black Hills' most prolific gold producers, was named for the indignant wife of the mine's discoverer, who insisted the mine be named in her honor.

Black Hills Daily Pioneer, Jun 1, 1878
Notice that he does own Little Nettie mine.

Black Hills Daily Times, Aug 3, 1881
J. Wertheimer. On executive committee of Franklin Mining Co.

Black Hills Daily Times, Sep 4, 1884
Col. Wertheimer chaperoned Gen. Allen and Msrs. A. T. Packard and J. C. Fisher through the Homestake.

Black Hills Daily Times, Jun 5, 1885
Paul Rewman and Jake Wertheimer scratching heads over Iron Hill shares.

Black Hills Daily Times, Aug 13, 1885
Hearst impressed with Carbonate Camp. George Hearst, Superintendent Grier, Jake Wertheimer and Mr. Fallonsbee, visited the Carbonate Camp yesterday.

HENRY WERTHEIMER

Like his father, young Henry Wertheimer was an outstanding citizen. He was editor of the Deadwood school paper, the "School Budget." He did, however, make headlines once in 1883, when at the age of 15 he drew $5,000 in checks and then managed to lose them. All was forgiven, and Henry's 17th birthday was celebrated with a party. Nathan Franklin, his childhood friend, who had also arrived in Deadwood at the age of 7, was one of the invited guests.

Black Hills Daily Times, Aug 18, 1880
Henry Wertheimer, Editor of the paper "School Budget."

Black Hills Daily Times, Sep 26, 1883
Henry Wertheimer, Drew $5000 in checks & then lost them.

MISFORTUNE STRIKES

Jake's luck began to run out in 1885, when he suffered a series of troublesome accidents which started on Jan 31st. He was thrown from a sleigh, injuring his leg, and requiring a month's convalescence. In June he was run over by a run-away horse and carriage, apparently causing only slight injury, but probably contributing to his chronic bronchial ailment. Then in October, already in an invalid condition, Jake was assaulted in the street by a drunken soldier. A friend who happened to witness the incident sprang to his defense, landing the assailant in the street, but this assault only made Jake's health issues worse.

Black Hills Daily Times, Jan 31, 1885

Jacob Wertheimer was thrown from a cutter while enjoying a sleigh ride, and the horse pushed the heavy vehicle over and fractured the colonel's leg. Surgical attendance was summoned.

Black Hills Daily Times, Feb 1, 1885

Wertheimer's leg sprained, not fractured. Jake Wertheimer was more fortunate than at first believed. His leg was not fractured—only sprained.

Black Hills Daily Times, Feb 12, 1885

Wertheimer is confined to his bed with a complication of maladies.

Black Hills Daily Times, Feb 22, 1885

Jake Wertheimer enjoyed a ride to Lead, yesterday. His convalescence is gratifying to his many friends.

Black Hills Daily Times, Jun 14, 1885

Jakey Wertheimer run over by run-away horses and carriage. He was slightly injured and thoroughly muddled.

The following January the chronic bronchitis that had plagued Jacob Wertheimer took his life. After a brief but remarkably successful ten years in Deadwood, having performed his final act of civic duty by testifying before a grand jury from his sick bed, Jacob died on January 26, 1886, at age 43, leaving his widow Henrietta and son Henry to go on without him.

Black Hills Daily Times, Jan 10, 1886

Wertheimer testifies from sick bed. Grand jury adjourned to the Merchants to take the evidence of Jake Wertheimer, at present on the sick list.

Black Hills Daily Times, Jan 27, 1886

Jacob Wertheimer, 43, proprietor of the Merchants Hotel, died last evening, after a long and painful illness, of chronic bronchitis.

Jacob Wertheimer's funeral took place at the Merchants Hotel with burial at Mount Moriah Cemetery. Henrietta, although surrounded by friends and family, was overwhelmed and unable to provide any information to the press at the time. The next two years would test the grit and resiliency of this wife, mother of their son, and now proprietress of the Merchants Hotel.

Black Hills Daily Times, Jan 28, 1886

The prostrate condition of Jacob Wertheimer's family renders it impossible to collect additional data. The deceased left a will.

Black Hills Daily Times, Jan 28, 1886

In memoriam. Retail Liquor Dealer's Association approves resolution in testimony to the wife and son of our departed friend, Jacob Wertheimer.

Black Hills Daily Times, Jan 29, 1886

Funeral of Jacob Wertheimer took place at the Merchants yesterday, burial at Mount Moriah. Attending Jacob Goldberg, Louis Reubens, Nathan Colman, Morris Liebmann, Seth Bullock,

Black Hills Daily Times, Feb 6, 1886,

Judge Nathan Colman reports Jacob Wertheimer's will bequeath all to his wife, Henriette Wertheimer, and appoints her executrix of estate.

Black Hills Daily Times, Feb 19, 1886

Judge Gordon busy with Wertheimer estate; Mrs. Wertheimer files bond as administratrix. Messrs.

Harris Franklin, John Treber and McDonough appointed appraisers of the estate.

Jacob had been well loved in the community, and his wife was presented with a life-sized portrait of her late husband.

Black Hills Daily Times, May 23, 1886
Mrs. Wertheimer has just received a beautiful life-sized portrait of her late husband.

Following Jacob's death things did not go well with the Merchants Hotel. M.J. Couch brought a case against the owner of the Merchants in court, and papers were served by the Board of Health condemning the rear end of the property, including the cesspool and the club room. It took a court battle to settle the matter, but the Merchants was finally returned to Henrietta's possession. The result was the addition of a spacious and elegantly equipped new bathroom in 1887, much the pleasure of her guests.

Black Hills Daily Times, Nov 16, 1886
Mrs. Wertheimer, owner of the Merchants, returned from Cincinnati and elsewhere in the east last evening. Henry will follow in a few days.

Black Hills Daily Times, Nov 25, 1886
Mrs. Wertheimer is experiencing no little difficulty in obtaining possession of her hotel property. The courts have been appealed to, and, as we understand, there the matter is likely to remain for months.

Black Hills Daily Times, Dec 1, 1886
The case of Mrs. Jacob Wertheimer vs. M.J. Couch before Justice Hall as per adjournment yesterday, and the court directed that proceedings be resumed, then writ of prohibition issued by Judge Thomas.

Black Hills Daily Times, Dec 9, 1886
Mrs. Wertheimer was served, yesterday, with papers from the board of health condemning the rear end of the Merchants Hotel, consisting of cesspool, club room, &c.

Black Hills Daily Times, Dec 12, 1886
Case of Henrietta Wertheimer vs. M.I. Couch called before Justice Hall yesterday. Change of venue granted.

Black Hills Daily Times, Dec 16, 1886
Wertheimer-Couch case called up in Henley's court at 5 o'clock last evening. It is understood Couch will vacate and there will be no further trouble. Mrs. Wertheimer announces she will again have possession of the Merchants Hotel this morning, and will at once proceed to place it in order ready for business.

Black Hills Daily Times, Dec 17, 1886
Mrs. Wertheimer re-opens Merchants Hotel. Tom Flynn is in charge of the office.

Black Hills Daily Times, Jul 17, 1887
Mrs. Wertheimer is constantly surprising guests of the Merchants, the latest is a spacious and elegantly equipped and furnished bath room.

It was time for Henry to pursue higher education. Henrietta, besieged and in mourning for Jacob, left Deadwood with young Henry for points east and Cincinnati, where he was to attend college. Still grieving for his father, Henry wrote to his mother of his homesickness, while assuring her of his steady improvement. Nonetheless, Henrietta traveled back to Cincinnati to console her son. In November, Henrietta returned to Deadwood, expecting Henry to follow within a few days. Then came the announcement that Henry would remain at school in the east until graduation. It was a very unsettled time in both their lives.

Black Hills Daily Times, Dec 17, 1886
Henry Wertheimer will not come home as was announced, but remain at school in Cincinnati until graduation.

Black Hills Daily Times, Jul 21, 1887
Henry Wertheimer in a letter to his mother, manifests great homesickness, but gives assurance of steady improvement.

In July word came back to Deadwood that Henry had suffered a small accident in Chicago, nothing of concern. Certainly it was reminiscent of the injury to his leg that his father had suffered only two years before. The fracture of a small bone in his leg, at first thought to be of little consequence, became a serious problem. Henrietta traveled to Chicago to be with her son, who was weak and confined to bed, but said to be improving. But soon, business demands required that she return to Deadwood alone in the spring.

Travel in 1887
Photo courtesy Centennial Archives,
Deadwood Public Library

Black Hills Daily Times, Jul 1, 1887

Henry Wertheimer reported to be suffering from a fracture of a small bone of the leg; nothing serious.

Black Hills Daily Times, Aug 20, 1887

Mrs. Wertheimer leaves for Chicago on Monday. Henry continues weak and confined to his bed, but is said to be improving.

Black Hills Daily Times, Oct 2, 1887

Mrs. Henrietta Wertheimer returned last evening from Chicago on a business trip that will keep her here for a week or two. She will return to Chicago to attend upon her son Henry at the Michael Reese hospital in a very precarious condition. Henry continues weak.

Black Hills Daily Times, Oct 23, 1887

Mrs. Charles Posner is advised by letter from Chicago of the very low condition of Henry Wertheimer. Hope of recovery is abandoned.

Although responsibilities had drawn her back to Deadwood for two weeks, she hastily returned to Chicago to be beside her 19-year-old son, whose condition had deteriorated. In late October of 1887 Harris Franklin back in Deadwood received word from Chicago that Henry Wertheimer, Jacob and Henrietta's only child, had died at Michael Reese Hospital. It was tragedy upon tragedy for the Wertheimers.

Black Hills Daily Times, Oct 30, 1887

Wertheimer dies at Chicago. Harris Franklin receives telegram, without particulars, of the death of Henry Wertheimer Oct. 29.

Bereft, Henrietta once again returned to Deadwood; this was still her home. Now she turned management of the Merchants Hotel over to her brother-in-law, Louis, as she tried to find a way to cope.

Meanwhile, brother-in-law M.J. had married. In September of 1889, sorrow struck once again, when the first child of Mr. and Mrs. M.J. Wertheimer died and was buried in the Jewish section of Mount Moriah Cemetery.

ENDINGS

In 1890, Louis sold the hotel, and subsequently the building went through a series of transformations. The new owner, John G. Keith, changed the name to the Keystone Hotel. In 1909, it was again seriously damaged by fire, and once again repaired. The building that had been the Merchants Hotel finally burned to the ground in December of 1951.

In the spring of 1893 Henrietta, apparently intending to spend the rest of her life in Deadwood, built two double residences on Shine Street.

Black Hills Daily Times, Feb 2, 1893
Mrs. Henrietta Wertheimer will build two double residences this spring on the old Kelly warehouse lot on Shine Street, corner Williams.

The Wertheimer brothers' business remained under family management for nearly 40 years. Their store had grown into one of the most extensive enterprises of its kind in the Black Hills. In 1909 they moved out and rented the building to the Zoellner Brothers' Clothing Store. M.J. and Louis Wertheimer finally left Deadwood in 1916.

Jacob Wertheimer only lived to the age of 43. In ten years of visionary expansion and diversification, Wertheimer had become a wealthy man, not just in money, but also in friends. Besides his businesses which had provided jobs for Deadwood's citizens, he had participated in the process of creating a stable government and bringing higher education to Lawrence County.

Although his legacy was not as widely noted as that of Harris Franklin or of Sol Star, Jacob Wertheimer's fortunes rose and fell with those of Deadwood, and he left a significant imprint.

The infant child of Mr. and Mrs. M.J. Wertheimer, the only other Wertheimer of record in the Mount Zion section of Mount Moriah, lies in an unmarked grave.

Jacob Wertheimer's grave marker is among the oldest tombstones in the Mount Zion section of Mount Moriah Cemetery.

The inscription, now seriously eroded, reads:

> *Jacob Ben Zvi Wertheimer*
> *Died January 28, 1886*
> *For these I cry*
> *My eyes pour forth water on*
> *The death of the godly one*
> *Jacob Ben Zvi Wertheimer*
> *Who died*
> *On the 26 day of Shevat 5646*

Photo courtesy Sihaya Reed

GOLDBERG

GOLDBERG'S GROCERY
670-672 MAIN ST.

Jacob Goldberg
Photo courtesy Adams Museum

Goldberg was the name that first assured me that there had indeed been a Jewish presence in Deadwood. How could there not have been other Jewish people here? The story of Jacob Goldberg and his grocery store reached back to 1876, the very beginning of settlement.

At the start of the excitement of the gold boom in 1876, a young man named Connors bought a supply of grocery stock from some disgruntled gold-seekers at 10 cents on the dollar. Connors and his partner, P.A. Gushurst, were determined to get their stock to Deadwood, but negotiations with the wagon boss were not going well. The two young men overcame the objections of the disinclined wagon boss, making their point frontier-style, with a pair of six-shooters. They had no intention of being prevented from getting their supply of groceries through. They reached Deadwood in August 1876, pitched a tent, and opened for business. Trade was lively; everyone needed their bacon and beans. The Big Horn Mountains of Wyoming to the west were having a gold rush of their own and Gushurst and Connors' store was the natural place to stop and stock up. The Big Horn Store, doing business out of a tent, had found its name.

When the weather turned seriously cold, young Gushurst paid $75 and a rifle, and purchased a lot, the first ever sold in Deadwood. The two men built a frame structure for their Big Horn Store, but the partnership was not to last. Connors died, Gushurst moved on to open a new grocery business in Central City, and 25-year-old Jake Goldberg became the new owner of the Big Horn Store, Deadwood's first grocery store.

Bighorn Store
Photo Stanley J. Morrow, courtesy Library of Congress

Jacob Goldberg was born in Germany in 1851 and came to America at the age of 18, where his family settled in New York City's lower Manhattan. Seeking new opportunities on the Western frontier during the Montana gold boom, the spirited young Jacob made his way to the mining city of Helena, where he engaged in the clothing business. Fire, always the arch-enemy, stole his possessions in a blaze that destroyed much of the city. Then gold discovery erupted in the Black Hills and Jake joined a large company of 140 hopeful Montana frontiersmen under the leadership of a Capt. Hardwick, heading for Deadwood. Along with Sol Star and Sam Schwarzwald, Jacob Goldberg was among the audacious young Jews in the Montana Party who rode from Helena through perilous Indian hunting grounds to reach the Hills. An attack near Devil's Tower resulted in the loss of one of their scouts, but the party remained vigilant, continued on, and the caravan of 60 wagons arrived at Deadwood in August of 1876. Many of the Montanans were experienced miners, but some, like Jake, came in other capacities, having previously established businesses and professions in Helena.

The Big Horn Store
Photo courtesy Adams Museum

After purchasing the small frame building, Goldberg took in Nicolas C. Mattheissen as a business partner. Notices of the partnership began to appear on September 24, 1877. In December, Jacob Goldberg's Big Horn Store, later to be known simply as Goldberg's Grocery, started to advertise in the newspapers, beginning a Deadwood tradition that would endure for over 100 years.

One of the earliest advertisements for the Big Horn Store appeared as a lottery for kittens. Although the store specialized in groceries, it also needed to fill various other needs of the community, and felines were considered indispensable to reining in the burgeoning rodent population. Alexander Davidson brought the first load of cats from Denver in 1876, following which shipments of cats arrived from time to time, appearances that couldn't help but attract attention. Even though the cats were a favorite of the ladies and a sign that society was developing, the animals tended to fight and howl, and became a mixed blessing. Their yowling irritated some residents enough to use the cats for target practice.

Black Hills Daily Times, Aug 1, 1877
Fellow on the road to Deadwood with load of cats.

Black Hills Daily Times, Sep 14, 1877
Cats "mew-sic by the band" singing at night.

Black Hills Daily Times, Apr 4. 1878
Big Horn Store proprietor, lottery for kittens

Black Hills Daily Times, Jan 24, 1878
A couple of thoroughbred Maltese cats in freight.

Black Hills Daily Times, Jan 30, 1878
Cats have been doing great executions in warehouse.

Black Hills Daily Times, Aug 26, 1880
Goldberg store received invoice of cats, day of playful mouse ends.

Black Hills Daily Times, Feb 3, 1881
Van with wild cats in cages attracts attention

In August of 1878 the partners began the process of building their first fireproof, a wise decision. They started laying in large stocks of merchandise, with shipments arriving from Bismarck and Fort Pierre on a regular basis. In December of that year they petitioned the city council to open up the thoroughfare of Main Street, initially little more than a clutter of mining claims, tents and makeshift shacks, with no protection against the conflagration that was about to descend into Deadwood Gulch.

Black Hills Daily Pioneer, May 12, 1878
Matthiessen & Goldberg, closing out their stock.

Black Hills Daily Times, Aug 1, 1878
Matthiessen & Goldberg building big fireproof.

Black Hills Daily Times, Sep 3, 1878
Matthiesesen and Goldberg, Doors of fireproof constructed by Lake's tinsmith.

Black Hills Daily Times, Dec 6, 1878
Matthiessen & Goldberg. Big Horn Store laying in large stocks.

Black Hills Daily Times, Dec 7, 1878
Matthiessen and Goldberg. Businesses wanting night watchmen for fire protection.

Black Hills Daily Times, Jul 19, 1879
Matthiessen and Goldberg. Erecting brick building to be used as grocery store.

Black Hills Daily Times, Aug 22, 1879
Matthiessen and Goldberg. Transferred stock to Wertheimer's during rebuilding.

The Great Fire struck in September of 1879, and although the partnership's losses were calculated at $4000, their fireproof building was largely spared. They were able to continue on with construction, adding a second story to their brick building.

Black Hills Daily Times, Oct 7, 1879
Has brick store completed above the first story.

Black Hills Daily Times, Oct 12, 1879
Capping on top of new building about completed.

Black Hills Daily Times, Nov 4, 1879
Matthiessen and Goldberg. Fire-proofs saved in the big Deadwood fire.

The partners placed notices in the Black Hills Daily Times, informing the public that they were still operating out of their fireproof quarters. Goldberg and Matthiessen would continue to operate their grocery together as the Big Horn store until 1882. In 1890 it became the Goldberg Grocery.

Black Hills Daily Times, Sep 27, 1879
Matthiessen and Goldberg. Losses in the big fire of September 27, $4,000.

Black Hills Daily Times, Sep 28, 1879
Matthiessen and Goldberg. Still in building where they moved a few weeks ago.

Black Hills Daily Times, Sep 30, 1879
Removing debris, putting in foundation to rebuild.

FEEDING THE POPULATION

The population had to be fed and Matthiessen and Goldberg were determined to be the leaders in that field. Considering the challenges of bringing food, especially perishables, into the Hills from outside sources, the variety and availability of groceries was surprisingly extensive, and tells much about the needs and tastes of the day. Although most of their trade dealt with such staples as flour and meats, as one reporter noted in 1881, the Big Horn Store also supplied Black Hills citizens with the little luxuries of life.

Black Hills Daily Times, Nov 29, 1879

Matthiessen and Goldberg have, since the fire, occupied quarters on upper Main St., but are now in their own building near the bank corners, with a full line of fine staple and fancy groceries. They are in daily receipt of fresh goods, and will not surrender their well-earned reputation of being the leading grocery house in Deadwood.

Black Hills Daily Times, Dec 2, 1879

Spearfish Mill sent in 7,000 lbs of flour yesterday.

Black Hills Daily Times, Aug 21, 1880

Bought fifty-three cheeses from Rapid City factory.

Black Hills Daily Times, Mar 13, 1881

Select stock of meats has just arrived.

Black Hills Daily Times, May 15, 1881

Received a mammoth Swiss cheese by ox express.

Black Hills Daily Times, Sep 15, 1882

J.Goldberg, Went east to purchase stock of goods, gone 2 weeks.

On September 15, 1882, the partnership dissolved. The newspapers reported that N.C. Matthiessen was retiring and leaving Deadwood. In October it was reported that he had bought a large stock of goods in the east, and was opening a new grocery business in Montana. The former Big Horn Store co-owner later wrote to Jake from Livingston, where he had opened another grocery, sounding anything but cheerful, according to Goldberg. In 1885 Matthiessen suffered the consequences of another disastrous fire at Livingston, resulting once again in destruction of his property.

Black Hills Daily Times, Feb 1, 1883

Swiss cheese just arrived at Goldbergs

Black Hills Daily Times, Jun 21, 1883

Alphabetical soup, made of grandest vermacilla (sic).

Black Hills Daily Times, Aug 1, 1883

Gunpowder, English, basket & pan-fired teas.

Black Hills Daily Times, May 1, 1883

Genuine sugar house syrup & Vermont maple syrup arrived.

Black Hills Daily Times, Jul 1, 1883

Swiss cheese, made in Switzerland, not in Missouri.

Black Hills Daily Times, Jul 7, 1883

Repapering & otherwise improving Big Horn Store.

The railroad finally arrived at Rapid City, making that the closest terminal to Deadwood. Refrigerated freight cars made shipments of such perishables as seafood and dairy products practical. Goldberg partnered up for a time with John Herrmann and John Treber, and they opened a branch store in Rapid City. Treber, not Jewish, and Goldberg, one of Deadwood's original Jews, were fast friends for many years.

Herrmann, Treber, and Goldberg. Rapid City 1880
Photo courtesy David Strain

Black Hills Daily Times, Jul 28, 1883

Returned from Rapid, John Herrmann went that far with Goldberg.

Black Hills Daily Times, Jun 13, 1884

Limburger odorizers. Main Street thoroughly odorized. Atomizers circular in form and labelled "Limburger." Jake Goldberg stores in fire-proof safe.

Black Hills Daily Times, Jul 1, 1884

Home-made pickles at 75 cents per gallon at J. Goldberg's.

Black Hills Daily Times, Sep 9, 1884

Notice of dissolution of Herrmann, Treber and Goldberg.

Black Hills Daily Times, Dec 2, 1884

Neufshatel cheese, just received, at J. Goldberg's.

Black Hills Daily Times, Jan 3, 1885

Fresh Lake Superior trout and white fish, the finest ever come to town, cheaper than ever, at J. Goldberg's.

Black Hills Daily Times, Feb 1, 1885

A carload of creamery butter just arrived, which will be sold to the trade cheap at J. Goldberg's.

Black Hills Daily Times, Jun 9, 1885

Jake Goldberg was first Deadwood merchant to receive eastern flour after closing of mills here.

Black Hills Daily Times, Jun 10, 1885

Holland herrings and home-made pickles at J. Goldberg's.

Black Hills Daily Times, Jun 24, 1885

Jacob Goldberg in possession of the only 900 pounds of flour in the city. There is any amount of flour en route, but heavy rains make it a tedious process to roll in.

Black Hills Daily Times, Aug 11, 1885

Choice dried beef sliced to order at J. Goldberg.

Black Hills Daily Times, Nov 24, 1885

Jake Goldberg is down at Sand Creek, hunting up overdue freight.

Black Hills Daily Times, May 15, 1886

For a limited time only, J. Goldberg will give away with each pound of baking powder a sugar dish, cream pitcher or butter dish.

Black Hills Daily Times, Aug 1, 1886

J. Goldberg has a carload of choice butter en route here by refrigerator line from Chicago. It should arrive about August 5. Orders should be sent in early.

Black Hills Daily Times, Aug 14, 1886

Jake Goldberg proud to be first purchaser of James Anderson's platform counter scale.

Black Hills Daily Times, Aug 23, 1887

Goldberg acquires rye bread agency. Undersigned has this day acquired the agency for John Hage celebrated rye bread. Lovers of genuine rye bread will please leave orders every morning at J. Goldberg's.

Black Hills Daily Times, Sep 10, 1887

Jake Goldberg has arranged with John Treber to bring fresh oysters from St. Louis to Rapid City in refrigerator cars.

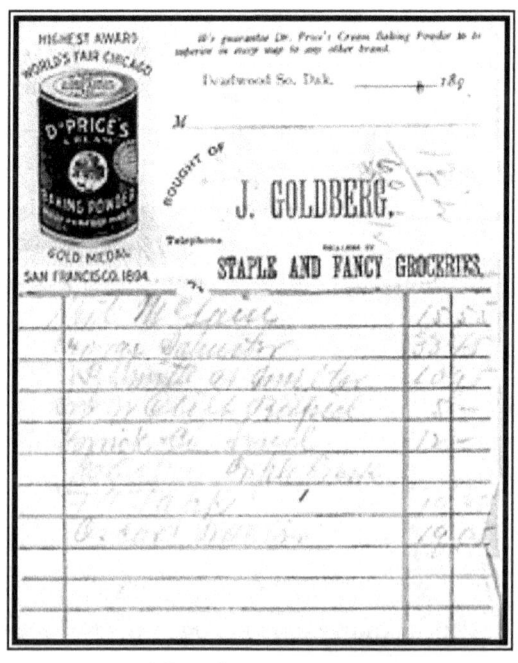

Goldberg's Grocery receipt
Photo courtesy Adams Museum

Described as gentle, sociable and "mild-eyed", and with a lingering German accent, Jake Goldberg was nobody's fool. The adventurous young man had a rougher side. Stories related in the Daily Times could be quite entertaining.

Black Hills Daily Times, May 12, 1882

Jake Goldberg, Rumored he will accept Morris Welsh's challenge to fight.

Black Hills Daily Times, March 14, 1884

Jacob Goldberg is a merchant, buys goods and sells, and occasionally goes out in the country for a ride. On one of these occasions he put up with a rancher in the valley for a horse feed and dinner, at the noon hour. The dinner was a good one, with the buttermilk accompaniments, and after the usual rest and smoke, he inquired the amount of his bill, and was told by the hoary headed granger, that the presence of his company more than compensated for the first cost of the provisions destroyed, and that he would in the future consider it a favor to have him call frequently and partake of his hospitality. Since that time he has been a solid friend of Mr. Goldberg, calls on him whenever he comes to town, asks after his health, and advises him in regard to the prospects of the coming vegetables. Last week he came to town, and told Goldberg in a very patronizing way that he had two sacks of potatoes, 200 pounds, of a superior variety, the last of a big load, and that he could have them for a cent a pound, $2 for the lot, sacks and all, the finest by all odds that had ever been offered in this market, the kind that first class housewives go crazy after, worth double the amount asked for them, but for old acquaintance sake he would let them go at that figure. Jakey took them at that figure, weighed them not, neither the sacks did he open to gaze upon their pristine loveliness, laid two dollars down, and then laid the two sacks of murphies down by the stove. The next morning the floor of the store was covered with water, and an examination proved that it came from the potatoes, they having been frozen solid before their entry into the store. The potatoes now lay on the sidewalk and a gentle, mild eyed youth, with a large fair complexion, awaits with Job-like patience and a club the coming of that big-hearted rancher.

The Big Horn Store ledgers show that Goldberg's trade extended to such distant points as Chadron, Hot Springs, Custer, Pierre, and even Sioux Falls. Names like Seth Bullock, Chinese merchant Sam Wing, Mike Russell, the Homestake Mess, and the Golden Reward Mining Company, all central to the colorful history of the booming mining camp, are but a few of those noted in the ledger books. The entries are often annotated with characterizations like "woodchopper," "prospector," or "lawyer."

While most of Goldberg's early customers included such respectable clientele as the World's Fair Restaurant of Lead and the Golden Reward Mining Company, one of the more infamous names appearing repeatedly in the ledgers is the name of Martha Burke Cannary, better known as Calamity Jane. According to Dr. Watson Parker, this *"boozy old bawd ... ran up a bill at Jake Goldberg's grocery, and anywhere else that wanted to give her credit, and most places did give her credit, for she became a sort of public charity and in addition was a nuisance when she was crossed or hindered."*

Calamity Jane did run up a tab at Goldberg's Grocery, leaving a lasting souvenir of her patronage. Either the Big Horn Store or Shoudy's Meat Market, next door to the Big Horn, depending on which source you prefer to believe, was most likely the site of the capture of Jack McCall, the man who killed Wild Bill Hickok on August 2, 1876. Rumor had it that McCall tried to escape through Goldberg's back door and was captured there. There are different versions of the capture of Jack McCall, and although neither Calamity Jane's veracity nor accuracy were ever considered exceedingly reliable, according to Calamity's Jane's own version of the story, McCall was captured in front of Shurdy's (sic) Meat Market. Other versions have McCall being captured next door, in front of Goldberg's Grocery. Either way, the sidewalk outside Goldberg's was the scene of wild excitement on August 2, 1876.

Just as Jake Goldberg had his tougher side, Calamity Jane, despite her hard exterior, had her softer side. Estelline Bennett, daughter of Pioneer Judge Granville Bennett, in her memoir, "Old Deadwood Days," recalled how as a child she met Calamity Jane face-to-face on the street in front of Goldberg's Grocery. Although Calamity's nefarious reputation preceded her, Estelline did not recognize her; however, her girlfriend Maude Dennee did. Calamity invited the two girls into Goldberg's where she offered to buy them some candy. Too frightened to refuse, they followed her into the store where Calamity tossed a silver dollar onto the counter and ordered Jake to "give these little girls some candy." The girls, still stunned, left with a large amount of hard candy, wondering how they would explain this to their mothers.

Those who knew her, and those who only knew of her, have spent years trying to decide which of Calamity Jane's complexity of attributes predominated. Dr. Valentine T. McGillycuddy, surgeon, surveyor of the Black Hills, Indian agent at Pine Ridge, and a leading citizen of Rapid City, drew his own conclusions about Martha Jane Cannary, referring to her as "loud and rough in all her ways, but kind-hearted, always ready to nurse a sick soldier or miner." He said she'd had many husbands, since license shops and preachers were hard to come by in those days. Calamity Jane drifted from mining camp to mining camp all over the northwest until her death in August of 1903. Jacob Goldberg, Sam Schwarzwald, and many other original pioneers, were acquainted with the infamous Calamity Jane, and attended her funeral on Mount Moriah.

ADVERTISING

The Big Horn Store advertised extensively in the newspapers, keeping their name in front of the public— and their delivery wagon busy. A popular publicity technique in the 1800s was the balloon release, a minor spectacle eagerly anticipated by the public.

Black Hills Daily Times, Feb 17, 1883
Jake Goldberg, Delivers goods in brand new wagon, all painted up.

Black Hills Daily Times, May 13, 1883
Jake Goldberg, Delivery wagon requisitioned to take drunk to jail.

Black Hills Daily Times, Jul 22, 1883
Gave free balloon exhibition in front of his store.

Black Hills Weekly Times, July 12, 1884
A very pretty six-foot balloon was released by Jake Goldberg and George Bews from in front of the Big Horn store last evening. Attached were orders, a presentation of which will secure a finder a bottle of Mumm's extra dry and a sack of flour.

Black Hills Daily Times, Dec 23, 1884
Christmas in Deadwood. The season of gift selecting and gift making at hand; the dilemma where to buy and what to buy; extensive, costly and magnificent stocks on every hand.

CHARITABLE, COMMERCIAL, & FRATERNAL ENDEAVORS

Jake's other interests included the public library's board of trustees and several charities. He was an active member of the board of directors and bank officer of the First National Bank of Deadwood, and held stock in the Merchants National Bank. He also held shares in the Carbonate Mining Company and Black Hills Oil Company.

Black Hills Daily Times, Jan 30, 1880

Leading businesses have stock in Merchants National Bank.

Black Hills Daily Times, Aug 2, 1881

Jake Goldberg, Shareholder in Carbonate Mining Co.

Black Hills Daily Times, Feb 24, 1883

Acted as floor manager for Library Assoc. ball.

Black Hills Daily Times, Jun 3, 1883

J. Goldberg, Contributions for construction of Deadwood St. bridge.

Black Hills Daily Times, Feb 1, 1884

Notice of meeting of stockholders of Black Hills Oil Company. Mr. McPherson, president of the board; Mr. Goldberg, secretary.

Black Hills Daily Times, Mar 2, 1884

First assessment of the Black Hills Oil Company was levied by the board of directors, of one-half of one cent per share of stock, payable immediately, as per assessment notice published in another column. The secretary, J. Goldberg, requests us to announce that all persons interested in the company who have not received their certificates of stock, should call on him at his place of business, Big Horn store, Deadwood, after Tuesday next, March 4th, and he will issue to them.

Black Hills Daily Times, Mar 7, 1884

We are requested to announce that all members of the Black Hills Oil company who have signed a deed of transfer for their landed interests to the company can procure their certificates of stock by calling upon the secretary, Jacob Goldberg.

Among his fraternal associations, which included the Masonic lodge, he was most involved with the Knights of Pythias. As with many in the Jewish population, Jake held offices in Knights of Pythias, sincere in his belief that this organization was dedicated to improving the individual as well as serving the community.

Black Hills Daily Times, Jan 9, 1882

J. Goldberg, To be installed as Knights of Pythias officer.

Black Hills Daily Times Jun 23, 1883

J. Goldberg, Endowment Rank of Knights of Pythias elect officer.

JACOB AND LENA

Jacob Goldberg's personal life was noteworthy in that he was outspokenly committed to finding a bride, planting roots, and making his future in Deadwood. Fundamentally a family man, bachelorhood did not suit him. He was determined to attend every dance and every picnic. He would leave no stone unturned until he found the right woman with whom to share his life. The young bachelor was plainspoken about his plans and determined to succeed, but his first few attempts at securing a wife didn't work out as he'd hoped.

Black Hills Daily Times, Jan 27, 1880

Hope Goldberg has better luck in east, finds a rib. Hope he has better luck, doesn't return home alone.

Black Hills Daily Times, Jan 8, 1881

Jake Goldberg, Old bachelor makes a point to attend every dance.

Black Hills Daily Times, Feb 1, 1881

He is ready and willing to marry.

Black Hills Daily Times, Mar 17, 1881

Jake Goldberg, Late for grand jury, was visiting with his girl.

Black Hills Daily Times, Mar 25, 1881

Have ordered a telephone for their store. Merchant wants phone so he can talk to his girl.

Black Hills Daily Times, Nov 25, 1882

Number of old bachelors planning Thanksgiving dinner,

Black Hills Daily Times, Dec 28, 1882
Wears a smile not unlike a crack in a dried lemon.

Black Hills Daily Times, Jun 9, 1882
Jakey Goldberg, Failed to make it to Sturgis, lost wheel on wagon

In 1884 the young lady who would share his future, Jacob Goldberg's "rib," at last came into view. Lena Weissner, like Jacob, hailed from New York City. Her sister, Mrs. Heineman of Spearfish, made the introduction, and the couple knew within a short time that they were meant for each other. The betrothal took place at the Heineman home in Spearfish on Sept 26, 1884, and the Times made the announcement. The couple began planning for their October wedding which was expected to take place as soon as the apartment Jake was preparing above the Big Horn Store could be outfitted in a suitable manner.

Black Hills Daily Times, Oct 3, 1884
Jake Goldberg was on last Saturday betrothed to Ms. Weissner at the residence of Mrs. Heineman, Spearfish. The marriage takes place as soon as their future home can be furnished- perhaps four weeks. Ms. Weissner is a sister of Mrs. Heineman.

Black Hills Daily Times, Nov 1, 1884
Jake Goldberg is fitting up the floor over the Big Horn Store for a manner most magnificent and significant.

Black Hills Daily Times, Oct 14, 1884
Judge G.G. Bennett is moving his office to the Miller building to make room for Jake Goldberg and his new wife over Jake's store.

Black Hills Daily Times, Nov 26, 1884
The marriage of Jacob Goldberg to Miss Lena Weissner, is announced to take place at Spearfish next Sunday.

Black Hills Daily Times, Nov 29, 1884
Jake Goldberg received from brother and sister-in-law a magnificent set of solid silver knives and forks. Marriage to Lena Weissner takes place tomorrow.

Black Hills Daily Times, Dec 2, 1884
Jacob Goldberg marries Lena Weissner at the residence of the bride's sister, Mrs. Jacob Heineman, Spearfish, on Nov. 30.

At the age of 23, Jacob Goldberg became a bridegroom. Among the wedding guests were Jacob's brother, Leo Goldberg, from Salt Lake City; Joseph Hattenbach, Jonas Zoellner, Joseph Poznansky, Max Stern, Nathan Colman, Benjamin Welf, and M.J. Wertheimer.

The Goldbergs wasted no time in starting their family. Their marriage produced two sons, Sam and Joseph, and a daughter Julia, all of whom survived to adulthood, no small achievement in a day when infant and childhood mortality ran very high.

Black Hills Daily Times, May 24, 1887
"It's a boy, J. Goldberg, Jr.," making his appearance at 5:30 p.m. last evening.

Black Hills Daily Times, Sep 10, 1887
Jacob Goldberg, wife and children and nurse went out to Brownsville yesterday for a picnic.

Black Hills Daily Times, Dec 1, 1887
Yesterday was the 3rd anniversary of Jacob Goldberg's marriage and his 26th birthday.

Black Hills Daily Times, Dec 25, 1887
Mrs. Jacob Goldberg was the recipient of a handsome gold watch this morning, presented by her husband.

Jacob and Lena Goldberg
Photo courtesy Deadwood Public Library

Childhood diseases were epidemic in nature, and Julia became ill in the winter of 1888, but she recovered and the children survived. Goldberg's sons, Joe and Sam, grew up to be associated with their father's grocery business for many years.

Black Hills Daily Times, Nov 2, 1888
Julia, daughter of Mr. and Mrs. Jacob Goldberg, has been quite sick for a day or two. Dr. Rogers is in attendance. It is to be hoped she is not dangerously ill.

Following the Jewish principle of remembering to give charity, Jacob participated where he found the need. His character was such that he was warmly embraced by the community.

Black Hills Daily Pioneer, Feb 1, 1878
Miss Augusta Chambers to be given benefit, Jacob Goldberg,

Black Hills Daily Times, Nov 29, 1881
Donated money to help Jews.

Black Hills Daily Times Jun 30 1882
Jakey Goldberg parts his hair in the middle (likely reference to his being an upright fellow).

Black Hills Daily Times Sep 16 1883
Donated sugar & coffee for raffle at Catholic Fair

Roots and religion were important to Jacob Goldberg, and despite the distance, he kept in close contact with his extended family. When his 13-year-old brother Emanuel was confirmed at the Reform synagogue on E. 22nd St. in New York City, Jacob offered Emanuel's confirmation speech to the Black Hills Daily Times, who saw this as an opportunity to present to its readers an unfamiliar aspect of this curious, but significant, segment of Deadwood's society. The boy's eloquent expressions of regard for his parents and grandmother were truly moving, and the Times printed the speech, complete with prayers, in its entirety.

Black Hills Daily Times, Sep 7, 1884
A JEWISH CONFIRMATION: Among most people outside of the Jewish church, little is understood of the ways of that church, notwithstanding they are mostly laid down in the Bible. Mr. Jacob Goldberg of our city, the other day received the words of an address by his brother (Emanuel) on his confirmation at the Jewish synagogue on East 22nd Street, New York. If most young man would bear him to their parents occasionally it would be a benefit to themselves as well as telling to their parents that there is ever a spot in their hearts that goes out towards them. The following is Emanuel Goldberg's address to his parents:

Almighty Father. With my heart filled with gratitude do I thank Thee for having spared my beloved parents and Thy young servant to witness this joyful season of "confirmation". Oh, cause this new path of my young life to be illuminated with kindness and mercy; continue to watch and protect me for Thou art gracious; purify my heart so that I may serve Thee in truth and may my prayer be accepted with grace and favor. Amen

Dear relations and friends. In behalf of my dear parents, do I extend you a hearty welcome on the ever memorable occasion of my Jewish initiation. Today my thoughts are directed towards you, my honored parents, who have so willingly and lovingly provided me with all life's necessities; caused me not alone to be educated in the language and history of my land, but in the language and sublime history of Israel; the duties I owe to that Heavenly Being and to my ever-living religion, a religion founded upon the sublime doctrines of that divine Law of which I have read a portion, and whose inspired teachings have been Israel's hope, glory, comfort, and pride.

That Law ordains me first, to love the Lord with all my heart and soul, to perform my religious duties, to worship in public and private His everlasting and holy name, to observe his sacred Sabbath, and to ever practice love, justice, humanity, and charity to all my fellow creatures. Secondly, that holy Law commands me to honor father and mother. What words can I express to you dear Father to sufficiently give you my thanks for the interest, care, and maintenance you have so willingly extended me and my dear brothers and sisters? With a firm hand you have led me and by precept and example you have taught me to honor the holy Sabbath and to regularly perform my duties as an Israelite. Again, dear Father, do I heartily thank you.

And to you, my dear mother, the watchful guardian of my childhood and infancy. What words can I render to justly convey my thanks and gratitude for all the loving and tender care, affection and devotion? How many an uneasy night has sleep fled as you waited eagerly, watching me as I helplessly laid for weeks and weeks upon my sick bed, and how your loving eye wistfully gazed upon me, vigilantly watching my every movement. How your gentle hand protected and aided me; how your sympathetic heart troubled with pain on beholding my sufferings, and how you earnestly prayed to heaven for my recovery. Your prayers were answered and yesterday you experienced that great joy by God's kindness and mercy of beholding the day to witness my confirmation.

And to you, my dear grandmother, whose whole heart is centered in the love and comfort of all your grandchildren, fondly and devoted have you anxiously and affectionately watched over us, participating in our joys and willingly sharing in our sorrows and sufferings. Gratefully do I acknowledge your kindness of heart, your devotion, and never-failing interest in our behalf. Many, many thanks good and honored Grandma.

And now, dear father and mother, freely do I confess that I can never partially repay you for the trials, cares, and sufferings you have so willingly endured in rearing me feel this joyful hour, while I also cordially confess at times I have caused human vexation and pain by innocent and childish acts of the past, but I am sure they are all forgotten and forgiven, while I assure you I will endeavor to amend my wrongs by accepting your good counsels, and appreciating all your endearing efforts for my welfare and success. From this day I will strive to meet your approval so that at the end I will be a joy and pride to you, my honored parents, and an ornament to my people and an honor to that religion in which I have been so solemnly confirmed.

Almighty God, cause Thy all-seeing eye to watch and protect me with Thy mighty hand; strengthen me in my resolution to amend in this new life. Bless, O my Heavenly Father, my beloved father and mother; Grant them many years of health and happiness, prolong their days to a good old age, so that they may witness the joy and prosperity of all their children. Bless my dear grandmother, spare her many years in our midst so that she may behold the joy and happiness of all her grandchildren. Bless my dear brothers and sisters; bless my dear uncles, aunts, and cousins, and bless all assembled at this joyful celebration with all Thy manifold and gracious blessing, now and forever more. Amen."

The synagogue on E. 22nd St. where Emanuel delivered his *Bar Mitzvah* speech was

Congregation Tel Aviv, which served the community in New York's East Village long after the Goldbergs' membership. In its early days the synagogue saw waves of immigrants, families like the Goldbergs, who held dear their Jewish heritage as their lives underwent the radical changes that the New World presented.

When Jacob Goldberg wasn't tending his Big Horn store, he was traveling and hunting and spending time on his ranch in Wyoming. This was an adventurous family. Their enthusiasm for discovery took the Goldbergs far from the life of crowded eastern city streets.

Black Hills Daily Times, Jul 12, 1882
Jacob Goldberg, Left for his ranch near Sundance Mountain.

Black Hills Daily Times, Jul 13, 1882
Goldberg, Buffalo hunters start out from Spearfish today.

Black Hills Daily Times, Jul 25, 1882
Jake Goldberg, Did not return with other hunters, after lone bear.

Black Hills Daily Times, Jul 26, 1882
Goldberg, Says buffalo hunting is splendid sport to read about.

Black Hills Daily Times, Sep 15, 1882
Hattenbach in charge of Big Horn Store while Goldberg gone.

Black Hills Daily Times, Aug 8, 1883
Writes from Chicago, goes to Salt Lake before returning.

Black Hills Daily Times, Sep 11, 1883
Returned home on Sunday from his trip around world.

Black Hills Daily Times, Mar 15, 1884
Leopold Goldberg, a brother of Jake, writes to him from Salt Lake that the Coeur d'Alene mining excitement is at fever heat in that country, and that it is estimated that at least one-third of the mining population of Utah will go there within the next month. They have become perfectly wild over the excitement.

Black Hills Daily Times, Jun 26, 1887
Ed Grossfeld, Spearfish businessman, has agreed to accompany Jacob Goldberg as guide and scout through the mountains to Bear Gulch.

There were other Goldbergs in Deadwood, some from New York City and some from Salt Lake City, some of whom were related in some way to Jacob. An F. Goldberg was elected officer of a Deadwood fire hose company. In 1879 Ralph Goldberg was elected one of the original officers of the Deadwood Athletic Club. A clothing firm of D.& J. Goldberg appears in 1877. One of the firm's owners, Mr. Dave Goldberg, and his wife were guests at the wedding of Oscar Silver and Rebecca Loewenthal in 1882.

Black Hills Daily Times, Apr 1, 1879
D. & J. Goldberg, Clothing at 20 % discount, come one, come all. ad

Black Hills Daily Times, Sep 28, 1879
D.&J. Goldberg, Opened store on old lot, selling "fire" goods cheap.

Black Hills Daily Times, Apr 1, 1880
D. & J. Goldberg, Fine line of fancy percale and white shirts, ad

Black Hills Daily Times, Jan 1, 1880
D. & J. Goldberg, Offer their clothing 30% less than ever before, ad

Black Hills Daily Times, Mar 12, 1880
Smith swindled the clothier out of a $35 suit.

Black Hills Daily Times, Oct 29, 1882
Dave Goldberg, Selling "sheap cloding" at Billings, formerly here.

CIVIC ACTIVITIES

Jacob Goldberg volunteered many hours of his time preparing for community picnics and fairs. He was committed to his work of establishing the first public library and sat on the library board of directors. He was instrumental in founding the first college in the northern Hills, Spearfish Normal School, a training school for teachers.

Spearfish Normal School, ca.1909
Photo courtesy Leland Case Collection,
Black Hills State University

Fourth of July celebrations were especially busy as he served on committees arranging for parades, fireworks, music, and decorations through the years.

Black Hills Daily Times, Jun 13, 1879
J Goldberg, Chairman of the committee on procession for Fourth.

Black Hills Daily Times, Jun 26, 1879
J Goldberg, Authorized to make arrangements for music on 4th.

Black Hills Daily Times, Jun 23, 1882
Booming Fourth, bound to be a success.

Black Hills Daily Times, Jul 1, 1882
Jake Goldberg, Glorious 4th of July ball at Keimer's Hall, ad

Black Hills Daily Times, Sep 13, 1882
J Goldberg, German citizens giving a picnic at Nelson Park.

Black Hills Daily Times, Jul 6, 1883
Fourth dawned clear, celebration was splendid success.

Black Hills Daily Times, Jul 3, 1884
Fourth of July celebration ready. Arrangements complete for celebration; city gaily decorated for the occasion; fireworks received; programme of exercises.

Goldberg had other friends and business partners through the years, but John Treber and Jake were close friends. The two men traveled around the region extensively, in some cases scouting out fresh opportunities, such as their branch in Rapid City. Although their business partnership dissolved in 1884, the Goldbergs and the Trebers kept their social relationship strong.

Black Hills Daily Times, Jun 12, 1883
Mr & Mrs J. Goldberg. Celebrated at Wooden wedding anniversary of Mr & Mrs Treber.

Black Hills Daily Times, Jul 24, 1883
Goldberg, Treber & others played "Solo" last night.

Black Hills Daily Times, Mar 8, 1884
John Treber and Jake Goldberg went to Spearfish yesterday for a sleigh ride.

Black Hills Daily Times, Jan 24, 1885
John Treber and Jacob Goldberg visited Sturgis yesterday.

Black Hills Daily Times, Oct 11, 1885
John Treber and Jake Goldberg visited the Carbonate camp yesterday.

Black Hills Daily Times, Oct 22, 1886
John Treber and Jake Goldberg were visitors at Spearfish yesterday.

Black Hills Daily Times, Oct 28, 1886

John Treber and Jake Goldberg, enjoyed a ride to Scoop (Sturgis), yesterday.

Black Hills Daily Times, Apr 14, 1887

Friend of Jacob Goldberg, remembering him as living away off here, made up a box of delicacies and sent it by express. Jakey paid express charges $1.95, and opened it to find perhaps a dollar's worth of pineapples and strawberries.

Goldberg Grocery, June 1952
Photo courtesy Homestake Adams Research and Cultural Center

Goldberg's Grocery with Jake and employees, 1915
Photo courtesy Adams Museum

Sons Joe and Sam worked alongside their father, but life in Deadwood presented fewer opportunities for the sons than it did for their father. Eventually both brothers left Deadwood and moved to San Antonio, Texas. Julia married M.A. Rosenthal and moved to Los Angeles, California.

James O'Hara, Goldberg's associate, employee and partner for nearly 30 years, bought the store in 1934, complete with name, and carried on as Goldberg's Grocery. After legalized gambling came to Deadwood in 1990, everything changed. Deadwood once again was being transformed, and Goldberg's Grocery took on the name of the Gold Dust Casino. The store had been in business for over 100 years.

Jake had purchased a burial plot in the Mt. Zion section of Mt. Moriah in 1897 for the sum of $22, but he never used this piece of real estate. In 1934 Lena's failing health required the Goldbergs to move to California, but Jake returned to the Hills every year to visit. He remained active in managing the business, finally disposing of Goldberg's Grocery and making California his permanent home. Lena died there in 1936 and Jake followed in 1937 at the age of 86. One of Deadwood's most lasting and wholehearted supporters, his name was synonymous with integrity and fairness.

Jacob Goldberg
Photo Courtesy Adams Museum

REWMAN
TELEPHONE COMPANY BUILDING
668 MAIN ST.

Paul Rewman
Photo Courtesy Adams Museum

COMMUNICATIONS

Paul Rewman, one of the most influential and perhaps least recognizable, of Deadwood's earliest Jewish population, was brilliant and audacious. Rewman was born into the age of fast-moving technology. He applied his skills to the introduction of such advances as bringing the telephone and electric power to the Black Hills. The demands of the burgeoning mining sector for communication and electric power for mining operations, as well as for public and private use, were marked and immediate. Remote little Deadwood, far off the beaten path, tucked away high in the mountains of northwestern Dakota Territory, accessible only by the most primitive modes of travel, but brimming with mineral and timber treasure, was among the first places in the country to enjoy the fruits of modern innovation. Technology was changing the world, and Rewman would be at its forefront in the Black Hills.

1866: The dynamo was the first electrical generator capable of delivering DC power for industry. The modern dynamo, fit for use in industrial applications, was invented independently by Sir Charles Wheatstone, Werner von Siemens and Samuel Alfred Varley. Varley took out a patent on 24 December 1866.

1866: The White House installed its first telegraph office.

1876: Deadwood installed first telegraph.

1876: Alexander Graham Bell received a patent for his revolutionary new invention–the telephone.

1877: President Rutherford B. Hayes had the White House's first telephone installed in the mansion's telegraph office. President Hayes embraced the new technology, though he rarely received phone calls. In fact, the Treasury Department possessed the only other direct phone line to the White House at that time. The White House phone number was "1." Phone service throughout the country was in its infancy.

1878: The first telephone exchange in Deadwood was established and managed by Paul Rewman.

1880: Thomas Edison brought the incandescent electric light bulb into practical use and patented the incandescent light bulb.

1883: First electric lights in Deadwood. The DC power was supplied by a dynamo installed on Lee Street.

1891: Electricity was installed in the White House.

Paul Rewman can be placed as one of the earliest Jewish pioneers of the Black Hills Gold Rush. Based on the history of the Deadwood's Jewish population written by Blanche Colman, we have it on good authority that Rewman was an English Jew. Estelline Bennett, not Jewish, but also a child of Deadwood's Black Hills Gold Rush days, recalled Rewman being present when gold dust was the accepted local currency. Miss Bennett wrote of Rewman telling her of the rousing welcome given to General George Crook, a heroic military figure, who was credited with saving Deadwood from a disastrous Indian raid. On the night of the grand opening of McDaniels Theater, one of Deadwood's many impromptu entertainment establishments, General Crook held an informal reception up and down Main Street, shaking hands along the way, remembering everyone he had ever seen, including Captain Tom Russell, a member of the gold-seeking Gordon Party. As for the theater, had Mr. McDaniels been aware of the fact that he was building on a placer claim, things might have gone differently. No sooner was it finished than the miner descended upon it with pick and shovel and pan to work his claim, and the crude structure soon collapsed into the dust of Deadwood's Main Street. Rewman recalled distinctly that he had been working on a roof, and had driven the last nail into the last shingle the night after General Crook arrived in the camp. Rewman took his pay for work in tickets to the event instead of gold dust, the current coin of the camp.

Shelter in an unforgiving climate was the most immediate need. Small sawmills were soon erected, and Rewman became one of those most busy with construction.

In 1832, Samuel Morse, a professor of art with an interest in science, began experimenting with a new system. Fascinated with the possibilities of electricity, Morse set out to find a way to send signals along an electrical cable. The technology had its own language, in which alternating long and short bursts of electrical current represented individual letters. Morse code spawned a number of independent telegraph services. By 1860 all independent telegraph lines had joined into one organization, the Western Union Telegraph Company. The telegraph spread rapidly across Europe, and in 1866 the first transatlantic cable was laid.

Communication via telegraph was vital to Deadwood and Lead. The telegraph system allowed the exchange of national and international news to be shared by different newspapers, and in 1846 newspaper publishers from around the country gathered to create an organization to promote cooperative news-gathering by wire. In 1846, Richard Hoe invented the steam cylinder rotary press, making it possible to print newspapers much more rapidly and cheaply than had been possible in the past. Also, the rotary press spurred the dramatic growth of mass-circulation newspapers.

On March 7, 1876, 29-year-old Alexander Graham Bell received a patent for the telephone, his revolutionary new invention. There was a dispute over the patent, but Bell prevailed. In 1878 Bell and his partners, Hubbard and Sanders, offered to sell the patent outright to Western Union Telegraph Company for $100,000, but the president of Western Union balked, countering that the telephone was nothing but a toy. Two years later, he told colleagues that if he could get the patent for $25 million he would consider it a bargain. By then, the Bell Company would no longer sell the patent, and Bell and his investors went on to become millionaires.

Telephone purchase receipt, Caledonia Mining Co.
Courtesy Jerry L. Bryant

Telephone service was now a priority in Deadwood. In March of 1878, under the leadership of Paul Rewman, Deadwood had the Black Hills Telephone Exchange, the first telephone exchange established in Dakota Territory, which also included areas that encompassed present day Montana and most of Wyoming. The exchange offered calls between Deadwood and Lead for 50 cents— 25 cents cheaper than stagecoach fare, and considerably faster and more secure. The completion of the line was celebrated with a gathering and a bonfire, followed by a splendid ball at the Grand Central Hotel.

Black Hills Daily Times, 1881

We have a telephone, and it is a source of great comfort. We can hitch onto Gayville, Central and Lead cities and talk face-to-face with any person we desire.

Yesterday we called up A.M. Barnes of Central City and told him that Thomas Burns and his female dog were in the office, and asked what disposition we should make of them. In a moment it came: "Kill the dog and kick Burns out of the office." We did neither and the dog is alive and Burns is on the warpath looking for Barnes…

With the aid of the telephone there is nothing for the local editor to do but sit in the Bank Saloon and drink Tom and Jerry."

ELECTRIC POWER

The other priority was for electrical power. According to Dick Dunwiddie, historian born and raised in Deadwood, telegraph, telephone, and electricity technology had "three different wire development histories. Each had to have unique wire for outside and inside. There were few standards. Lengths of cable runs for each were limited. Electric DC power in late 1800s was dangerous and called 'old sparky.' There was a dynamo power generator on Lee Street that had a limited length and number of end devices. Initially, the Lee Street dynamo had capacity of around 5-6 bulbs. Each had its own wire run. The telegraph, telephone, and power shared poles."

According to Dunwiddie, the first Deadwood High School graduation was held in 1886 in the Deadwood Theater across from yet-to-be Franklin Hotel. *"It had one DC electric light hanging from the ceiling… AC didn't happen until early 1900s. It required new AC generators and new distribution and internal home wiring. That was when Black Hills Power and Light got its start."*

The Consolidated Light and Power Company was a combination of two former companies – Black Hills Electric Light Company, and Belt Light and Power Company. The plant, with a generating capacity of about 20 arc lights, was operated without any great success for several years. The service at times was uncertain and patronage began to fall away. It was on the verge of collapse when it was bought by Harris Franklin, Sol Star, and Paul Rewman in 1884.

With the new owners, new life was infused and plans were set for giving the people service as good as conditions at the time would permit. The dynamos were moved to the flour mill of Sol Star, and the mill boilers, used to furnish power to grind grain during the day, produced steam for the light plant during the night, and the plant was run on a fairly economical plan.

Business increased, and in 1886 improvements were decided on. To the arc-light generator there was added a small incandescent machine, which was the first to be brought into the Hills. The business of the company still continued to improve, and in 1889 a brick structure was built. The old equipment was replaced by new and much larger equipment, and business was done on an increased scale.

Black Hills Daily Times, Jul 15, 1886
Electric fire alarm installation. Chief Engineer McDonald and Sol Star closeted with Supt. Rewman relative to the construction of lines connecting signal boxes with the striker.

In 1895, Paul Rewman, titled "superintendent," placed a newspaper advertisement by a "first class firm" for a "Western Electrician." Rewman required "an energetic and pushing traveling salesman well acquainted with electric light stations of the United States, to sell on commission an article of regular and large consumption..."

Fort Meade, the U.S. Army post at nearby Sturgis, needed electric power. Bids were let for wiring the stone residence building, and on Dec.1, 1900, it was announced that Paul Rewman's bid of $370 was accepted.

On June 1, 1903, the plant at Pluma was reconstructed and modern machinery was installed, so that on January 1, 1906, the Deadwood plant went out of commission and all electric energy for Deadwood and Lead was generated at the Pluma plant. It was one of the most complete and best equipped west of the Missouri River.

Rewman was also engaged in a growing coal business. In 1903 he filed a complaint with the South Dakota Board of Railroad Commissions, protesting that the rate of fares and freight charged by the Chicago and Northwestern Railway Company on the shipment and transportation of coal from Deadwood to various points in the northern Black Hills was discriminatory and excessive. Rewman was advised that the complaint would be satisfied without a hearing, and the case was dismissed.

FAMILY

Rewman, who was a prominent and influential player in the Deadwood scene, found a woman to match his ambition and achievements. Paul Rewman married Mabel Fontron on July 10, 1911. They spent a full year honeymooning in Europe and the British Isles.

Mabel Rewman was Catholic and a Republican. She was also a strong suffragette and a gifted speaker who earned a reputation as an early campaigner for women's rights. As an activist she participated in marches in Washington and gave speeches in South Dakota, Nebraska, Ohio, and Illinois. In 1920 Governor Norbeck appointed Mrs. Rewman to the Board of Charities and Corrections, the first woman ever to hold a position on one of the constitutional boards of the state.

Mabel Fontron Rewman and Paul Rewman were acclaimed and accomplished people of their time, both of whom were recognized in Who's Who in South Dakota. Oscar Stanley Rewman, their only child, died tragically at age 2. Whether Rewman left Judaism and joined Mabel in the practice of Christianity remains a mystery, but Paul and Mabel, and their son, Oscar, are buried in Deadwood's Saint Ambrose Catholic Cemetery under the statue of an angel.

Rewman Family grave marker
Courtesy How To Enjoy The Black Hills.com

COLMAN

ROSENTHAL'S PALACE - 652 MAIN

Nathan Colman
Photo courtesy Al Alschuler

Continuing southward along Main Street, I soon arrived at 652 Main St., a lovely brick building with a bay window on the second floor that projected outward over the street. From its bay window, one might observe the goings on in the street below. The guidebook I was following called the building Rosenthal's Palace, and it said that Nathan Colman had conducted one of his many business enterprises in this building. The Daily Times offered a glimpse into some of what transpired in this building in 1886.

Black Hills Daily Times, Jun 8, 1886
Rosenthal talk of the town. Sale of Sol Rosenthal to Messrs. Goldberg and James Carney of his stocks has been the talk of the Black Hills the past week. Sale of purchased goods commences today.

Black Hills Daily Times, Jul 1, 1886
Rosenthal transfers back accounts. Notice is hereby given that I have this day transferred all my back accounts, notes and debts due me to Jacob Goldberg and James Carney. All persons owing me will settle with them. Sol Rosenthal, Deadwood, Dakota.

Black Hills Daily Times, Jul 15, 1886
James Carney and Jacob Goldberg have entirely closed out Sol Rosenthal stock, Isaac H. Chase taking what remained Tuesday — $400 worth.

NATHAN, AMALIA & FAMILY

Nathan Colman's story and that of his family could be a book of its own. They were a family with a long history of achievements and firsts. Nathan's was a life of courage, perseverance, enterprise, and faith. He seemed to have an endless spirit of adventure that took him from place to place and from one endeavor to the next. In each venture he displayed a wide variety of interests and talents. He was admired and respected in his community, and in a place with so many reasons to be wary of your neighbor, Nathan Colman was trusted.

Nathan was born in Hof, Germany in 1850, and in 1871, when he reached the age of 21, Nathan emigrated to the United States. The American Colman family name likely started in Europe as Kugelmann, or even Kalman. Young Colman, drawn by the opportunities on the western frontier, headed for Fort Sumner in New Mexico Territory. He is still accorded New Mexico Jewish Pioneer status at the New Mexico History Museum in Santa Fe. Nathan made his way from New Mexico to Denver, Colorado, where he met Amalia. Amalia Oppenheimer, born in 1852, was also a German Jewish émigré. Her family lived in the small town of Schluchtern, Germany, near Frankfurt am Main. Michel Oppenheimer, her father, was a writer and translator of Hebrew and Jewish religious works. At the age of 17, Amalia displayed the characteristics of a spirited young woman.

Following the death of her mother, Amalia immigrated to the United States where she stayed with relatives in Baltimore, Maryland. After a short stay in the east, she made the long journey across the country to Denver, Colorado, where she had other relatives. When they met, Nathan and Amalia had a lot in common, and they were meant to share a life together. They were married in Denver in 1874, and perhaps prophetically, their first child, daughter Anne, was born in 1876, the year of the opening of the Black Hills Gold Rush.

Stagecoach
Photo courtesy Adams Museum

Reports of happenings in the Black Hills were irresistible to the young couple. There was a Gold Rush taking place, and great opportunity awaited those bold and resolute enough to reach for it. The Colmans began to make plans to travel to Deadwood. Nathan would lead the way, courageously making the winter journey into Dakota Territory. Amalia and baby Anne would follow a few months later by stagecoach. By 1877, with enormous reserves of daring, the couple would start a new life in the Black Hills. They could never have anticipated the degree of difficulty, or just how much their decision would help shape the future of their chosen destination.

Like most Gold Rush pioneers, with no one to meet him and only his hardy resources to draw upon, Nathan Colman was on his own. He first went to Custer in 1877, thereafter traveling to Deadwood with his supplies. Nathan had come equipped to start a little tobacco and confectionery shop. Setting to work, he opened his business, readied a home, and awaited his family's arrival.

In a late April afternoon of 1877, a stagecoach bumped and clattered its way north along a rutted trail on the eastern edge of the Black Hills. The coach had left Sidney, Nebraska, early that morning, and was bound for Deadwood, Dakota Territory. The cramped passengers, those who'd been fortunate enough to secure inside spaces, were tired and disgruntled, their bottoms aching from long hours on the horsehair-stuffed seats. Able-bodied men who hadn't been able to grab seats inside, clung to the sides or rode on top. The stagecoach lines were kept busy night and day, transporting would-be millionaires into the Black Hills. With gold fever at fever peak, the stagecoach companies could barely keep up with the demand for space.

Stagecoach stop at Elk Creek
Photo Courtesy Adams Museum

Except for the occasional jarring thud, the swaying of the coach helped the infant sleep, but when she awakened, she was hard to console. Her young mother pleaded with the gentlemen squeezed in beside them to not light up another cigar.

The coach was seriously behind schedule, as they often were, and the husband awaiting the stagecoach's arrival in Deadwood had plenty of reason to worry. A multitude of hazards lay in travel in Dakota Territory; there were countless possible explanations for a delay, none of them comforting. Road agents, holdup men, were only too eager to relieve the passengers of their money and possessions. Stage holdups happened all the time; outlaws preyed upon travelers, and travelers employed every form of ingenuity to conceal their money. Only yesterday a coach had been held up on this very route. Most terrifying of all were the hostile Indians along the road, preparing the next ambush. The trail through Red Canyon had been abandoned altogether because the Indians had made that route so treacherous.

Nathan took no comfort from the story he had heard about Calamity Jane, one of Deadwood's more renowned denizens. Calamity Jane knew of Indian attack first-hand. Earlier that year of 1877, as she was riding to Crook City, about 12 miles outside of Deadwood, she came upon a stricken coach carrying passengers and overland mail from Cheyenne to Deadwood, in dire need of help.

> "Upon looking closely I saw they were pursued by Indians. The horses ran to the barn as was their custom. As the horses stopped I rode along side of the coach and found the driver John Slaughter, lying face downwards in the boot of the stage, he having been shot by the Indians. When the stage got to the station the Indians hid in the bushes. I immediately removed all baggage from the coach except the mail. I then took the driver's seat and with all haste drove to Deadwood, carrying six passengers and the dead driver."
>
> — **Autobiography of Calamity Jane**

Rumors flew in Deadwood that the stagecoach carrying Nathan Colman's family had been attacked by marauding Indians. The stage lines hired only the sharpest and toughest of applicants, men like Boone May, of stalwart character. He could be overwhelmed, but for most purposes, a stagecoach driver was equipped to fulfill his assignment. In time, the stage companies would employ armed guards to defend their passengers and shipments of bullion, "riding shotgun" beside the driver or as outriders alongside the coach. There were some forces against which a stagecoach was defenseless, however, and this was Dakota Territory, where weather could prove an unexpected adversary. April in Dakota was, above all, unpredictable. Blizzards were a strong possibility. There could be impassably muddy gumbo trails through the Badlands. Occasionally the Cheyenne River overflowed its banks, making crossing impossible for days at a time.

Had they been flooded out, or snowed in, or held up, or broken down? Were they just exchanging coaches outside of town, as was the practice of the stagecoach lines? Were the passengers being made to wait beside the road while the company swapped the road-weary coach and team for a more impressive Concord coach and fresher team of horses before making its final grand swoop into Deadwood Gulch? Nathan Colman, a religious man, prayed for the safety of his wife and daughter. As difficult a voyage as Amalia's was, Nathan's had been much harder. He had traveled part of the way from Denver by muleback, finding shelter where and when he could, through a savage Dakota winter. This was a capable and unbendable couple.

The coach, delayed by road conditions, finally appeared over the hilltop and came rolling into Deadwood Gulch. The horses pranced up Main Street, and the coach rolled to a stop at the Sidney-to-Deadwood Stage Company office. With joy and relief, the family was reunited that spring night in 1877. Preparing to face the unknown, the young family began their pioneering life in Deadwood. Little Anne Colman was the first of what might have been a large family of brothers and sisters, had four of her siblings not been stricken with fatal childhood diseases. Amalia would bear three sons and four daughters, but only three of her children, Anne, Blanche, and Theresa, would survive the epidemics of scarlet fever, diphtheria, typhoid, and other early-day diseases that ravaged Deadwood's children and filled its cemeteries.

Nathan, Amalia, and children
Photo courtesy Al Alschuler

Amalia, Nathan, and Anne Colman
Photo courtesy Adams Museum

In September of 1879, when Deadwood was almost totally destroyed by the Great Fire, both their home and their business were in the path of the fire. Amalia and her first son, who was only a few days old, had to be rescued from their home. Another son was stillborn in 1880. Time after time, the Colmans were tested. They dealt with the raw realities of life on the frontier as they were forced to cope with fire and flood, illness and death.

Black Hills Daily Times Sep 20, 1879
Birth, twelve pound boy at Justice Colmans.

Black Hills Daily Times May 7, 1880
Judge is having severe time with sickness in family.

Black Hills Daily Times, Feb 9, 1886
Sickness among children reported increasing. Jessie Belding ill last week, but better yesterday. The baby now an object of concern. Colman child also reported very sick.

Black Hills Daily Times, Dec 28, 1887
Six-year-old Rosa, daughter of Mr. and Mrs. Nathan Colman, died suddenly Christmas morning.

Black Hills Daily Times, Aug 16, 1888
Nathan Colman is the fond father of a brand new girl baby. It arrived on Saturday last and is a perfect image of its past.

Black Hills Daily Times, Aug 17, 1888
Baby arriving at Nathan Colman's residence a boy, not a girl.

Black Hills Daily Times, Jan 3, 1891
Nathan Colman is nursing severe attack of rheumatism. His boy is confined to his house with quite a severe cold.

Nathan (in vest) in front of his store.
Note the misspelled name, Coleman, on the awning.
Photo courtesy Al Alschuler

Just as the Colmans repeatedly looked to the future and chose to start over after the Great Fire of 1879, they had to make the same choice once again when a fire in 1894 destroyed both their home and business. Each new structure was stronger, more fireproof, more resilient. Despite the hardship, Nathan and Amalia Colman kept their family and their faith strong.

RABBI COLMAN

Nathan Colman was an observant Jew, devout and learned in Hebrew, in Jewish ritual, and tradition. His skills and education were welcomed by his fellow Jews in the growing town. True to the spirit of frontier Judaism, with those skills, he was called upon to lead the little Jewish community in religious services, for holidays, and other religious functions. Nathan's service to Deadwood as its lay rabbi, was a position he would hold for the rest of his life. He officiated at most of the Jewish rites and celebrations in the community, conducting High Holiday services and leading Passover Seders, weddings and burial rituals. In late November of 1891, the Hebrew congregation of Deadwood showed their appreciation for Nathan's contribution to their community with a surprise party and a beautiful gold-topped, inscribed ebony cane.

Daily Pioneer Times, Dec 1, 1891

"Surprised. Such was the condition of Nathan Colman on calling at the residence of J. Goldberg, by invitation, on last Sunday evening to participate in social games. The judge was a little late, and on his arrival found the commodious residence filled with members of the Hebrew congregation of Deadwood, who had assembled there to cane their acting Rabbi. The meeting was called to order. Nathan Halle, as spokesman, in a short and appropriate address told Mr. Colman what the congregation thought of him and at the close presented him, on their behalf, with an elegant gold mounted ebony cane, handsomely engraved, bearing the following inscription: 'To Nathan Colman from the Hebrew congregation of Deadwood, South Dakota, 5653.' The judge was entirely taken by surprise and at the moment was at a loss for words to reply. He soon recovered himself and in his usual bright and witty matter thanked the congregation for their valuable and handsome gift..."

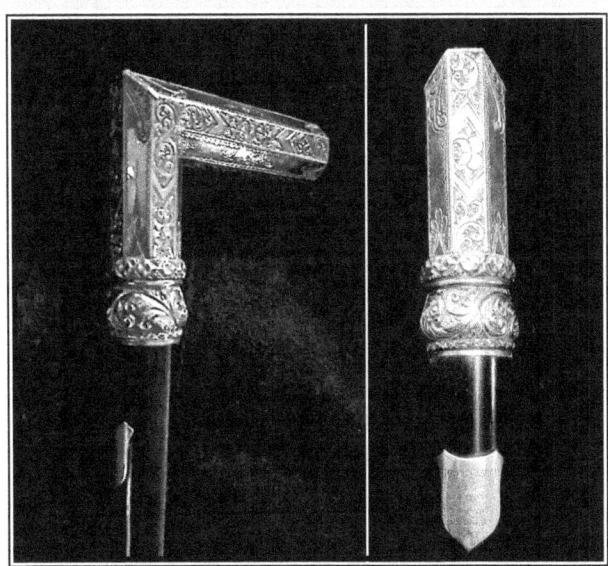

Photos courtesy Joyce and Michael Neiderman

Nathan was elected secretary of the Chevreh Kaddishe, the group charged with performing the requirements of Jewish burial. There were also the happier occasions, such as the wedding on Nov. 4, 1879, of Rebecca Reubens and David Holzman. This milestone event was the first "Hebrew" wedding in the Black Hills, and one of the earliest Jewish events of record in Deadwood. It was described as "beautiful and unique."

Black Hills Daily Times, Nov 4, 1879

... Mr. David Holzman, one of our bonanza clothing dealers, and Mrs. Rebecca Reubens, the beautiful and accomplished daughter of Mr. Louis Reubens, were joined in the holy bonds of wedlock. The interesting ceremony took place at the residence of the bride's parents in Ingleside, in the presence of at least 60 ladies and gentleman of our best Hebrew society and of all other nationalities...

In 1893, when the Jews formed the Deadwood chapter of B'nai B'rith, an international association dedicated to preserving Jewish heritage and performing acts of service. Nathan Colman, one of the 24 charter members, was once again elected to office.

According to family history, Nathan's mother was a Hattenbach, a relative of the Deadwood Hattenbachs, another pioneering family, also charter members of the local B'nai B'rith.

Black Hills Daily Times, Jun 27, 1893

Order of B'nai B'rith instituted with 24 charter members; officers elected. Israel Cowan, Nathan Colman, Jacob Goldberg, M. Stern, Gus Cohen, Louis Minzer, Joseph Hattenbach, Ben. Blumenthal, Aaron Hattenbach, Jonas Zoellner, M.J. Wertheimer.

In December of 1903 Nathan had the honor of officiating at a second Jewish wedding- that of his daughter Anne to Maurice Neiderman, a young businessman. This wedding took place at the newly opened Franklin Hotel, and was the first Jewish wedding to be held there. Nathan performed the ceremony, acting as both Rabbi and Justice of the Peace. His new son-in-law, a Hungarian Jew with American roots in Chicago, was well liked in Lead and Deadwood.

PUBLIC SERVICE

Like so many of his Jewish neighbors, Nathan was a naturalized American citizen and highly patriotic. These people welcomed the opportunity to participate in all levels of government, from jury duty to city council to county commissioner, all the way to the state legislature. In 1878 Nathan was appointed Postmaster of the Beaver precinct, adjacent to Deadwood. Noted for his fairness and honesty, a title earned through his role as Deadwood's Justice of the Peace, he was referred to as Judge Colman, an office he was elected to in 1879 and continued to hold for life. In 1880 he was appointed probate judge and held that position well into the 1890s.

Black Hills Daily Times, Aug 19, 1879

Arraigned before Colman, bond set at $3,000.

Black Hills Daily Times, Dec 3, 1879

Moody made decision for Colman as Justice of Peace.

The community approved of his work, and when he ran for re-election as Justice of the Peace in 1879, the Black Hills Daily Times took a position strongly in support of Judge Colman, affirming that he was an honest "western man," well suited for the job.

Black Hills Daily Times, Sep 7, 1979

"If you want a man to settle your little difficulties in an honest and comprehensive manner, elect Judge Colman [who] ... is familiar with the practice of this Territory. In fact he is no slouch of a lawyer himself... Mr. Hall, the old gentleman running [as Colman's opponent]... is comparatively a stranger to the frontier and on account of his extreme age, his fogy notions... would make a good Justice down East where puritanical and blue laws are still in vogue. Mr. Colman is a western man and consequently better fitted out here."

Black Hills Daily Times, Jan 21, 1880
Fined Happy George $25 and costs, plus 30 days.

Black Hills Daily Times, Apr 29, 1880
Three robbers brought before Judge Colman.

Black Hills Daily Times, Jun 13, 1880
Moved his office into his new building on Sherman,

Black Hills Daily Times, Mar 31, 1880
Judge convened his court yesterday, in his office.

Black Hills Daily Times, Apr 23, 1880
Judge made $.50 for acknowledging a deed.

Black Hills Daily Times, Aug 20, 1880
Wrestled all day yesterday with grand larceny case.

Black Hills Daily Times, Sep 17, 1880
Judge in running for office of probate judge.

Black Hills Daily Times, Oct 30, 1880
Citizens of South Deadwood well satisfied with Judge.

Black Hills Daily Times, Jan 28, 1892
Charles R. Dwyer protests Nathan Colman's petition for letters of administration in Hattie Belle Lockwood estate. Dwyer alleges that deceased had no property at time of her death.

Colman assumed a wide variety of positions of civic responsibility. In addition to his jobs as Justice of the Peace, Notary Public, and postmaster in the Beaver district, in 1881 he was elected secretary of Deadwood's fire department. He later acted as one of the judges of the territorial election in 1889, the year South Dakota achieved statehood. He was also one of the enumerators of the 1890 census. In 1891 he sat on the Lawrence County Commission, whose job it was to decide on issues regarding taxes, bridges, and roads, as the county laid down its infrastructure. Nathan inevitably became involved in politics, casting his vote with the Republican Party. He was sent as a delegate to state Republican conventions representing South Deadwood in 1880 and 1882.

Black Hills Daily Times, Sep 24, 1880
Clans gather on stormy banks of river of politics.

Black Hills Daily Times, Oct 26, 1880
South Deadwood Republicans place his name in nomination.

Black Hills Daily Times, Nov 12, 1880
Colman determining the equities of colored saloon.

Black Hills Daily Times, Jun 15, 1881
Elected secretary of fire department.

Black Hills Daily Times, Oct 15, 1882
Delegates and alternates selected to attend convention.

Black Hills Daily Times, May 27, 1890
Area names of census enumerators for South Dakota.

Black Hills Daily Times, Nov. 11, 1891
Lawrence County commission meeting November 10. County commissioners met and spent day wrestling with tax petitions, bridge petitions and road petitions. Nathan Colman.

BUSINESSMAN

Unafraid to tackle a new undertaking, Colman embarked upon one widely disparate commercial venture after another. Underlying everything were his civic duties, but his personal businesses were numerous. To the tobacco and confectionery shop, he added groceries. He later introduced ice and coal into this business.

Nathan Colman's store
Photo Courtesy Adams Museum

In 1879 a "great bonanza" was discovered on the hill overlooking Deadwood from the east. A tunnel was run from the area opposite Star and Bullock's Hardware Store toward the hill in order to access the gold strike. Nathan staked his claim and got to work, becoming one of the first to prospect in that hill. Because of the number of Jewish citizens owning claims there, it picked up the name of "Hebrew Hill." Although the town at large couldn't see the harm in the name, the Jewish community took offense at the name Hebrew Hill and voiced their objections. Despite their protests, the name stuck. The hill that later would bear Mt. Moriah Cemetery, kept the name of Hebrew Hill, although it was mainly applied to the Jewish section of the cemetery. Colman was still working his claim as late as 1884.

Black Hills Daily Times, Mar 31, 1879
Hebrew Hill. Practical name as many claims are owned by Hebrews.

Black Hills Daily Times, Mar 31, 1879
Nathan Colman, one of the first to stake a claim on Hebrew Hill.

Black Hills Daily Times, Apr 2, 1879
Some of our Hebrews said to be offended by name Hebrew Hill.

Black Hills Daily Times, April 4, 1884
Nathan Colman has gone to work on his claim on Hebrew Hill.

In addition to his law practice, in 1880 Colman started a shoe repair shop. In 1881 he dropped all his judicial duties to open a billiard hall/saloon on Sherman Street. For a while he dealt in marble such as that used in tombstones and construction projects. In 1882 he opened a curiosity shop on Sherman Street. Following this, in 1883, he started the Berlin Bakery on Sherman Street, advertising a "full line of goodies." That was quite successful, and later that year he opened a branch of the bakery on Main Street.

Black Hills Daily Times, Feb 20, 1880
To have shoe repair shop in addition to law practice.

Black Hills Daily Times, Feb 24, 1880
Judge has gotten his shoe repair shop set up.

Black Hills Daily Times, Jan 20, 1881
Has opened saloon since laying off judicial ermine.

Black Hills Daily Times, Jun 5, 1881
Erecting addition to Sherman St. saloon.

Black Hills Daily Times, Jun 11, 1881
Judge will have addition erected to his building.

Black Hills Daily Times, Jun 17, 1881
Judge intends to re-open his billiard hall/saloon.

Black Hills Daily Times, Sep 1, 1881
A fine garden for sale.

Black Hills Daily Times, Jul 23, 1882
Most remarkable curiosity shop on Sherman Street.

Black Hills Daily Times, Jun 30, 1883
Bought out & took charge of Berlin Bakery on Sherman St., has full line of goodies.

Black Hills Daily Times, Aug 22, 1883
Overhauling & remodeling Lindbloom's old building.

Black Hills Daily Times, Aug 25, 1883
Colman opens out Main St branch of Berlin Bakery.

In addition to doing some of his own prospecting, like most of Deadwood's merchants, Colman held mining shares. He was an investor in the Carbonate Mining Company, along with Harris Franklin, Ben Baer, and Jacob Goldberg.

Black Hills Daily Times, Aug 3, 1881
Shareholder in South Deadwood Carbonate Mining Co.

Colman also went into the second-hand business, but in 1886 he sold his entire stock of new and used goods, disposing of everything including the showcases and shelving, and opened a real estate and brokerage firm. Already experienced in collections, he added a loan and collections agency in 1890. By this time Nathan was 43 years old, and his eldest daughter, Anne, was 14. In the space of less than 14 years he'd already started at least 11 different businesses and he was far from through.

Black Hills Daily Times, May 30, 1886
Judge Nathan Colman has opened a cozy brokerage office in the McHugh building, adjoining the Times office.

Black Hills Daily Times, Jan 26, 1887
Nathan Colman, who went to Rapid after absconder John Oleson, had a lively time in accomplishing his mission.

Black Hills Daily Times, Apr 30, 1890
As I am about to engage in the real estate and brokerage business, I offer my entire stock of new and second hand goods, shelving, show cases etc., cheap for cash — Nathan Colman.

Black Hills Daily Times, Jul 1, 1890
Nathan Colman is going into the collection and loan agency business on Main Street. Before doing so, however, he will pass a week or two at the Minnekahta Hot Springs.

Black Hills Daily Times, Feb 13, 1892
M. Goldsmith arrived from Chicago to manage business of Nathan Colman, who will take a vacation owing to ill health.

One of the ways the Colmans participated in the social life of the community was through their enjoyment of music. Nathan played the cornet and with some of his fellow musicians organized a brass band in 1880 that played at concerts around the area. His German roots ran deep, and in 1890 he helped establish the Deadwood branch of the Liederkranz Society, a club for those with an interest in German music, arts, language and culture. The German-American citizens held a congenial picnic at Nelson Park on September 13th of 1882, with German festivities and food. Nathan's performance on the cornet brought less than rave reviews, probably mostly tongue-in-cheek, from the reporter at the Black Hills Daily Times.

Black Hills Daily Times, Sep 29, 1880
Musicians from South Deadwood organize a brass band.

Black Hills Daily Times, Nov 4, 1880
More hideous noise from Colman on silver cornet.

Black Hills Daily Times, May 31, 1881
To perform at St. John's benefit concert

Black Hills Daily Times, Sep 13, 1882
German citizens giving a picnic at Nelson Park

Black Hills Daily Times, May 27, 1888
Nathan Colman, the Sherman street merchant, celebrated his 41st birthday yesterday, with liquid refreshments and cigars.

Black Hills Daily Times, Aug 7, 1888
Nathan Colman has become possessor of a patent folding canvas boat, complete arrangement with folding beds, stools and tent for a party of picnickers.

Black Hills Daily Times, Mar 5, 1890
Deadwood Liederkranz Society elects officers.

Nathan Colman continued in his position as lay rabbi to the Jewish community until his untimely death on June 4, 1906, at the age of 56, at the Colman home on Williams Street. According to his doctor, the cause of death was Bright's disease, characterized by kidney inflammation.

Deadwood Pioneer Times, Jun 5, 1906
As a relief to his sufferings, Nathan Colman, 56, one of the first settlers, breathed his last at his Williams Street residence. He had been confined to his home for many weeks with Bright's disease. He was a patient sufferer and had courage... He asked for no flowers... he had been Justice of the Peace since 1878, a sterling tribute to his honesty and popularity. Few men possessed a kinder heart. He was a man who searched out the right path and followed it, even to his own detriment.

Amalia Colman survived Nathan by 33 years, and died in Deadwood on April 1, 1939. She is buried beside her husband and six of her seven children in the family plot in the Mt. Zion section of Mt. Moriah Cemetery.

ANNE COLMAN NIEDERMAN

Anne, also known as Annie or Anna Colman, born in Denver in 1876, had been brought to Deadwood as an infant. She was raised and educated in Deadwood, and was the only one of the Colman sisters to marry and leave Deadwood permanently as an adult. One of the earliest newspaper articles concerning Anne relates to her riding in a parade, representing the state of New Mexico, where her father had first made a home in America.

Black Hills Daily Times, Jul 2, 1882
Anna Colman, Will ride in car of state representing New Mexico.

Black Hills Daily Times, Dec 23, 1885
Closing exercises of the fall term in the high school and junior departments.

Black Hills Daily Times, Jul 25, 1890
Professor Louis Werker and class will give grand vocal and instrumental concert at Opera house this evening. Anna Colman will perform.

Black Hills Daily Times, Jun 27, 1891,
Graduating and closing exercises at high school. Annie Colman.

Anne Colman, top row, second from right
Photo courtesy Adams Museum

Anne's marriage to Maurice Niederman in December of 1903 was the first Jewish wedding to be performed at the Franklin Hotel. Nathan officiated, acting as both Rabbi and Justice of the Peace. The event was described in the Deadwood newspaper (unnamed and undated):

"The wedding of Mr. Morris Niederman and Anne Colman took place Sunday in the presence of the more intimate friends of the young couple, and more

particularly of the bride's family. This ceremony was performed in the hotel parlors at 8:15 by Nathan Colman, father of the bride. The civil contract was first prescribed by Mr. Colman, Justice of the Peace. Following this the Jewish marriage service was read in Hebrew by Mr. Colman as acting Rabbi. It was one of the most beautiful and unique services ever observed in this city.

Miss Blanche Colman, sister of the bride, was maid of honor, and Miss Julia Goldberg, daughter of Mr. and Mrs. Jacob Goldberg, bridesmaid. The groom was attended by Paul Chamison and Charles Levy of Lead. The parlor was decorated with potted palms and presented a very attractive scene. After this ceremony a few moments were offered for felicitations, after which the company adjourned to the hotel dining room for the wedding dinner. A large number of handsome, costly, and useful presents were received by the newly married couple, which will prove highly serviceable in their new home. Mr. Niederman is a young businessman, well known in Deadwood and Lead. He was in business in Lead before locating at Deadwood. The bride belongs to one of the oldest and most esteemed of Deadwood's families."

Maurice, or Morris Niederman, was a Hungarian Jew, also born in 1876, who immigrated to America as a youngster. At the age of 14 he was employed as a dishwasher in Omaha, following which he became an itinerant peddler, canvassing the West, living for a time in Ardmore, Oklahoma. Maurice went to Dakota Territory where he settled in Lead and established a liquor business in partnership with Max Friedwald. From there he relocated to Deadwood where he opened the Family Liquor Store. This was Deadwood, with unreliable drinking water, awash in alcohol. Maurice was well liked in the community, and it was a suitable match for Anne's parents. Two sons, Nathan and Norman, were born in Deadwood, but some years later the couple sold their business and moved to Chicago. It must have been a tearful departure for this close family. The Niedermans' two daughters, Sarah and Dorothy, were born in Chicago.

Deadwood Pioneer Times, April 9, 1932

Mrs. N. Colman, pioneer resident of Deadwood, is in receipt of word from Chicago, Ill., conveying announcement of the marriage of her grand-daughter, Sarah Niederman to Harold Alschuler, Gary, Ind., the wedding to take place today at the home of the bride's parents, Mr. and Mrs. Maurice Niederman of Chicago. The bride, who has visited in Deadwood on several occasions, and will be remembered by a number of local people, and the groom, were classmates at the University of Illinois. They will establish their home in Gary.

Parade on Main St. Family Liquor Store on awning, lower left of picture
Photo Courtesy Adams Museum

BLANCHE COLMAN

Blanche Colman in 1926
Photo courtesy Al Alschuler

Blanche Colman, Anne's younger sister, was the first female attorney to have passed the South Dakota bar to practice law in the Black Hills. The last of the original Jewish pioneers to die in Deadwood, Blanche lived to the age of 94 and saw some momentous changes in her lifetime.

Blanche was born in Deadwood in 1884. She was an outstanding student who had all the stalwart characteristics of her parents. On the 1894 morning after one of Deadwood's fires, despite the Colmans' home having been caught up in the conflagration, 10-year-old Blanche appeared at school wearing a skimpy combination of clothing she had rescued from her room, but punctual as always, not wanting to spoil her perfect attendance record. After graduating from Deadwood High School in 1902, she was appointed private secretary to newly elected Congressman William Parker, who brought her to Washington, D.C.

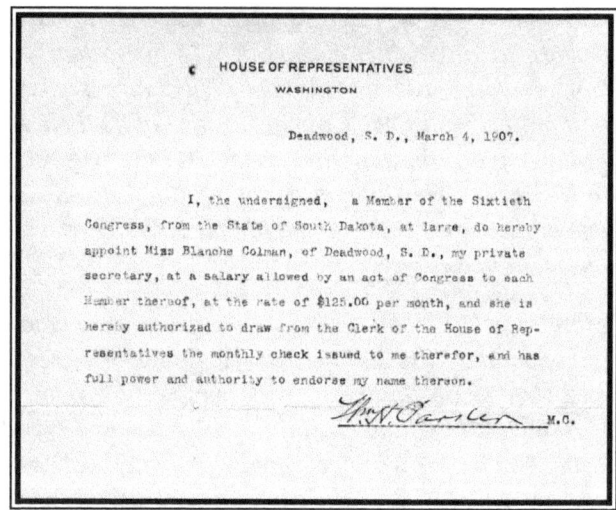

Letter appointing Blanche Colman private secretary to Congressman William Parker, March 4, 1907.
Photo courtesy Al Alschuler

Blanche was unhappy in Washington and longed to return to her home in the Black Hills. In 1903, she returned to Deadwood for the wedding of her sister Anne in December. The tiny, dark-eyed brunette, looking beautiful in her embroidered chiffon dress and carrying pink roses, was her sister Anne's Maid of Honor, once again at home in Deadwood.

In 1914, W.H. Bonham, publisher of the Deadwood Pioneer Times wrote, "The Deadwood Bar was made up of the best legal talent from the mining states and territories of the west and were surpassed by none..."

Her father was a strong influence in her life, and she also turned to law as a career. She took a job working for Chambers Kellar, attorney for the Homestake Mining Company, studying law in her spare time. She became a top-notch legal assistant, doing Kellar's homework backstage. She became the second woman in South Dakota to be admitted to the Bar; the first woman was admitted without having submitted to the bar examination, having been automatically admitted upon graduation from her school's Law Department. In 1911, at the age of 27, according to the Lead Daily Call, Blanche was the first woman admitted to the South Dakota bar to practice law in the Black Hills, and one of a very few women lawyers in the United States at the time.

Like her father, Blanche was especially adept at probate law. At Kellar's firm, Blanche did most of the research for one particular probate case that established legal precedent in the Supreme Court of the State of South Dakota. She worked as legal counsel for Homestake for 50 years, assisting Kellar with Homestake's litigation issues involving water rights and labor problems, finally retiring from that firm in 1950.

Lead Daily Call, Dec 31, 1960

Blanche Colman, Deadwood, was complimented on the occasion of her 76th birthday. She is the first woman in South Dakota to take the bar examination. A three-tiered cake, topped with miniature scales of justice was presented to Miss Colman by the hosts, Mr. and Mrs. Kenneth Kellar. Kellar also gave her a Black Hills Gold pen on behalf of the firm of Kellar and Kellar and Driscoll. She became associated with the law office of Chambers Kellar around 1902 until her retirement.

In 1961 the South Dakota State Bar Association awarded her a gold lapel pin for her 50 years of service as a practicing attorney in South Dakota.

Deadwood Pioneer Times, Jun 28, 1961

The first woman to receive a 50-year award as a practicing attorney in South Dakota is a native of Deadwood, Blanche Colman. The state bar of South Dakota will accord special recognition to eight attorneys who have practiced law in this state for 50 years, including Miss Colman. Each will receive a solid gold lapel pin, indicative of the fact at the annual meeting in Yankton on June 30.

Noted Deadwood historian, George Moses, recalled that Blanche would leave her little apartment in the Franklin Hotel and climb the 2 miles up the hill to her job at the Homestake Mine offices in Lead every day, a routine that may have contributed to her longevity.

During World War I, in the midst of the devastating 1918 flu epidemic, Blanche volunteered her services as secretary to the American Red Cross chapter. Emergency hospital facilities had to be set up at the Homestake Recreation Center to care for victims of the epidemic that claimed over 100 lives around Deadwood.

Blanche in her Law Office
Photo Courtesy Al Alschuler

Summertime meant visits from Chicago nieces and nephews who came to visit their aunts Tess and Blanche, but also to enjoy the fun of Deadwood, picnics in the hills and the Days of '76 parades. Sarah Niederman Alschuler recalled catching a ride with some good-looking cowboys in a parade— and catching a scolding when Aunt Blanche found out about it. With no children of her own, Blanche doted on her sister Anne's children. Blanche and Tess lived most of their later years in their apartments in the Franklin Hotel. Blanche could be demanding, but she was much loved and respected by her neighbors. Everyone from the bellhop at the Franklin, to the Supreme Court judge, who affectionately indulged her frugality and resistance to change as the years progressed, cared about her. Although she was personally thrifty, Blanche was a generous lady. An avid reader, she kept up on current events, preferring the Wall Street Journal and U.S. News & World Report. She avoided gossip, and would rather converse about current events and topics of national importance. True to her faith, Blanche kept a wooden mezuzah on the doorpost of her apartment in the Franklin Hotel. Long after her Jewish family and friends had vanished, she read alone from her prayer book, spending solitary Sabbaths in prayer and reflection. Alone and in her 90s, she would recite the weekly and festival services from her *siddur* (prayer book). In the 1970s she was befriended by young student rabbi, Howard Berman, who recalled Sabbaths spent visiting with Blanche, enrapt as she recounted stories of her beloved Jewish community in Deadwood. She told Rabbi Berman of how services were held in private homes and in rented halls. She remembered with pride how her father had officiated at Jewish religious events, High Holy days' services, Passover *seders*, weddings, and funerals. Her mind, never permitted to languish, was sharp to the last.

Deadwood Pioneer-Times, Feb 8, 1971
Miss Blanche Colman of the Kellar and Kellar Law Offices and her sister Theresa Colman, County Auditor, will leave Rapid City on the Milwaukee this evening for Chicago, Ill. for a visit with their brother-in-law and sister.

Blanche is remembered by those who knew her as a dignified, brilliant, reserved, but articulate lady. She loved to sing and recite poetry. Helen Rezatto, in her book, Mount Moriah, "Kill a Man- Start a Cemetery," tells us that Blanche's favorite poem was "Barbara Frietchie," by John Greenleaf Whittier. The words seem a fitting homage to Blanche Colman:

Over Barbara Frietchie's grave,
Flag of Freedom and Union, wave!
Peace and order and beauty draw
Round by symbol of light and law;
And ever the stars above look down
On thy stars below in Frederick town.

Because Nathan had arrived in Deadwood in February of 1877 rather than 1876, he was excluded from membership in the Society of Black Hills Pioneers. Years later, eligibility was changed to admit those who arrived before 1880. Blanche was invited to become a member, but out of respect for her father, Blanche politely, but adamantly, declined. This was a proud woman.

A Deadwood girl from the start, she lived during the early days of Deadwood's history where she saw, and took part in, some of the most exciting changes of the modern world. She lived to see rugged transportation by way of stagecoach give way to the magic of airplane travel. She saw the introduction of the telephone and television. She saw her tiny wilderness community go from a raucous mining camp to the stable and civilized commercial hub of the Black Hills. She saw Deadwood's population swell and later contract with the initial frenzy and subsequent subsidence of the Black Hills Gold Rush. And she saw her beloved Jewish community, under the religious leadership of her father thrive, until none of the younger generation were left at all.

She and Tess knew of the horrors taking place in Europe during the Holocaust years and did what they could to help. Blanche was ultimately alone, the last of Deadwood's living Jewish pioneers.

During her final illness, Blanche was confined to the Catholic hospital in Deadwood. Her niece, Sarah Neiderman, returned from Chicago to attend her ailing aunt. The Mother Superior honored her Jewish patient by reserving special kitchen utensils and preparing foods which she knew Blanche could eat in order not to violate her religious beliefs. Blanche died there at the age of 94 in 1978. No longer able to speak, the Mother Superior recited the *Shema* (Hebrew declaration of faith) for Blanche, the affirmation every Jew recites each day and at the hour of death. On the day of her funeral the carillon atop the Adams Museum tolled the melody to the Hebrew hymn *Adon Olam*.

Blanche Colman rests in the Colman family burial plot in the Mount Zion section of the cemetery. A historical marker at the foot of Jerusalem Avenue, sponsored by the Jewish American Society for Historic Preservation and maintained by the City of Deadwood, honors the Jewish community, and portrays Nathan Colman and two of his daughters.

Theresa, Nathan, and Blanche Colman
Photo courtesy Adams Museum

THERESA COLMAN

Theresa Colman, youngest of the three surviving sisters, was born in Deadwood in 1891. Tess or Tessie, as she was known, also carried on the family tradition of ability and talent.

Theresa in her office.
Photo courtesy Adams Museum

In 1907, Theresa received a certificate for proficiency in shorthand and typing, valuable skills for a woman of that day. She graduated from Deadwood High School where she focused her education on bookkeeping, and began her working career as a secretary to W.H. Bonham, editor of the Pioneer Times newspaper. She left in 1916 to work as bookkeeper for the Beatrice Creamery Company in Chicago until 1925, returning to Deadwood to work in public service. Tess worked in the Lawrence County Treasurer's office, and then served as Lawrence County auditor.

Like Blanche, Tess was an independent woman who never married.

Ida Israel Levinson (Mrs.Joseph Levinson), Tess Colman, Blanche Colman, and Amalia Colman in front
Photo courtesy Centennial Archives, Deadwood Public Library

Weekly Pioneer-Times, Mar 17, 1938

Miss Tessie Colman will leave on the Northwestern today for Chicago, going to the big city for the purpose of attending the wedding of her nephew, Nathan Niederman, which will take place in a few days.

Aunt Tess, as she was affectionately known by her sister Anne's children, died at the age of 81 on April 30, 1972, predeceasing Aunt Blanche by six years. When she died, the flag at the Lawrence County courthouse was lowered to half-mast out of respect.

Theresa is buried in the family plot on Mt. Moriah along with Nathan, Amalia, Blanche, and four other siblings who died in childhood. Their older sister, Anne, rests beside her husband, Maurice, in Chicago.

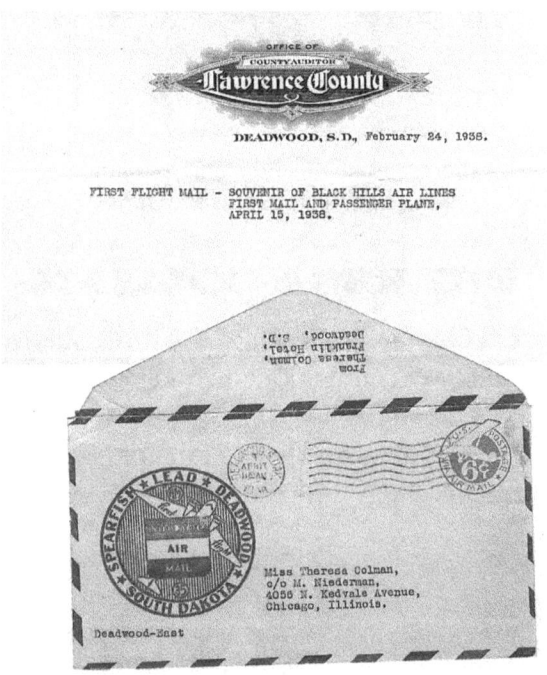

First Air Mail letter to Deadwood addressed to Theresa Colman, April 15, 1938
Photo courtesy Al Alschuler

Colman family burial plot in Mount Zion Section of Historic Mount Moriah Cemetery
Photo by Ann Haber Stanton

As the direct descendant of the Deadwood congregation, the Synagogue of the Hills in Rapid City honors its past by reciting the memorial Yizkor list each year on the High Holiday of Yom Kippur. At the beginning of the list are the names of Blanche and Theresa Colman, of the pioneering Colman family of Deadwood, true Jewish-American originals.

BAER
626 MAIN ST.

Benjamin Baer
Photo courtesy Deadwood Public Library

BUSINESSMAN

At the start of the Black Hills Gold Rush, Ben Baer, 25, was one of the first Jewish pioneers to arrive in Deadwood. He was born in Paris, France, in 1846, and arrived in the United States in 1871, first spending some time in St. Joseph, Missouri, before traveling to St. Paul, Minnesota, where he developed some long-lasting connections.

Black Hills Daily Times, Aug 31, 1877
Ben Baer, returns from St. Joseph, Mo.

Baer got his start as a dealer in wholesale and retail liquor in Yankton, in southeastern Dakota Territory. Drawn by the excitement in the Black Hills, Baer traveled the 400 miles to Deadwood in August of 1876 with a plentiful supply of alcoholic spirits. In 1876 revenue agents from Nebraska and Wyoming were kept busy preventing whiskey shipments from getting into Indian territory. Traveling from Yankton by way of the Missouri River and Fort Pierre, avoiding both Indians and unwelcoming federal agents, Baer arrived in time to help avert a dry spell in Deadwood.

Liquor was legal in Deadwood, provided it was not sold on Sunday. Drinking water was not always trustworthy. Alcohol was a way of life, as much necessity as luxury, and would become part of the scene at all levels of Deadwood society. Up until the enactment of Prohibition, there was no stigma attached to trade in alcohol, and as fertile ground for the liquor trade, there was a fortune to be made in the Black Hills. Trash heaps of discarded bottles in later years remained as testimony to the zealous consumption of alcohol.

Black Hills Daily Pioneer, Sep 1, 1878
Wines & Cigars, ad

Black Hills Daily Times, Sep 21, 1878
Incoming Freight from Fort Pierre.

Black Hills Daily Times, Nov 30, 1878
Incoming Freight from Sidney.

Black Hills Daily Pioneer, Dec 1, 1878
Importer & dealer in Kentucky Whiskies, ad

Black Hills Daily Pioneer Dec 8, 1878
Most complete wholesale liquor establishment, Baer.

Baer needed to protect his goods from the ravages of fire and flood, and in June of 1879 he started building a warehouse for his merchandise. Like other merchants in Deadwood, he suffered losses in the Great Fire of 1879, his damages amounting to $2,000, but his stock was intact and he planned to be back in business soon.

Black Hills Daily Times, Jun 19, 1879
Broke ground for two-story fire-proof in rear.

Black Hills Daily Times, Jul 2, 1879
Work of laying the foundation for fire-proof begun.

Black Hills Daily Times Aug 21, 1879
Baer & Whitehead have combined their fire-proof.

Black Hills Daily Times Sep 11, 1879
Made donation to the fire department to buy hose.

Black Hills Daily Times, Sep 27, 1879
Losses in the big fire of September 27, $2,000. His stock is still intact, will be in business soon.

Black Hills Daily Times, Nov 4, 1879
Fire-proofs saved in the big Deadwood fire. Improvements were being made to the streets, with new wood plank sidewalks being laid.

Black Hills Daily Times, Dec 19, 1879
Having broad plank walk laid in front of business.

Black Hills Daily Times, Mar 24, 1880
Stone for foundation of new brick block arriving.

Black Hills Daily Times May 11, 1880
To commence the erection of brick block next week.

Max Fishel's Stationery Store
Photo courtesy Centennial Archives, Deadwood Public Library

As did many Deadwood businessmen, Ben Baer had a number of businesses and affiliations going on simultaneously. In 1880, Baer and Max Fishel, another Jew, built a double-front brick building on Main St., with Baer operating a liquor store on his half, and Fishel running a stationery store on his.

Black Hills Daily Times, Nov 29, 1881
Ben Baer, Donated money to help Jews.

Baer formed a partnership with Harris Franklin in a wholesale liquor and cigar business which branched out, including one outlet in Rapid City.

Franklin and Baer, Rapid City
Photo courtesy David Strain

Black Hills Daily Times, Mar 25, 1881
Shipped 2 wagon loads of goods to Rapid customer.

Black Hills Daily Times, Dec 6, 1881
Will be in Rapid a few days.

Travel anywhere was time-consuming and risky, but in late May of 1881 Baer took time out to return to his native France to visit family. Word came back in mid-July that he had reached his destination and was in Paris.

Black Hills Daily Times, May 25, 1881
Ben Baer, Leaves Deadwood via Sidney coach.

Black Hills Daily Times, Jul 19, 1881
Ben Baer, Is visiting Paris.

A Deadwood card game could win or lose a fortune. One classic photograph entitled "The Poker Game" whimsically re-creates the moment of an extraordinary win at the poker table. At the table sits Ben Baer, surrounded by Jewish friends Gus Cahn, Ed Haas, Aaron May, Sam Hess, Emanuel Fist, Louis Deutsch, Ben Oppenheimer, and Sol Ehrman. Stunned by his winning hand, Baer appears dazed.

At just such a card table, Baer's winnings were to be paid in cattle, but drought had rendered those cattle perilously close to starvation and practically worthless. He went to bed believing that he had acquired a starving herd, but awoke the next morning to a pouring rain. Rain had broken the drought, and the dry prairie sprang to life. With a stroke of amazing good luck, fresh green grass and plentiful feed saved the cattle and made Ben Baer, and by association, Harris Franklin, overnight cattle barons.

Black Hills Daily Times, Jan 12, 1882
Ben Baer, On board of directors, First National Bank.

Black Hills Daily Times, Mar 15, 1882
Wagered Ingleside lots in game of seven-up.

High-stakes luck!
Photo courtesy Adams Museum

As a silent partner in Harris Franklin's cattle business, Baer's name seldom appeared on their deals, but the two had extensive cattle holdings in the country north of the Black Hills. Their company absorbed the Hash Knife and Turkey Track, as well as some other large adjoining cattle outfits. Under the name of the Franklin Cattle Company, the Franklin and Baer herd also included horses, and extended on the open range from Texas to Saskatchewan and Eastern Alberta. From a herd of 45,000, it shipped 10,000 head to market annually. The partners later sold their cattle holdings and organized the Golden Reward mine, which would become one of the most productive gold mines in the northern Black Hills.

Black Hills Daily Times, Jan 28, 1883
Introducing brand of cigar called "Bear", 1st class.

Fireproofing was no protection against floods. A major flood in the spring of 1883 gave consumers of Baer's merchandise reason to celebrate—free of charge.

Black Hills Daily Times, May 19, 1883
Ben Baer: Fireproof is very badly demolished.

Black Hills Daily Times, May 20, 1883
Ben Baer: Statement of losses by the Deadwood citizens from flood.

Black Hills Daily Times, May 23, 1883
Liquor barrels floated, enjoy drinking from stream.

Black Hills Daily Times, May 26, 1883
Sent ox team out to pick up supplies stuck in mud.

Black Hills Daily Times, May 27, 1883
Human hyenas take advantage of flooding.

Black Hills Daily Times, Jun 22, 1883
Fireproof repaired, now better than before flood.

In the early 1880s Baer started the American National Bank of Deadwood. He remained president until it later consolidated with Harris Franklin's First National Bank, still Franklin's silent partner. Besides formation of their 1884 liquor and banking partnership, the business alliance of Franklin and Baer held investments in cattle and mining, and would become among the most significant in Deadwood's history. Baer formed other business relationships, but none would be as long-lasting or profitable as his partnership with Harris Franklin.

Black Hills Daily Times Jan 1, 1884

Two firms of Harris Franklin and Ben Baer have consolidated, now able to do an immense business.

Black Hills Daily Times Jan 6, 1884

Two large wholesale liquor firms unite to form Franklin and Baer. They will occupy both buildings, but hold office in the former Franklin and Gottstein building.

Black Hills Daily Times, Jan 13, 1884

First (ox) train over the road arrived from Dickinson, consisted of three wagons of freight for Ben Baer and Jensen and Bliss.

Black Hills Daily Times, Jan 30, 1884

Mr. Baer has returned from Rapid City.

Baer must have considered going into business in Idaho. To relieve Baer of any doubts regarding starting a new business venture further west in Idaho, in 1884 Dave Holzman wrote from Coeur d'Alene, assuring Baer and his friends back home in Deadwood that business wasn't very good, not to be in a hurry to start a new business there.

Black Hills Daily Times, Feb 27, 1884

Letter to Ben Baer from an old fellow townsman, Dave Holzman, regarding Coeur d'Alene states, "I would advise all my friends to stay away from here for the present. All along this road business is dull, with the exception of a few saloons and lodging houses, so I say stay away for the present, don't be in a hurry to get here. This is the best advice I can give."

In partnership with Sol Star, Harris Franklin, and Daniel McLaughlin, in 1884 Baer helped to start the Deadwood Flouring Mill Company, in which three of the four officers were Jews.

Black Hills Daily Times, Oct 9, 1884

Deadwood Flouring Mill Company formed. A new organization completed by election of officers for the Deadwood Flouring Mill Company. Sol Star, Harris Franklin, Ben Baer, Daniel McLaughlin.

Black Hills Daily Times, Sep 5, 1885

Ben Baer is on a visit to Rapid and intermediate points.

Black Hills Daily Times, Sep 10, 1878

Citizens give donations to yellow fever sufferers Baer

Black Hills Daily Pioneer, Sep 11, 1878

Gives money for yellow fever victims in South.

Black Hills Daily Pioneer, Sep 15, 1878

Charity Ball for Yellow Fever Sufferers.

Giving charity was a basic necessity. Yellow fever, or American plague as it was known at the time, is a mosquito-borne disease that appeared intermittently. In 1793 an epidemic hit Philadelphia. By the time it ended, 5,000 people were dead.

FAMILY

By 1884 Ben Baer had already become quite wealthy, but his life was still incomplete. The press did not overlook his marital status.

Black Hills Daily Times Nov 8, 1883

Ben Baer has returned, but so far as we can see he came alone.

Baer had a sweetheart in St. Joseph, Missouri, Ida Flarsheim, whom he wished to marry. Ida's family needed some convincing, but in 1884 Ben was able to assure the father of his beloved that he had secured enough of a fortune to provide for a wife. The couple was married in March in St. Joseph.

Black Hills Daily Times Mar 9, 1884

Yesterday's Sidney coach took out Ben Baer, and Benjamin was so sly about it that he slipped off as though the Times local was not up to his little racket. For luck, we will state that on Wednesday, March 19th, at an early hour in the evening, he will lead one of St. Joe, Missouri's, fairest daughters to the altar, and he has our consent. The Times congratulates.

Black Hills Daily Times Mar 14, 1884

George Bewes received by mail yesterday an artistic and finely executed card that read as follows: "Ben Baer, Ida Flarsheim, to be married March 19, at 8 p.m. at the residence of the bride's mother, No. 615 North Fourth street, St. Joseph, Missouri. The Times, with the groom's numerous friends in the Hills, extend their congratulations.

Black Hills Daily Times Apr 1, 1884

Ben Baer and new bride to reside at Ingleside. The furniture occupied by Ben Baer in his bachelor quarters in the First National Bank building was moved yesterday to the residence preparing for him and his bride in Ingleside. They are expected in soon, as he wrote they would leave Chicago on the 25th.

Black Hills Daily Times Apr 15, 1884

Ben Baer and wife arrived here at a late hour last night. The Times extends congratulations to Mr. and Mrs. Baer, hoping the lady may be pleased with the country she has adopted as her home.

Ben and Ida built a home on Lincoln Avenue in Ingleside. Ida returned to Missouri for the birth of their first child, Ira B., but all their other children were born in Deadwood. The couple found that family life in the Black Hills was fraught with hazards far beyond those money could overcome. It was not uncommon in that day to lose children to the ravages of contagious diseases. The Baers lost two children in Deadwood, a baby of 16 months in 1896, and a girl who died in 1899. Burial records in the Jewish section of Mount Moriah are incomplete, but both of these children are believed to be buried somewhere in the Jewish cemetery. Four other children, Helen (Stamm), Jerome B., Fernand B., and Edwin B., survived.

Black Hills Daily Times, Aug 29, 1886

Ben Baer returned from a protracted eastern visit, accompanied by Mrs. Baer, last evening.

Black Hills Daily Times, Oct 6, 1886

Girl wanted: Mrs. Baer seeking help A competent girl wanted immediately. Mrs. Ben Baer, Lincoln Avenue, Ingleside.

Black Hills Daily Times, Dec 21, 1890

Ben Baer's family are quite sick, and he is detained at home caring— for them.

Black Hills Daily Times, Mar 24, 1892

M.J. Flarsheim, brother of Mrs. Ben Baer, left for his home, St. Paul, yesterday after a pleasant visit in this city of a week's duration.

HORSES

Like Sol Star, Paul Rewman, and many others in Deadwood, Baer had a penchant for fine horses. He worked hard with the Deadwood Driving Park Association for the successful completion of the park.

Black Hills Daily Times, Jan 22, 1880

Thoroughbred Missouri steed attracting attention.

Black Hills Daily Times, Jun 1, 1880

Secretary of the Deadwood Driving Park Association.

Black Hills Daily Times, Jun 24, 1880

John Looby, Gave away trotter for $500, to Ben Baer.

Black Hills Daily Times Feb 2, 1884

Ben Baer stepped out of his buggy onto uneven frozen ground and sprained his ankle.

Black Hills Daily Times, Sep 22, 1886

A great event. Driving Park association working unceasingly in the interest of the fall meeting, the complete success of which is abundantly assured. Ben Baer, Paul Rewman.

GOVERNMENT

Governance was an immediate factor in everyone's life in the Black Hills, and those elected to office had a heavy responsibility in the rapidly developing towns. Clean government was always something to strive for.

Black Hills Daily Times, Oct 23, 1885

Lawrence County. The public safety. Meeting of citizens to take action called for by crookedness of ex-officials.

Baer, along with some of Deadwood's other Jewish businessmen supported Sol Star in his 1885 run for mayor. Those also endorsing Star included B.H. Kohorn, Mr. Weidenfeld, A. Kone, Mike Gottstein and Sol Rosenthal.

MINING

Baer was heavily invested in mining, particularly of the silver being extracted from the mines around Carbonate. In 1885 he was elected one of the officers of the Liberty Mining Company.

Black Hills Daily Times, Feb 5, 1885

Ben Baer, Stockholders of Liberty Silver Mining Company elect officers.

LEGACY

Franklin and Baer together held 2250 shares of stock in the new Franklin Hotel. If Harris Franklin was the "richest man in Deadwood," surely Ben Baer was a close second. With his preference to remain in the background when conducting business, Baer's propensity for privacy kept his wealth much less obvious.

A notice appeared in the Deadwood Daily Pioneer Times of January 24, 1899, saying Ida Baer had died, their marriage cut short after 15 years. *"The remains of the late Mrs. Ben Baer were shipped from this city yesterday to St Joseph, Missouri, where they will repose in a vault until Mr. Baer is able to travel, when he will take them to New York City for interment in the family ground. Following the request of the deceased, there was no funeral service."*

At the turn of the century Baer returned to St. Paul, followed a few months thereafter by his family. In St. Paul, Baer started the American National Bank, where he remained as president. The American National Bank later became known as the Bremer Bank. Their building was renamed the Bremer Bank Tower in early 2005.

On Jan. 4, 2012, a notice appeared in St. Paul's Pioneer Press saying that the old Bremer Bank building had been demolished to make room for the new light-rail train connecting St. Paul to Minneapolis. The new Bremer Bank Tower is a now 27-story high-rise building in St. Paul, Minnesota.

SCHWARZWALD
NATHAN, LOWENTHAL, SILVER, ALDRICH
620 - 622 MAIN ST.

Sam Schwarzwald
Photo courtesy Adams Museum

SCHWARZWALD BUSINESSMAN

Further down Main Street, in the Badlands area, I reached a furniture store with the name Schwarzwald written on the window. It occupied two storefront spaces— furniture stores need room for their merchandise— and it was busy with shoppers. A kindly-looking gentleman approached and introduced himself as Leo Aldrich, and started a friendly chat. I told him who I was, and that I was researching the history of Deadwood's Jews, and that Schwarzwald sounded to me like a Jewish name. Could it be? Leo smiled and invited me to have a seat on a nearby sofa. "Yes," Leo said," let me tell you a little about this store and the family that's kept it in business for over 80 years." That little chat began the unfolding of a Jewish-American family's epic history.

The founder of Schwarzwald's Furniture, a Jewish pioneer named Samuel Schwarzwald, was born February 16, 1848, in Prussia, the son of Jacob and Fuerda Kohn Schwarzwald. His family immigrated to New York City in 1857 where he attended public schools until he was 16. Sam worked in various states including Georgia, Missouri, and Montana. In 1876 he joined a party leaving from Fort Benton, Montana, heading for the Black Hills by way of Bismarck, in what is now North Dakota. From Bismarck the group of 128 Montanans including Sol Star, and Jacob Goldberg, followed the old Custer Trail into Deadwood, arriving on August 12, 1876, shortly after Wild Bill Hickok was killed.

His first business dealings in Deadwood, Dakota Territory, were in grain and produce, and before long Sam was handling all such commodities. He and his business partner, a man named Stone, traveled to Fort Pierre by ox train to purchase stock necessary to furnish homes and businesses, returning with such essentials as cookstoves, crockery, tables and chairs. They established this first furniture store in a tent off Deadwood's muddy main street. From that tent the business moved into a log building.

In the fall of 1877 he opened his first new and used furniture business in a frame house on the west side of Deadwood at the north end of Broadway Street, under the firm name of Stone and Schwarzwald, later becoming the sole owner. From 1879 on he devoted all his time to furniture, stoves, and crockery. The merchandise was brought into Deadwood by ox train from the ferry at Fort Pierre. In 1894 he built a brick and stone building at 620 Main St., and in 1897 he expanded, acquiring the adjacent building at 622 Main St.

The business was quite successful, and in 1900 he built a second two-story brick building on the left side of this lot, connecting the two buildings on the interior with a 20-foot-wide arched opening. In 1911, Schwarzwald decided that this end of Main Street was no longer part of the retail district. He leased space in the Syndicate Block, across Main St., and moved his store to that location, but by 1919, he had returned to his old stand, where the store remained for the rest of Sam's life. Upon Sam's death in 1927, the furniture store passed into the ownership of his wife Augusta (Gussie) and her children by a prior marriage. Sam had encouraged Charlie Nathan, a step-son, to attend business college in Nebraska, and after graduating, Charlie took over the major share of the store's operation. It was destroyed by fire in 1948, and during the reconstruction Schwarzwald had offers to move to Rapid City. He declined, instead choosing to rebuild in the same Deadwood location, but doing business out of the Deadwood Auditorium until the new building was completed. The new store was constructed in the most modern of styles, with glass block windows and cement walls. Charlie had been groomed to operate the business, continuing under the Schwarzwald name. By 1950 Charlie Nathan had turned Schwarzwald's into the largest furniture store in Western South Dakota and one of the most long-term mercantile establishments in Deadwood's history.

In 1977, the building was sold, and the furniture store moved to 608-610 Main Street. The new owner dealt in Indian artifacts, and remodeled the building in the trendy Southwestern style.

Schwarzwald's Furniture Store was a fixture of Deadwood's Lower Main Street scene through all of Deadwood's many fires and floods, two World Wars and the Great Depression, almost continuously doing business within 200 feet of the store's original location.

Balloon-raising across from Schwarzwald's Furniture Store, ca. 1891
Photo courtesy Adams Museum

NATHAN AND LOWENTHAL

The story of Sam Schwarzwald's life in Deadwood brings with it the lives and loves of other names and other Jewish families. It takes us from Brooklyn to Deadwood, to Central City, and on to Lead in territorial days. We meet the Lowenthals and the Nathans, the Silvers and the Aldriches, all of whom are descended from, or related in some way to patriarch Sam Schwarzwald.

New Yorkers from Brooklyn, and later the Bowery in lower Manhattan, Max, Ben, Pauline, Esther and Augusta (Gussie) were the Lowenthal children. The family left New York City for greener pastures in Gold Rush country, where the parents started a business in Central City, a town midway between flourishing Deadwood and Lead. Gussie, who was born in 1863, met her first husband, Louis Nathan, a 26-year-old Central City businessman, and on

Oct. 12, 1884, when Gussie was 21, she and Louis were married.

Ben Lowenthal and family
Photo courtesy Marc Aldrich

Black Hills Daily Times, Oct. 14, 1884

CUPID'S CAPERS: Following is a copy of a neatly printed invitation received at the Times of his last evening, for which would return thanks and expand congratulations. No young man is more deserving of a good wife and companion than Louis, and no young lady more deserving of a good husband than Ms. Lowenthal. "Mr. and Mrs. Lowenthal request the pleasure of your company at the marriage ceremony of their daughter, Gussie, to Louis Nathan, at their residence, Central City, Sunday evening, October 13, 1884, at 7 o'clock.

Among the guests at the wedding of Louis Nathan and Gussie Lowenthal were Sam Schwarzwald, Joe Hattenbach, J. Chamison, Nathan Jacobs, Gus Fishel, L. Cohn, J. Wertheimer, Sol Rosenthal, B. Holstein, David Goldbloom, Bertha Goldbloom, Max Abrams, Charles Hyman, M. Stern, L. Pincus, L. Epstein, M. Frank, Charles Posner, M. Rosengarden, Ben Lowenthal, Max Lowenthal, Harris Franklin, and Louis Minzer. Of note was that Sam Schwarzwald was among the list of guests.

Family situations were changing. Theresa married Levander Aldrich and they started a family in Deadwood. The Lowenthal parents eventually moved to Chadron, Nebraska. Years later, Max and Ben left the Black Hills and moved to Chadron, where the Lowenthal brothers operated a clothing business. Ben married and had sons. Brother Leo died in the flu epidemic of 1919.

The marriage of Louis Nathan and Gussie Lowenthal did not last. They divorced around 1888 but by then they had three children, Charles, Leo, and Theresa. Sam Schwarzwald was still in Deadwood and single, owner of a successful business, and now Gussie was free. In 1903 Gussie re-married, this time to Sam Schwarzwald, and the couple built a home on the hillside at 340 Williams Street in Deadwood. Gussie's children remained close to their mother and Charlie, Leo and Theresa became family to Sam.

Leo Nathan
Photo courtesy Marc Aldrich

Charlie and Leo Nathan
Photo courtesy Marc Aldrich

Gussie Schwarzwald
Photo Courtesy Centennial Archives,
Deadwood Public Library

Gussie Schwarzwald in the furniture store
Photo Courtesy Marc Aldrich

Deadwood had a great building boom in 1936. Whereas the rest of the country was deep in a Depression, the price of gold was exceptionally high and prosperity abounded in the Deadwood, Lead, and Trojan mining areas. Ranchers and farmers were forced off their land because of the drought and the Depression, and some came seeking work at Homestake, which was paying comparatively good wages. Employees of Homestake were offered interest-free loans to build homes, and they needed to furnish those homes. The furniture business prospered. Even then, people came from out of town to gamble in Deadwood, but the women also did their shopping in Deadwood's thriving business district.

Charlie Nathan, Gussie Schwarzwald
Photo courtesy Marc Aldrich

Black Hills Daily Times, Jan 3, 1879
Secretary of the Lead City Social Club, Oscar Silver

Black Hills Daily Times, Feb 21, 1879
Oscar Silver will furnish the music for the Miners Union Ball, Lead

Black Hills Daily Times Jun 23 1883
Endowment Rank of Knights of Pythias elect officer, Oscar Silver

Black Hills Daily Times, Jan. 6, 1886
Officers installed Monday for Dakota Lodge, No. 6, Knights of Pythias.

Black Hills Daily Times, Jan. 10, 1888
Knights of Pythias installation at Lead a grand affair. Oscar Silver

Black Hills Daily Times Jan. 9, 1892
Ancient Order of United Workers installs officers. Oscar Silver

Like most Deadwood merchants, Sam had dealt in mining investments quite successfully. He was a member of the Society of Black Hills Pioneers, and also active in the Republican Party. His societal activities included membership in the Elks and Eagles lodges.

SILVER

By 1879 Oscar Silver was already well established and doing a brisk jewelry business in Lead. Like many of the Jews of that time, he was an active member of fraternal organizations. The Jews were especially active in Knights of Pythias and the Masonic Lodges, Elks and Eagles Lodges.

Pauline Lowenthal, Charlie Nathan, Esther Silver
Photo courtesy Marc Aldrich

In January of 1882 Oscar asked for the hand of Esther Lowenthal in marriage. A celebratory betrothal party was held at the Lowenthal residence. In September, Esther and Oscar were married in Ingleside, and settled in Lead where Silver had his business. In 1885 a son was born. They also had at least one daughter.

Black Hills Daily Times, Jan 30, 1882

Celebrated betrothal at Lowenthal residence with party, a Jewish custom. Guests at Lowenthal-Silver betrothal party (included) Mr and Mrs.D.Goldberg

Black Hills Daily Times, Sep 28, 1882

Oscar Silver, Marriage, to Esther Lowenthal, in Ingleside.

Black Hills Daily Times, Jun 7, 1885

Son born Friday evening to wife of Oscar Silver, Lead

Black Hills Daily Times, Nov 27, 1886

O. Silver is on the sick list.

Black Hills Daily Times, Jun 16, 1887.

Mrs. Oscar Silver, Lead, is visiting her parents in Central.

Black Hills Daily Times, Sep 16, 1887

Silver and wife return from the east. Oscar Silver and wife came in on the coach from the east last evening and went on up to home in Lead City.

Black Hills Daily Times, Apr 24, 1890

Mrs. Oscar Silver and children, Lead, returned yesterday from Europe. For the last week or so they visited at Chadron.

Black Hills Daily Times, Sep 13, 1891

Oscar Silver received a telegram Friday from Chadron stating that his father-in-law, Mr. Lowenthal, died at 3:40 p.m. of old age. Deceased was well known in the Hills.

Black Hills Daily Times, May 20, 1892

Mrs. Oscar Silver is reported quite seriously ill.

PARTNERSHIPS

Many Deadwood and Lead businesses branched out into neighboring towns such as Belle Fourche, Sturgis, Spearfish, Rapid City and Chadron. Centrally located Buffalo Gap was about 100 miles south of Lead and one-third of the way to the nearest railhead at Sidney, Nebraska. Speculating that Buffalo Gap would be the next business boom-town, Silver joined with Sol Star, Louis Nathan, Sol Bloom, and others who had bought lots, and some who started businesses in Buffalo Gap, locally known as the Gap. Disappointingly, Buffalo Gap turned out to be less than the roaring success they'd all been anticipating, and Silver's plan was thwarted.

Black Hills Daily Times Feb 12, 1884

Oscar Silver and H. Monheim, Lead, have returned from trip to Custer.

Black Hills Daily Times, Sept15, 1885

Deadwood merchants in Chadron. Chadron Journal reports Felix Poznansky in with large stock of goods to take immediate possession of new building purchased of Ben Lowenthal. Gottstein and Owens will soon be ready for business.

Black Hills Daily Times, Jan 24, 1886

Oscar Silver and Ben Lowenthal left by last evening's coach for the Gap.

Black Hills Daily Times, Jul 14, 1886

Oscar Silver arrived from the Gap yesterday afternoon

Black Hills Daily Times, Jul 15, 1886

Mr. O. Silver has moved his branch store from the Gap to Lead. The manager, Mr. A.W. Tranth, will assist in the main store in Lead.

Black Hills Daily Times, Apr 25, 1886

Board of Trade elects officers. Pincus Cohen, Oscar Silver, Louis Minzer.

Black Hills Daily Times, Oct 21, 1886

Mr. Silver has disposed of his clothing store on Main Street in Lead, and will confine all his business to one store on Mill Street.

Black Hills Daily Times, Aug 2, 1887

The store of Oscar Silver at Lead was broken open by burglars Sunday night and caused much excitement. Silver says he misses no goods, but one, or both burglars may be identifiable.

In 1889 Silver was also selling men's, youth's, and children's clothing out of his Mill Street establishment in Lead.

Black Hills Daily Times, Jun 2, 1889

Special hat sale till June 5th, 1889. J.B. Stetson's light colored clear Nutria hats, worth $5 and $6, will sell at $2.50 each; fine quality dark brown felt hats, worth $3.50, will sell at $1.50 each. Men's, youth and children's fine and perfect fitting clothing will sell for less than original cost of cloth and trimming — Oscar Silver, Mill Street, Lead City, Dak.

Black Hills Daily Times, Mar 23, 1892

J.C. Collins came to Lead yesterday to auctioneer for Oscar Silver.

ALDRICH

Theresa Nathan, the sister of Charles and Leo Nathan, married Levander Aldrich, and they had three children: Leo (named for Theresa's brother); Wilmot (Willie); and Kenneth (Kenny). Theresa died in her 30s when her son Leo was 16 years old. The boys lived with their father during part of the Depression, but then were "farmed out" to area rancher/farmers around Rapid City. Later they were reclaimed and raised in Deadwood by grandmother Gussie Schwarzwald and uncle Charlie Nathan.

Leo Aldrich
Photo courtesy Marc Aldrich

The three brothers worked at the store under Charlie's supervision. Later Willie and Kenny left to start their own businesses, but Leo remained, becoming the owner/manager of Schwarzwald's Furniture in the late 1960s or early 1970s. Charlie married Irene North, of Finnish background. She died in the 1980s and is buried by her family in Galena, South Dakota. Charlie Nathan died around 1979 in his 90s and is buried in the Mt. Zion section of Mt. Moriah Cemetery.

Rapid City Journal, Oct 8, 2008.

Leo was born March 20, 1920, to Levander and Theresa (Nathan) Aldrich in Rapid City and lived there with his parents until his mother's death. He was 16 years old. He then moved to Deadwood to live with his maternal grandmother, Gussie Schwarzwald and uncle Charles Nathan.

At this point Leo suggested I cross the street and talk to Bert and Ruth Jacobs at the New York Store on my way back northward along Main Street. He said they also had quite a family history, and we smiled as we embraced for good-byes. I saved his advice for the following day, so glad to have met such a lovely man.

In the mid-1980s Leo retired and closed the store that had been in his family since the beginning the Black Hills Gold Rush, over 100 years before. Some Black Hills people still have memories of that store, and many more have furnishings that were purchased there, when Deadwood was still the hub of the Black Hills economy. Leo Aldrich died in 2008 at the age of 88 and rests in Mt. Zion.

Mt. Zion graves of Theresa Nathan, Gussie Schwarzwald, Charles Nathan
Photo by Ann Haber Stanton

STAR

BULLOCK HOTEL 631-633-635 MAIN ST.

Solomon (Sol) Star, Deadwood's First Jewish Mayor
Photo courtesy Adams Museum

STAR AND BULLOCK PARTNERSHIP

This engrossing journey into Deadwood's history was leading me across Main Street's cobblestones to the Bullock Hotel. My guidebook said that Sol Star, who had been Deadwood's mayor for 14 years, was the business partner of Seth Bullock, that they'd started a hardware business on this very corner in 1876. Their store had equipped the earliest gold-seekers with some of their most immediate needs. But the hotel is named for Star's longtime business partner, Lawrence County Sheriff, Seth Bullock. I wondered why Star's name was not on the hotel's sign.

The serene countenance belies the intrepid spirit of Deadwood's first Jewish Mayor, Solomon Star. Few photographs remain of Sol Star. Those we do have portray a dignified gentleman with a benevolent demeanor and a quiet strength. This was a man with high principles but a firm grip on reality. His leadership helped guide Deadwood from an unruly Wild West frontier mining camp to a civilized town that was for many years the center of commerce for the Black Hills region. Sol Star's sound judgment, his resourcefulness in emergencies, his ready generosity, and his concern for the interests of his community made him a popular icon, prominent socially and politically. Sol's sturdy and level character saw him through some trying times. Of all the Jewish pioneers who left their imprint upon Deadwood, the Black Hills, and South Dakota, Sol Star is undoubtedly the most recognizable.

The handsome Bullock Hotel stands where Star and Bullock's Hardware began in a tent in August of 1876, at the beginning of the Black Hills Gold Rush. The tent soon gave way to a frame building, which in 1880 became a sandstone building, the front of which functioned as a hardware store. The rear part, a warehouse, was sturdy enough to withstand the major fires of 1879 and 1894.

Star and Bullock Hardware
Photo Courtesy Adams Museum

The partnership of Sol Star and Seth Bullock that began in the gold mining town of Helena, Montana, would become one of the most dynamic and successful of Deadwood's many business affiliations, contributing significantly to the economic development of Deadwood, Belle Fourche, and many other western Dakota Territory towns.

Solomon Star, fifth child in a family of 10 children, was born in the Kingdom of Bavaria, Germany, on December 20th, 1840. In 1850, before Solomon reached the age of ten, his Bavarian-born parents, Marcus Star, a merchant, and Minnie Friedlander Star, sent him to Cincinnati, Ohio, to live with his mother's brother, uncle Abraham Joseph Friedlander, a clothing merchant. After a year in Cincinnati, Sol and his uncle moved to Circleville, Ohio, where they resided from 1851 until 1857. Census records of 1900 indicate that Sol spoke both German and Yiddish. Sol worked as a clerk as he continued his education, which stopped short of college. Between the years 1857 and 1861 he moved to Terra Haute, Indiana, and in 1861 Sol left Indiana for Saline County, Missouri, where he established his own business. In 1865, carefully considering the opportunity that lay ahead in the booming gold fields of the West, Sol packed up and left for Montana Territory. He was 25 years old.

From the clothing business in Helena and Virginia City, Montana, he branched out into banking, and became remarkably successful. In 1870, at the age of 30, Sol's assets were valued at more than $10,000.

Sol also began to distinguish himself in public affairs, and he was asked to serve as personal secretary to the governor of Montana. Then, in 1872 President Ulysses S. Grant appointed Star registrar of the United States General Land Office at Helena. The land office registrar also functioned as mining registrar, of particular importance to miners staking their claims. In this crucible Sol was educated in the business of mining. In 1874 he was appointed to the post of Territorial Auditor of the Commonwealth of Montana, a position he held until 1875.

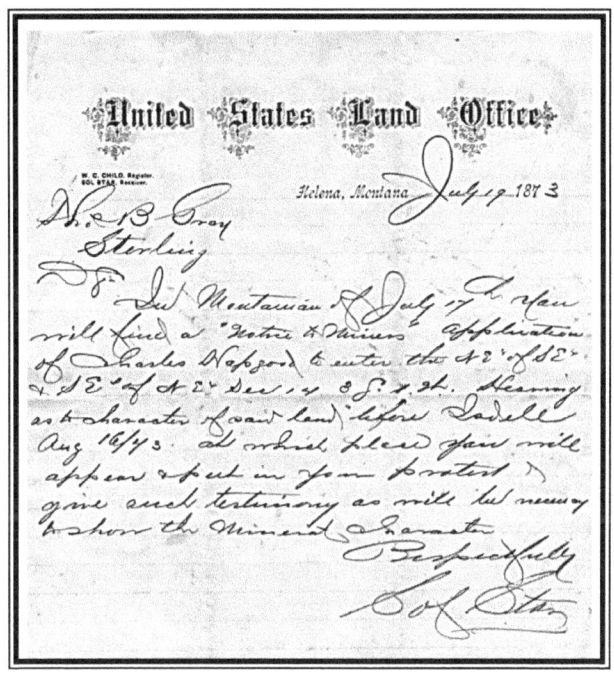

Photo courtesy Jerry L. Bryant

Seth Bullock was a tall, impressive-looking man with a jutting jaw and a steely demeanor from under bushy eyebrows. Ads in the Helena paper show that Bullock was in business as an auctioneer and commission merchant. In 1873 he was elected Sheriff of Helena—maintaining law and order was his specialty. The popular Republican knew how to take command of an unruly crowd or demonstrate leadership in the legislature. Seth Bullock had become a young leader on the Montana frontier.

They formed a business partnership in hardware and mining supplies, a joint venture which would last for many years. The business partnership of Star and Bullock made headlines in Montana in June of 1876. They had been transporting a load of hardware between Helena and Benton, when they had to cross the Prickly Pear River, just above a spot where the water became much deeper and swifter. The horses spooked at some floating brush, pulling their freight wagon downstream. After a mighty struggle, the two men managed to get the wagon back to shore, although it was on that same side as it had started out. Once back on shore, the wagon, its contents, and the partners had taken a soaking, but they managed to make it to a nearby ranch for repairs. The next day they were able to complete the crossing successfully, but the misadventure was newsworthy to the Butte Miner.

Bullock married his Michigan childhood sweetheart, Martha Eccles, in Salt Lake City in the spring of 1874, and by 1876 they had a daughter, Madge. For safety's sake, Seth sent Martha and Madge back to Michigan while he and Sol aimed their sights on the stampede into Deadwood, Dakota Territory. Upon learning of their intentions, the Butte Miner published a farewell message to Sol:

> *"Mr. Sol Star, who had recently shipped a large inventory of Queensware to Helena and designed the opening of a store, has taken the Black Hills fever, shipped his goods back from Benton to Bismarck, and designed today to start for Deadwood City. Sorry you are going Sol, but good luck to you."*

Star and Bullock had both "taken the Black Hills fever." They had previously combined their capital and purchased a stock of goods in the East, intending to have these shipped to Helena. Now they decided to head off the shipment and have it freighted to the Black Hills via Bismarck. That summer of 1876, the partners packed up their remaining stock of hardware and mining supplies, and joined a large wagon train of Helena prospectors and businessmen in a trip that would take 27 days. They traveled to the Missouri River and downriver by boat to Bismarck, and then overland with heavily laden wagons pulled by oxen along a route that would later become the Bismarck-Deadwood stage road. Among the 1876 Montanans headed across the plains for Deadwood were two other notable pioneers of European Jewish origin, Jake Goldberg and Sam Schwarzwald.

In the wake of the recent calamitous events surrounding the Custer Massacre at the Little Big Horn, the Indian threat was a serious issue; the Sioux were enraged and ready to defend their territory. As the Montana party approached, they learned that a skirmish between whites and Indians had been fought the previous night. An attack on the outlying settlements or an ambush upon travelers spelled trouble, and the travelers were jittery. There were fresh signs of Indians on Big Bottom, below Whitewood. Perhaps foreshadowing the good fortune that lay ahead, their wagon train was unharmed and they proceeded safely toward Deadwood.

The partners arrived in Deadwood, Dakota Territory, on July 31, 1876, two days before the shooting of Wild Bill Hickok. Deadwood City, a mucky collection of tents and shacks, was one of a string of mining camps in Deadwood Gulch. On August 4, Star and Bullock purchased their first lot on the corner of Main and Wall Streets and hung their shingle from a tent pole. The price they paid for their lot, along with many other historical documents, was later lost in a fire which destroyed Lawrence County courthouse records.

The Deadwood that Star and Bullock arrived at was disorderly and uncontrolled, with gold seekers by the thousands, as well as suppliers, gamblers, saloon-keepers, journalists, doctors, lawyers, hobos, lawmen and dance hall girls. Crudely built saloons, wood frame buildings, supply stores and gambling joints were being slapped up overnight. Shelter could best be described as rudimentary. By the fall of 1876 the population of Deadwood was estimated at from 10,000 to 25,000. With new gold-seekers arriving daily, Star and Bullock, two men deeply rooted in order and stability, found themselves in a chaotic environment.

With their stock of Dutch ovens, fry pans, dynamite, axes, rope, pans ($8), picks ($12), and shovels ($10), all supplies essential to miners, the partners set to work. They had used foresight and brought an inordinately large supply of chamber pots. These sold very well, considering the lack of indoor toilet facilities and the needs of a Deadwood winter. They announced to the Black Hills Daily Times their intention to open an "auction, commission, and storage house," calling it Star and Bullock Auctioneers and Commission Merchants. In 1877 they purchased an adjoining lot from Henry Beaman and Sam Schwarzwald, and expanded their stock to include general merchandise. Their business flourished.

Black Hills Daily Times, Aug 5, 1876
Star and Bullock to open auction and storage house.

Black Hills Daily Times, Apr 21, 1877
Star and Bullock buy lot from Beaman and Schwarzwald.

Black Hills Daily Times, May 26, 1877
Star and Bullock own general merchandise store.

When it was finally judged to be safe, Martha and Madge Bullock followed Seth back to Deadwood, and the Bullocks eventually built a large house near the home of Harris Franklin on Van Buren Street. The Bullocks went on to have another daughter, Florence, whom they called Floy, and one son, Stanley, as well as another adopted boy whom they raised as their own.

Black Hills Daily Times, Aug 6, 1877
Erecting very tasty building in South Deadwood, home at 28 Van Buren St, Deadwood.

In April of 1877 the Times announced that Seth Bullock was Deadwood's new sheriff, succeeding the brief tenure of Sheriff Isaac C. Brown. Sheriff Brown had been involved in the notorious trial of Jack McCall. McCall was accused of shooting Wild Bill Hickok. Three weeks into his job, Brown was killed in a shot through the heart, leaving the post of sheriff vacant.

Black Hills Daily Times, Aug 5, 1876
Isaac Brown, was elected sheriff, McCall trial.

Black Hills Daily Times, Aug 26, 1876
Isaac Brown, shot through the heart, Sunday 20th.

Black Hills Daily Times, Mar 3, 1877
Bullock dispersed crowd in South Deadwood.

Black Hills Daily Times, Apr 9, 1877
Seth is Deadwood sheriff.

POSTMASTER

Among Star's earliest ventures into public service was accepting an appointment as Deadwood's postmaster. In 1876 Deadwood was relatively isolated, with few routes of communication. The issue of mail to and from "the states" had to be addressed. U.S. mail service was instituted in April of 1877 and Richard O. Adams was commissioned Deadwood's first postmaster. Mail was of prime importance; arrivals and departures of mail were announced in the newspapers on page one, column one, right below the masthead, along with publication information and the weather report. Business communications were imperative. Besides, a miner had to get a letter to his sweetheart or a letter from home. He had to share news of his grand success, or unburden himself of his dismal luck. But the mail was subject to the vagaries of unpredictable weather, unreliable transportation, and local delays created by blocked streets.

Black Hills Daily Times, Apr 27, 1877
Deadwood Post Office, 6000 letters to hand out.

Black Hills Daily Times, Apr 28, 1877
63 men stood in line for mail.

Black Hills Daily Times, May 5, 1877
Seventy-five men wait in line for mail.

Black Hills Daily Times, May 7, 1877
South Deadwood scuffling over mail.

Black Hills Daily Times, May 8, 1877
Deadwood Post Office received 500 pounds of mail.

Black Hills Daily Times, May 15, 1877
"Patiently wait and trust the Lord."

Black Hills Daily Times, Apr 23, 1878
Mail so wet you could catch cold reading it.

Black Hills Daily Times, Apr 29, 1878
Mail pouch lost in Cheyenne River, recovered.

Black Hills Daily Times, Aug 16, 1878
Mail sack seems to be lost again.

The mail was a particularly sensitive aspect of the government's service, and presented temptation to those placed in that position. Postmaster Adams, after spending two years on the job, from April 1877 through June 1879, was arrested for stealing $2,000 and convicted of mail fraud. He was summarily dispatched to the penitentiary in Sioux Falls.

Black Hills Daily Times, Jun 26, 1878
Alleged deficiency in postmaster Adams' account.

Black Hills Daily Times, Aug 17, 1878
Mail sack seems to be lost again.

Black Hills Daily Times, Aug 19, 1878
Missing mail bag is found. Where was it?

Black Hills Daily Times, Aug 20, 1878
More postal outrages.

Adams was pardoned and released in February of 1881, but meanwhile, Deadwood needed a postmaster. The area's citizens, trusting Sol Star, petitioned the government to appoint Star to the job. The word was out in March that a new postmaster had been appointed for Deadwood, and the Black Hills Daily Times, wondered with a wink, "Did Adams write 'Twinkle Twinkle Little Star"? On June 1, 1879, Sol Star received confirmation of his appointment from President Garfield, and his commission as postmaster was announced in newspapers nationwide. A corner of Star and Bullock's hardware store on Main Street was set aside, and on July 1, Sol Star opened the post office for business.

Black Hills Daily Times, Mar 6, 1879
Has been appointed new postmaster for Deadwood.

Black Hills Daily Times, Apr 7, 1879
Postmaster at Deadwood has celestial name Sol Star.

Black Hills Daily Times, May 24, 1879
Confirmation by Senate of Sol Star as postmaster.

Black Hills Weekly Times, May 31, 1879
Chicago Tribune announces position as postmaster.

Black Hills Daily Times, Jun 1, 1879
Received his postmaster commission from president.

Black Hills Daily Times, Jun 21, 1879
Our new postmaster returned by Bismarck coach.

Black Hills Daily Times, Jun 24, 1879
New post office to be in store on corner of Main. New postmaster will take charge on first of July.

Black Hills Daily Times, Jul 9, 1879
Should have post office all fixed up by week's end.

Sol often received letters from people wanting to come to Deadwood to work, a large majority of these being single women looking for positions as domestic servants. A letter from a young lady and her sister told of how girls wished to come to the Black Hills, but not knowing anyone there, they were afraid to come without the guarantee of a job. Sol handed over one such letter to the editor of the Black Hills Daily Times, who in turn wrote a column encouraging young women to come to the Black Hills for legitimate employment.

Black Hills Daily Times, May 9, 1880
Women write from states to postmaster wanting jobs. "We are able to say the local demand for maid-of-all-work is very strong and active. Several dozen modest and industrious girls could find employment in our best families at much greater salaries than are paid in the states."

Already heavily occupied with his hardware business and deeply engaged in his many civic obligations as well as his local fraternal and social duties, the go-getting new postmaster had accepted this additional responsibility of a demanding federal position. Star was considered the best man for the job and proceeded to apply himself to his new tasks with his usual vigor. He knew what he was up against; any irregularity was an instant public issue. When the mail failed to arrive or when it was late, Star was accountable. Mail had to be handed over in person, requiring miners to come in from their diggings to collect their letters, a situation that almost everyone found inconvenient and irritating.

However, the timing of his confirmation together with his name, Star, were an unfortunate coincidence. The Star Route trials were about to erupt. Sol's confirmation coincided with a time when this added responsibility would weigh him down, implicate him sideways in a nationwide mail fraud scandal, and come close to tarnishing his reputation.

Black Hills Daily Times, Jul 16, 1879
New postmaster is in trouble so soon.

Black Hills Daily Times, Aug 13, 1879
After evaluating postmasters feels he is the best.

Black Hills Daily Times, Sep 30, 1879
Farmer Tyler in town helping Postmaster Star.

Black Hills Daily Times, Oct 17, 1879
Central City friends enduring hardship on mail delivery.

Black Hills Daily Times, Dec 18, 1879
Postmaster wants to know where lock boxes are.

Black Hills Daily Times, Dec 28, 1879
Postmaster Star has fixed up P.O. second to none.

In 1880 real trouble set in. Within six months of Star's assuming office, the United States Postmaster General requested an additional $2 million from the U.S. House Appropriations Committee to cover a shortfall in the star mail routes. The star routes were, as they are today, rural mail routes serviced by private contractors, and designated on post office maps by asterisks or stars. The public erroneously began associating his name, Star, with the major investigation of mail fraud in the star routes taking place in Washington at the time. A debate in the House resulted in a resolution authorizing an immediate investigation of the situation. This caused a shortage in post office funding and consequent slowdown of mail delivery, raising a great furor throughout the West which relied heavily upon these star routes for their postal service. The investigation revealed that indeed there had been mail fraud in some cases. The fact that those found responsible were friends of sitting President James A. Garfield made prosecution difficult, and further action came to a halt. Following Garfield's assassination in 1881 by Charles Guitteau, a thwarted applicant for the post of ambassador to France, the investigation resumed, and under President Chester A. Arthur the Star Route Trials, an infamous national scandal, resumed. The defendants were accused of such crimes as forgery and creating fraudulent rural post offices with spuriously distant addresses in order to increase their pay. A defense attorney for the Star Route Trials summarized what the mail meant to people living in the mining camps: *"These men went all out through the mountains, men that went out there... to hunt for silver and for gold, live in little camps of not more than twenty or thirty, maybe, but they wanted to hear from home just as bad as though there had been five hundred in that very place. And a fellow that had dug in the ground about eleven feet and had found some rock with a little stain on it and had had the stain assayed, wanted to hear from home right off. He stayed there and dreamed about fortune, palaces, pictures, carriages, statues, and the whole future was simply an avenue of joy upon which he and his wife and the children would ride up and down. He wanted to write a letter right off. He wanted to tell the folks how he felt... He felt rich; he was sleeping right over a hole that had millions in it..."*

The government now looked with suspicion on anyone associated with the postal service. A special federal mail investigator was named and John Furay was sent from Washington to examine Deadwood's postal records. His assignment was to obtain depositions from Sol Star and other postal workers and report his findings back to Washington. Furay's report to Washington asserted that he had obtained a "confession" from Sol Star. Although the press would have gleefully printed such juicy gossip had this been made available, it was clear there was little merit to the claim. The alleged "confession" never saw the light of day, and the allegation remained dubious.

Star, meanwhile, continued to improve the post office and the mail service, carrying out his duties in the best way possible despite the hovering cloud of suspicion and the occasional jibe from the press. For all his good work, however, damage had already been done.

Black Hills Daily Times, Jan 1, 1880
Postmaster at the Deadwood Post Office.

Black Hills Daily Times, Jan 6, 1880
Bloated [post] office holder here to make report.

Black Hills Daily Times, Feb 21, 1880
Postmaster to be notified when mail coming in late.

Black Hills Daily Times, Feb 25, 1880
Disgruntled pointing at him as post office problem.

Black Hills Daily Times, Feb 26, 1880
Something of great importance to the Black Hills.

Black Hills Daily Times, Feb 28, 1880
Receives notice from Sidney stage of mail cutback.

Black Hills Daily Times, Mar 5, 1880
Spearfish to receive mail four times a week now.

Black Hills Daily Times, Apr 24, 1880
Postmaster at Sturgis says there was no mail bag.

Black Hills Daily Times May 15, 1880
Postmaster, there is irregularity in mail service.

Black Hills Daily Times, Nov 18, 1880
Cause for complaint against Post Office too limited now.

Black Hills Daily Times, Dec 3, 1880
Daily mail service on Pierre route starts next Sun.

Black Hills Daily Times, Jan 8, 1881
Telegram from Rapid, 25 sacks of mail at office.

Black Hills Daily Times, Jan 12, 1881
He says blame weather not stage & railroad for late mail.

As the scandalous affair continued to evolve, most of the citizens of Deadwood stood solidly behind their popular postmaster. Clearly, he didn't need the money, as his thriving businesses demonstrated, and it was unlikely that he would have jeopardized his standing in the community for whatever small profits he would have gained. Moreover, his integrity was beyond question. The Black Hills Daily Times offered support, referring to his accusers as "persecutors," claiming that removing him as postmaster would "cause a public calamity" and that Star had brought the post office "almost to perfection."

Black Hills Daily Times, Mar 8, 1881
Removal as postmaster would cause public calamity.

Black Hills Daily Times, Apr 13, 1881
Brought post office almost to perfection.

Black Hills Daily Times, Apr 21, 1881
Takes trip down the road to prospect eastern mail.

Black Hills Daily Times, Apr 22, 1881
Went to Rapid in search of mail, found only mud.

Black Hills Daily Times, Apr 26, 1881
Left Deadwood on mail hunting expedition.

Black Hills Daily Times, Apr 29, 1881
Brings mail back from trip down the road.

Black Hills Daily Times, Jun 5, 1881
Gentlemanly postmaster has vanished from our midst.

Black Hills Daily Times, Jun 7, 1881
Postmaster returns from trip to his farm.

Black Hills Daily Times, Jul 2, 1881
Says we shall have 2 daily mails without delay.

Black Hills Daily Times, Jul 6, 1881
Helped lower price of post office box to $1.

Black Hills Daily Times, Jul 19, 1881
Postmaster to spend a day or two at home.

Black Hills Daily Times, Jul 26, 1881
His placid smile again haunts the post office.

Black Hills Daily Times, Sep 5, 1881
His reports didn't agree with Furay's.

Black Hills Daily Times, Sep 6, 1881
To be investigated by mail agent Furay.

Black Hills Daily Times, Sep 7, 1881
The return of an indictment would be an insult.

Black Hills Daily Times, Sep 15, 1881
No reason why he should be hauled over the coals.

Star was prepared to explain what he knew about the Star Route situation, but he never got the chance. In October of 1881 he was dismissed by President Chester A. Arthur for alleged complicity in the Star Route mail frauds. A replacement named J.A. Harding was appointed Sol's successor. Temporarily disheartened, Sol sought refuge in the seclusion of his S&B ranch at DeMores.

Black Hills Daily Times, Sep 20, 1881
Harding appointed to succeed postmaster. Has gone east to call on agent Furay.

Black Hills Daily Times, Sep 21, 1881
Rumors that Harding will succeed him confirmed.

Black Hills Daily Times, Sep 29, 1881
Furay endeavored to have post master indicted. President has him removed as Deadwood post master

Black Hills Daily Times, Oct 1, 1881
His confession of star route fraud. What he says about the indictment against him. Confesses to making false certificates of star route.

Black Hills Daily Times, Oct 3, 1881
His persecutors in star route fraud case.

Black Hills Daily Times, Oct 7, 1881
President removes him on charge of complicity.

Black Hills Daily Times Nov 10, 1881
Burying himself in seclusion of ranch.

The post office suffered substantial loss because of the investigation and trials; however, the result was acquittal of everyone involved. Historians now agree that the charges against Sol were baseless and believe that he was the victim of a false accusation by an ambitious investigator bent on destroying the reputation of an innocent man for purposes of furthering his own career.

1882 brought a public outcry demanding that Star be reinstated as postmaster, but Star was already looking forward to other means of participating in leadership in Dakota Territory. Despite the pointless degradation, Star would continue to pursue a lifetime of public service.

Black Hills Daily Times, Jan 25, 1882
Will tell what he knows of former mail service.

Black Hills Daily Times, Mar 9, 1882
Should be reinstated as postmaster.

Black Hills Daily Times, May 3, 1882
Was most efficient & popular postmaster Deadwood ever had.

STAR & BULLOCK HARDWARE

By July 1877, Star and Bullock were prospering as local merchants in Deadwood Gulch. Construction of their store totaled $385. Their letterhead, under a date of July 2, 1877, states "Office of Star and Bullock, Auctioneers and Commission Merchants, Groceries, Queensware, Glassware, Lamps, Boots and Shoes and Miners' Supplies." Beneath that reads, "Fireproof Storage, Deadwood, Black Hills, Dakota Territory."

The partners advertised liberally from the very start; however, their line of goods needed little promotion. Stock moved quickly, and the optimistic young firm grew. In time Star and Bullock Hardware Company would prove to be one of the most successful businesses in the Black Hills, providing equipment and supplies to the prospectors, miners, mine owners and operators, farmers and ranchers, townspeople and their families. By following the progress of their business one also tracks glimpses of the region's progress. By 1878 Star and Bullock were expanding their services, becoming building contractors for local development, providing fencing, iron shutters, fireproof doors, and roofing for business and public projects.

Black Hills Daily Times, April 17, 1878
Bids for fencing and clearing the new cemetery.

Black Hills Daily Times, Feb 8, 1879
Manufactured iron fire-proof doors for Wertheimer.

Black Hills Daily Times, Feb 24, 1879
Putting iron shutters on court house.

They made frequent buying trips eastward to keep up with their customers' needs. Of necessity, stock became more varied. Besides the usual mining and agricultural hardware and merchandise, they supplied the region with some of the amenities of modern civilization. Everything from tableware to birdcages to buggies were regularly advertised in the newspapers. They offered cupboards with doors to keep the flies away from the food, quite innovative according to some of their less domesticated customers. Freight brought in by ox train from Bismarck and Sidney and Cheyenne sold as quickly as it arrived.

In May of 1879 they erected an unusually large sign on a hill on the west side of the Gulch. They also installed a large sign high above the roof of their building with 6-foot-tall gilded letters. Their famous sign could be seen from great distances.

Black Hills Daily Times, Apr 11, 1879
Sol Star goes east on Monday.

Black Hills Daily Times, Apr 12, 1879
Star & Bullock. Onion seeds & onion sets just received at store.

Black Hills Daily Times, Apr 14, 1879
Went east on a purchasing tour this evening

Black Hills Daily Times Apr 23, 1879
Bullock tending the store since Star went east.

Black Hills Weekly Times, May 10, 1879
Star & Bullock. Erected a way up sign on hill below Boulder flume.

Black Hills Weekly Times, May 17, 1879
Have 2 car loads of harvesting implements on way.

Their storefront proclaimed their supply of Queensware crockery, a popular variety of English tableware, which they imported from London and Liverpool. Shipments from Liverpool in 1879 arrived in 55 days, fairly amazing considering the obstacles to shipment.

Black Hills Weekly Times, May 31, 1879
Star & Bullock. Received crates of crockery 55 days from Liverpool.

Black Hills Daily Times, Jun 1, 1879
Importing some crockery directly from London.

Black Hills Daily Times, Jul 4, 1879
Received a (ox) train load of reapers & mowers.

Black Hills Daily Times, Jul 11, 1879
Star & Bullock. Have sold 10 reapers & 14 mowers this season.

Black Hills Daily Times, Jul 27, 1879
Sol Star was in Chicago yesterday.

Black Hills Daily Times, Aug 19, 1879
Received lot of grind stones from Chicago in 16 days.

Black Hills Daily Times, Aug 26, 1879
Threshing machine turning out 1,000 bushels a day.

In August 1879, as part of an improvement to the hardware store, the partners built a 25-foot addition to their warehouse in Ingleside.

Black Hills Daily Times, Aug 29, 1879
Erecting 25' addition to warehouse in Ingleside.

Black Hills Daily Times, Sep 5, 1879
Has $150 French plate windows in position.

Black Hills Daily Times, Sep 12, 1879
Star and Bullock. Only merchants to pledge $100. to fire fund.

Black Hills Daily Times, Sep 18, 1879
Have hoisted a chandelier to match French windows.

1879, the year of the Great Fire, was a landmark year for all of Deadwood. Four weeks after making a sizable donation to the fire fund in hopes of improving the fire hose company's capacity to fend off the dread enemy, the unthinkable happened. On Sept. 26, 1879, a day that Seth Bullock termed Black Friday, more than 300 homes and businesses were lost in the Great Fire. Their hardware store incurred losses in the amount of $18,000. Like many other businesses in town, the fearless young businessmen were not to be defeated. The value of a fireproof building to Deadwood was confirmed, and within three days, temporarily operating out of a fireproof part of the building that had survived the blaze, they were back in business, preparing to rebuild. Like their fellow citizens, the partners were compelled to adjust to each new set of circumstances and move on.

Black Hills Daily Times, Sep 27, 1879
Star & Bullock. Losses in the big fire of September 26, $18,000.

Black Hills Daily Times, Sep 30, 1879
Operating out of fireproof, building new store.

Black Hills Daily Times, Oct 1, 1879
Star & Bullock erected a tin shop in rear of fireproof since fire.

Black Hills Daily Times, Oct 1, 1879
Canary & bird cages at Star & Bullock, ad.

Black Hills Daily Times, Oct 2, 1879
Star & Bullock. High wind yesterday blew in sides of new building.

Black Hills Daily Times, Oct 5, 1879
Star & Bullock will occupy their new quarters today.

Black Hills Daily Times, Oct 14, 1879
Star & Bullock Foundation of building ready, adjoining Beaman's.

Black Hills Daily Times, Nov 4, 1879
Star & Bullock Fire-proofs saved in the big Deadwood fire.

Black Hills Daily Times, Dec 6, 1879
Freight Bound hillwards from Bismarck.

Black Hills Daily Times, Jan 10, 1880
Incoming freight from Bismarck.

Black Hills Daily Times, Feb 29, 1880
Freight bound hillwards from Sidney.

Their Deadwood headquarters alone couldn't keep up with the demand; they were obliged to branch out. By 1886 Star and Bullock were selling hardware and equipment from stores in Billings, Carbonate (now a ghost town), DeMores (today's Belle Fourche), Spearfish, Whitewood, Sturgis, Rapid City, and Custer.

Black Hills Daily Times, Mar 28, 1880
Arranging for a branch at Rapid of Star & Bullock

Black Hills Daily Times, Apr 30, 1880
Have large force of laborers & stone masons at work.

They placed more orders for merchandise from the east, hired a sizable force of laborers and stonemasons, and set to work building a large brick warehouse with a 2-story wood frame store facing Main Street. By May of 1880 the basement of their new structure was completed and by June the brick work was almost finished. This time around, the new addition would have fireproof metal doors. By September they had installed the plate glass windows and were ready to start operating out of their new fireproof building.

Black Hills Daily Times, May 19, 1880
Have basement of new building completed.

Black Hills Daily Times, Jun 9, 1880
Brick work is nearly finished on new building.

In one advertisement in the Times, their hardware store offers a treadmill for dog-power as a creative, if questionable, way to churn butter.

Black Hills Daily Times, Jul 3, 1880
Have tread mill to churn butter by dog power.

Black Hills Daily Times, Aug 1, 1880
Moved goods out of store, carpenters at work

Black Hills Daily Times, Sep 14, 1880
Putting new plate glass front in hardware store

Great new inventions were being patented and released. Star and Bullock were prepared to present the latest in technological advances to their customers. In 1877 Thomas Edison patented his cylinder, or tin foil phonograph. In 1880 Deadwood's first phonograph showed up on Star and Bullock's shelves and those who saw it at the hardware store recommended it to others. When telephone service came to Deadwood, Star and Bullock's Hardware Store was among the first to subscribe. The new technology would further enhance their business.

Black Hills Daily Times, Oct 13, 1880
Those seeing phonograph recommend others view it.

Black Hills Daily Times, Apr 3, 1881
Star & Bullock. Deadwood merchants have a telephone.

Business was booming, yet it was necessary to conform to the mores of the community, closing on Sunday, as did the other merchants.

Black Hills Daily Times, Oct 29, 1881
Seth Bullock. Agrees to close business on Sundays.

Black Hills Daily Times, Jun 2, 1882
Star, Bullock & Co. Opening hardware establishment at Billings, Mont.

Black Hills Daily Times, Oct 8, 1882
Subscriptions secured for telephone line extension.

Black Hills Daily Times, Jun 16, 1883
Star & Bullock. Making arrangements to open out at Sturgis.

Black Hills Daily Times, Jul 1, 1883
Star & Bullock Purchased Harmon's store, in Sturgis, $8,000.

Black Hills Daily Times, Jul 3, 1883
Sol Star, Leaves for Chicago, purchase goods for Sturgis store.

Black Hills Daily Times, Jul 7, 1883
Star & Bullock. Not leaving Deadwood, establishing a branch at Sturgis.

In a tongue-in-cheek ad, the Crowning Glory brand stove was claimed to do everything but "start itself and cut its own firewood."

Black Hills Daily Times, Mar 1, 1883
Crowning Glory, handsomest cook stove made, saws & cuts its own wood, ad

The difficulties of transporting goods over trails in the 1870s and early 1880s were formidable, and increased their costs significantly. Nothing in Deadwood came cheaply or easily. It's hard to imagine the obstacles to transporting window glass under these conditions.

Black Hills Daily Times, Jul 10, 1884
Bull train finally arrives. Star & Bullock's bull train arrived from Medora yesterday, loaded with window glass. It encountered rough weather and road the entire distance; was nineteen days enroute, and was compelled to unload and load five times.

The one-story brick they built in Spearfish in 1885 underwent remodeling and in February of 1886 they announced an addition, a two-story stone structure in an adjoining building, to replace their salesroom. They would fit out the upper story as an opera house.

Black Hills Daily Times, Apr 28, 1885
Star, Bullock and Bishop will erect a 50-60 one story and basement brick block at Spearfish, work to begin at once.

Black Hills Daily Times, Jul 15, 1885
Star and Bullock to build with stone. Owing to poor quality of brick manufactured at Spearfish, Star and Bullock will build their new block (building) largely of stone.

Black Hills Daily Times, Aug 14, 1885
Joe Henry over from Spearfish and says Star and Bullock's new block is under roof; music hall closes for the season.

Black Hills Daily Times, Sep 10, 1885
Deadwood, through its representative business houses, is becoming closely allied with Sundance.

Black Hills Daily Times, Sep 22, 1885
Anchor and Suttler is the name of a new firm that embarks in the saloon business at Spearfish today, in the old Star and Bullock building.

Black Hills Daily Times, Feb 3, 1886
An entire business block at Sundance destroyed by fire.

Black Hills Daily Times, Mar 1, 1887
Star and Bullock, wholesale and retail dealers in mine and mill supplies, hardware, tinware, iron, nails, steel, cook stoves, ranges, heaters, etc., wagons and buggies, agricultural implements, wallpaper, oils, paints, window glass, cutlery, silverware, glassware and Queensware. Deadwood, Dak. — branch houses at Custer, Spearfish, Sturgis, and DeMores.

Black Hills Daily Times, Feb 21, 1886
Star and Bullock will this season build a brick block at Spearfish, adjoining the one now occupied by the firm. They will also replace their sales room, this city, with a magnificent brick, the upper portion to be fitted as an opera house.

Black Hills Daily Times, Aug 1, 1886
Loftiest bulletin in the territory. Star and Bullock are having their elevated sign regilded, 350 feet above the roof of their building, with six-foot letters.

Black Hills Daily Times, Aug 17, 1886
Powder unloaded in Deadwood and Lead. Noah Newbanks on Sunday and yesterday unloaded 125,000 pounds of powder at Deadwood and Lead. Star and Bullock's new magazine, Deadwood gulch, received its first consignment.

In October of 1886 a fire charred many of Spearfish's major business buildings, damaging the building housing Star and Bullock's Hardware, but it was restored and was doing business again in 1887.

Black Hills Daily Times, Oct 12, 1886
Spearfish in ashes. One of the principal business blocks of Spearfish burned; 10 business houses and contents, including the hotel, destroyed; as many more buildings damaged to a greater or less extent involving a loss of $70,000.

Their hardware business branched out into the neighboring territories of Wyoming and Montana, with stores in Sundance, Wyoming, and Billings, Montana. New homes were springing up to accommodate the growing population. In addition to such mining necessities as dynamite, Star and Bullock offered housewares. In January of 1883 they advertised having received 5,000 rolls of wallpaper. A mountainous selection, stacked almost to the ceiling, could actually present something of a hazard to the unwary shopper.

Black Hills Daily Times, Mar 3, 1887
A rack of wallpaper toppled over at Star and Bullock's, nearly burying Johnnie Ayres. He received a number of bruises.

Black Hills Daily Times, Apr 3, 1887
Old and well-known firm of Star & Bullock, hardware and agricultural implement dealers, incorporated with the firm name of the Star & Bullock Hardware company, absorbing the Sherman street and its Carbonate branch of James Anderson.

Black Hills Daily Times, May 1, 1887
Star & Bullock Hardware Company's primer: A - axes, adzes, anvils, augers, ammunition, agate iron ware; B - belting, bellows, babbitt, bolts, brushes, buckets; &c., &c. Full page advertisement

Although mining and housewares remained their mainstay, contracting was a significant division of the hardware business. They secured the contract for the roof of the Masonic-Odd Fellows temple at Lead as well as the tin roof of the Molitor building.

Black Hills Daily Times, Oct 19, 1887

Star & Bullock have the contract for putting the roof on the Masonic building at Lead, instead of Geo. Hearst as stated previously.

Black Hills Daily Times, Nov 2, 1887

Star & Bullock Hardware company have just completed the tin roof of the Molitor building and are now at work on roof of Masonic-Odd Fellows building at Lead.

Black Hills Daily Times, Jun 1, 1888

Star & Bullock to open hardware store at Whitewood.

AGRICULTURE—S&B RANCH

Unidentified man, Sol Star, and Seth Bullock on bridge over Redwater River near S&B Ranch
Photo courtesy Adams Museum

By 1879, despite the early threat to the outlying regions by Indians, Star and Bullock had extended their interests into the fields of agriculture and stock-raising, a fast-growing segment of the local economy.

Homesteaders and ranchers settled in the rich agricultural bottomland along the Redwater and Belle Fourche rivers, which became the primary source of livestock and food for the flourishing gold camps of Lead and Deadwood. As homesteading and agriculture increased in the fertile valley east of Deadwood, farm implements and equipment were in heavy demand.

Black Hills Daily Times, Mar 31, 1879

Star and Bullock received 50 plows on Saturday and the demand for them up to noon today was so active that the entire lot will readily be sold. This will be in addition to the number given in our editorial on Thursday that justifies an increase in our estimate fully 1/4. Of course, we have no data upon which to base an estimate made of the crop that will be raised this year, but the sale of two or three hundred plows by the merchants of Deadwood is a gratifying fact that our agricultural development of the year will be on a scale that no one hardly (sic) dreamed of and we confidently anticipate with it a result that will astonish the country and have a most important and beneficial effect on our material growth and prosperity.

Black Hills Daily Times, Sep 10, 1879

Six threshing machines are running in the valley.

Black Hills Daily Times, Apr 4, 1880

How they are crowding into our valleys.

Black Hills Daily Times, Apr 6, 1880

Extended tour of our tributary valleys.

Black Hills Daily Times, Jul 18, 1880

Samples of wheat and rye on exhibition at store

Black Hills Daily Times, Sep 29, 1880

Wanted-Three men to work on a ranch.

Black Hills Daily Times, Oct 5, 1880

Corn on exhibit that was raised on their ranch.

In 1881 the ranch produced the first crop of alfalfa in Dakota Territory. They exhibited their livestock and prize-winning grain crops at the various state and county fairs. Meanwhile, their hardware business was kept busy selling agricultural equipment and implements.

Black Hills Daily Times, Mar 23, 1881
Have 5 car loads of fence wire coming from Pierre.

Black Hills Daily Times, Jul 16, 1881
Have sold 4 steam threshing machines this year.

Their S&B Ranch, at the confluence of the Belle Fourche and Redwater Rivers, made up of land purchased from homesteaders in the Belle Fourche valley, became a major cropland and cattle-raising area. The ranch dealt in first-quality livestock, thoroughbred horses, and high-quality varieties of grains. The S&B became renowned for its thoroughbred trotting horses.

As they built their line of livestock, gradually their Star and Bullock Stock Farm Company's reputation grew. The ranch was acclaimed for producing some of the finest horses to be found. Announcement of a livestock sale at the S&B Ranch attracted buyers from around the country.

Black Hills Daily Times, Feb 1, 1881
Negotiating for Col. Benteen's thoroughbred stallion.

Black Hills Daily Times, Feb 17, 1881
Purchased Col. Benteen's celebrated stallion.

Black Hills Daily Times, Apr 17, 1881
Have put in 300 acres of small grain at Redwater.

Black Hills Daily Times, May 1, 1881
Slowly increasing worldly possession in stock line.

Black Hills Daily Times, May 18, 1881
Bought mare from the late M.G. Chase's stock.

Black Hills Daily Times, Aug 4, 1881
Are exhibiting oats grown on their ranch.

Black Hills Daily Times, Oct 24, 1881
Contributed varieties of wheat to Nebraska fair.

Through their heavy engagement in agriculture, in 1882 both Sol and Seth became members of the local Agricultural Review Society.

Black Hills Daily Times, Mar 30, 1882
Sol Star, Seth Bullock, Soon to become members of Agricultural Review Society.

Black Hills Daily Times, Apr 25, 1883
Have over 200 acres finished in wheat.

Black Hills Daily Times, Sep 27, 1887
St. Patricks Day, the trotting colt, was purchased of Star & Bullock by Barnes & Co., who will take him to Rapid.

Sol enjoyed his weekend trips to the ranch whenever he could escape his many responsibilities in town. He attached particular importance to fine horses, and at the ranch he could ride one of his splendid mounts, oversee the livestock, or assess the agricultural situation in the valley.

Black Hills Daily Times, Feb 25, 1885
Mayor Star went out to his ranch on yesterday, to be absent until tomorrow.

Black Hills Daily Times, Mar 26, 1885
Mayor Star took a spin out to his ranch yesterday. He will return today.

Black Hills Daily Times, Mar 27, 1885
Sol Star and Seth Bullock came in from the ranch, last evening. Farmers are busily engaged seeding.

Black Hills Daily Times, May 3, 1885
Mayor Star went out to his Belle Fourche ranch last evening.

Black Hills Daily Times, Sep 8, 1885
Mayor Star returned from trip through the northwestern portion of the county, finding grain damaged

to some extent, but the situation far from what represented.

Black Hills Daily Times, Jul 11, 1886

Messrs. Bullock and Star left for their Belle Fourche ranch last evening.

The Elkhorn Railroad reached Whitewood from Rapid City and points south in 1887, three years before it ever arrived in Deadwood. Star and Bullock were able to ship their valuable livestock to Chicago via Rapid City along that line.

Black Hills Daily Times, Aug 14, 1888

First and valuable shipment of blooded stock from Star and Bullock Stock Farm Company to ship from Whitewood to Chicago via Railroads.

Names for Sol's horses and his interest in politics intermingled. One horse was named for a Montana politician, Joe Toole. Another favorite horse was named Valentine for his friend Dr. Valentine McGillycuddy, mayor of Rapid City.

Black Hills Daily Times, Oct 6, 1889

Mayor Star back in the saddle. The sylph-like form of Mayor Star was seen in the saddle yesterday, the first time since '78. He rode Valentine for which handsome animal he now has a very tender regard.

Black Hills Daily Times, Jan 1, 1890

Star and Bullock Stock Farm Company. Williamsburg — brief sketch of an interesting horse.

Black Hills Daily Times, Jan 31, 1890

Star & Bullock sustain loss of "Joe Toole" from distemper, horse named after Montana's illustrious democrat.

Black Hills Daily Times, May 18, 1890

Stallion loss a heavy one. Dakota Onward, handsome and valuable stallion imported by S&B. stock farm, died of lung fever.

Black Hills Daily Times, Jun 6, 1891

Isaac G. Pfantz of Pennsylvania is here to look at mines and attend sale of S&B Stock Farm horses at Belle Fourche.

Black Hills Daily Times, Jun 11, 1891

Young gets well-deserved thrashing. John H. Young bid in a number of horses at Star and Bullock stock sale, but didn't have a cent to his name.

The railroad's decision of where to locate a bridge, a town, or even a whistle-stop, could make or break a prospective community. Under highly competitive circumstances, the town of Minnesela, just three miles to the southeast of the Star and Bullock Ranch, lost its bid for a station when a speculator purchased the right-of-way to Minnesela and demanded a high price from the railroad. Star and Bullock stepped up to the challenge and offered the railroad 40 acres of free right-of-way across their land, convincing the railroad to continue on to the ranch. Anyone moving from the town of Minnesela was offered free lots in the newly founded town of Belle Fourche, formerly called DeMores. Belle Fourche subsequently became the Butte County county seat and the largest railhead for livestock in the territory, and Minneselans were irate.

DEADWOOD FLOURING MILL

During the initial years of the gold rush, flour had to be freighted into Deadwood from points east. This situation began to change with the construction of a flouring mill in Spearfish in 1879. The new mill was a combination grist mill and saw mill, and the first flour from the Spearfish mill found its way into Deadwood stores in March of 1880. The example set by Spearfish was soon followed by Crook City, followed by one on the Redwater at Minnesela. Now Deadwood needed its own flouring mill. A contract was let to Robert Hood for the construction of a mill, and by July of 1881 carpenters were putting up the framework for the mill on upper Main Street, on the property adjoining the parochial school. The owners of the new mill were Sol Star, Seth Bullock, Robert Hood, and Harris Franklin.

Sol was now the part-owner and new general manager of the Deadwood Flouring Mill. He rented a log house near the shingle mill where he could be close to his work. His brand of flour, "S.S.S." flour, for Senator Sol Star, a name that seemed to meet the approval of the community, was advertised as the best in the West.

Black Hills Daily Times, Apr 15, 1881
To rent log house near the shingle mill.

Black Hills Daily Times, Dec 31, 1881
Brand of flour called "S.S.S" named for him.

Sol wanted no one to go hungry. In 1883 he delivered a supply of flour to the Indian Reservation, spending the next five weeks at the agency among the Sioux, and visiting with his friend, Indian agent Dr. Valentine McGillycuddy, one of the most influential men in Western Dakota Territory.

Black Hills Daily Times, Jul 27, 1883
Took flour from Deadwood Flouring Mill to Indian agency.

Black Hills Daily Times, Aug 7, 1883
Returned from 5 weeks' picnic with the Sioux.

When the company's prestigious name seemed to be in danger of faltering, Star resolved to keep his company strong. In July of 1884 the original company was dissolved and reorganized as Deadwood Flouring Mill Company. Comprising the new board were Sol Star, Harris Franklin, Ben Baer, and Daniel McLaughlin.

Black Hills Daily Times Jul 1, 1884
Notice of Dissolution. Notice of partnership between Seth Bullock, Sol Star, Robert Hood and Harris Franklin, doing business as the "Deadwood Flouring Mills," is this day dissolved.

Black Hills Daily Times Jul 19, 1884
We understand that Sol Star and Mr. Wager, of the Deadwood mill, go east the first of the month, for the purpose of purchasing additional machinery. The Deadwood flour mill has always been considered one of the best in the west, and Mr. Star does not propose that it shall lose its prestige.

Black Hills Daily Times, Oct 9, 1884
A new organization completed by election of officers for the Deadwood Flouring Mill Company.

Star devoted whatever spare time he had to working at the flour mill. He traveled east with W.A. Wager, the mill's supervisor, to purchase new equipment. They installed a rather startling alarm whistle, an alert to assure the necessary continuous flow of water to the mill. In July of 1886 they gave the mill a thorough overhaul just to keep the equipment in good condition.

Black Hills Daily Times, Jan 10, 1885
Continued blast of whistle merely a preemptory call for Star and Wager to inform them the water supply had ceased at the flour mill. Flow did not reach Deadwood until toward evening.

Black Hills Daily Times, Jul 16, 1885
Messrs. Star and Wager working unceasingly, despite the idleness of the flour mill, placing the establishment in thorough repair.

Black Hills Daily Times, Sep 10, 1886
Mayor Star puts in his spare moments firing at the flour mill.

Wheat crops from the S&B ranch were processed at the flouring mill. In October of 1886 they had harvested 300,000 pounds of wheat at the ranch which awaited transportation to the mill.

Black Hills Daily Times, Nov 13, 1886

Transportation wanted for 300,000 pounds of wheat on Star and Bullock ranch to flouring mill.

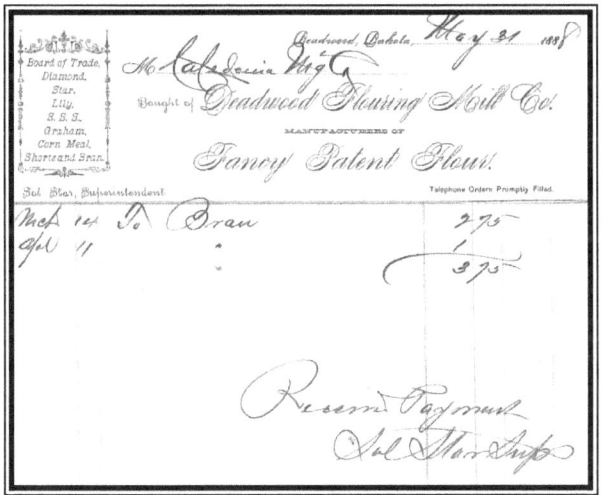

Photo courtesy Jerry L. Bryant

FIRE PREVENTION

Fire, natural or human-caused, was the formidable enemy of the early settlers of Deadwood Gulch. Dry, dead pinewood and thick underbrush filled the narrow three-mile strip of canyon, which soon after the initial discovery of gold began filling up with tents, log cabins and wood frame buildings jam-packed together. It was tinder for a blaze. In December of 1876 a committee of three men, including Star, felt it was critical to take some action to prevent a disaster. This committee would inspect chimneys, provide ladders for reaching the upper stories, and require fire buckets and water barrels in each building. They began forming the first volunteer hose companies, practicing regularly, and engaging in competitions to sharpen their skills. In June of 1877 the first hook and ladder company was organized and in October 1877 a fire watchtower was built on a mountain overlooking Deadwood to monitor the city and the surrounding forests. Whether as private citizen, city councilman, or mayor, fire control was one of Star's primary concerns.

Black Hills Daily Times, Sep 6, 1877

Star and Bullock's fireproof caves in.

Black Hills Daily Times, Jan 3, 1878

Sol Star, committee appointed to raise funds for fire safety.

Black Hills Daily Times Jan 4, 1879

Special meeting of Board of Fire Commissioners.

Black Hills Daily Times Jul 24, 1884

Ordinance No. 73: An ordinance concerning the storing and sale of kerosene or coal oil, gun powder, and nytro glycerine (sic). Restricts kerosene or coal to 200 gallons without obtaining permission; gun powder and nitro to 100 pounds.

Black Hills Daily Times, Feb 18, 1885

Mayor Star ordered 500 feet of hose, a play pipe, one dozen spanners and hydrant wrenches combined, and two pick axes for the department.

Black Hills Daily Times, Feb 9, 1888

Fire at Central (City) seriously threatened destruction of the entire town. Eaves' stable, a large log two stories in height, entirely enveloped in flames. Eaves' loss was from $100 to $200.

Black Hills Daily Times, Oct 29, 1889

Neat job on city hall. N.J. Tuplin is heartily congratulated for successful raising of new fire bell to new city hall belfry.

Black Hills Daily Times, Apr 6, 1890

Alarm sounds for ugly blaze in stable owned by Star & Bullock. Inflammous character of building made it impossible to more than prevent spread of flames. Report circulated that tramp perished in the flames.

In order to support the hose companies and to purchase equipment, frequent fundraising social events were held. These events brought out some of the finest of legitimate entertainment and recreation, sometimes local talent, but also outstanding performers from the outside.

Black Hills Daily Times, Mar 19, 1885
South Deadwood hose company entertained with a musicale in its parlor last evening. Aaron Hattenbach,

Black Hills Daily Times, Jan 3, 1886
A happy event universally and enjoyably observed; elaborate receptions by the fire department largely attended; other events.

Black Hills Daily Times, Mar 17, 1886
Solomon Star, L. Reuben, Department meeting at South Deadwood hose to appoint committees to act on electric fire alarm and arrange forthcoming benefit performance.

Black Hills Daily Times, Mar 23, 1886
The laddies and their alarm fund. Electric alarm fund to be supplemented by performance of Pearson's Theatre group.

Black Hills Daily Times, May 19, 1886
Red-letter day for South Deadwood Hose. Pomp and circumstance laud arrival of new hose cart. Herman Bischoff thanks Deadwood band for their services.

Black Hills Daily Times, Jul 7, 1886
Deadwood contingency returns from Rapid. Mayor Star and city officials and the Hook and Ladder and South Deadwood companies returned from Rapid.

Black Hills Daily Times, Jan 22, 1887
To benefit fire department. Blind Boone to present benefit concert for South Deadwood Hose company.

Black Hills Daily Times, Dec 10, 1889
Reception and dance committees named. Fire board names reception and floor committees for Christmas night dance.

Black Hills Daily Times, Dec 27, 1889
Deadwood fire department Christmas evening reception and dance a most pleasurable event; description of new fire hall.

Black Hills Daily Times, May 1, 1890
Solomon Star, Fire alarm ready for active service. In sounding alarm by hand, from six to ten rapid strokes should be given, followed by signal for each ward.

In 1891 sparks from the flouring mill started a grass fire behind the building. A team of young firefighters, including young Morris Liebmann, doused the flames, averting a serious blaze.

Black Hills Daily Times, May 7, 1891
Gallant fire laddies. Sparks from Deadwood flouring mill set fire to grass behind the building and started a conflagration, that but for prompt action of juvenile hose team would have proved serious.

The flouring mill survived several fires, but in 1896 a fire broke out in the boiler room. Because of a delay in getting the hose and water on, the mill was destroyed and never rebuilt. When he disposed of his interests in the flour mill, for a time Star lived practically retired. But in 1899 public duty again called, and Sol was elected to Clerk of Courts

GOVERNMENT

In 1876 white people were trespassers on Indian land. The territorial government at Yankton was powerless to control the area. According to the Fort Laramie Treaty of 1874, the Black Hills were still part of the Great Sioux Reservation. Deadwood was in Dakota Territory, not yet truly part of the United States. It remained without legitimacy or local government, and except for the jerry-rigged miner's meetings, there was little in the way of a legal system. One of Deadwood's earliest needs was for some form of legitimate organization and governance. As former register of the land office at Helena, Montana, Sol Star brought with him valuable experience.

The year 1877 ushered in major changes. The first county commissioners were named by

Governor Pennington, bringing the first "legal" law to the Black Hills. The county commissioners authorized a survey of Deadwood in order to plat the city. An election was held, and Deadwood won by 340 votes, making the city the seat of Lawrence County. Proposals for a 50 x 50-foot courthouse were accepted. The busy calaboose was moved to South Deadwood and became the Lawrence County jail. A county recorder was needed to keep records on mines and real estate. John Lawrence, the county treasurer, was authorized to issue licenses and collect taxes.

There were pressing needs for regulations governing sanitation, building codes, and business license fees to provide operating funds. In Deadwood's first election, held in September of 1876, 1139 men (women had yet to gain the vote!) voted on organizing a provisional city government. 1,082 voted for organization and 57 voted against. E.B. Farnum was elected Deadwood's first mayor and ex-officio justice of the peace. Con Stapleton was elected city marshal. The large Montana contingent had considerable voting strength during its first summer in Deadwood.

One of the main responsibilities of the fledgling city government was to establish a system of taxation in order to fund its activities. Revenues were crucial if Deadwood were to develop. Businesses of all types were the first to be taxed.

Local merchants, influential in city government, were determined to retain business in their own hands. Along with the more traditional targets of taxation, licenses were created for every type of business, and some were specifically aimed at outsiders. Hawkers and peddlers were taxed, quite exorbitantly, at $25 per quarter, under the proposition that they were itinerants.

Black Hills Daily Times, Nov 25, 1879

Patronize home institutions, don't buy from salesmen. Rosenthal.

Black Hills Daily Times, Sept 17, 1885

D. Goldberg and his auctioneer, Milinix, neglect to take out any of the required territorial or county licenses as peddlers or auctioneers. Complaint lodged and Goldberg fined $50. Complicated application to county commission results in no license.

LEADERSHIP

Sol Star's integrity was widely acknowledged, and as such he was accorded many positions of confidence. That he was highly regarded by his fellow citizens was demonstrated by the number of personal estates entrusted to his care.

Black Hills Daily Times, Dec 8, 1877

Sol Star made special administrator, Kitty LeRoy estate.

Black Hills Daily Times, Jan 6, 1877

Sol Star, administrator of Ben Keller estate.

Black Hills Daily Times, Apr 1, 1879

Sol Star, administrator of the estate of Charles E. Barker.

A committee was formed in April of 1877 to decide on permanent organization of the city and Sol Star was among the committee members. He won a seat on the first official city council, receiving more than half the vote, to become one of the five city council members.

Black Hills Daily Times, Sep 16, 1876

Sol Star runs for Council in Deadwood.

Black Hills Daily Times, Oct 28, 1876

City Councilmen. Sol Star, Keller Kurtz, Joseph Miller, H. C. Philbrook.

Black Hills Daily Times, Dec 30, 1876

Sol Star, Sign notice of City meeting.

Black Hills Daily Times, May 8, 1877
Sol Star delegate to the Convention.

Black Hills Daily Times, Sep 13, 1877
Sol Star on executive committee in New Territory.

Black Hills Daily Times, Oct 2, 1877
Sol Star on committee to view Deadwood's streets.

Black Hills Daily Times, Oct 4, 1877
Sol Star calls for general election.

Black Hills Daily Times, Dec 2, 1877
Sol Star on committee appointed to secure patent for townsite.

Black Hills Daily Times, Feb 11, 1879
Bills allowed by new board of County Commissioners.

Black Hills Daily Times, Jun 4, 1879
Sol Star. Deadwood Corresponding Society of the Washingtonians.

Sol Star was once more elected to the board of aldermen, or city council, and would again serve from 1882 to 1884.

Black Hills Daily Times, Oct 22, 1885
The people's movement. Petitions or calls were circulated and numerously signed for a citizen's meeting, Re: management of county affairs — the undersigned request people to meet Oct. 22 to discuss the situation.

Black Hills Daily Times, Oct 24, 1885
Lawrence county Committee of safety meeting of the committee of 15 held last evening.

Star's leadership was appreciated, although appreciation could take a quirky turn, as when a specialty cigar was named for "our popular mayor" by the firm of Lowerre and Hathaway during Sol's last term in office. At other times tribute was bestowed by more traditional means.

Black Hills Daily Times, Feb 1, 1890
Star portrait at fire parlor. Magnificent portrait of Hon. Sol Star placed in fire department parlors yesterday. It was taken by John H. C. Grabill.

Black Hills Daily Times, Jan 12, 1892
Mayor Star presented handsome scarf pin, symbol of executive position.

Sol Star's leadership skills rewarded him with a steady stream of public offices, city, county, state, and federal. He was endorsed as Republican nominee for U.S. Congress in 1890. The citizens of Deadwood nominated Star for mayor repeatedly and Star accepted. He had his opponents, but attempts to oppose him vanished into thin air; no one could compete with his charisma or the many benefits Star brought to Deadwood. Once Star made his first bid for the mayoralty of Deadwood, winning over K.G. Phillips in 1884, it was the beginning of a 14-year run of holding the mayor's seat. In 1886 Sol's name once again appeared on the city ticket. In 1887, a petition was circulated asking for Sol to accept another term as mayor. He obliged, overcoming opponent Miller by nearly a clean sweep in the election of 1888. In election after election the citizens knew who they wanted. The press, also in support of Sol, exhorted the public to participate in performing their civic duty by voting, and in 1892 Sol once again prevailed in Deadwood's mayoral election. The position of mayor paid the princely sum of $300 per year or $25 a month, considerably more than he had earned as alderman, which was zero.

Star was a fearless leader. In 1882 the Deadwood city council had been under the control of an entrenched group of influential local politicians, known in the town as the "Solid Six." The stage was set for corruption, and Sol's acceptance of the nomination to city council was acknowledged as a direct challenge to a precarious situation. A successful race would mean breaking up this group. Sol confronted the "Solid Six" and by defeating an opponent named Lawrenson in the councilmen's race, he redefined Deadwood's city politics.

Black Hills Daily Times, Mar 27, 1882
Star accepts nomination as councilman.

Black Hills Daily Times, Apr 19, 1882
Solid 6 thought themself shrewd in "Third Ticket"

Black Hills Daily Times, Apr 28, 1882
Success of Star means breaking up of solid six.

Black Hills Daily Times, May 2, 1882
Vote for him will assist in removing solid six.

Black Hills Daily Times, May 3, 1882
Star defeats Lawrenson in Councilman's race.

Black Hills Daily Times May 7, 1884
Results of mayoral race in Deadwood. Sol Star beat K.G. Phillips. Winning council seats: Second Ward; H.H. Kiemer.

Black Hills Daily Times, Apr 15, 1885
Who the people want. Names of those endorsing Sol Star as mayor.

Black Hills Daily Times, Apr 28, 1886
City ticket carries Sol Star for mayor.

Black Hills Daily Times, Apr 12, 1887
Petition asking Sol Star to accept another term as mayor. Star accepts.

Black Hills Daily Times, May 2, 1888
Victorious — practically a clean sweep at yesterday's election; Star elected; Mr. Miller defeated for mayor and alderman.

In a headline endorsing Sol Star for Clerk of Courts, the Black Hills Pioneer Times in October 1906 summarized Star's political career as well as their esteem of his character.

Black Hills Pioneer Times, Oct 21, 1906
With such a man as Sol Star, the able clerk of courts, numbered among its candidates, strength is conceded to the Republican ticket. Name over the list of old-timers, and find if you can the man without a host of friends to swear by him, and then add to this the friends gained through a career of impartial, judicious, and liberal treatment to all and you have Sol Star. One of Mr. Star's strongest endorsements for re-election is the known fact that he handles every phase of his work with a precision that shows he has it at his fingertips and that no matter what the nationality of anyone with business at the clerk of courts office, he invariably goes away satisfied.

Underlying his work, and to which is largely due his success, is the long experience that Sol Star has enjoyed in political circles. Personal contact with every branch of city and county affairs, and a personal acquaintance with the men who have and are conducting the business of state, together with the knowledge of their work, has taught him the secret of getting on in politics— and for that matter, in life— the ability to correctly read the character of all with whom he comes in contact. His charity is one of the strongest of his own characteristics, and many a man has sought and found the aid that Sol never refuses.

Personally he is an optimist, full of dry wit that is always appropriate and to the point, and always the master of any situation in which he finds himself. A fluent talker and speaker, an able parliamentarian, courteous and affable, it is small wonder that members of the bar requested his renomination and that he invariably runs ahead of his ticket.

Sol Star was raised and educated in the Buckeye state where he arrived at the age of 9 years. Early in 1865 he emigrated to Montana, reaching Deadwood August 1, 1876. He engaged in the mercantile business and was for 13 years Mayor of Deadwood and the man to whom is due to credit for nearly all of the present city improvements. He was president of the Republican state convention held under statehood, elected to the first state legislature in the 1889 and (blur), aided in the election of United States Senator

G.C. Moody in 1893, was elected to the Senate, being unanimously chosen president of the body and has since been identified with every enterprise in the city. He is a prominent member and officer of several secret societies.

Black Hills Daily Times, Mar 1, 1885
Mayor Star is in receipt of a magnificently engraved invitation to the inaugural ball at Washington, next Wednesday.

He was chosen president of the first Republican convention at Huron. Sol was twice elected to the South Dakota House of Representatives, initially in 1889, while Dakota was still a territory, and then again in the fall of 1892. In 1892 he was elected state senator and served one term in the upper house. Applying his characteristic intrepid opposition to measures he did not agree with, he quickly gained a reputation for his thoughtful attention to the work of government, and was elected president of the Senate without opposition. Sol was endorsed for a seat in the U.S. Congress, but he preferred to remain in South Dakota.

Black Hills Daily Times, Jan 31, 1890
Representative Star sends copy of house bill creating office of mine inspector in Deadwood.

Black Hills Daily Times, Feb 1, 1890
Deserved compliment to Representative Star. From Pierre — Legislature has member from Black Hills, Sol Star, fast gaining a strong foothold in the house because of careful consideration he gives all subjects and the fearless way he has of opposing measures he does not think to be right.

Black Hills Daily Times, Jan 3, 1891
Persons who left by special car for Pierre to attend organization of legislature.

Black Hills Daily Times, Feb 23, 1891
Seth Bullock and Lawrence County Republicans want Deadwood's mayor for Congress strongly endorsed by the convention held here yesterday of the Independents.

No-one achieves the prominence, influence, and financial status of Sol Star without incurring some measure of antipathy. There were those who might have welcomed an occasional change in the pattern of Deadwood's habit of re-electing Star mayor. Even these citizens understood the importance of what Sol Star was doing for Deadwood, and continued to support him. Perhaps Star's greatest compliment came not from one of his supporters, but from one of his critics.

Rapid City Journal, May 5, 1891
"I don't like Star altogether, but I have voted for him a number of times and will do so again. He's one of the most charitable men I ever knew. His charity is not of the kind that parades itself, but it has done a great deal to relieve poverty and distress wherever he has found it. Many a poor person has received aid from his private means. I don't know that this is any great part of the secret of his popularity, but it has done much to make me a Star man."

Black Hills Daily Times, Sep 23, 1891
Lawrence County Independents and Republicans want Deadwood's mayor for Congress; strongly endorsed by the convention held here yesterday; they were all for Star.

Black Hills Daily Times, May 3, 1892
Every voter owes it to himself and to the good of the city to vote at the city election. Run-down on candidates. Solomon Star,. L. W. Gilman, John Treber, L. R. Graves, J. F Edmonds.

Black Hills Daily Times, May 4, 1892
Victorious! We elect our mayor and three out of four aldermen; Solomon Star.

Black Hills Daily Times, Aug 30, 1884
Sol Star, Republican primaries will be held throughout the county today.

Black Hills Daily Times, Sep 26, 1884

Lawrence county delegation to Rapid City convention departs today.

Black Hills Daily Times, Oct 13, 1886

District convention. The ticket for members of council and brief report on Republican convention, Solomon Star, Harris Franklin.

Black Hills Daily Times, Mar 2, 1888

Local representatives of territorial committee. Republican: Sol Star.

Black Hills Daily Times, Aug 15, 1888

All citizens who desire success of Republican party requested to meet Aug.15 for organization of Republican club.

Black Hills Daily Times, Mar 17, 1892

Lawrence County Republican convention held, resolution passed, committees appointed.

In the spring of 1879 Deadwood was still a ward of Lawrence County. Campaigning for Deadwood city autonomy, in a strongly-worded letter, somewhat reminiscent of the United States Declaration of Independence, Sol Star wrote to the Black Hills Daily Times:

Black Hills Daily Times, Apr 10, 1879

THE CITY OF DEADWOOD: Webster's dictionary gives this definition of the city: "a corporate town; in the United States account of collective body of inhabitants, incorporated or organized by a mayor or aldermen." Under this definition the city of Deadwood only exists in the collective body of its inhabitants, and we are a city without a name or duties and without those common rights that belong to every American city. We are utterly powerless to enforce or to protect any of those rights, and the only privilege we have is that of beggars who may humbly supplicate the power that holds the destiny of the country within its all-powerful grasp, to bestow upon us such protection as they may deem proper. We are forbidden the privilege of electing our own officers; we can pay taxes but we cannot vote to choose our own rulers for the purpose of helping to bear the burdens of government; we are full grown men and citizens, but for the purpose of enjoying its rights and principles, we are puny children- wards of the County- incapable of taking care of ourselves. And so the county commissioners become our guardian, and furnish our officers ready made, who are liable to be mere political favorites, with no character and nothing to recommend them to the people they are to govern and control.

A city of the population of Deadwood should have a local self-government whereby they could choose their own rulers who should be directly responsible for their own laws affecting their municipal rights and city interests. The result as it now stands is that the people of the county make the laws and furnish the officers for the city. The theory of municipal inferiority and dependence and that we are incapable of self-government is fully carried out in practice.... signed, Sol Star

Fully engaged in many areas of public affairs and commerce, Sol held memberships on a multitude of committees and boards.

Black Hills Daily Times, Feb 6, 1881

Sol Star, Corresponding secretary, Deadwood Board of Trade.

Black Hills Daily Times, Feb 24, 1881

Bill for erection of Dakota College.

Black Hills Daily Times, May 31, 1881

Chairman of Citizen's Central Committee.

Black Hills Daily Times, Dec 12, 1882

Deadwood Library Association met at court house.

Black Hills Daily Times, May 13, 1882

Sol Star, Board of trade meeting.

Black Hills Daily Times, Oct 3, 1884

Regular monthly meeting of the Board of Education authorizes borrowing of $2,000.

Black Hills Daily Times, Jan 7, 1887
School Board met to allow bills; heard report from city clerk on delinquent tax report; receive and act upon report of Judge McLaughlin.

Black Hills Daily Times, Jan 22, 1887
First step for organization of Deadwood Stock Exchange taken last evening. Charter obtained last summer, but nothing done towards organization.

Black Hills Daily Times, Jun 21, 1890
Black Hills Electric Light Company elects officers. Harris Franklin, Solomon Star, Paul Rewman.

Sol's participation in federal, state and local government lasted through the administrations of 11 Presidents, beginning with Ulysses S. Grant (1869-1877), Rutherford B. Hayes (1877-1881), James A.Garfield (1881), Chester Allen Arthur (1881-1885), Grover Cleveland, (1885-1889), Benjamin Harrison (1889-1893), Grover Cleveland, (1893-1897), William McKinley (1897-1901), Theodore Roosevelt (1901-1909), William Howard Taft (1909-1913) and finally Woodrow Wilson (1913-1921). While Mayor of Deadwood, Sol was invited to the inaugural ball of Grover Cleveland, whose second term as President came to a sudden and tragic end on September 19th of 1881, when he died as the result of bungled medical treatment following a shooting.

DEVELOPMENT

Between Star's work on Deadwood's City Council and his years as mayor, he either participated in or presided over much of Deadwood's earliest development. He saw the expansion of civic improvements, from the most basic to some of the most eventful in Deadwood's history.

Black Hills Daily Times, Aug 30, 1884
Mayor Star and Marshal Tyler, surveyed the ground preparatory to building an east approach to the Lee street bridge.

Black Hills Daily Times, Dec 10, 1884
Pound ordinance. Notice is hereby given that all livestock found within the city limits of Deadwood on and after the 11th last, will be impounded under the city ordinance. By order of Sol. Star, Mayor.

Black Hills Daily Times, Dec 30, 1884
Sol Star: Telegram received that order prepared for removal of land office from Deadwood. Return telegram asked stay of proceedings.

Black Hills Daily Times, Apr 10, 1886
Notice of resolution for paving Main and Lee streets.

Black Hills Daily Times, May 11, 1886
Committee on right-of-way for proposed railway to Hay Creek coal fields requests meeting with property holders.

Black Hills Daily Times, May 26, 1886
Deadwood City council authorizes contract for immediate macadamizing of Main Street

Black Hills Daily Times, Jul 13, 1887
Sidewalk resolution approved by council.

Black Hills Daily Times, Jul 28, 1887
Raising property values in Deadwood. The assessed valuation of Deadwood increased over $40,000.

Black Hills Daily Times, Sep 8, 1887
Notice of adoption of resolution for bulkheading Whitewood Creek.

Black Hills Daily Times, Dec 30, 1890
Passenger train welcomed. Dec. 29 a historical day for Deadwood, with arrival of first passenger train.

Black Hills Daily Times, Jun 18, 1891
Resolution providing for construction of sidewalks.

Black Hills Daily Times, Jan 1, 1892
Black Hills Electric Light company organized in 1883 and is a credit to any city in the country.

Black Hills Daily Times, Feb 16, 1892

Star reports on federal building. Letter to Sol Star from J.A. Pickler that we are assured by sub-committee that it will report Deadwood public building bill to whole committee.

Black Hills Daily Times, May 5, 1892

Notice of special election for bonds in sum of $40,000 for sewer and water improvements.

LAW AND ORDER

Shortly after arriving in the Hills, Sol's partner, Seth Bullock, began his career in public service with an appointment to the Board of Health and Street Commissioners, a direct response to a sudden outbreak of smallpox. This was the first public body of any permanence and authority to exist in the northern Hills gold camps. The board was authorized to assume virtual control of Deadwood as long as the threat of smallpox existed. Assured that its orders would be backed up— with firearms, if necessary— they began by acquiring a public subscription building fund to locate a "pest house" where smallpox victims could be confined. Then, as now, the "not-in-my-backyard" mentality prevailed, and finding a location proved to be a dilemma.

By 1877 his partner Seth Bullock was well-established as Deadwood's sheriff.

Black Hills Daily Times, Oct 13, 1877

Sheriff Bullock, wants fumigation of 2 "pole-cats"

Deadwood was a magnet for outlaws of all kinds— horse thieves, road agents, and gunslingers were the most obvious. But pickpockets, swindlers, and other bad actors mingled with the gamblers, drunks and prostitutes. Star was determined to establish law and order. He and Bullock used their influence, Star, the administrator, and Bullock, the lawman, in a battle against the odds to tame the town.

Black Hills Daily Times, Aug 11, 1885

City lock-up. It has been suggested that the city purchase of the county the two iron cells now in use at the county bastille.

Black Hills Daily Times, Aug 22, 1885

Star performed a very wise act in directing Marshal Dunn to order Baldy Ford to leave town instantly.

Black Hills Daily Times, Apr 27, 1886

Six piratical appearing individuals of the genus tramp were arraigned before Justice Hall yesterday. They were guaranteed safe escort beyond the city, and proceded towards Sturgis and Rapid.

Black Hills Daily Times, May 4, 1886

Dan Dority shot three times and seriously wounded by Pat Casey.

Black Hills Daily Times, Jul 1, 1886

John Donaldson and Al Marx refused permission to fight by Mayor Star on basis of ordinance against prize fighting. Donaldson declares intention of meeting Marx on the date set, July 3, at any place to be designated by Marx.

Black Hills Daily Times, Nov 19, 1886

City prisoners not wanted at new jail. Deadwood city council to meet in special session to discuss resolution of Lawrence County to not accept city prisoners.

Black Hills Daily Times, Nov 20, 1886

Mayor Star denies statement in yesterday's Pioneer, that he had "very emphatically expressed himself on the question (care of city prisoners) and gave it as his opinion that the action of the board was illegal...."

Black Hills Daily Times, Feb 3, 1887

Entire police force issued caps with words "city police" by Mayor Star.

Black Hills Daily Times, Aug 16, 1888

A neck-tie party is not beyond possibility if a certain gang of pick-pockets and rollers do not cease their work.

Sol was concerned with the upbringing of the youngsters of the town, encouraging good behavior in boys with offers of a cadetship to Maryland Military and Naval Academy at a reduced rate to nominees. Rowdyism was met with putting parents and guardians on notice, and imposing a curfew. A saloon-owner could risk revocation of his license if caught allowing a minor to frequent his establishment.

Black Hills Daily Times, Sep 4, 1886

Mayor Star in receipt of letter offering to confer a cadetship at reduced rates upon son or any other young man nominated to Maryland Military and Naval Academy.

Black Hills Daily Times, Jan 19, 1887

City council adopts resolution to revoke licenses of saloons that minors are permitted to frequent.

Black Hills Daily Times, Mar 1, 1887

Notice of parents and guardians – A certain class of boys have existed in this community to the constant annoyance of the police, and the utter disgrace of the city. From and after this date, boys under the age of 21 years will not be permitted on the streets of Deadwood after the hour of 9 p.m. o'clock, unless accompanied by parent or guardian.

Black Hills Daily Times, Dec 23, 1887

A party and present for every Deadwood child organized.

Star and Bullock had as much to do with laying down law and order in Deadwood as any two individuals. In 1878 there was little doubt who would be the Republican choice for sheriff of Lawrence County. Sheriff Bullock kept a tight grip on his domain, locating the first jailhouse behind the Star and Bullock building.

The gold boom attracted personalities who ensured that Deadwood was never dull. Profanity was rampant, and it was irksome, particularly in the presence of respectable women and young children. Star's administration acted to rein in the use of bad language as part of their effort to clean up the town. In 1891 the consequence of cussing could occasion a stay in the calaboose.

Black Hills Daily Times, Aug 1, 1891

A.B. Stockmorton, Louis Jones, E. Westinger, R.B. McDonald, Andrew Palmer and Robert Evans, laborers employed by J.H. Damon, arrested for their language.

As long as they paid their taxes— and Deadwood entrepreneurs paid exceedingly well— local government was obliged to permit businesses of all stripes to operate, including the saloons, dance halls, and brothels. There was a great deal of profit for those who supplied the freely flowing alcohol, a reality that conflicted with the personal values of Star, himself a temperance man.

Black Hills Daily Times, Aug 4, 1885

In cleaning Mayor Star's private rooms, yesterday, the janitor discovered a bushel basket full of temperance tracts.

Except in the most egregious of cases, Sol was compelled to balance the need for building a city with keeping the most unwholesome element in check, while keeping his personal convictions steadily in front of him. He had learned well from his days at in Helena. Life in a frontier mining town meant whiskey and prostitution and criminally bad behavior. This was a rough crowd.

Black Hills Daily Times, Jul 31, 1887

Mayor Star receives telegram from Omaha stating, "our wives, professionally known as Misses Fenton and Saunders, are forcibly detained at Gem theatre." Law responds to find women leisurely strolling the street.

Black Hills Daily Times, Nov 18, 1890

A matter of fancied revenge. "The saloon men of Deadwood showed how little manhood they possessed when they made a fight on Sol Star."

With lofty principles as his guide, during his years as mayor he worked for prohibition and higher moral standards in the wide-open town, one-third of whose population consisted of a criminal element. His policies occasionally raised eyebrows. One of his opponents in a mayoral race was Romeo Dwyer, owner of a local saloon and son of the madam of a brothel. As mayor, Star found the mother-son operation particularly obnoxious and Dwyer's candidacy, above all, brazenly arrogant. He raided the brothel and closed down Dwyer's saloon, causing some of his local constituency to object. They pressured Star to reopen Dwyer's saloon, pointing to the considerable revenues generated by those businesses needed to support the economy.

MINING

Not only had the partners found a mercantile gold mine in Deadwood, but like most of their contemporaries in business, they were invested in mining as well.

Black Hills Daily Times, Aug 15, 1881

Star & Bullock. Promoters of new Mining Co. Iron Hill

Among other mines, they held stock in the Carbonate Mining Company, whose main resource was silver. Star was elected president of the new Franklin Mining Company in August of 1881.

Black Hills Daily Times, May 3, 1877

Star, Bullock, and Wiser owner Portland lode.

Black Hills Daily Pioneer, May 9, 1878

Application for a patent, Notice No. 23.

Black Hills Daily Times, Aug 2, 1881

Star & Bullock, Stockholder in 2nd Carbonate Mining Co.

Black Hills Daily Times Aug 3, 1881

Selected president of the new Franklin Mining Co.

The Iron Hill Mine at Carbonate Camp, a short-lived boom-town, was one of the more hopeful prospects for Deadwood's mining investors. The Iron Hill was producing high-grade silver, and in January of 1885, 200 tons of sacked silver ore sat on the sidewalk in front of Star and Bullock's Hardware, awaiting shipment to the smelter.

Black Hills Daily Times, Dec 8, 1885

Messrs. Star and McPherson returned from Iron Hill Mill with three handsome bricks. The high state of purity speaks loudly to the credit of those in charge.

Black Hills Daily Times, Jan 5, 1885

A large pile of Iron Hill ore, sacked, ornaments the sidewalk in front of Star and Bullock. Two hundred tons will be shipped.

Black Hills Daily Times, Jun 11, 1886

J.K.P. Miller and Seth Bullock went over the proposed route of new free Carbonate road yesterday and are convinced that the road is not only practicable but can easily be constructed.

Black Hills Daily Times, Nov 18, 1887

A trip to Carbonate camp and back by Times reporter with Sol Star and John Treber, behind his matched span of flyers.

Despite the investment and prospects, the Iron Hill and the other mines of Carbonate soon played out, and Carbonate, once a flourishing community with several Jewish residents and investors, became an inaccessible ghost town within a few short years. Other mining investments were more profitable.

HEALTH

Spirited and energetic as he was, Sol Star's health was a problem. He was plagued with discomfort from headaches and "rheumatism," or arthritis. He tried what remedies were available, including trips to Hot Springs, where the warm mineral waters occasionally offered some temporary help.

Black Hills Daily Times, Feb 11, 1881
Sol Star took to his little bed with sick headache.

Black Hills Daily Times, Sep 23, 1884
Seth Bullock contracted rheumatism while at Pierre and on his return became absolutely helpless.

Black Hills Daily Times, May 15, 1885
Mayor Star is badly crippled with rheumatism, and immediately upon organization of the new council will proceed to Hot Springs, Fall River county.

Black Hills Daily Times, May 19, 1885
Mayor Star and W.A. Wager leave in the morning for Hot Springs.

Black Hills Daily Times, Jun 2, 1885
Head miller Wager returned from the Hot Springs last Saturday. Mayor Star is improving and will remain until the last rheumatic kink disappears.

Black Hills Daily Times, Jul 3, 1885
Mayor Star will return from Hot Springs tomorrow. His health is greatly improved.

Black Hills Daily Times, Jul 8, 1885
Mayor Star speaks in the highest terms of the curative properties of the water of Minnekata.

Seth Bullock was subject to a similar ailment, which also crippled him up on occasion.

Black Hills Daily Times, Jul 3, 1886
Mayor Star is again much of an invalid with rheumatism.

Black Hills Daily Times, Sep 26, 1886
Mayor Star is confined to his room with a cold.

Black Hills Daily Times, Sep 28, 1886
Mayor Star continues on the sick list. He ventured out yesterday, but for a short time only.

Black Hills Daily Times, Sep 29, 1886
Mayor Star was much better yesterday.

Black Hills Daily Times, Sep 30, 1886
Mayor Star is rapidly recovering from his, at one time, threatening illness.

Black Hills Daily Times, Dec 1, 1886
Mayor Star again wears a cane, rendered necessary by a periodical attack of rheumatism.

Black Hills Daily Times, Jan 4, 1887
City council meeting Jan. 3. Deadwood City council met minus Mayor Star, absent through indisposition.

Black Hills Daily Times, Jan 11, 1887
Mayor Star continues a great sufferer with rheumatism.

Black Hills Daily Times, Dec 7, 1887
Mayor Star was confined to his room yesterday with a violent attack of neuralgia, a chronic malady with his honor.

Black Hills Daily Times, Dec 8, 1887
Mayor Star is on his feed and feet again.

Medicine was still very primitive. Popular remedies and treatments appealed to those desperate for relief. Sufferers were willing to grab at almost anything that appeared promising.

Black Hills Daily Times, Dec 10, 1887
Tom Powers sent up galvanic battery received by Will Frasier and set up to relieve rheumatism. When it wouldn't work, Fred Eccles observed Pat Lynch holding wires tightly, quietly remarking, "Well, no wonder; the darned thing's grounded. Pat, go wash your hands." Pat complied, it worked.

Black Hills Daily Times, Feb 7, 1888
Mayor Star was on the sick list yesterday.

Black Hills Daily Times, Dec 2, 1888
Mayor Star was confined to his bed yesterday, with a nervous headache.

Black Hills Daily Times, Mar 29, 1890

Harris Franklin, Mayor Star and Jack Gray return from Hot Springs, Mayor Star very little, if any, benefited.

Black Hills Daily Times, May 9, 1890

Mayor Star is confined to his bed with a periodical sick headache.

At the time, 90% of all physicians in the United States had no college education. Instead, they attended medical schools, many of which were condemned in the press and by the government as "substandard." There was nothing to limit medical quackery in the Black Hills. With a serious lack of regulation or understanding of medicine among the populace, anyone could set up a practice, advertise at will, and extract money from the desperate and the gullible.

Rapid City Daily Journal, May 1, 1891

DR. WINGARD, DEADWOOD, SOUTH DAKOTA, advertisement

Opposite the Keystone Hotel

Successfully Cures: all forms throat, lung, nerve and blood diseases; all chronic diseases and deformities far in advance of any institution. Those who contemplate going to Hot Springs for treatment in any private or blood disease can be cured at one-third the cost here at home.

LADIES: That tired feeling and all-female weakness promptly cured. Bloating, headache, nervous prostration, general debility, sleeplessness, depression and indigestion, ovarian troubles, inflammation, and ulceration, falling and displacements, spinal weakness, kidney complaints and change of life, consult Dr. Wingard.

EYE AND EAR: Acute or chronic inflammation of the eyelids or globes, far and nearsightedness, inversion of eyelids, scrofulous eyes, ulcerations, inflammations, abscesses, dimness of vision one or both eyes, and tumors of the lid. Inflammation of the ear, ulceration or catarrh, internal or external deafness or paralysis, singing or roaring noises, thickened drums, etc.

SYPHILIS: A disease most horrible in its results, completely eradicated without the use of mercury. Scrofula, erysipelas, fever sores, blotches, pimples, ulcers, pains in the head and bones, syphilitic sore throat, mouth and tongue, glandular enlargement of the neck, rheumatism, catarrh, etc., permanently cured when the others have failed.

PRIVATE DISEASES OF MEN: A special study and practice for many years. Over 2000 cases treated yearly. Recent cases of private diseases cured in a short time. Ulcers, tumors, blotches on the face or body cured without giving mercury or other poisons. By a remedy of great curative power he has arranged his treatments that it will not only afford immediate relief but permanent cures.

In an era when doctors might be distrusted, people often sought lay practitioners and snake oil vendors. They applied home remedies or purchased patent medicines through mail-order sources. Some pernicious medicinal concoctions were actually poisonous, such as those that included mercury or arsenic, but many more were alcohol-based. Some had other harmful or addictive ingredients like opium and cocaine. Addictive disorders were a serious health issue throughout the country, particularly in rural areas where physicians and hospitals were scarce.

Star understood suffering. One of his great hopes was to bring a better way of treating illness to Deadwood. In 1892 he met with a small group to form a division of the Hagey Institute, a nineteenth century organization intended to provide health care, with particular attention to addictive problems. The efficacy of their claim remains doubtful in light of today's medicine, but the Hagey Institute of Deadwood also guaranteed a cure.

Black Hills Daily Times, May 6, 1892
Hagey Institute. Organization of company and officers elected.

Black Hills Daily Times, May 15, 1892
Hagey Institute of Deadwood — a cure guaranteed.

EVENTS

Star and Bullock took part whenever a celebration, fair or parade needed to be assembled. Whether by contributing money or services, exhibiting livestock or entering a horserace, it would have been unusual not to have their participation.

Black Hills Daily Times, Jul 1, 1879
Star & Bullock Executive committees on July 4th celebration meet.

Black Hills Daily Times, Aug 22, 1881
Will exhibit 2 thoroughbred bulls at fair.

Black Hills Daily Times, Sep 16, 1881
Exhibited thoroughbred stallion at fair.

Black Hills Daily Times, Sep 19, 1881
Contributed thoroughbred horses to fair.

Black Hills Daily Times, Sep 26, 1883
Citizens who have contributed to Deadwood Driving Park.

Black Hills Daily Times, Jul 3, 1884
Fourth of July celebration ready. Arrangements complete for celebration; city gaily decorated for the occasion; fireworks received; programme of exercises.

Black Hills Daily Times, Sep 16, 1885
An auspicious opening of the exposition, with a very fine display and additions coming in hourly; extensive display of horses and livestock; Deadwood wins.

Black Hills Daily Times, Sep 19, 1885
Fair ending. Another day's pleasure and a large crowd at the fair ground; a large number of distinguished visitors; Meade vanquishes Rapid by a narrow margin; horse and hose races featured for today. Seventh Cavalry band.

Black Hills Daily Times, Oct 7, 1886
Auspicious opening of Black Hills Fair. Better weather and conditions generally for a successful turf event could not well be enjoyed, and with stables full of trotters and runners of repute, it would be strange indeed if the meeting now in progress was not a complete success.

Black Hills Daily Times, Jul 6, 1887
The Fourth: how observed at Deadwood and neighboring points; magnificent display and parade by our laddies at Deadwood, and at the opening of the tournament.

Black Hills Daily Times, Sep 21, 1887
Second day of fair more of a success; attendance larger and everybody seemed to enjoy themselves with horse racing and mining contests.

Black Hills Daily Times, Sep 29, 1887
At Rapid fair, Patrick's Day a Star & Bullock colt, takes first money.

Black Hills Daily Times, Sep 8, 1891
Board of trade. Black Hills world's fair convention to meet tomorrow to formulate plan for securing representation at Chicago in '93.

Black Hills Daily Times, Sep 10, 1891
To be represented at world's fair Board of trade. Plan evolved by world's fair convention to secure an exhibit; question to be submitted to vote of the people.

Mayor Sol Star (far right) officially greeting visiting orator William Jennings Bryan, and his family in Deadwood.
Photo courtesy Centennial Collection,
Deadwood Public Library

In July of 1882 Sol had joined a group of buffalo hunters, starting out from Spearfish, returning suntanned and relaxed the following week. Those hunts did have tragic long-term implications for the Indians and the buffalo they depended upon, but unfortunately, this was not of particular concern to the settlers at the time.

Black Hills Daily Times, Jul 13, 1882
Buffalo hunters start out from Spearfish today.

Black Hills Daily Times Jul 25, 1882
Returned from hunt brown as Injun, happy as clam.

FRATERNITIES

Sol's fraternal associations, a major social activity of the day, were no less outstanding than his place in civic affairs. While still in Montana, he was the First Grand Master of the Grand Lodge of the Great State of Montana. July of 1877 marked the establishment of Lodge #7, the Masonic Temple in Deadwood. Sol was one of the primary installing officers at the ceremony, representing the Masonic temples of Montana. He reached the 32nd degree of the Masonic order, and his membership in the Golden Arch Masons would last a lifetime. His extensive Masonic record as reported in the newspaper showed that he was affiliated with all the Masonic bodies.

Black Hills Daily Times, Dec 20, 1877
Sol Star, Masonic social, St. John's Eve.

Black Hills Daily Times, Mar 3, 1885
Sol Star elected officer of Dakota Masons. At a convocation of Chapter Masons, the grand chapter of Dakota organized and Sol Star elected as E.G.S.

Black Hills Daily Times, Nov 21, 1886
Speaking of handsome badges, we are reminded that Mayor Star has, without doubt, the largest, handsomest, and most costly jewel in the territory, presented by Masons of Montana in 1871.

Sol was a prominent member of most of the fraternal orders. He was a charter member and first exalted ruler of Deadwood's Elks Lodge, a member of the popular Olympic Club of Deadwood, a member of the Knights of Pythias and of the order of Red Men, as well as a member of the Ancient Order of United Workmen.

He was a friend to the Chinese, who appreciated his fellowship. Sol had the rare privilege of being invited to their exclusive Masonic Temple and was also invited to a Chinese funeral.

Black Hills Daily Times, Oct 30, 1885
Finely executed oil painting of Sol Star on exhibition at Hamilton's. It was sent to his honor by a celestial female admirer.

JUDAISM

Star openly identified as a Jew, was a Yiddish speaker, and was a member of the Hebrew congregation. He was known to spend the occasional Sabbath at the ranch or in town, possibly taking time from his busy schedule to pass some quiet hours. As a German Jew, Sol no doubt was most comfortable with the more liberal Reform Judaism. His reading from Hebrew scripture at Anna Franklin's funeral would indicate that he learned this as a youngster, and was likely to have been either *bar mitzvah* or confirmed.

Black Hills Daily Times, Nov 29, 1881
Donated money to help Jews

Black Hills Daily Times, Jul 28, 1885
Mayor Star passed the Sabbath in town, returning on yesterday to Spearfish for a week or two. Flour mill expected to start up about the first of September.

He was among the Hebrew congregation which assembled on Dec.1, 1891, to honor Nathan Colman, their long-time acting rabbi, presenting him with an ornate, inscribed gold-topped ebony cane.

Black Hills Daily Times, Dec 1, 1891
Colman surprised by Hebrew congregation. Nathan Colman, on calling at residence of J. Goldberg, finds residence filled with members of Hebrew congregation who had assembled there to cane their acting Rabbi. Sol Star.

SOCIAL LIFE

Estelline Bennett, who grew up in the 1880s, observed the incongruous amusements of the respectable ladies and gentlemen of Deadwood, with their picnics, tennis games, church socials, sleighing parties, and dances, as compared to the rowdy, shabbily sinful behavior that took place every day in the Badlands of lower Main Street. She wrote, *"...it seems so extraordinary that a proper Victorian society flourished in proximity to the nefarious activities of the Badlands."*

The perennial eligible bachelor, Sol was admired by the ladies. He seemed to enjoy a full social life where he attended dances, was a congenial skating partner at the rink, and was involved in organizing the frequent public and private gatherings of the town, yet he remained single.

Black Hills Daily Times, Dec 16, 1876
Grand ball for reopening of General Custer House.

Black Hills Daily Times, Sep 15, 1877
Sol Star at dance at Spearfish House.

Black Hills Daily Times, Jul 12, 1879
Postmaster Star, Sol trying to keep girls from kissing clerk.

Indications are that he did have his eye out for a wife. On December 17 of 1880, a Times reporter got what seemed to be a scoop when he stopped by the post office to pick up his mail. Two of the postal clerks, Tyler and Ickes, wreathed in smiles, informed the correspondent that the postmaster had gone east in a clandestine manner for the sole purpose of getting married. The reporter ended his speculative article by stating, "A new postmistress may be looked for after the holidays, which will be sad news for belles of this vicinity. The boys in the office are jubilant and will make preparations for their chief's return."

The lady in question may have been an entertainer who occasionally appeared in Deadwood. This attractive out-of-town singer and actress, Miss Ida Livingstone, was said to be possessed of a "wonderful voice and a costly wardrobe." Miss Livingstone's reputation varied from notorious adventuress to bestower of great generosity whose "heart and purse were ever open to the needs of the suffering " This was a self-confident and independent woman who could grant a benefit performance at the Lead Opera House one week, and sue the city of Omaha for a defective crosswalk the next.

Being endorsed by the clergy, as Miss Livingstone claimed to be, did lend a certain legitimacy to her performances in the "entertainment district" at theaters such as the Langrishe, the Central, the Combination, and the Metropolitan, all of which were also known to feature acts of far less cultural value. Her performances did not meet with universal approval in Deadwood, however. Perhaps Gilbert and Sullivan operettas were considered a bit high tone in some circles. At the Central Theatre, the performer was *"hissed and insulted."*

Black Hills Daily Times Jul 6, 1879

Ida Livingstone. Combination Theater Company preparing "Pinafore."

Black Hills Daily Times, Jul 8, 1879

Ida Livingstone was hissed and insulted when performing at Central Theatre

Still, Ida's irresistible charms dazzled Sol, who threw her a farewell benefit following her 1880 appearance in Deadwood. Shortly after Ida's departure for Chicago, Sol left for the east, ostensibly on post office business, raising hopes by hinting that he would return with a bride.

Black Hills Daily Times, Dec 5, 1880

Sol Star, Offer to tender Ida Livingstone a farewell benefit.

Black Hills Daily Times, Dec 16, 1880

Postmaster goes to Washington on R.O. Adam's business.

Black Hills Daily Times, Dec 17, 1880

Has gone east for holidays, will return with wife.

It was not to be. The failure to engage a bride did little to bolster Sol's spirits, already dampened by the ongoing Star Route trials. We're left to wonder whether the gentlelady found fault with either life in Deadwood or her suitor, or both. Her theatrical career may have held greater attraction than the dust of a frontier mining town. Whatever the reason, Sol returned to Deadwood in that same state of bachelorhood as he'd left, and remained so for the rest of his days.

Black Hills Daily Times Feb 15, 1881

Sol. Returned from pleasure sleigh ride to Rapid City.

Black Hills Daily Times, Oct 31, 1884

Kiemer hall crowded from early until late last evening. Contests for graceful waltzing, most popular bachelor, and best housekeeper.

Black Hills Daily Times, Dec 10, 1884

The Kazoo band has been engaged to pipe their liveliest dirge as the Early Hour-ers go rolling 'round the rink.

Black Hills Daily Times, Dec 31, 1884

The attraction at the rink last evening—prizes for the most graceful lady skating.

Black Hills Daily Times, Jan 10, 1885

Articles of incorporation prepared for the "Bald Headed Club" of Deadwood.

Black Hills Daily Times, Jan 18, 1885

Not exactly on ice; but the next thing to it — conditions and affairs at both the new and old rink.

Black Hills Daily Times, Jan 28, 1885

Rollerskating clubs organize.

Black Hills Daily Times, Jan 30, 1885

What this great country needs at present is a roller skate with an air brake attachment, and other roller skating tidbits.

Black Hills Daily Times, Apr 2, 1885

Early Hour club entered upon its lease of the new rink yesterday. Polo to be played in strict accordance to Western League rules. Officers re-elected.

Black Hills Daily Times, Apr 18, 1885

Rink crowded last evening for polo event to raise money for fire department.

Black Hills Daily Times, Aug 8, 1885

Judge Hastie is in receipt of a letter from Miss Jean Glass, at El Paso, Texas, in which she wishes to be remembered to her many friends, Mayor Star included.

Black Hills Daily Times, Mar 9, 1886

Hat appropriated for cigar debt. Paul Rewman invited Mayor Star and others into Bews for cigars. He then attempted to give them the slip. His $5.50 hat was appropriated to cover expense.

BULLOCK HOTEL

In 1894, after doing business at Wall and Main Streets as Star and Bullock's Hardware Store for 18 years, fire destroyed the original wood-frame hardware store building and annex for the second time. Discord had erupted in their relationship, and Star had had enough. Bullock wanted to rebuild, but Star backed away, choosing to focus his attention on his other business interests, especially the flouring mill. Ayres had opened a hardware store across the street and Deadwood now needed lodging-places. On the site of the former hardware store, Bullock constructed an impressive hotel decorated in an "Italianate" and Victorian style, with imposing arched windows and a splendid lobby, ideal for visitors or salesmen. This hotel was Bullock's alone, and Star's name was gone. Whatever their disagreement, their partnership dissolved, but their friendship remained solid.

The sandstone for the hotel's blocks was quarried from nearby Boulder Canyon and transported to Sturgis where it was tooled, and then loaded back on the train for Deadwood. The annex on the south which adjoined the hardware store was incorporated into the hotel. The original Bullock Hotel had 64 rooms, a bathroom on each floor, and was quite luxuriously appointed for its time. The first floor boasted a large dining room in the rear, a kitchen and pantry, a sample room where salesmen could store their cases, and offices in the front. The grand opening was held in April of 1896.

Bullock Hotel annex
Photo by Ann Haber Stanton

Bullock had been elected to the territorial Senate in Helena, Montana, where he introduced legislation to create Yellowstone Park. He had earned the rank of captain through his service in Theodore Roosevelt's Rough Riders during the Spanish-American war. He was a close friend of Roosevelt, and in 1905 he organized a group of cowboys to ride in President Roosevelt's inaugural parade in Washington. For all that, even while occupying the post of U.S. marshal, Bullock listed his occupation simply as "gold miner" in the 1900 census. Despite his many accomplishments and contributions to the Black Hills and to the country, Capt. Seth Bullock, remained a strong but modest man.

TRAIL'S END

In 1901, Doane Robinson, South Dakota State Historian, wrote of Sol Star:

"Some men have a genius for popularity. With no effort on their part they become a sort of social or political center from which there seems to radiate an aroma of good fellowship, permeating the entire community. Frank and generous; genial in disposition; ever ready with a helping hand for a fellow in distress; jovial and social, yet, in serious

matters keen and penetrating; sound in judgment; full of resources in emergency; energy unbounded, and a public spirit ready for war in the interests of his town, country, or state. These are some of the characteristics of a naturally popular man.

The combination is not common, it is true, but it exists now and then, as if to demonstrate the possibilities of human nature. Solomon Star, of Deadwood, S.D., comes very near to this ideal, if his fellow-citizens who know him best are fair in their estimate of him.

He writes his name 'Sol,' and is known everywhere as 'Sol' Star. He came to the Black Hills in 1876 with a stock of goods and settled in Deadwood as a merchant. From the very outset, with no public desire on his part, he became a leader. No public gathering was complete without his presence; no enterprise began without his active influence; no delegation left the "Hills" to a convention but Sol. Star was the animating spirit and "set the pace." Without assuming superior wisdom or ability, he was spontaneously accorded a leadership, if not even a guiding hand. He never sought to use his popularity for his personal advantage, but for his friends he was a great power.

His peculiar influence in the Black Hills spread his name throughout the territory of Dakota, from Bismarck to Yankton. Solomon Star was born in Bavaria, Germany, in 1840. He came to this country when young and received a good academic education, although he is not 'college bred.' He is a stalwart Republican. He has filled numerous positions of honor and trust with fidelity and credit. He was appointed by President Grant register of the United States land office in Montana territory. He was also auditor of the same territory. He was postmaster of Deadwood under President Garfield. He was mayor of the city of Deadwood for thirteen years—a very remarkable career in a western city. It is doubtful if a parallel run can be found in the history of the Northwest. It is likewise strong testimony to his executive ability and integrity.

He was chairman of the first state Republican convention, when the state of South Dakota was admitted to the Union. He was also state auditor of South Dakota. In 1898 he was elected clerk of the circuit and county courts of Lawrence County, S.D., and was re-elected in 1900, receiving the highest vote and largest majority. Mr. Star is unmarried.

Although his interest in public affairs has been so conspicuous, his activity in fraternal affairs has been scarcely less marked. He is a member of the popular Olympic club of Deadwood. He is a member of the Masonic order in which he has reached the thirty-second degree. He is also a Knight of Pythias and a member of the order of Red Men, as well as a member of the Ancient Order of United Workmen. This brief epitome of Mr. Star's career gives only a meager idea of his strong personality, which has drawn to him in close friendship more associates than it is the good fortune of many men to enjoy. He is just in the prime of life, and whatever good fortune the future has in store for him, there are but few, if any, of whatever social or political position, high or low degree, but will rejoice in his success [1901]."

Encyclopedia of South Dakota, Robinson, Doane. First Edition, Pierre, S.D., 1925; pp 669-670

An active public servant to the last, Sol Star had served in public office most of his adult life. In his post as Clerk of Courts until the time of his death from pneumonia following a lengthy illness in 1917, Sol Star was said to have been a punctual, careful, obliging and competent official. It was said that his friends found him still on the job, working when he was quite unfit for work and should have been in bed. It took considerable pleading on their part to get him to finally consent to go to the hospital. This was his last service for the county, a service practically unbroken from the first day he stepped to the clerk's desk in January 1899.

On October 10, 1917, at the age of 77, Sol Star died. The death certificate listed chronic pulmonary tuberculosis as his cause of death, the third leading cause of death in the United States at the time.

The Deadwood newspapers carried lengthy, detailed obituaries. As accolades filled the papers, mourners filled the Masonic Temple where an elaborate memorial service was held. Honorary pallbearers included his old partner Seth Bullock; fellow hardware merchant George V. Ayres, and Jewish friend Paul Rewman, all of Deadwood; A.J. Poznansky of Belle Fourche; and Moses Morris, an old friend from his days in Helena, Montana made up the remainder of the group. The lodge room could hardly accommodate the assembled crowds. The Honorable E. W. Martin, representing the Lawrence County bar association, pronounced the eulogy in which he told of the life of Sol Star among the people of the Hills, his goodness, his kindness of heart, and of his unbounded charity. He recalled the active part Star had taken in the civic life of Deadwood, of the interest he had taken in the affairs of the county, territory, and the state, and the part he had taken in their direction. He spoke of the politics and the good that Star's participation in them had done. One newspaper article called it a splendid tribute to the worth of a good man. P.A. Gushurst, vice president of the Society of Black Hills Pioneers, of which Sol Star had been president at the time of his death, spoke of Sol's pioneer experiences and of his career as one of the trailblazers of the country.

Deadwood Daily Pioneer-Times, Oct 13, 1917

All pioneers are urgently requested to attend the funeral services of our late president, Sol Star, at the Masonic temple, Deadwood, Sunday afternoon at 2:30 o'clock. Paul Rewman, Secretary.

"No man was more highly respected in any community nor had more worthy appreciation of people given him, and few men have given a life of as useful endeavor extending over so long a period as has Sol Star. Everyone was his friend and he was friends to everyone. If he had any enemies they were of the political sort, which passed with the sweeping up of the ballots after the election. In the passing of Sol Star the West loses one of those sturdy Pioneers whose efforts have largely, if not entirely, contributed to the bringing of the civilization of the East to the West and the opening up of a wild hunting ground and making it safe for people to come, work, build homes and live."

The Pioneer-Times' observations about Star's character and accomplishments fully agreed with those of his colleagues and fellow citizens. In a life's career that included participation in some of the most historic changes ever witnessed in South Dakota, Sol Star had helped steer Deadwood from a wild mining camp to a stable, prosperous city, and helped to lay the foundation for a strong and respected state.

Star's fraternal affiliations brought him honors from his early days in the West, as Grand Master of the Masonic Temple of Helena, Montana, to Deadwood's Lodge #7, and a long-time member of the Montana Pioneer Society.

President Theodore Roosevelt, the conservationist with whom Seth Bullock had explored Yellowstone, determined that the area be set aside as a great national park. On January 3, 1903, Roosevelt signed legislation creating Wind Cave National Park. Capt. Seth Bullock was appointed supervisor. Thirteen years later, Roosevelt's administration would create the first National Park Service and appoint Seth Bullock its first director.

In September of 1919, Sol Star's long-time friend and business partner, Seth Bullock, died of cancer at his home on Van Buren St. He and Martha are buried high atop Mount Moriah, above Mt. Zion, on the trail to White Rocks. Their grave faces Friendship Tower on Mount Roosevelt, the stony monument Seth helped build to another of his good friends, President Theodore Roosevelt.

Both Sol Star and Seth Bullock recognized the magnitude of events taking shape in their day, and contributed to their documentation. They believed in the necessity for accurate preservation of the history, and as such both served as presidents of the Society of Black Hills Pioneers.

> "He (Sol) has been a resident of South Dakota since pioneer days and has seen a marvelous development that has taken place in the almost 40 years that have elapsed since his arrival in 1876. When he came to Deadwood he moved his goods with a team of oxen and although he crossed the Sioux reservation was unmolested by the Indians. A few years previously when he had moved his goods from Missouri to Montana he also made the journey by ox team. On his arrival in the Black Hills there were still many buffalo, deer, and elk; everywhere were evidences of primitive conditions. He has not only witnessed the change that has transformed this region to a settled and prosperous section, but has done his full share in bringing this about and he deserves the honor and respect that are paid to those who by their labors have made possible the development of today. His reminiscences about pioneer life do much toward giving the present generation some idea of life in the early days of the state".

Kingsbury's History of South Dakota

Solomon Star, this symbol of Western character, also exemplified some of the highest ideals of Jewish living. While practicing his personal values of honesty, fairness, morality, and charity, his spirit of service to his community can be seen in the long years of devotion to public office and his many quiet acts of generosity. Of all the outstanding accomplishments of his lifetime spent in Deadwood, perhaps one of the greatest was that while Sol Star owned his flouring mill, no one in Deadwood went hungry.

Louis Swarts, Sol's nephew from St. Louis, arrived in Deadwood to accompany his uncle's body back to St. Louis for further services and interment. With no children of his own, all he had he left to his relatives.

Deadwood Daily Pioneer-Times, Oct 13, 1917

Mr. Swarts, a nephew, arrived from St. Louis to accompany the body back to that city for burial. Honorary pallbearers included Seth Bullock, Deadwood; George V. Ayres, Deadwood; Paul Rewman, Deadwood; A. J. Poznansky, Belle Fourche; Moses Morris, Helena, Montana.

Sol Star was buried in New Mount Sinai Cemetery and Mausoleum, Affton, St. Louis County, Missouri.

Photo courtesy Jerry L. Bryant

LEVINSON

LEVINSON BUILDING - 657 MAIN ST.

Continuing up Main Street, I arrived at a building whose cornice proclaimed the name Levinson. I learned that Sol Levinson was born in Russia and came to the United States at the age of 18. He settled in Chicago where he engaged in business. In 1886 he married Rebecca Marx of Detroit and for a time they lived in Eagle Grove, Iowa. In 1898 they moved to Deadwood. He first started out in the hide business and later started a jewelry business on Lee St., on the west side of Main St. Later he moved to the Rosenthal building on the east side of Main St. In 1905 he bought property on the west side of Main, and in 1910 he began remodeling that building, expecting to spend $10,000 in the process.

The Levinson Building at 657 Main St. is a reminder that Deadwood's Jewish population was not without its Wild West scandals.

Daily Pioneer-Times, Mar 1, 1902

Winsberg is Guilty; The jury convicts him of the attempted killing of Sol Levinson; a plea of self-defense; Attorney Joseph B. Moore decided to entirely abandon insanity theory.

The jury in the case of the State against Leo Winsberg charged with the attempted killing of Sol Levinson brought in a verdict of guilty in Circuit Court yesterday afternoon at 4 o'clock. There was no great surprise at the finding of the jury, although it was conceded that Attorney Joseph B. Moore put up a strong defense and made the best of the material at hand. The prosecution was taken somewhat by surprise when the line of defense was explained by the defendant's attorney. It had been generally understood that a plea of insanity would be introduced on the defendant's behalf, but Mr. Moore decided to leave that line entirely and make an attempt to acquit his client solely on the grounds of self-defense.

Sol Levinson, the complaining witness, told a straight-forward story of the shooting and maintained that he had done nothing to Winsberg to provoke him to such an act. A number of other witnesses were introduced by the state including Levinson's son Joe who was an eye witness to the shooting.

The defendant took the stand in his own behalf and impressed one as being a good witness for himself. Whether he told the truth or not he doubtless thought that what he said was true. He said that early in the evening of the shooting he was in Lead with Abe Fink. He had for some time been brooding over the trouble he had which resulted from his business dealing with Levinson. He maintained that Levinson brought him out to the Hills from the east to engage in the hide business with him and had given the defendant the worst of it in money matters. The matter had preyed upon his mind to such an extent that he determined to kill himself and for that purpose purchased the gun with which he shot Levinson.

On the evening in question he had decided to come to Deadwood and commit the act of self-destruction here, as he had friends in Lead and was desirous of being away from them when the deed was done.

On learning of his intention to go to Deadwood, Abe Fink asked the prisoner to step in at Sol Levinson's place and hand him a small sum of money that was owing to the latter. He executed the commission from Fink but before leaving the store got into an argument with Levinson about their old business relations. A question arose as to whether or not Levinson had paid a certain bill. Levinson was sitting at his desk while Winsberg stood on the opposite side. Levinson reached down into one of the lower drawers to procure the receipt, and Winsberg, knowing that a six-shooter was kept there, imagined that Levinson contemplated an armed attack upon him and in self-defense drew his gun and opened fire on Levinson.

This is Winsberg's story as told from the witness stand and although he would impress a person as one who at least thought he spoke the truth it was evident from the verdict that the jury was satisfied that the acts of Levinson were not sufficient provocation for the shooting and that there was no reason for the belief on the part of Winsberg that his life was in danger. Judge Washabaugh has set Friday, March 7, as the date upon which he will sentence the prisoner.

Sol Levinson survived the shooting; Winsberg went to jail.

In 1909 Sol and his son, Joe, again moved their jewelry business. The new jewelry store occupied the one-story, double-front brick building constructed in 1880 by Ben Baer and Max Fishel. Baer had operated a liquor store on his half before going into partnership in 1884 with Harris Franklin in a store across the street. Fishel had a stationery store on his half of the building. For a time in the 1920s Sol Bloom operated his clothing store in this space.

The next year, Sol added a new front and a second story, and to announce to the world that he was alive and thriving, had the name Levinson engraved in the cornice of the second story.

Sol became ill, and suffered from what was finally diagnosed as stomach ulcers, which led to two operations. Sol Levinson passed away in St. Joseph's Hospital in 1910 at the age of 51 after the second operation. Sadly, he died two months before his new project was finished, never having lived to see its completion.

Sol Levinson was a member of Masons and Modern Woodmen, and services were conducted at the Masonic Temple. The Masonic funeral service was read as well as a Hebrew prayer by Sidney Jacobs. Among the pallbearers were Sol Star, Nathan Franklin, Jonas Zoellner, Sol Rosenthal, and Sidney Jacobs.

Levinson Building, Deadwood
Photo by Ann Haber Stanton

Deadwood Daily Pioneer-Times, Sep 13, 1910

Sol Levinson, who was a man of great business ability and straightforward in his dealings, had always believed in Deadwood as a commercial center of promise, and proved the truth of his belief by his success here. He is survived by two sons, Joseph and Bernard. He leaves a brother, Dan Levinson of Eagle Grove, Iowa, who arrived here Sunday and was with him when death came... There are also two sisters and a brother in Russia.

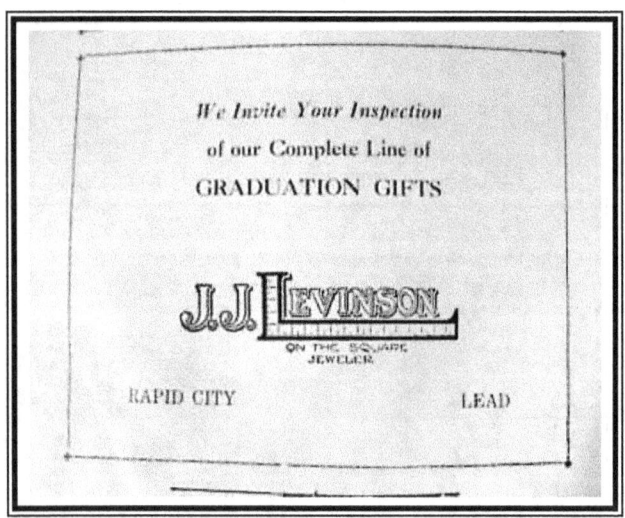

Photo courtesy Jane Mattila-Eide

Sol's son Joseph Jacob Levinson opened jewelry stores in Lead and Rapid City. He married Ida Israel, a tall and pretty woman, friend of the Colmans of Deadwood. Joseph operated the Rapid City branch of Levinson's jewelry store for many years. Although their jewelry stores are long gone, an elegant stained glass sign bearing the Levinson name adorns the doorway of a shop in the historic Buell building on 7th St. in Rapid City.

Photo by Ann Haber Stanton

Joseph died in Rapid City in February of 1934. The Levinson family, including Solomon, Ida, Joseph, Bernard, and Rebecca are buried in the Mount Zion section of Deadwood's Historic Mount Moriah Cemetery.

BLOOM

669 MAIN ST.

Solomon (Sol) Bloom was well known in the Black Hills and Sheridan, Wyoming, but much of what appeared in print about Sol was in the form of advertisements for his clothing business. He was a true pioneer, coming to the Black Hills in 1876 where he soon established his clothing and shoe store in Deadwood. It was notable for the great quantity of inventory, the racks and shelves stacked high with merchandise. His stores became among the most extensive mercantile establishments in the Hills, with branches in Spearfish, Sturgis and Sheridan, Wyoming.

Black Hills Daily Times, Oct. 12, 1886

Spearfish in ashes. One of the principal business blocks of Spearfish burned; 10 business houses and contents, including the hotel, destroyed; as many more buildings damaged to a greater or less extent involving a loss of $70,000.

Businesses often relocated. For a time, Sol Bloom operated his Deadwood clothing store at 657 Main St., that same building where Levinson later had his jewelry business. Bloom's Shoe and Clothing Deadwood store later did business in the Syndicate Building on the corner of Lee and Main Streets.

Bloom's store was long since gone by 1987, when the Syndicate Building was destroyed in yet one more major fire. Bloom's location at the opposite corner of Main and Lee Street in Deadwood is still known as Bloom's Corner.

Bloom Store, Deadwood
Photo courtesy Steve Norquist

Bloom store, Deadwood, Syndicate Block
Photo courtesy Steve Norquist

Bloom Store– 1890s
Photo courtesy Adams Museum

Charles VanMeter, Ned Hall, Charles Hyman and Sam W. Brown, Bloom's long-time salesman.
Photo courtesy Adams Museum

Sol's long-time bookkeeper, Morris Stern, was also an early arrival in Deadwood, accruing 25 years as Sol's associate.

Weekly Pioneer-Times, Sep 14, 1901

M. Stern, who has been book-keeper at Sol Bloom's clothing house of this city for many years, expects to leave about the 19th of the month for Chicago, where he will engage in business. A number of his friends had arranged to give him a farewell banquet at the Bullock Hotel tomorrow night, but it has been put off on account of the death of President McKinley.

Weekly Pioneer-Times, Sep 19, 1901

Morris Stern is Charmed. Morris Stern who has been book-keeper and manager of Sol Bloom's Deadwood store, was presented with a handsome charm last night by his fellow Bloom employees. It was a magnificent jewel in the form of a Prussian eagle, emblematical of the thirty-second degree of Scottish rites of Masonry, and it came from D. Kahn, manager of Bloom's store at Sheridan, Wyoming; Ed Gavin, manager of the Sturgis branch; and C.J. Hyman, of the Deadwood store. The jewel was presented by Henry Frawley in a few chosen remarks, on the eve of Mr. Stern's departure from Deadwood.

There was a happy assemblage of friends of Mr. Stern last night to bid farewell and God-speed. Some twenty five got together, and the evening was passed with a lunch and refreshments and cigars. Some of those present were in a reminiscent mood, and found ready listeners while they looked into a Havana haze and told of the doings of an earlier period. They all testified to a sincere regret at Mr. Stern's departure, and they were profuse in wishing success in his new location. Mr. Stern has resided in Deadwood since 1877, and he has been manager of Bloom's Deadwood store since 1878. He and his family will leave Deadwood tomorrow for Chicago, and there is a genuine feeling of sadness at their leaving.

After Sol Bloom died in Sheridan, Wyoming, his salesman Sam Brown continued operating the business as owner until 1937.

JACOBS
BLUMENTHAL, SALINSKY, AND MARGOLIN

677 MAIN ST. HUB STORE, NEW YORK STORE

Sidney Jacobs
Photo courtesy Centennial Archives,
Deadwood Public Library

CLOTHING BUSINESS

As I approached the New York Store, I noticed that the apparel in the window was quite fashionable. The shop was owned by a Jewish couple named Berthald (Bert) and Ruth Jacobs. They were among the tiny remnant of Deadwood's former population. Their sons, Sheldon and Doran, had moved to New York City. The couple had time to sit and reflect on some of their memories. They said the lives of four Jewish families converged at their New York Store, dating back to 1886. The first women's clothing shop was owned by I. Salinsky and operated as the Ladies Bazaar, located at 639 Main Street.

Salinsky's Ladies Bazaar
Photo courtesy Centennial Archives,
Deadwood Public Library

In 1912 Salinsky sold the store to Sam Margolin and his wife, Sarah Blumenthal Margolin, who moved it further north up Main Street to this beautiful old building known as the Phoenix Block, so named for its resurrection after Deadwood's many fires. The Margolins operated it as the New York Store.

Phoenix Block ca. 1880
Photo courtesy Leland Case Library

They told me Sarah Blumenthal Margolin was the eldest daughter of Benjamin and Frieda Blumenthal, the couple responsible for bringing the Torah to the Black Hills. So here was an answer to a key question: Deadwood did have a Torah! The Jacobses could tell me how the Torah got here. Generations of families had a part in this. I asked Bert, where do we even start? Start at the beginning, he said. Start with my grandparents, the Jacobses. I knew at once I had struck historical gold.

DEADWOOD TORAH

Simon and Dora Jacobs, a German-Jewish couple who had moved from St. Louis, were established in Deadwood by 1886. Simon had opened a little tobacco and candy store, and as a rather improbable sideline, he also dealt in diamonds. Bert told me that Benjamin Blumenthal, like so many immigrants, preceded his younger brother, Joseph, immigrating to America in order to help the rest of the family. Ben had left his sweetheart, Frieda, in Germany, planning to settle in America before he could ask for her hand in marriage. However, Frieda's devoutly religious family, including her uncle Joseph, a famous rabbi, insisted she live a *Torah*-centered life if she were to travel to that Dakota wilderness.

The *Torah* is the essential core of the Jewish religion and learning. A *Sefer Torah* is the hand-inscribed parchment scroll containing the five books of Moses, the sacred text of historical wisdom and law which embodies the scripture that guides Jewish religious life. Because Deadwood had no *Torah,* Ben's friends, Bert's grandparents, Simon and Dora Jacobs, together with the Jews of Deadwood, made a plan to bring a scroll to America. The young couple was sent on a lengthy, precarious, but necessary, mission. They would travel to Germany to accompany Frieda and a *Torah* scroll back to Deadwood. Such a voyage in the 1800s entailed travel by steamship across the Atlantic, by train overland across the country, and by stagecoach through the Black Hills— hardly an easy journey.

Once the Jews had a *Torah*, they established the Hebrew Congregation of Deadwood. Lacking a brick-and-mortar synagogue building, the *Torah* was sheltered in the Ingleside home of the Blumenthal family, to be taken out for sabbaths, High Holy Days services, or for other special occasions. Most services were held at the Masonic Temple.

BLUMENTHAL FAMILY

Benjamin and Frieda Blumenthal
Photo courtesy Florence Hawki

Sarah and Saul Blumenthal ca. 1893
Photo courtesy Florence Hawki

Blumenthal children
Photo courtesy Florence Hawki

Blumenthal children
Photo courtesy Florence Hawki

The Blumenthals were a large and musically talented family. They had a family band that performed for various occasions, sometimes entertaining in the city park. For their livelihood, though, the Blumenthals had a long-lasting family clothing business. Their business eventually branched out to a ladies' wear shop in Rapid City known as "Dorothy's," which operated into the 1980s. In time, one of the brothers, the popular Abe Blumenthal, joined the roster of Deadwood's Jewish mayors, which included Sol Star, Nathan Franklin, and Artie Welf.

Sol, Abe, and Gus Blumenthal
Photo courtesy Adams Museum

Russian-born Sam Margolin had come to America with his mother, brothers, and sisters to join their father, Henry, who had escaped from Russian oppression in 1890. This was a common theme for Jews from eastern Europe. Sam left school to help the family and eventually became a salesman for a meat company whose territory would take him to Deadwood, and then Jew Flats, a remote farming settlement near Quinn, South Dakota.

Sarah moved with Sam to Jew Flats and the Margolins spent a few challenging years homesteading. When they left, they moved to Sioux City and then Hawarden, Iowa, where they ran a family store. Shortly after the birth of Hugh, their first child, they returned to Deadwood and purchased the New York Store, where Sarah had once worked making hats. In 1927, the year they built their house on Lincoln Avenue, their second child, Peggy, was born. Another daughter, Faye Jean, was born in 1930. In 1950, Peggy and her husband, Lawrence Gavenman, joined the Sam Margolins in the New York Store and in 1960 they sold the store to Bert and Ruth Jacobs.

Sarah Blumenthal and Sam Margolin
Photo courtesy Faye Gitter

Sam and Sarah Margolin
Photo courtesy Faye Gitter

SIDNEY JACOBS AND FAMILY

As the Jacobs' chronicle continued, the most entertaining part of their yarn had to do with Bert and his father Sidney Jacobs. Sidney could have held the title of the Most Flamboyant of Deadwood's Colorful Jewish Characters. How Sidney and Jennie became a couple was a Jacobs-meets-Jacobs series of coincidences.

Black Hills Daily Times, Dec 23, 1890
Program of exercises at city public school Dec. 24. Jennie Jacobs.

Jennie Jacobs, a daughter of Simon and Dora Jacobs, attended school in Deadwood and graduated from Deadwood High School. After graduation she was visiting her cousin in Kansas City, Missouri, while New York stage actor and vaudevillian Sidney B. Jacobs happened to be performing there. The lively and personable Sidney knew from their first meeting that he wanted this charming young Jennie for his bride, and within two weeks he proposed. Jennie was a Deadwood girl, had been since age 12, and she agreed to accept Sidney's proposal under one condition: Sidney must trade his life on the stage for a stable home in Deadwood. When he agreed to Jennie's stipulation, Jennie Jacobs never had to change her name. Sidney gave up touring and the stage, and took on a new role as a tailor and clothier.

Stories about Sidney were never dull. As trim and slender as Bert was, his father was a remarkable figure of a man at 265 pounds, standing five feet, seven inches tall, with a 52-inch waistline. No-one could say this was a healthy size, and the doctor in Deadwood sent Sidney to the Mayo Clinic in Rochester, Minnesota. At Mayo he was recommended a special diet and further ordered to stay at the Carlton Hotel while he attended a clinic for two weeks, eating only in the prescribed diet dining room. To the dismay of all, he failed to lose any weight. Seven years later, Bert had occasion to go to the Mayo Clinic and stay at the Carlton Hotel as his father had done. Recognizing the name and the town on the register, the hotel clerk asked Bert if he was Sidney Jacobs's son. When Bert said he was, the clerk cleared up the mystery as to why the elder Jacobs lost no weight in spite of the prescribed diet. The clerk recalled that after each meal in the diet dining room, Sidney would go into the regular dining room at the hotel and have another meal.

Sidney was founder of the Hub, a retail menswear business in Deadwood that was in business for 50 years. The store was notable for having clothing covering the counters and hanging from the ceiling. Pictures of the founder's son, Bert, at the age of 10 months, adorned all the company's boxes, stationery, statements and checks. In addition to founding the Hub store, Sidney branched into the wholesale end of the business, supplying merchandise for retailers in the western end of South Dakota, eastern Wyoming and Montana. His theory of merchandising was found on his business card: *"You can work like the devil and be Johnny-On-The-Spot, but you can't make a profit on goods you haven't got."*

Black Hills Daily Times, Jan 8, 1887
Messrs. Gumbiner and Jacobs, accompanied by Pincus Cohen and wife went to Rapid by way of horses and sleigh. Return delayed by sick horse.

Daily Pioneer-Times, Mar 1, 1902
The Hub Clothing Store will sell at a special sale Saturday and Monday, the best $10 suit made in our own factory. "Union Mail" clothing. These suits are worth $15 anywhere. COATS!!

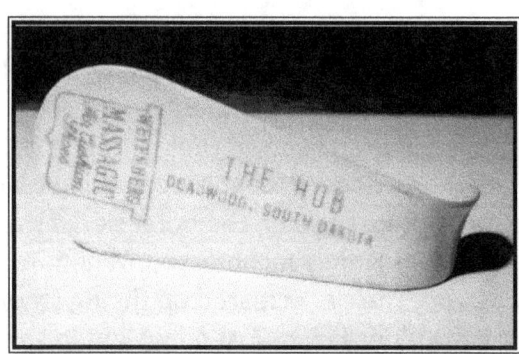

Souvenir of The Hub
Photo courtesy Steve Norquist

Sidney believed in the power of roadside advertising. His signs could be found along roadways throughout the Black Hills and as far as Wyoming and Montana, proclaiming the merits of the Hub in Deadwood. At one point there were 106 signs within three miles of Deadwood, so many signs that there were complaints that they were obscuring the Black Hills' scenery. Such a top-heavy sign display resulted in a letter from the state highway department warning there were too many signs and that some should be taken down.

A practical joker himself, Sidney was often the butt of jokes on Deadwood's Main Street. The numerous signs advertising "The Hub for Suits" were perfect targets for a good prank. His friends would pull out a sign, take it back to Deadwood, and tell Sidney that they had found it out in the country somewhere and thought he needed it back in Deadwood. Of course, everyone up and down the street watched for the show when a sign came back to Deadwood, with exasperated Sidney aiming to thump the pranksters with his cane.

Another amusing prank took place when Sidney was having dinner at Sundance, Wyoming, with two of his friends, both traveling salesmen. The three hung their overcoats on the hall tree and when Sidney wasn't looking, his friends slipped some silverware into Sidney's coat pocket. When they had finished their meal, the two called the owner of the cafe over to the table and told him there was missing silverware on the table. The owner called the police who searched the overcoats and found the silverware in Sidney's pocket. The story of Sidney's "stealing" the silverware made the rounds of Sundance and Deadwood, and they had a good laugh.

Once, when they stayed overnight in Hulett, Wyoming, his friends got up early, left Sidney sleeping, and drove to another town. Sidney was sure they had gone back to Deadwood and was furious. Of course, they came back three hours later to pick him up.

Sidney was never much of a sports fan, but he was a great supporter of the Deadwood baseball team, and in 1931 he donated enough money to provide the entire team with the finest uniforms in western South Dakota. The team became the champions and Sidney proudly declared that their suits made them the winners.

Sidney brought his son, Berthald, into the business. Bert had been a traveling salesman for Phillips Jones, a collar and shirt wholesale concern. Father and son did not always agree on how to manage the Hub, and merchandise that failed to sell could remain on the shelves year after year. Sidney needed a "sale," and Bert knew that was the only way to dispose of all the outdated merchandise. Bert prevailed, and with old shoes going for as little as 10 cents a pair, some items being packed and sent to an outlet in Chicago, the old merchandise disappeared.

Of commodious girth and jovial nature, Sidney was well liked. That outgoing aspect of Sidney's nature remained with him throughout his life. In 1910 he was appointed by Governor Byrne to represent South Dakota at the National Mining Congress. He was an executive member of the

Deadwood-Lead '76 Centennial Committee. Jennie, too, was active in civic affairs and was a member of the Deadwood chapter of the Order of Eastern Star, the women's branch of the Masonic Order.

When Nathan Colman died in 1906, Sidney Jacobs stepped into Colman's shoes, and assumed the role of lay Rabbi, a position he held until his death in 1934. He was remembered for his generosity, and respected for his intelligence, his religious knowledge, and his leadership.

Both father and son had had youthful aspirations for a life behind the footlights, but in each case, fortune, and a woman, drew them in different directions. Bert was about to chuck his job with a shirt manufacturing concern for a career as a tap dancer, when he met Ruth Ashe of Fargo, North Dakota, the girl who was to become his wife. Ruth persuaded him to remain in the clothing line rather than trying for the chorus line. Their clothing business prospered and they expanded, with branches in Belle Fourche, Sturgis, Rapid City, and even Los Alamos, New Mexico. Bert and Ruth eventually closed all but the New York Store in Deadwood. They kept the New York Store until 1974, when they retired, but their sons had gone on to build extraordinarily successful careers elsewhere.

Bert Jacobs, seated at left
Photo courtesy Centennial Archives, Deadwood Public Library

Unidentified woman and Ruth Jacobs (right)
Photo courtesy Adams Museum

A number of people with the common Jewish surname of Jacobs appear in Deadwood's early history, some related, some not. Some settled in Deadwood, and others just passed through. Morris Jacobs opened a saloon, a sure-fire path to prosperity, but he may not have been related to other Deadwood Jacobses.

Black Hills Daily Times, Jan 6, 1886

Officers installed Monday for Dakota lodge, No. 6, Knights of Pythias. M. Jacobs, Oscar Silver

Black Hills Daily Times, Jul 1, 1886

M. Jacobs is bound to keep up with his neighbors, as his saloon looms up in fine shape.

Black Hills Daily Times, Aug 4, 1886

A.J. White has accepted a position with Mr. Jacobs in the saloon business. Mr. M. Jacobs has just received a fine stock of liquors and cigars which fills his place of business up nicely.

Black Hills Daily Times, Aug 22, 1886

Mr. M. Jacobs, while at work in his place of business yesterday, fell and wrenched his hip in such a manner that he will be laid up for some time to come.

Black Hills Daily Times, Jan 1, 1888

Lawrence County commission met and approved retail liquor dealers bonds. Morris Jacobs.

Black Hills Daily Times, Sep 4, 1890

Prohibition. Raid of extensive proportions inaugurated by enforcement league against dealers in original packages. Morris Jacobs, Ben Blumenthal.

Black Hills Daily Times, Nov 9, 1890

Circuit court report November 9. State vs. Morris Jacobs; Harry Williams protests pre-emption proof of C.L. Kane. Morris Jacobs.

Black Hills Daily Times, Sep 29, 1891

Petit jury panel constituted of 23 free holders; John Roony exonerated and released; civil calendar called. Morris Jacobs

Black Hills Daily Times, Dec 10, 1889

Pioneer reports first white woman to ever ascend to summit of Bear Butte was Miss Amelia Jacobs; hundreds of women possibly accomplished that feat previous to the time mentioned.

Black Hills Daily Times, Jun 4, 1891

A. Jacobs today opens a sample room in Central, in the building vacated by I. Cohen, where you can find the best in town. A. Jacobs, I. Cohen

Louis Jacobs
Photo courtesy Centennial Collection, Deadwood Public Library

Nathan Jacobs
Photo courtesy Centennial Collection, Deadwood Public Library

Besides Sol Star and Nathan Franklin, Deadwood has had its share of Jewish mayors. Among them were Abe Blumenthal and Artie Welf.

Deadwood Mayor Abe Blumenthal (center)
Photo courtesy Florence Hawki

Simon Jacobs, unidentified friend, and Deadwood Mayor Artie Welf
Photo courtesy Adams Museum

Of those who made a life and were finally laid to rest in Deadwood, there are several Jacobs' graves in the Mount Zion section of Mount Moriah Cemetery. Jennie Jacobs died September 25, 1945, after a rather lengthy illness. Berthald died in 1990, and Ruth in 1994. Bert and Ruth were buried in the family plot in the Mount Zion section of Mount Moriah, and son Sheldon joined his parents there in 2015.

The last available gravesite, that set aside for Sheldon's brother, Doran, will never be filled. Doran died suddenly two years after his brother, and was buried in New York to be closer to children and grandchildren. The historic cemetery is now formally closed to further interments. Mount Zion has seen its last Jewish burial.

HATTENBACH

79 SHERMAN ST.

As I started walking northward up Sherman Street I was struck by the handsome brownstone building with the name Hattenbach inscribed in the parapet. Some research revealed this building was all that remained in Deadwood of a large family of pioneering Hattenbachs, six brothers and one sister, along with their spouses and children. Their grocery business had served the region through the early years of the Black Hills Gold Rush, through Deadwood's ascendancy, and on into the next century. Not only were the Hattenbachs influential in the culture and economy of the northern Black Hills, but their participation in Jewish society helped keep the flame of Judaism alive in the region. In June of 1893 they were noted as charter members of the newly organized Deadwood Chapter of B'nai B'rith.

Black Hills Daily Times, Jun 27, 1893
Order of Bnai Brith instituted with 24 charter members; officers elected. Nathan Colman, Jacob Goldberg, M. Stern, Gus Cohen, Gus L. Minzer, Joseph Hattenbach, Ben Blumenthal, Aaron Hattenbach, Jonas Zoellner, M.J. Wertheimer.

Their parents, Godfrey (Gedalya or Gottfried) and Frances Hattenbach, immigrated from Germany, and the children, six sons, Nathan, Ludwig, Joseph, Aaron, Mitchell, and David, and one daughter, Adelia, were all American-born. Like many of their neighbors, the gold rush held an irresistible attraction, compelling the young Hattenbachs to hitch their fortunes to Deadwood's rising star. After much moving around the country, the parents made their home in Sioux City, Iowa, but the adult Hattenbach siblings struck out for greener pastures.

Groceries and general merchandise were the mainstay of the Hattenbachs' livelihood in Deadwood, but these were industrious and enterprising people. If we could cut a trail back through the highest hills and the deepest forests of the northern Black Hills, after about 10 miles from Deadwood we would come to a clearing in the woods that was once known as Carbonate Camp, or Carbonate, where the adventurous Hattenbach spirit helped turn a mining camp into a real town— for a short time. The Hattenbachs set their stamp on this mining district, where silver was the main treasure. But other minerals, such as gold, tin, and lead, all helped to make the Carbonate mining district one of the fastest-growing mining regions of the Black Hills, with a meteoric flash of prosperity… and an even more swift plummet.

Credit for the origins of Carbonate Camp belongs to a pair of non-Jewish Virginian horticulturists, James Redpath and his son, L.B. Redpath. They came to the Hills to plant apples and ended up staking out a claim alongside their orchard, for carbonate, a silver-lead combination. They named the mine the Virginia for their home in West Virginia.

While Homestake and the majority of other Black Hills miners were preoccupied with gold, the Hills were rich in a wide variety of mineral wealth. In January of 1878, R.J. Porter climbed the hill to the Carbonate mining district to investigate its possibilities. He located a carbonate deposit, and named that the Red Cloud Mine. The mining district was revealing major deposits of hard carbonate silver ore. Word soon got out and silver mining took off. In the summer of 1880 Porter found the largest silver strike of all, and that became the Iron Hill Mine. The town of Carbonate was named for the abundant mineral, which by 1881 was attracting miners from everywhere. They dug for silver in every hill and valley of the Carbonate district.

By June of 1884, Carbonate Camp was a thriving Hills community. The roads to Lead and Deadwood were well traveled, and the town was well provided for. Hacks, local horse-drawn coaches, did a profitable business running taxi service trips between Deadwood and Carbonate Camp. John McClintock operated a stagecoach line between Deadwood and Carbonate Camp. There was even some talk of a trolley. The difficulty arose during rainy or wintry weather when bad roads and deep snows made it hard to get people, machinery, and supplies in and out.

Black Hills Daily Times, Nov 4, 1884

Carbonate Camp. The Hattenbach smelter, we learn from Mr. Craig, will start up again day after tomorrow on Iron Hill ore. It is at present under repairs. Mr. Plummer has started a general merchandise store.

The camp is steadily improving, there is always a demand for workmen. An application has been forwarded to the department for a post office, a thing greatly needed at present. An express is running daily from Central to the camp, driven by Joe Johnston, leaving Frank's store at 8:00 a.m.

Houses were being built for the burgeoning population, and there was plenty of work for everyone. By late 1884 Carbonate Camp had two streets, a school, churches and a cemetery. There were banks, a stock exchange, and a newspaper called the Carbonate Miner. There were boarding houses and hotels; the Hugginson Hotel alone had 63 rooms. Sol Star and Seth Bullock opened the first branch of their Star and Bullock Hardware Store in Carbonate Camp, naturally enough, since both of these businessmen were also heavily invested in Carbonate's Iron Hill Mine. There were restaurants, a bakery and a drugstore, at least three Chinese laundries, and a barbershop. A Jewish merchant named Kessler opened a dry goods store, and there were other shops and services as necessary to provide for a small town. The doctor from Central City charged $10 for a house call to Carbonate Camp. The citizens filed an application for a post office. There were also the ubiquitous saloons and gambling halls, and, as always in a frontier boomtown, a red light district. At its peak, Carbonate Camp was said to have had a population of several thousand, and felt worthy of dropping the "Camp" part of its name. The newspapers, however, out of habit, still referred to it as Carbonate Camp.

Sol Star's partner, Seth Bullock, toured the area, and seeing the obvious mineral potential, set up two mining companies, the Utica and the Iron Hill Mining Company, both stock-based corporations. A one-foot-wide vein of ore there glinted so brightly, that he placed samples of the ore in the window of the Merchant's National Bank for all to see. The town was soon buzzing with expectation, clamoring for a chance to buy stock. They had stamp mills to crush the ore. Now all they needed was a smelter to process it, and Nathan Hattenbach found one in Chicago.

That ore smelter that Nathan Hattenbach purchased in Chicago, which had offered so much promise at the start, was making them a fortune when functioning properly, but it was plagued with problems. The Hattenbachs were said to have been very mechanically minded, and although Nathan applied his skills to the snags, the smelter would persistently break down, causing work stoppages, legal issues, and in one case there was an arrest for malicious mischief. As problems multiplied, some of the investors sued, with the partners demanding their money, pitting Hattenbach against Hattenbach.

The large amount of arsenic needed in the smelting process was bound to cause an air pollution problem. In 1887 fumes from the smelter which were said to have killed all the cats in town, were now causing respiratory problems for the humans. At this point the boom had subsided. Most of the population, including the Hattenbachs, simply packed up and left. That was the death knell for Carbonate. The camp that would be a town became a ghost town almost overnight.

GODFREY AND FRANCES HATTENBACH

Godfrey Hattenbach
Photo courtesy Charlotte Hattenbach

The American Hattenbach story begins with the birth on March 13, 1813, of a boy with the Hebrew name of Gedalya ben Nosson (Godfrey) Hattenbach, son of Eddel Isaacs Michaelis (1781-1848) and Nathan ben Joseph Hattenbach (1780-1830) of Hof (now Hoof), near Kassel, Germany.

The Hattenbachs had acquired their family name in the early 19th century. They came from the same town in Germany as the Colmans, and were related through Nathan Colman's mother, who was also a Hattenbach.

At around the age of 26, Godfrey, now an ambitious young German-Jewish shoemaker, set his sights on America. In the late 1830s, about age 27, he immigrated to the United States through the port of Baltimore where he listed his occupation as "farmer."

Godfrey and Frances were married in Baltimore and first settled in Joplin, Missouri, where he bought some land and planted his first crop of corn. Times in Joplin were hard; family lore tells that the Hattenbachs had corn at every meal for a whole year. In 1848 they moved to St. Joseph, Missouri, and opened a general store while Godfrey also helped lay out the town. They moved from place to place, never staying in one location for very long. After Missouri they moved to Cincinnati where Godfrey had an auction, commission and clothing business. By then they already had three children, all listed in the 1854 census as having been born in Missouri. That was followed by a move to Council Bluffs, Iowa, where he started another general store. Then in 1855, they moved to the new town of Omadi, Nebraska. 1857 found them in Covington, Nebraska, where they also helped lay out that town but is now a ghost town. In South Sioux City, west of the Missouri River, opposite Sioux City, Iowa, Godfrey built a hotel which was twice destroyed by storms. In 1858 he became a fisherman. He started Sioux City's first billiards room. He is credited with being the first Jewish settler in Sioux City, where he donated land for the first Jewish cemetery. In 1863 due to fear of Indian raids, the family moved back to Cincinnati and there he was in the cigar business. Their children all made successful lives in Gold Rush country, but there is no indication that either the Hattenbach patriarch or his wife ever lived in Deadwood.

Godfrey died in 1879 at the age of 69 while in Chicago, and was buried there. His son, Aaron, and son-in-law, David A. Magee, later brought Godfrey's remains back to Sioux City's Mount Sinai Cemetery for re-burial in the land he'd originally donated. That cemetery was later sold and all the bodies in Mount Sinai exhumed and reburied in the Floyd Cemetery, near the Floyd River. Peripatetic even in death, at last Godfrey Hattenbach rests in peace.

Frances Hattenbach
Photo courtesy Charlotte Hattenbach

Frances Hattenbach, born in 1820, was also of German-Jewish origins. She was known to be a good cook, which may have been one reason they ran a hotel. In 1863 the Hattenbachs moved to Cincinnati, Ohio, where Godfrey started a cigar business. Frances lived to age 60, and was buried in Sioux City.

NATHAN AND DENA HATTENBACH

Nathan Hattenbach
Photo courtesy Charlotte Hattenbach

Nathan Hattenbach was born in 1843, in St. Joseph, Missouri. Eldest of the Hattenbach sons, in 1871 Nathan was in business in Sioux City with brothers Ludwig and Joseph, manufacturing and dealing in cigars and tobacco. Nathan's name begins to appear in the Deadwood newspapers in January of 1878, with the purchase of mining real estate. In February he traveled back to Sioux City to purchase a herd of cattle. Nathan is perhaps the most intriguing in terms of his participation in the headlong rush for Black Hills treasure. Although the Hattenbach name is applied to several of the mines within the Carbonate mining district, the one most often associated with the ghost town that once was Carbonate, is that of Nathan Hattenbach. His confidence in Carbonate was secure enough that he moved his young family to the new boomtown.

Black Hills Daily Pioneer, Jan 15, 1878

Nathan Hattenbach, Real Estate & Mining Transfers.

Black Hills Daily Times, Feb 25, 1878

Nathan Hattenbach, To Sioux City for a herd of cattle.

Black Hills Daily Times, Jun 12, 1878

Nathan Hattenbach, One of the owners of the Mary Mine.

In 1881 Nathan Hattenbach appears as one of the first shareholders in the South Deadwood Carbonate Mining Company, but he also traveled eastward to supply the Hattenbach store.

Black Hills Daily Times, Jun 3, 1881

N. Hattenbach, In the east buying stock of groceries & dry goods.

In June of 1881 the Black Hills Daily Times notes that Nathan traveled eastward, ostensibly on a grocery and dry goods buying trip. In truth, he was seeking much more than merchandise in Chicago— he had a woman in mind. Nathan's intended bride, Dena Wolf, was born in 1860, which made her 17 years his junior, but Nathan presented an optimistic future. Dena accepted and they were married in June in Sioux City. Soon, the newlyweds, together with their stock of groceries and dry goods, set out for Deadwood.

Black Hills Daily Times Jun 20, 1881

Nathan Hattenbach, Sherman St. grocer returns from east with bride. Blushing bride returns from east with husband.

Nathan and Dena Hattenbach
Photo courtesy Charlotte Hattenbach

Black Hills Daily Times, Jul 22, 1881

Mrs. Hattenbach, to arrive in Deadwood with husband.

In the days before railroad links to Deadwood, rail service ended at Sidney, Nebraska. Stagecoach was the common means of conveyance of the day, certainly a grueling journey that probably added little luster to the young bride's enthusiasm for her prospects. Nathan carried his Chicago bride across the threshold and into a new world.

Cooking for miners in Deadwood was as far from life in Chicago as she could have imagined, yet that became one of Dena's responsibilities. Her new existence was a challenge, but it did expose her to a wide variety of experiences and people. She was said to have made friends with Calamity Jane, who taught her to shoot tin cans off a fence. Nathan and Dena had six children, three boys and three girls, Arthur, Flora, Maurice, Leah, Zetta, and Laurence, all, according to family history, born in Dakota Territory.

Black Hills Daily Times, Aug 3, 1881

Nathan Hattenbach, Shareholder in South Deadwood Carbonate Mining Co.

By 1883 excitement over Carbonate Camp was mounting. Impressive specimens of hard carbonate silver ore were being extracted from the Far West silver mine in which the Hattenbachs were already heavily invested.

The mining district was in dire need of a smelter to process the more difficult, refractory silver ore they were digging. Years prior to this, gold ore was actually shipped to Wales for smelting. Before the railroads arrived, this would have been a lengthy and extremely costly process.

The Sioux City Journal reported that they had discovered a 5-foot vein of silver ore, enough to warrant keeping a smelter running continuously.

Black Hills Daily Times, Oct 2, 1883

Nathan Hattenbach, Reported at Sioux City, en route to Chicago.

Black Hills Daily Times, Nov 20, 1883

Nathan Hattenbach yesterday received by express some superb specimens of hard carbonate silver ore from a mine which he owns in the Black Hills. Nathan proposes to put a smelter in at this mine, as he has a 5-foot vein of this ore in sight.—Sioux City Journal. This is about the third time that Nathan has threatened the Journal folks with a smelter. We of the Hills would like to see him erect one, as we all believe there is ore enough in the Carbonate camp at this time to keep a smelter running all the time.

In January of 1884 Nathan returned from Chicago with news that he had purchased a smelter for use in Carbonate Camp. When the smelter, being brought in piece by piece, began to arrive in Deadwood City on a wagon drawn by six oxen, it attracted the attention of everyone, although nobody except one group of miners from Carbonate Camp had any idea what this strange-looking "dynamo" was for. One Carbonate miner who understood what was happening threw his hat in the air and shouted, *"There it comes at last; Nathan Hattenbach's smelter. Now we're all fixed."*

Nathan was made superintendent and put in charge of the smelter. Seth Bullock's Iron Hill mine, about a mile from the smelter, contracted with him to smelt their ore. Soon 42 bars of silver-lead bullion, each weighing about 100 pounds, with an estimated value of over $67,000, went on display in the window of the Merchant's National Bank. The town's population jubilated, and the stock price soared.

With a capacity of 30 tons per day, the Hattenbach smelter could accommodate more ore than the Far West Mine could produce; it also had the capacity to process ore on contract for neighboring mines. The undertaking was roundly applauded with great expectations in the mining camps of the northern Black Hills.

Black Hills Daily Times, Jan 5, 1884

Nathan Hattenbach, Returned from Chicago where he bought a smelter for use in Far West Mine in Carbonate camp. The smelter has the capacity of 30 tons per day.

This smelter, like every other piece of equipment, every manufactured item in this remote outpost, had to be hauled overland and into the Hills by wagon train, and Lead and Deadwood were at the end of the line. From there on, everything had to be loaded onto wagons to be carted up the rutted mountain roads to the mines. Parts of the Hattenbach smelter continued to arrive at Carbonate Camp that winter of 1884. By March the snow in the Northern Hills was so deep that transportation into the camp was a real challenge.

Black Hills Daily Times, Feb 21, 1884

Portions of the Hattenbach smelter arrived Tuesday by one of the trains of the Northwestern Transportation Company and the balance within a few days.

Black Hills Daily Times, Feb 22, 1884

Teams loaded with Hattenbach's smelter passed through town yesterday for the Carbonate Camp. Whether all of the machinery or only a part has arrived we could not learn, but there was heaps of it.

Black Hills Daily Times, Mar 9, 1884

Nathan Hattenbach's smelter was being loaded on wagons yesterday for removal to the Carbonate Camp. The snow is so deep that it will be quite an undertaking to get it there.

Black Hills Daily Times, April 29, 1884

Men were at work taking down the machinery in the old Hidden Treasure mill at Central yesterday. Part of the machinery will be removed to the Carbonate Camp and used in the Hattenbach smelter.

Black Hills Daily Times, Jul 15, 1884

The last piece of the Hattenbach smelter was landed at the works, Carbonate Camp, on Sunday. The main building is complete, much of the machinery is in place, and preparations already under way for "blowing in" at an early day.

Nathan also bought up other machinery from the Hidden Treasure mill at Central City. Thus equipped, Nathan constructed a plant in Rubicon Gulch east of Carbonate Camp. When the smelter was completed, two teams were employed to haul the ore to the smelter.

Ore smelter
Photo courtesy Library of Congress

Black Hills Daily Times, Jun 11, 1884

New discovery at Carbonate Camp. Work resumes on the Iron Hill.

Convinced that Carbonate had a promising future, and with the Far West and its neighboring mines now prospering, due in part to the Hattenbachs' smelter, in 1884 Nathan decided to move his growing young family out to Carbonate. Unfortunately, at that point the Hattenbachs were unaware of the serious health hazard from arsenic fumes arising from the smelting process.

Black Hills Daily Times, Jun 4, 1884

Hattenbach family moves to Carbonate Camp. Bud Billington, who drives one of McClintock's hacks, moved Nathan Hattenbach and his family out to the Carbonate Camp yesterday.

Black Hills Daily Times, Jun 11, 1884

New discovery at Carbonate Camp. Work resumes on the Iron Hill.

In late October of 1884 the Hattenbach smelter was finally ready for operation, and the mining district was showing great promise. But the smelter gave endless problems that required constant maintenance and repair. It would freeze up and cause work delays for days on end. Nathan's innate mechanical ability, a Hattenbach family trait, no doubt kept the smelter going. When Nathan couldn't make his own repairs, he called on Homestake's help. There were many causes for the delays, but with Carbonate being the up-and-coming bonanza, and so much invested in the mines there, the entire community was vitally interested in happenings at Carbonate. The newspapers followed progress almost day by day.

Black Hills Daily Times, Sep 2, 1884

The Hattenbach smelter, Carbonate district, rapidly approaches completion and will be blown in in about ten days

Black Hills Daily Times, Sep 23, 1884

Nathan Hattenbach was at the Merchants yesterday. His new smelter, Carbonate Camp, is nearly complete, and will be blown in at an early day.

Black Hills Daily Times, Sep 28, 1884

Nathan Hattenbach and Mr. Goodkind came over the Carbonate Camp yesterday. The new smelter will be blown in the last of the week.

Black Hills Daily Times, Oct 9, 1884

William Selbie returned from the Carbonate Camp with a quantity of rock to make the eyes water. It is from the Utica, and is all very rich.

Black Hills Daily Times, Oct 10, 1884

Supt. Hattenbach, of the Carbonate smelter is in the city. Smelter blow-in waiting for sufficient coal.

Black Hills Daily Times, Oct 18, 1884

Hattenbach application for patent.

Black Hills Daily Times, Oct 22, 1884

Nathan Hattenbach, of the Carbonate Camp, was in the city yesterday. Arrangements are complete for blowing in the smelter today. The daily delivery of ore from the Iron Hill is large.

Black Hills Daily Times, Oct 23, 1884

John Heard, the popular quartz hauler, of Golden Gate, has the contract for furnishing Iron Hill ore to the Hattenbach smelter, Carbonate Camp.

Black Hills Daily Times, Oct. 25, 1884

Deacon Selbie and Rev. Mr. Sample returned from trip to Carbonate Camp. Singular discovery of fossils was made in the Yankee shaft.

Black Hills Daily Times, Oct 29, 1884

Hattenbach smelter blown in. After months of toil, the Hattenbach smelter begins operations; resulting in developing the richest district in the Hills; plenty of high grade ore on hand, and any quantity in sight.

Black Hills Daily Times, Oct 31, 1884

Hattenbach smelter shut down for one week. Hattenbach smelter working satisfactorily until crack discovered in the water jacket. The works will not be idle to exceed a week. Result of initial run of 12 hours amounted to 800 pounds of bullion.

Black Hills Daily Times, Nov 1, 1884

Nathan Hattenbach came over from the Carbonate Camp yesterday. He assures the Times that the smelter will be in repair and operation again in a day or two.

Black Hills Daily Times, Nov 2, 1884

Nathan Hattenbach was in Lead yesterday looking after his water jacket. He expects to start up again on Wednesday next.

Black Hills Daily Times, Nov 8, 1884

Hattenbach Smelting Company organized. Notice given of special partnership for the purpose of establishing and carrying on smelting and mining works.

Black Hills Daily Times, Nov 12, 1884

The Hattenbach smelter resumed operations yesterday. It is in thorough repair, and with competent men in charge, permanent and successful work is reasonably anticipated.

Black Hills Daily Times, Nov 14, 1884

Hattenbach smelter started up, then "freeze up" occurred, necessitating a cessation of work. Assured works will be idle only a few days.

Black Hills Daily Times, Nov 15, 1884

Wm. Hanley, boilermaker for the Homestake company, went out to the Carbonate Camp yesterday to repair the Hattenbach smelter.

Black Hills Daily Times, Nov 16, 1884

The Hattenbach smelter will be in operation again today. It has been placed in thorough repair. That the public have faith in the enterprise is indicated by a lively demand for Far West stock.

Black Hills Daily Times, Nov 18, 1884

The Hattenbach smelter started up yesterday morning. Hattenbach smelter contributes 128 bars of bullion.

In November of 1884 Nathan formed a new partnership, re-organizing the Hattenbach Smelting Company with Meyer Wheeler and William Goodkind.

Freeze-ups, slowdowns, disagreements, stock slumps and rallies, all made the papers.

In between work stoppages for necessary repairs, the smelter was producing. The Iron Hill Mining Company brought in about 1,000 tons of ore that contained between 90 and 250 ounces of silver per ton and about 20 percent lead. The owners of the smelter were paid $26 per ton by the Iron Hill, and the smelter company returned 90 percent of the silver and all of the gold.

On November 21, 1884, 42 bars of base bullion, each weighing about 102 pounds, were brought into Deadwood by a 4-horse team. It was estimated that it contained 400 ounces of silver per ton. Another delivery arrived the following day, this one containing 2 tons. The entire shipment was sent to Chicago for refining and marketing. Mining stocks in the Iron Hill shot up to 80 cents per share— if you could buy stock in the Iron Hill at all. The Hattenbach smelter was making a ton of money for the stockholders.

Bullion awaiting the treasure coach
Photo courtesy Adams Museum

Many of the Black Hills' leading businessmen were invested in the mines around Carbonate, which now numbered in the hundreds. The mining district map was a maze of mining claims, some dangerously overlapping. Sol Star, Harris Franklin, Ben Baer, Paul Rewman, and Valentine T. McGillycuddy all had interests in mines like the Iron Hill and the Seabury-Calkins, which were producing silver, gold and galena in rich quantities.

Black Hills Daily Times, Nov 22, 1884

Excitement increasing over the Iron Hill and neighboring mines. False rumor quelched. Supt. Hattenbach, of the Carbonate smelter is in the city. Smelter blow-in waiting for sufficient coal.

Black Hills Daily Times, Nov 23, 1884

Iron Hill Mine, Far West Mine, Eureka Mine, Enterprise Mine. Forty-four bars of bullion were contributed by the Hattenbach smelter to the world's wealth, yesterday, making 128 during the last three days.

Black Hills Daily Times, Nov 25, 1884
Horse shoes sent over to Hattenbach smelter. Load of horse shoes provide Hattenbach smelter with iron for reduction for large amount of arsenic.

Black Hills Daily Times, Nov 26, 1884
The Hattenbach smelter "froze up" Saturday, causing a suspension of work until last evening. It is again in full blast.

Black Hills Daily Times, Nov 30, 1884
Iron being gathered for Hattenbach smelter. John Hess was around the Lead shops gathering iron for the Hattenbach smelter.

Black Hills Daily Times, Dec 5, 1884
Hattenbach smelter resumed operations yesterday, and is believed no further difficulty will be experienced.

Black Hills Daily Times, Dec 6, 1884
The Hattenbach smelter continues in successful operation, and all interested are happy. It is now believed that the iron ore famine has been overcome.

Malfunctions resulted in several disputes and dips in the price of stock when the smelter failed to function properly. Friction arose between the Hattenbachs and Seth Bullock, presiding officer on the board of directors of the Iron Hill Mining Company.

Black Hills Daily Times, Dec 9, 1884
Rumors were numerous and various yesterday respecting affairs at the Carbonate Camp. Stock sold down 40 cents, rallied, and none could be purchased at any reasonable price.

Black Hills Daily Times, Dec 10, 1884
Iron Hill ore brought in. Forty-one and a half bars of bullion, came over from the Hattenbach smelter yesterday, the result of the last day or two's run on Iron Hill ore.

The Iron Hill Mining Company, owned by Seth Bullock, eventually took over the smelter. The drama was played out in the newspapers. The Black Hills Daily Times printed whatever was offered as news, each party presenting their own side of the story, with the result that the public probably never received objective reports.

Black Hills Daily Times, Dec 11, 1884
McMaster explains Iron Hill lore. Thomas McMaster, Supt. of Iron Hill, writes letter to the editor in reply to Noliston, and presents true facts regarding Hattenbach smelter.

Black Hills Daily Times, Dec 12, 1884
The Iron Hill company began action for damages against the Hattenbach Smelting company, for violation of contract.

Black Hills Daily Times, Dec 16, 1884
Pay day at the Iron Hill, four men at work on the Eureka, plus more news from Carbonate.

Black Hills Daily Times, Dec 19, 1884
A report that the Hattenbach smelter had been leased to the Iron Hill without foundation.

Meanwhile, Nathan had taken his place among the outstanding citizens of Lawrence County. His seat on the county commission was important at a time when precincts were being established and judges appointed.

Black Hills Daily Times, Sep 2, 1880
N. Hattenbach, Republican Club organized in South Deadwood.

By 1885 Dena was well acclimated to her new home. Deadwood had become a special gathering place for Hattenbachs and extended family. Dena's sister Frieda from Chicago and her fiancé, Simon Mayer, arrived in May of 1885. The couple was married at Wertheimer's Merchants Hotel on May 19th.

Black Hills Daily Times, May 20, 1885

Simon Mayer and Miss Frieda Wolf, all of Chicago, married May 19 at the Merchants Hotel.

Despite the friction with Seth Bullock, the issues with labor, and all the delays, Carbonate was still the New Eldorado and the object of excitement in the Hills. Investors of the town remained alert and interested. The Hattenbach smelter made the processing economically feasible, and when it worked, it made them money.

Black Hills Daily Times, May 9, 1885

Important meeting in the interest of a new road; rich strike, stampede and excitement in the New Eldorado. Harris Franklin, Seth Bullock.

Black Hills Daily Times, Aug 15, 1885

Ore from the Hercules will shortly be worked upon by the Hattenbach smelter. Four hundred tons of excellent ore is on the dump at present.

Black Hills Daily Times, Sep 19, 1885

Supt. Millett and 12 Iron Hill employees were arrested and brought to the city yesterday for malicious mischief.

Black Hills Daily Times, Sep 25, 1885

Supt. Millett and nine employees arraigned before Justice Henley. Millett and Thos. H. White placed under bond. All others in arrest were discharged. Nathan Hattenbach.

In 1886, the Our Mines section of the Black Hills Daily Times continued to report heavy bullion shipments, new advances in dividends, and an upward trend in stocks. The Iron Hill, in which the Hattenbachs, Sol Star, Ben Baer, Paul Rewman, Harris Franklin, and so many of the Jewish businessmen were invested, appeared to be doing well.

There was a second boom of prosperity; silver was assaying highly. The Iron Hill, however, came upon hard times in the form of fire, litigation, and stock speculation. There was still a fortune to be made if you were willing to take the risk. The Spanish R Mine dug out $50,000 in silver before it closed in 1904.

Black Hills Daily Times, Apr 1, 1886

Harris Franklin made a tour of the Carbonate Camp yesterday. He reports great activity and enthusiasm throughout the district.

Black Hills Daily Times, May 1, 1886

The boom continues; Iron Hill advances; ten cent dividend anticipated.

Black Hills Daily Times, Jun 2, 1886

A manifest better feeling and strong upward tendency in stocks; Iron Hill declares another divvy; numerous meetings; mining miscellany.

Black Hills Daily Times, Jun 4, 1886

Over 8,000 ounces sent over from Iron Hill; heaviest bullion shipment sent east; important strike reported in the Champagne.

A stamp mill is a type of machine that crushes raw material utilizing gravity, by pounding rather than grinding, either for further processing or for extraction of metallic ores. In June of 1886 the Iron Hill was preparing for 10 additional stamps.

Black Hills Daily Times, Jun 14, 1886

Iron Hill preparing for 10 additional stamps; mining miscellany.

Problems with the smelter continued and were again causing dissent. In June of 1886, legal issues erupted. Seth Bullock's Iron Hill Mine began an action against the Hattenbach Smelting Company. Nathan Hattenbach was seen to be in violation of their contract. The family was now pitted, brother against brother, Joseph and Aaron on one side, and Nathan on the other. It resulted in having Bullock take possession of the Hattenbach smelter.

Black Hills Daily Times, Jun 1, 1886

Judge William E. Church refuses to dispossess Seth Bullock at the Hattenbach smelter.

Black Hills Daily Times, Mar 15, 1887

Joseph Hattenbach and Aaron Hattenbach, plaintiffs, vs. Meyer Wheeler, William Goodkind and Nathan Hattenbach, defendants. Summons — money demand.

Black Hills Daily Times, Sep 13, 1887

Mrs. N. Hattenbach departs on this morning's coach for Sioux City. Arrivals and departures via Northwestern. - 29 arrivals and departures. Mrs. N. Hattenbach.

It was all too much. On the morning of Sept. 13, 1887, young Nathan Franklin, son of mining magnate and financier, Harris Franklin, and Estelline Bennett, daughter of Judge Granville Bennett, left on the stagecoach for Sioux City, Iowa. Also on that coach were Dena Hattenbach, wife of Nathan, and her children. Nathan Hattenbach's family was leaving for Sioux City.

Nathan was soon to follow. There he started afresh, with a new business, opening the Fair Store, which sold glassware, crockery, and china. In 1900 they moved to New York, and then on to Chicago, where he had a grocery, and then a furniture and appliance store. At the age of 68, Nathan died in Chicago on November 5, 1911.

JOSEPH AND JENNIE ROSENTHAL HATTENBACH

Joseph Hattenbach
Photo courtesy Charlotte Hattenbach

At the news of the 1876 Black Hills Gold Rush, Joseph was bitten by the gold bug. Second of the Hattenbach boys, Joseph, born in 1848 in St. Joseph, Missouri, led the way into Dakota Territory. The young Sioux City entrepreneur could foresee tremendous business potential. Traveling up the Missouri River by the steamboat Far West— the same boat that had carried the news along with the survivors of Custer's Last Stand at the Little Big Horn back to civilization— Joseph made his way into Deadwood in 1876. His younger brother Aaron soon joined him and together they started their Hattenbach grocery business.

Newspaper notices show that Joseph began investing in mining as early as 1878, but it was probably earlier than that. In 1881 he organized a mining company in order to sink a shaft at the Mary Mine. He then traveled as far as

Chamberlain, a town on the Missouri River, a good 250 miles to the east, to sell stock in the Deadwood Enterprise Mining Company. His name was associated with the Mary Mine, the Surprise Mine, the Adelphi Mine, and the Far West Mining Company. Soon, their brother Nathan joined them.

Black Hills Daily Times, Jun 12, 1878

Hattenbach, One of the owners of the Mary Mine.

Black Hills Daily Pioneer, Jul 11, 1878

Joseph Hattenbach, Real Estate & Mining Transfers.

Black Hills Daily Times, Jun 4, 1881

Joe Hattenbach, Organized mining company to sink shaft at Mary mine.

Black Hills Daily Times, Jan 4, 1882

Joe Hattenbach, Was at Chamberlain selling stock.

Black Hills Daily Times, May 9, 1882

Joseph Hattenbach. Went east in interest of Far West Mining Co, returns.

Joseph's plan to return from Cincinnati to Deadwood with a 20-ton smelter never materialized.

Black Hills Daily Times, Jun 3, 1882

Joseph Hattenbach, Bringing back 20 ton smelter from Cincinnati.

Black Hills Daily Times, Mar 20, 1883

Hattenbach, Returned from Deadwood to Sioux City, got lost there.

Black Hills Daily Times, Apr 5, 1890

Real estate filed for record; a lively day. Joseph Hattenbach. Harmony Mining Company, Double Standard Mining Company, Tornado Mining Company. Plutus Mining Company.

The young bachelors of the town made some time for socializing. In Deadwood, a respectable young lady was where you could find one. In 1884, five of Deadwood's most eligible Jewish bachelors competed in waltzing contests at the Catholic Fair at Jewish-owned Keimer Hall to see who could charm Deadwood's best housekeeper.

Black Hills Daily Times, Oct 31, 1884

Final day of Catholic fair. Keimer Hall crowded from early until late last evening. Contests for graceful waltzing, most popular bachelor, and best housekeeper. Sol Bloom, Joe Hattenbach, Paul Rewman, Jake Goldberg, Sol Star.

Black Hills Daily Times, Dec 2, 1884

Deadwood Enterprise Mining Company by Joseph Hattenbach files application of patent for Surprise mine.

Black Hills Daily Times, Apr 21, 1885

A caucus of Fourth ward residents held for purpose of nominating a councilman. Joseph Hattenbach.

Black Hills Daily Times, Jun 14, 1885

Departure of South Deadwood hose team for Sioux Falls tourney. H Stein, Joseph Hattenbach.

Black Hills Daily Times, Jan 4, 1887

New Year's Day. The day celebrated in this city and in surrounding camps, with a general closing of business houses, an abstinence from work, roast turkey with cranberry sauce on the side, egg nog, also on the side. M. Liebmann, M.J. Wertheimer, Sol Bloom, Joseph Hattenbach.

Black Hills Daily Times, Jan 20, 1887

Roadster attempts run-away. Joe Hattenbach's roadster, not to be outdone (by a horse?), took it into his head, twice yesterday, to run away, and almost succeeded, but not quite, a thorough good time was made.

Black Hills Daily Times, Mar 26, 1887

Joe Hattenbach goes out this morning for a visit to Rapid.

Black Hills Daily Times, May 17, 1887

Hattenbachs return from brief trip. Joe Hattenbach returned Sunday from a protracted visit at Sioux

City and elsewhere. The trip accomplished a world of good for the boy, physically, mentally and — otherwise.

Black Hills Daily Times, Oct 9, 1887

A delightful company. Miss Christina, daughter of James Anderson of Centennial, surprised by party of Deadwood friends arriving for cards and dancing. Joseph Hattenbach.

Joseph's name, as well as that of his brother Aaron, often comes up in connection with Deadwood's Hose companies. Competition between hose companies, volunteer fire departments, was a practical challenge as well as a source of entertainment. Hose company competitions drew crowds of onlookers at parades.

Black Hills Daily Times, Dec 3, 1884

Hose company elects officers. Annual meeting of South Deadwood Hose company. Joseph Hattenbach.

Much of local social life centered around membership in various lodges. Joseph was an officer in the International Order of Odd Fellows. Like his brothers, Joseph was involved in a variety of civic and cultural affairs.

Black Hills Daily Times, Dec 14, 1887

Black Hills encampment, I.O.O.F., elects officers. Joseph Hattenbach.

Black Hills Daily Times, Jul 13, 1888

Masonic Lodge. I.O.O.F. — Interesting installation exercises last evening for Eureka and Golden Center lodges. Joseph Hattenbach.

Black Hills Daily Times, Jul 29, 1888

Contest at primaries. Many citizens of Lawrence County will be surprised that a contest occurred at yesterday's primaries. L.A.Reubens, Solomon Star, Aaron Hattenbach.

Black Hills Daily Times, Aug 1, 1888

Joe Hattenbach. Dr. Bennett and his Wizard Oil Excelsiors gave very fine entertainment last evening. Prizes followed. A delightful surprise.

Black Hills Daily Times, Aug 3, 1888

Lawrence County Commission meeting minutes July 17, 18, 19, 20. Joseph Hattenbach.

Black Hills Daily Times, Aug. 5, 1888

A double header — Republican convention. The Moody faction unable to control, bolts the convention, holds a little side show and will send a contesting delegation. Regular convention elects delegates Joseph Hattenbach, Solomon Star.

Black Hills Daily Times, Mar 14, 1893

Lawrence County Commission minutes special session March 8-9. Joseph Hattenbach, Isaac Cohn, Adolph Fishel, Henry Rosenkranz.

With a little help from a local entrepreneur and neighbor of brother Aaron, Joe's quest for a mate met with success. Jennie Rosenthal was the niece of Deadwood's Sol Rosenthal, and in October of 1889 Joe Hattenbach traveled to Missouri to marry his bride, returning to Deadwood with Jennie. The couple arrived by Northwestern stagecoach, and registered at the Keystone Hotel.

Black Hills Daily Times, Oct 4, 1889

Joseph Hattenbach returns accompanied by his bride, nee Jennie Rosenthal, niece of Sol Rosenthal. Keystone register, J. Hattenbach and lady.

Joseph built a comfortable home for his family at the corner of City Creek and Centennial Avenue, suitable for entertaining houseguests.

Black Hills Daily Times, Aug 6, 1890

H.B. Young and wife are comfortably domiciled in the Hattenbach residence, corner City Creek and Centennial Avenue.

Black Hills Daily Times, Dec 20, 1892

Miss Lena Rosenthal, sister of Mrs. Joseph (Jennie) Hattenbach, arrived via B. & M. (Burlington and Missouri Valley Railroad) yesterday from Warrensburg, Missouri, to visit for a few weeks with her sister.

Black Hills Daily Times, Jan 1, 1893

Jolly sleighing party. Mr. and Mrs. Joseph Hattenbach, Miss Laura Rosenthal, Clara L. Fishel and Miss Friedlander constituted a jolly sleighing party around the belt yesterday.

In 1883, funds had been raised for a normal school, or teacher's college, in Spearfish. Donors funded the $790.85 needed to purchase the land, and a building was constructed. Jennie Hattenbach and her mother, Mrs. Rosenthal, of Warrensburg, Missouri, looking to the future of Jennie's children, took an interest in Dakota Territorial Normal School. This training school for young lady teachers would in time evolve into Black Hills State University.

Black Hills Daily Times, May 14, 1893

1893 NORMAL SCHOOL Mrs. Rosenthal, mother of Mrs. Joseph Hattenbach and daughter, Warrensburg, Mo, young lady teachers and students of Normal School.

Joseph lived to the age of 67, dying in 1915. His widow, Jennie, died in Sioux City in 1938. They were both buried in the Jewish cemetery in Sioux City, and were survived by three of their children, Monroe, Jay, and Frances. Like many of the Jews of the midwest, Sioux City was their home-away-from-home.

LUDWIG AND EMMA HATTENBACH

Ludwig Hattenbach
Photo courtesy Charlotte Hattenbach

Ludwig was born in St. Joseph, Missouri, in 1846. The Sioux City directory of 1871 lists him in partnership with brothers Nathan and Joseph in the manufacture and dealership of cigars and tobacco. In 1878 he moved to Deadwood to join in the family's business enterprises. For a time he was put in charge of the ore smelter for the brothers' business, but family history tells of the mines filling up with water while he was there, the result being that there was nothing to smelt.

Black Hills Daily Times, Jul 23, 1882

Arrivals at Cosmopolitan Hotel. Ludwig Hattenbach, Brother of Hattenbach Bros, here from Sioux City.

Black Hills Daily Times, Aug 3, 1882

Ludwig Hattenbach, Going to Sioux City in interest of the Far West. Passed through Central on way to Carbonate Camp.

Ludwig did not stay in the Black Hills as long as his other brothers. In 1892 he married Emma Leve. The Sioux City directory later shows him there as a partner in the grocery business with brother-in-law David Magee. That business was destroyed by a financial panic and the partnership terminated in 1901.

Ludwig and Emma were later instrumental in starting Mount Sinai Temple in Sioux City. They held a fundraiser for the Ladies Aid Society at their home. The Sioux City Jewish Directory tells of this fund-raiser taking place on June 12, 1886: "The Strawberry Festival given at the home of Mr. and Mrs. L. Hattenbach was a grand success. About 200 people attended for the benefit of the Hebrew Ladies Aid Society." That this festival attracted 200 people shows that the Ludwig Hattenbachs were probably quite prosperous, with a large home, and Sioux City had a sizable Jewish population. His last occupation was as a grocer in Sioux City, where he died in 1920 at the age of 74.

ADELIA HATTENBACH MAGEE AND DAVID MAGEE

Adelia Hattenbach Magee
Photo courtesy Charlotte Hattenbach

Adelia was born in 1855, in Omadi, Nebraska, fourth of the seven Hattenbach children, their only daughter, and was said to be adored by her family. She was an artist who painted in oils and decorated Haviland china, a pastime favored by ladies of that era. Adelia was a talented musician who played piano and violin, and also gave piano lessons.

1876 was an important year for the Hattenbachs. Besides being the opening year of the Black Hills Gold rush, Adelia, the only female sibling of the Hattenbach brothers, was to be married on June 20th. This was no ordinary Jewish wedding. David Magee, a Gentile, had courted Adelia in secret. Her parents forbade her to marry out of her religion. In fact, they refused to let her see him at all. The beleaguered girl would drop messages from her window to this man whom she loved. Resolute in his determination not to let religion stand in their way, David traveled to Cincinnati, home of Hebrew Union College. There, at America's oldest Jewish seminary, founded in 1875, David studied for conversion to Judaism. Satisfied with his sincerity, Adelia's parents relented at last, and the couple was united in marriage in Council Bluffs, Iowa, on June 20, 1876, by Justice Berk on behalf of the state, and Rabbi Hertzman on behalf of the "Israelite church."

Dave Magee integrated thoroughly into the Hattenbach family; his attachment to both his new family and his new faith were highly regarded. He was even called by some in the family, "a better Jew" than the other Hattenbachs. Certainly, Magee applied himself to full participation in Sioux City's Jewish community life. He was one of the founding officers of Mount Sinai congregation, and Secretary of the Mount Sinai Cemetery association when it was formed in the 1884.

All the Hattenbachs, in fact, were committed to their Jewish responsibilities. The Deadwood Hattenbachs helped to organize Deadwood's first Jewish congregation. They also participated in founding the first, and only, chapter of B'nai B'rith in Western Dakota Territory.

Although the Magees maintained their primary residence in Sioux City, where David ran for sheriff in 1887, they had a substantial interest in Deadwood. They owned a large piece of the Far West Mine of Carbonate, as well as the Hattenbach Brothers' grocery business. The fortunes of the Magees rose and fell along with the rest of the Hattenbachs.

Black Hills Daily Times, Nov 10, 1887
David A. Magee, brother-in-law of Aaron Hattenbach, predicted winner of Sioux City election for sheriff. He is a large owner of Far West mining property.

Adelia was one of the charter members of the Hebrew Ladies' Aid Society in Sioux City in 1884. She died in Sioux City, Iowa, in 1926, at the age of 71. Adelia and David are buried there in Mount Sinai Cemetery together with Godfrey, Frances, and most of the other Hattenbachs. None of the Hattenbachs are buried In Deadwood.

AARON AND BELLE HATTENBACH

Aaron Hattenbach
Photo courtesy Charlotte Hattenbach

Aaron Hattenbach, born in Covington, Nebraska, on May 22, 1857, was the most long-lived of all the Hattenbach siblings. Aaron joined his brother Joseph in Deadwood in 1876 in the grocery business on Sherman Street. In 1878, when Nathan joined them, they pooled their money to operate the Far West mine near Carbonate, but the grocery store was their most dependable source of income.

Black Hills Daily Times, Apr 10, 1880
Small blaze behind store scared Sherman St citizen.

Black Hills Daily Times, Sep 14, 1880

Hattenbach Bros. Small fire in shed, passer-by set off alarm.

Black Hills Daily Times, May 28, 1881

Hattenbach Bros. Gave money for July 4th celebration.

In December of 1882 Aaron married Belle Holstein, daughter of Deadwood merchant Ben Holstein. The ceremony took place at the home of the bride's parents, Mr. and Mrs. Ben Holstein.

Black Hills Daily Times, Dec 6, 1882

Aaron Hattenbach, Marriage, to Belle Holstein, at bride's parents.

Aaron was musically talented and he contributed to the cultural scene in the Black Hills with his gifts. He played the organ, the zither, and the cornet. In time he formed an orchestra which performed for dances, concerts, parties, and benefits.

Black Hills Daily Times, May 11, 1882

Best organist in Hills, assists Al Frank, at Galen.

Black Hills Daily Times, Apr 17, 1885

Costly instruments are all the rage: Frank Knopf a zither, Aaron Hattenbach a cornet-a-piston, and Fred Clary's new silver cornet accompanied by bagpipes for resident of Central. Now we can announce receipt by Judge Alexander of a perfect gem of an instrument.

Black Hills Daily Times, May 5, 1885

Vocal and instrumental concert at Keimer Hall for benefit of South Deadwood Hose company next Tuesday.

Black Hills Daily Times, May 22, 1887

Aaron Hattenbach, Benefit performance for South Deadwood Hose opens Pearson's Opera House.

Black Hills Daily Times, Oct 27, 1887

The dance given by the Miners' Union at Lead last evening was the event of the season. Hattenbach band. European restaurant.

Black Hills Daily Times, Feb 9, 1888

Instrumental concert Monday eve, Feb. 20, by Deadwood orchestra. Deadwood Opera House. Aaron Hattenbach, Peter Eixenberger.

Black Hills Daily Times, Feb 18, 1888

Aaron Hattenbach, Programme for orchestral concert next Monday evening.

When called upon, he was noted for filling in for an absent church organist. Evidence of Aaron Hattenbach's orchestra continues to appear in the Times until 1893.

Black Hills Daily Times, Jun 10, 1888

Owing to the absence of Mrs. Bartels, Aaron Hattenbach will preside at the organ. Methodist church today, children's service.

Black Hills Daily Times, Sep 25, 1891

Deadwood's new opera house to go up on the Christy corner, Sherman Street. Deadwood Opera House. Hattenbach Brothers.

Black Hills Daily Times, Feb 6, 1892

Aaron Hattenbach's orchestra of three went down to Whitewood to furnish music for a dance.

Black Hills Daily Times, Feb 19, 1892

Pretty home of Mr. and Mrs. Byron P. Dague was scene of enjoyable dancing party. Hattenbach orchestra.

Black Hills Daily Times, Mar 3, 1893

Gray-hairs to speak. Programme of Grown Folks Elocutionary Contest. Hattenbach Orchestra.

Aaron also sat on the Deadwood City Council, responsible for setting up local government, maintaining a legal system, and laying down an infrastructure that would make Deadwood a safer and more governable community.

Black Hills Daily Times, Oct 8, 1884
County commission arranges election precincts and appoints judges; adopts resolution to handle liquor money. Aaron Hattenbach, Louis Reuben

Black Hills Daily Times, Jan 6, 1885
Grand and petit juries summoned. Ten grand jury men and twenty-five petit jury men summoned. Aaron Hattenbach, B.H.Kohorn

Black Hills Daily Times, May 15, 1885
Notice of special election for purpose of erecting a county jail. Lawrence County Commission. Lawrence County Jail. L. Reuben, Aaron Hattenbach

Black Hills Daily Times, Aug 18, 1885
Common council met to discuss petition from residents and property owners of Washington Avenue, Jackson, Jefferson and Madison streets; school levy; bills and miscellaneous. Sol Star, Harris Franklin, Aaron Hattenbach, Sol Rosenthal.

Black Hills Daily Times, Jan 19, 1888
Aaron Hattenbach, County commission appointments. Lawrence County Commission Board of county commissioners last evening concluded 12 busy days.

Black Hills Daily Times, Feb 4, 1888
Lawrence County Commission meeting minutes Jan. 18. Aaron Hattenbach, Louis Minzer.

Black Hills Daily Times, Sep 22, 1891
City Council meeting September 21. Petition from residents of Fourth ward; bond of M.A. Tipton presented; roads and bridges. invitation to Col. Sumner to visit Deadwood with his command; Lee Baxter reported aversely on electric light proposition; attention directed to pollution of Deadwood water supply. Solomon Star. Aaron Hattenbach.

Joseph and Aaron were among the major trustees and officers in the Far West Mining Company as well as several other of the many silver mines located in the Carbonate mining district. Pleased with the quality of silver ore issuing from the Far West mine, they displayed a sample of their findings at their Sherman Street grocery store in July of 1885. Aaron also held stock in the Gustin Minerva Consolidated Mining Company, Monitor Mining Company, the U.S. Grant, and the Maggie Mine.

Black Hills Daily Times, Jul 17, 1885
Annual stockholders meeting of Far West Mining company. An election for trustees and officers resulted. Aaron Hattenbach , Joseph Hattenbach.

Black Hills Daily Times, Sept 19, 1885
Atty. for Myer Wheeler and William Goodkind, files application for patent. Aaron Hattenbach.

Black Hills Daily Times, Nov 15, 1885
The Iron Hill Company Friday, filed an adverse to the application of Aaron Hattenbach for a patent for the Katie mine, Carbonate camp.

Black Hills Daily Times, May 28, 1887
Gustin Minerva Consolidated Mining Company notice of delinquent stock sale. M. Lowenthal, B. Goldbloom, Zoellner Brothers, H. Stein, H. Rosenkranz, Aaron Hattenbach, Fred Rosenkranz.

Black Hills Daily Times, Jan 7, 1890
Mineral world Jan. 7. Newcastle coal; Maggie annual; Uncle Sam partial clean-up; Monitor statement; mining brevities. Syndicate smelter. A. Hattenbach, Maggie Mining Company. Uncle Sam Mining Company. Monitor Mining Company.

Aaron served as an officer in the Knights of Pythias, a fraternal organization popular with their Jewish friends.

Black Hills Daily Times, Sep 1, 1888
Marco Bozzoris lodge No. 3 K. of P. presented C.F. Sheldon, C.C., with an elegant watch seal of the Pythias pattern. Aaron Hattenbach elected to the position vacated by Sheldon on his moving to Texas.

Black Hills Daily Times, Dec 11, 1889
South Deadwood Hose elects directors and officers.

J Hattenbach, Aaron Hattenbach, Nathan Colman.

Black Hills Daily Times, Dec 6, 1890

The carnival — grand and magnificent displays of business; ladies' marching full equal if not superior to anything ever had in the Black Hills. Hattenbach Brothers.

Despite setbacks, their grocery business continued to grow and prosper.

Black Hills Daily Times, May 10, 1887

The footprints of civilization were plainly visible yesterday at Hattenbach Bros. with robbery of safe. Entrance gained to Hattenbach grocery house, blew the safe and extracted cash and valuables as listed.

They relocated twice, first to the James Anderson building, and in 1891 they purchased two lots on Sherman Street from Sol Star and Seth Bullock, and began building their brick store. The new grocery store was especially well located to benefit from the arrival of the railroad in 1890. Wired for electricity in September of 1891, they moved their stock into the new brick store, using the adjoining building as a warehouse.

Black Hills Daily Times, Nov 5, 1891

Hattenbach Bros. have commenced moving their grocery establishment into the James Anderson brick store on Sherman Street.

Black Hills Daily Times, Nov 11, 1891

Store illuminated by electricity. Electric light wire put in Hattenbach Bros., new Sherman Street store.

Aaron and his wife had three children: Esther, Godfrey Walter, and Dorothy. By September of 1885 Aaron had built a home for his family in Deadwood's prestigious Presidential neighborhood of Washington, Jackson, Jefferson, and Madison Streets. Aaron's family counted Seth Bullock among their neighbors, as well as successful Jewish businessmen Harris Franklin, Sol Star, and Sol Rosenthal.

Black Hills Daily Times, March 11, 1892

Freight car containing 30,000 pounds of sugar backed right up to door of Hattenbach Bros.

Black Hills Daily Times, Apr 21, 1892

The porch in front of Hattenbach's old building, Sherman street, collapsed yesterday under weight of snow.

Black Hills Daily Times, Mar 26, 1892

Hattenbach Bros. purchased stock of Kendall & Smith, and will put in large stock of choice brands in adjoining building.

Aaron eventually sold his interest in the Hattenbach businesses to Joseph and moved to Goldfield, Nevada. From Goldfield he moved to Wilmington, California, where he ran a general store. In 1910, at the age of 51, he was living in Los Angeles. He also lived in Long Beach, California. In retirement he went into the apartment rental business, and died on April 7, 1943, at the age of 86.

MITCHELL HATTENBACH

Mitchell Hattenbach was born in October of 1859 in Covington, Nebraska. He first makes his appearance in the Black Hills Daily Times in 1879, when he won $5,000 in a lottery, a huge sum of money for that time. There were no photos of Mitchell available.

Black Hills Daily Times, Oct 12, 1879

Mitchell Hattenbach, In Deadwood. Draws $5,000 in lottery.

Notices regarding incoming freight from Bismarck indicate that Mitchell was involved in the family's early grocery business.

Black Hills Daily Times, Mar 30, 1880

M. Hattenbach, Incoming freight from Bismarck

Black Hills Daily Times, Mar 25, 1882

M. Hattenbach, On incoming coach.

Like all the Hattenbach siblings, Mitchell had interests in mining, and his name is connected to the Resumption Gold Mining Company. The year 1900 found Mitchell back in Sioux City, engaged in the jewelry business with his younger brother, David. The brothers bought pearls from men working the oyster beds in the Floyd River. At some point he married Belle Holstein, but the 1900 census lists him as a 40-year-old, living alone on Fifth St. in Sioux City. Mitchell died in Sioux City, Iowa, in 1911.

DAVID HATTENBACH

David Hattenbach
Photo courtesy Charlotte Hattenbach

David Hattenbach, the seventh child of Frances and Godfrey, lived from 1862 to 1929, and died at age 67. He was the first Jewish child born in Sioux City, Iowa. David makes only a brief appearance in Deadwood's press with his arrival by stagecoach in early January of 1887.

Black Hills Daily Times, Jan 7, 1887
Dave Hattenbach goes out this morning to Sioux City, Iowa; Chicago, and other cities, on business in connection with the business of the company in this city.

He returned to Sioux City, but like his brothers, David kept the interest of their family business in the forefront. In Sioux City he was in the jewelry business with his brother Mitchell. He was also the first mail carrier in Sioux City. Other occupations included selling life insurance for New York Life. The census of 1900 shows him living in Sioux City with his wife and daughter. David died there in 1929.

HATTENBACH LEGACY

Joseph and Aaron were the first of the Hattenbachs to arrive and the last to leave Deadwood. As a family, the Hattenbachs participated fully in the civic, cultural, and economic life of the region. They also managed to combine groceries and mining, their two main commercial enterprises.

Black Hills Daily Times, Sep 26, 1885
Hattenbach Brothers have a fine lot of ore on exhibition at their Sherman street store, from recent discovery in the Far West, Carbonate Camp.

Black Hills Daily Times, Dec 11, 1889
South Deadwood Hose elects directors and officers. Joseph Hattenbach, Aaron Hattenbach, Nathan Colman.

The Hattenbachs added their names to a long list of mine owners and businessmen pledging to support a railroad link.

Black Hills Daily Times, Jan 1, 1890
Black Hills resources - with particular reference to mines and mills and the ore and bullion output of Lawrence County, respectfully submitted to railroad companies pointing lines in this direction; businessmen pledge to aid and support railroad line.

To prosper, Deadwood needed a rail link. The Hattenbachs took a position in a bit of Deadwood turmoil that came to be known as the Water Wars. In an effort to bring the railroad from the valley east of the Hills through the canyon alongside the natural water course of Whitewood Creek, concessions would have to be made. It had already been decided that safety demanded track be 50 feet from the creek, but a group of businessmen felt that 25 feet would be sufficient. They finally settled on 45 feet of clearance as a compromise.

Black Hills Daily Times, Jul 29, 1890

That water way. Open letters from Councilman Carney replying to James K.P. Miller; S.P. Romans; consensus of opinion, relative to width of channel. M. Liebmann, Sol Rosenthal, Joseph Fink, Zoeckler Brothers, Harris Franklin, Hattenbach Brothers.

By now I knew some of the story of this large family who had left such a substantial imprint in the dust of Carbonate. Their history is at once inspiring and disappointing, but it reveals an indomitable spirit of people unafraid of striking out into new ventures. Mining was a significant part of their contribution to the economy of Deadwood, but their role as suppliers of retail groceries was far longer lasting. When their new construction was completed, they moved their stock from the Anderson building into their new store. That legacy lives on in the fine, durable brownstone building on Sherman Street.

Black Hills Daily Times, Sep 17, 1891

Deeds filed by which Star & Bullock conveyed two lots on Sherman Street, opposite the court house, to Joseph and Aaron Hattenbach. Purchasers will shortly begin erection of a handsome brick store.

Black Hills Daily Times, Nov 5, 1891

Hattenbach Bros. have commenced moving their grocery establishment into the James Anderson brick store on Sherman Street.

Black Hills Daily Times, Nov 11, 1891

Store illuminated by electricity. Electric light wire put in Hattenbach Bros., new Sherman Street store.

Hattenbach store on Sherman Street
Photo by Ann Haber Stanton

FINK

LEAD AND DEADWOOD

As several tombstones in the Mount Zion section reveal, including that of Joseph Fink, a number of Deadwood's Jews shared Koenigsburg, in the German province of East Prussia, as their birthplace. Prussia was a kingdom founded in 1255, with Koenigsburg as its cultural and economic center as well as its capitol. This was a multiethnic territory, where people spoke diverse languages such as Latvian, Lithuanian, Polish, and Yiddish. Prior to 1945, the region was cut off from the main part of Germany by a narrow strip of Polish territory known as the Danzig Corridor, and the city-state of Danzig, which is now the Polish port of Gdansk. The Jews who left were the lucky ones.

My pursuit was leading me from Deadwood, up Sherman St., to Central City, which had been the home of Barney (Benjamin) Franklin, the lesser-known brother of Harris Franklin who ran a general store. Barney had a large family, including at least one boy and a set of twins. There had once been a small community of Jews here.

I continued up the hill to the little city of Lead, location of the Homestake Mine, source of the golden motherlode that was fueling this fervor. At the beginning of the Gold Rush, most of the activity and commerce took place in Lead. Joseph and Anna Fink's elaborately engraved tombstone on Mt. Moriah predicted that this family would have an interesting story to tell. Their Black Hills story starts with father, Joseph Fink, in Deadwood and ascends with son Wolff to Lead. For all its noise and smoke, Lead had led the way, and Wolff Fink found his own gold mine.

JOSEPH FINK

Wolff's father, Joseph Fink, was the first of the two men to leave Koenigsburg for America, and the first to arrive in the Black Hills during early Gold Rush days. Notices of his presence appear in the papers as early as July 9, 1877. Starting out in business with a soda fountain, he next established a pawn-brokerage on lower Main St., in the Chinatown area of the Lower Main Street's Badlands. He was popular, and known around Deadwood as Uncle Joe. But Joseph Fink was a force to be reckoned with. This was a tough guy, well suited for a tough neighborhood. In addition to his various business dealings, he interacted with the law fairly regularly. In a setting already abounding with colorful characters and rowdy behavior, Joseph Fink got an unusual amount of attention in the press.

Black Hills Champion, Jul 9, 1877
Citizens to keep value of gold at $18 per ounce. Joseph Fink

Black Hills Daily Times, Jun 27, 1879
Elegant soda fountain now in running condition. Joseph Fink

Black Hills Daily Times, Oct 3, 1879
Petition for Boulder Ditch water. Joseph Fink

Black Hills Daily Times, Feb 1, 1880
Joseph Fink testified that Howard tried to pawn pocket relay.

Black Hills Daily Times, Apr 20, 1880
Pawnbroker Fink bought Burns gun from Smith.

Black Hills Daily Times, Apr 23, 1880
Joseph Fink claims to be innocent of buying stolen property.

Black Hills Daily Times, Jun 11, 1880
Joseph Fink had a tussle with Clark in his pawnbroker shop.

Black Hills Daily Times, Jun 17, 1880

Dead man has pawn ticket on him from Fink's shop.

Black Hills Daily Times, Oct 8, 1880

Pawnbroker putting business in shape in case of fire.

Black Hills Daily Times, Nov 27, 1880

Ida Clark's boarder attacked him, he had her arrested. Joseph Fink

Black Hills Daily Times, Jan 18, 1881

Our uncle Joseph Fink is suffering from a case of dropsy (swelling).

Black Hills Daily Times, Jan 20, 1881

Joseph Fink is much better, was able to set up in bed

Black Hills Daily Times, Jan 22, 1881

Joseph Fink is rapidly recovering, will attend to business.

Black Hills Daily Times, May 27, 1881

Joseph Fink donated money to July 4th celebration.

Black Hills Daily Times, Aug 1, 1881

Hydrant obstructs sidewalk in front of his shop. Joseph Fink

Black Hills Daily Times, Jun 20, 1882

Masquerade suits for rent or sale at Fink's pawn shop

Black Hills Daily Times, Jul 12, 1882

Green's attorney proved he pawned things for Beatty. Joseph Fink

Black Hills Daily Times, Feb 10, 1883

Opposed to division of Lawrence Co., pawnbroker. Joseph Fink

Black Hills Daily Times, Jul 26, 1883

Joseph Fink. Uncle of good many of the boys, back from Denver.

Black Hills Daily Times, Aug 14, 1883

Joseph Fink indicted for applying to his own use U.S. property.

Black Hills Daily Times, Aug 15, 1883

Joseph Fink plead not guilty to appropriating government property.

Black Hills Daily Times, Aug 17, 1883

Jury impaneled in case, (Judge) Parker for Uncle Joe.

Black Hills Daily Times, Aug 18, 1883

Joseph Fink. Jury came in with verdict of not guilty, discharge.

A mining dispute resulted in the arrest of two wagon-loads of workers from Laflin. Joseph Fink was involved in this, too.

Black Hills Daily Times, Jan 29, 1885

Arrival of another large batch of prisoners from Laflin in relations to Greenwood Mining Company. Joseph Fink, Herman.

Black Hills Daily Times, Mar 22, 1885

Services appreciated. Donations in appreciation of fire department efforts at Maillard building, lower Main street. Nelson and Parker.

Infrastructure, including water mains, was established by 1886. Joseph Fink's pawn shop, which had been washed out by flooding, needed water service restored. He enlisted the help of Mayor Sol Star, who resolved the problem.

Black Hills Daily Times, Mar 25, 1886

Mayor Star met with Supt. Grier, Homestake, and secured a promise to restore water main from John Farley and Co. to the former site of Joseph Fink's pawn shop, washed out by the flood.

Black Hills Daily Times, Jun 9, 1886

Superintendent Brelsford is restoring the Main street water main, to a point 200 feet north of Joseph Fink's pawn shop, and will establish a hydrant at the terminus.

Black Hills Daily Times, Jul 23, 1886

R.C. Lake has sold his store building on Mill street, Lead, to Mr. Fink of Deadwood, who will start his son in business as soon as the building is vacated.

Black Hills Daily Times, Dec 16, 1886

Fink the pawnbroker visited by colored man who walked out with cigar holder, then tried to sell. Property returned.

Black Hills Daily Times, May 7, 1887

Officer Duffy created a little consternation, First ward, yesterday, by ousting a number of poor, or undesirable tenants from the eyrie of Joseph Fink, east of Chinatown.

Black Hills Daily Times, Jun 2, 1887

George Roe, arrested for assaulting Joseph Fink, was fined $1 and costs by Justice Hall.

Black Hills Daily Times, Jan 9, 1887

Pat Welch assessed $16 fine or 11 days hard labor for boot theft; Charles Large 12 days each on charges of drunk and disorderly and assault. Now reclining in the bastile. Joseph Fink.

Black Hills Daily Times, Sep 6, 1887

Thomas Roberts case for embezzlement change of venue to Judge Murrin of Central; John Doe for assault and battery; George Bennett for assault and battery upon Joseph Fink.

Black Hills Daily Times, Sep 15, 1887

Joseph Fink will early next spring remove his family mansion from the island to a point nearly opposite Kidd & Benn's mill, and erect on the site a business block.

Black Hills Daily Times, Mar 2, 1887

Joseph Fink, with the aid of a man and shovel was enabled to keep his premises clear of water yesterday

Black Hills Daily Times, Apr 3, 1890

Jos. Fink is one of the happiest men in town. He sold part of real estate, proceeds of which settled all his bills and allowed an even thousand sent to his father as present on his 95th birthday.

Black Hills Daily Times, Apr 4, 1890

Jos. Fink started construction of a very unsightly frame building or shed on east side of Main street, Second ward. Acting Mayor Treber interfered and an eye-sore will be prevented.

Black Hills Daily Times, May 2, 1890

Joseph Fink erecting frame building on what was known for years as the island.

Black Hills Daily Times, Jun 10, 1890

Jos. Fink carries his left arm in a sling, result of endeavoring to remove cartridge from a revolver. Fink injured when weapon discharged.

Black Hills Daily Times, Sep 2, 1890

Sheriff Souter of Meade aroused from slumber to pursue burglar in nothing but gauze vest. George Monroy, Nebraska, is given as name of prowler. Joseph Fink

Black Hills Daily Times, Nov 1, 1890

Uncle Joe Fink to erect dance house, bowling alley and beer garden on side hill above B. & M. grade, opposite his store on lower Main.

Black Hills Daily Times, Dec 3, 1890

Real estate filed for record: J.K.P. Miller to Joseph Fink, a tract of land on the easterly side of M.C. No. 38, in Deadwood.

In 1890 Joseph was married to Anna, and he needed a home for his family. He bought land and by 1891 he was wealthy enough to build some houses in the fashionable Forest Hill neighborhood of Deadwood.

Black Hills Daily Times, Jun 7, 1891

Man known as Swede Pete had his foot nearly cut in two by a hatchet dropped by carpenter at houses Joe Fink is erecting.

Black Hills Daily Times, Jun 11, 1891

Deadwood improvements. Forest Hill. Dwellings being erected in Deadwood. Joseph Fink

WOLFF FINK

Joseph Fink's son Wolff immigrated to America from Koenigsburg in 1882, and worked with his father in Deadwood until 1883. Wolff chose to set up his first business, a jewelry store, in neighboring Lead which was a thriving Homestake company town.

He left the impression of being a bit more decorous than his father, and father and son did not always see eye-to-eye. They weren't above public engagement in fisticuffs. It could make for some lively local entertainment. The Times found their foreign accents added to the amusement.

Black Hills Daily Times, Jun 17, 1885

Lower Main enlivened by discussion "wid fishts" between Joseph Fink and his son. Uncle Joe got away with the fight.

Lead Daily Call Souvenir Edition – 1905 (Prussian/Jewish)

Lead's wide-awake diamond merchant and jeweler was born in Poland, but was raised in Koenigsburg, Prussia, where he attended school until he was 20 years of age. On leaving school he engaged in trade and for a number of years followed that line of business, selling his goods in principal markets of the old country. In 1882 he came to America on a visit to his father, who resided at Deadwood. It was not his intention to remain here, but his father prevailed upon him to make this country his home and he finally concluded to do so. He worked in his father's store at Deadwood for a year, when he came to Lead and opened a jewelry store of his own, his place of business being on the same lot on which his present brick business house now stands. This was in 1883. Since that date things have materially changed here in so far as the frame shacks of that day have given place to fine brick business stores, and in this respect Mr. Fink has kept up with the procession, as his well-stocked store will attest. Aside from his wife his family consists of one child, Louie, who is now at St. John's Military academy at Delafield, Wis.

Wolff's jewelry store in Lead specialized in diamonds, with the largest selection of diamonds in the area. He also sold watches, jewelry, clocks, and fine silverware, and became one of the area's most successful businessmen. He was also a pawnbroker on the side.

Wolff Fink Jewelry Store, Lead
Courtesy Adams Museum

Wolff Fink Jewelry Store. Lead
Courtesy Adams Museum

Black Hills Daily Times, Sep 1, 1886

Go to Fink, Jr., the Lead City pawnbroker, for watches, clocks and jewelry. That is the place where you can buy the cheapest. Ad

Wolff Fink Jewelry Store
Courtesy Adams Museum

Black Hills Daily Times, Apr 22, 1887

Great excitement at Lead when it was learned that Wolff Fink, pawnbroker, had been robbed of all he possessed, amounting to about $2,500, Wolff Fink, Russian Alice.

Black Hills Daily Times, May 18, 1887

Russian Alice sues Wolff Fink. A suit was on Monday brought before Judge Monroe by Russian Alice against Wolff Fink to recover a debt of $100.

Black Hills Daily Times, Jul 20, 1887

Much of the property stolen of Wolff Fink has been found in the possession of Grace Maynard, formerly inmate of Main street resort, Deadwood.

Black Hills Daily Times, Jul 21, 1887

Steal from the son, soak the sire. Nick Ivanovitch called in Deputy Sheriff Wilber Smith, giving him two pawn tickets with which he called on Uncle Joe Fink. They called for gold watch and two gold rings that Fink, the elder, had in stock. He gave them up and they were soon transferred to Wolff Fink at Lead City.

Black Hills Daily Times, Oct 25, 1887

On yesterday, Wolff Fink received a large safe. Mr. Fink says that he is not going to take any more chances in any robberies that may occur in the future.

In the late 1880s Wolff Fink got married. In 1888 his wife, delivered a baby boy whom they named Louis. Felix Poznansky, the local *mohel* was called from Rapid City to perform the *brit milah (bris)*, "covenant of circumcision", the physical symbol of a Jewish man's covenant with God. The parents link their son to thousands of years of Jewish heritage, affirming the child's Jewish identity. According to Jewish law, this should be done on the eighth day following a boy-child's birth, but in this case, allowing for distance, they probably had to make some exceptions. Felix Poznansky also circumcised the sons of Barney Franklin and Nathan Colman on this trip from Rapid City to Deadwood. Unfortunately, the mothers' names are not mentioned in the newspaper announcement.

Black Hills Daily Times, Aug 19, 1888

Felix Poznansky of Rapid is in the city and today will celebrate the Jewish rite of circumcision on the infants of Nathan Colman, Wolff Fink, and Barney Franklin.

Black Hills Daily Times, Feb 28, 1891

In civil suit of Wolff Fink vs. Joseph Brown, judgment of $80 and costs in favor of plaintiff.

Wolff went on to start a jewelry manufacturing firm in Lead that became a significant source of employment for the town.

Wolff Fink's jewelry factory, Lead
Photo courtesy Adams Museum

Tombstones of Joseph and Anna Fink, Mt. Zion
Photo by Ann Haber Stanton

Both Joseph and Wolff Fink's names appear in the Black Hills Daily Times until 1891. The names of Joseph and Anna Fink are inscribed on their elaborate tombstones on Mt. Moriah in Hebrew and English. Joseph's inscription tells of his origin in Koenigsburg, Prussia. Anna's birthplace was Grodno, Belarus.

Souvenir of Lead, South Dakota
Photo courtesy Adams Museum

STROOL

Benjamin Strool
Photo courtesy Janet Dunlap Rathbun

FOUNDING A TOWN

Following a story I'd heard, traveling many miles northward, I found myself in Perkins County, which shares a border with North Dakota, as desolate and isolated a stretch of prairie land as I'd ever seen. If there ever was a town here that was named for Benjamin Strool, there surely was no sign of it left.

A town on the prairie can flourish or wither for any number of reasons. The little town of Strool in the far northwest of South Dakota, a land of grass, sky, rocks, and hope, grew because it offered the opportunity to a handful of optimistic homesteaders for a place to settle and thrive. By following the minimum guidelines, for a filing fee of $10, the Homestead Act of 1862 ordained that one might stake a claim to 160 acres, a quarter section of the American West, and start a new life.

Young Bernhardt Stroohe, a 25-year-old Russian-speaking Jew, had newly arrived in New York City from Dublin, Ireland, aboard the Cunard liner R.M.S. Lucania in August of 1906. By the time he reached New York, he already had a remarkable story to tell. Stroohe was born in Latvia in 1881, and educated at Dorpat University in Estonia. He had fought for Latvian independence against the Russian Tsar Nicholai II in the Student Revolution of 1905. He managed to survive, afterward hiding out in the forests of Latvia. From Eastern Europe, Bernhardt made his way north and west, this time finding safety with his mother's family in Ireland. When he learned of free land being offered on the western plains of the United States where the federal government was promoting farming and development, he set his sights on some of the last homestead acreage still available in America.

In Hettinger, North Dakota, on April 9, 1908, he made his Declaration of Intention to become a United States citizen. As with many immigrants, his name became Americanized and he was now Benjamin Strool. He wasted no time staking his claim to this newly adopted country. On May 1, 1908, Ben filed a claim with the federal government on a barren stretch of prairie for 160 acres of American homestead land, far from the green forests and fertile farmlands of Latvia. He opened a general store under his name, giving Strool as a postal address. He invited other enterprising newcomers to start businesses to develop the community. Neighboring businesses and homesteaders began having their mail sent to Strool, making him the unofficial postmaster and founder of a newborn town named Strool.

Hitching posts in the middle of broad small-town Main Streets lined with wooden buildings were typical of the day. In 1908 through 1910 the town of Strool grew rapidly; in 1909 the town was already appearing on maps. But in 1911 the vagaries of a South Dakota weather pattern made an appearance. A drought caused a major agricultural setback, with some of the homesteaders selling out, enabling those who remained, including Ben

Strool, a chance to purchase some of the forsaken property at rock-bottom prices.

Main St. Strool
Photo courtesy Janet Dunlap Rathbun

In 1912, the town newspaper— even the smallest towns had newspapers— named The Perkins County Leader, reported a population of 200 in Strool Township. With good roads being developed for wagon and stagecoach service, settlers again flooded into the region. They often traveled by way of the Milwaukee Railroad in an "immigrant car," into the nearest railroad stop at Hettinger, North Dakota, sometimes with their farm animals and machinery. From there, for the price of $3.50, one might make the day-long trip with the Hettinger-to-Strool stagecoach, or continue by wagon over the wind-blown prairie to Strool. Some actually walked the distance. If one needed overnight accommodations, they might expect to sleep in a tent on a mattress stuffed with straw "prairie feathers." This was no-one's idea of luxury.

As more homesteaders arrived, putting up their tarpaper shacks and sod shanties in the surrounding townships, and starting farms and ranches, they needed goods and services. Strool's Main Street grew with the needs of the area. According to Janet Dunlap Rathbun's extensive research, in time there were *"three general stores, a bank, three hotels, two lumber yards, a hardware store, a smithy, a drug store, two livery barns, a restaurant, three real estate offices, a pool hall, a tavern, a creamery, a women's furnishings shop, a physician/surgeon's office, a barbershop, and a newspaper."* There were three 1-room schoolhouses, and two churches, one Catholic and another Protestant. Supplies were brought in by freight wagon, with lively traffic from Hettinger. Strool was becoming a regional supply center.

The newspaper was posting the essential legal notices of homesteading claims, charging $6.50 per announcement. The bank was encouraging real estate loans and inviting residents to start bank accounts. The real estate office promoted the good soil and water, and extolled the "healthful climate." Ben Strool's general store had vigorous competition. There was a traveling doctor and a visiting dentist. They had a winning baseball team competing with visiting rival teams, with small fortunes in bets riding on a game's outcome. There were Saturday night dances at the Town Hall with whiskey-drenched fights and midnight suppers, and Fourth of July fireworks with kids and ice cream. In 1917 the town's name appeared in bold print on maps, recognizing Strool as a major South Dakota city.

In 1930 the census showed 44 heads of households, and 122 dependents and workers in Strool Township. Most were from the Midwest, but, like Ben Strool, there were also immigrants from Europe. Ben theoretically charged residents a minimal annual rent of about $25 for perching on his property, which in practice was generally disregarded. He was owed quite a lot of money that he never tried very hard to collect.

Despite all the success, there was little confidence in the future of the town of Strool. There were no basements dug, no concrete foundations poured, and apparently little attachment to the land. For all the vitality of the town, people were making the most of their situation, at least for the time being, but with an underlying sense of impermanence.

The Great Depression of the 1930s was disastrous throughout the country, but on the plains it was cataclysmic. If it weren't the grasshoppers, it was the dust storms. Even when Ben reduced the rent during the "Dirty Thirties," his tenants ignored rental payments, which were probably beyond their reach at the time anyway.

Ben wasn't a particularly observant Jew, but he avoided pork in his diet. He wanted a wife, but Jewish women were rare in his neighborhood. Then Ben met Martha Jordan, a recently widowed dressmaker, a Catholic mother of two small daughters, far from her Sioux Falls home, friends, and family. In 1910 she and her children, Elizabeth and Marguerite, had crossed the state to claim 160 acres in Plateau Township, trying their hand at homesteading near Strool. Ben and Martha married and the next year they had a son whom they named Beryl. The Strool family made their home in the spacious 2-story, remodeled Hotel Grand on Main Street, where their nearest, and busiest, neighbor was a saloon.

Ben's interests extended beyond Strool. He had a wide variety of business, social, and political connections around South Dakota. In 1916, the family appears in Sioux Falls, with Ben operating a grocery story. In Mitchell he started the Palace City Jobbers, a wholesale tobacco and candy store, which became a life-long enterprise. Ben's main societal affiliation, like many Jews of the day, was with the Masonic Lodge, which he joined in Buffalo, South Dakota.

Ben Strool was regarded as a Democratic power in South Dakota, an exceptional achievement for a Russian Jew in a strongly Republican state. He was one of the organizers of the Perkins County Democratic Party Central Committee, and remained active with that political group for 30 years. He was the first Democrat elected State Commissioner of School and Public Lands, an office he held from 1933 to 1937, under the Democratic administration of Governor Tom Berry. He served the Democratic Party in Mitchell in various capacities, and in 1948 he acted as an alternate delegate to the Democratic Party National Convention. He served with the National Youth Administration, and in 1947, during World War II, he was a "price specialist" for the South Dakota Office of Price Administration.

After over 25 years of marriage, in 1937, Ben's wife Martha died and was buried in Mount Zion Jewish Cemetery in Sioux Falls. Twelve years later, in 1949, at the age of 67, Ben died in Kansas City, Missouri, where he had been undergoing treatment for cancer. His body was brought back to Sioux Falls, where his burial beside Martha was presided over by Rabbi Karl Richter. The children, Elizabeth (49), Marguerite (47), and Beryl (38), and their spouses, were listed in his obituary as the only survivors.

REIZEL STEPS IN

And here the story takes a bizarre turn. At the reading of the will, a stranger shows up with a marriage certificate verifying her status as the wife of Benjamin Strool. Reizel Hirschfield Strool claims she is Ben's wife, entitled to inherit Ben's estate and all of his property, which includes the town of Strool.

This is a complete shock. No-one in the family, not even Reizel's sister, Frances, is aware of this marriage. Reizel claims that she and Ben had met in Pierre where Reizel was working as a hospital dietitian. Reizel says that she and Ben had only been married for a short time and did not live together, but she produces probate papers containing Ben's Last Will and Testament, executed only three days before his death. The probate papers grant to "my beloved wife Reizel" the entirety of his estate, with the exception of bequeathing $100 to Beryl and $5 to each of his stepdaughters, Elizabeth and Marguerite. Beryl is furious, insists that this whole thing is illegal, that Reizel is not Ben's legal wife, and that the signatures on the Will are forgeries. Beryl sues, claiming that the witnesses did not know that his father, at this stage of his illness, was physically and mentally incapable of making a will, and did so under "menace, fraud, misrepresentation and undue influence." However, Beryl loses the suit, and only years later, in 1953, receives his $100 bequest. When the estate is settled, there is only $44.43 left.

In 1954, Reizel, the "rich widow," gets into her big Cadillac in Sioux Falls and heads westward across the plains of South Dakota to distant Strool to claim what she believes is rightfully hers. When she pulls into town, the townsfolk are not impressed. Clearly, this brash woman is not one of their own.

Waving the survey that Ben had commissioned in 1947, Reizel claims ownership of the land, demands the townspeople and merchants of Strool owe her back rent, and insists they purchase the land on which their homes and businesses are sitting. The citizens unleash a clear and simple Go-To-Hell message, and promptly move their untethered homes and businesses two miles north, where they create a new town which they name Prairie City. Strool is no more, and Prairie City, for a while, becomes the fastest-growing town in South Dakota. Outwitted, Reizel's dreams of instant riches are stymied… momentarily.

Who was this Reizel with such lofty aspirations? As it turns out, she was quite an accomplished woman with a strong streak of ambition. She was well educated, having spent her freshman year at Morningside College in Sioux City, Iowa, the University of South Dakota at Vermillion for her sophomore year, and finally graduating from the University of Iowa in 1937, prepared to enter the healthcare field as a dietitian. Although she claimed to have met Ben in Pierre, she may first have met Ben Strool while working as chief hospital dietitian at Saint Joseph's Hospital in Mitchell, South Dakota, in the 1940s. In his will, her address is given as the Veterans' Administration Hospital in Lyons, New Jersey, where she was again working as chief dietitian at the time of Ben's death in 1949. Who's Who of American Women, 1968-69 edition, credits her with other positions as chief dietitian, college-level instructor, and officer in professional societies.

In 1974, Reizel Hirshfield Strool Horel, now in her 90s and remarried, was living in Montauk, Long Island, a remote eastern suburb of New York City. She had sold her parcels of land in Strool, including the townsite, the ball field, and a pasture, for the sum $24,000— all in all, not a bad reward.

For a while, although Strool was no longer a town, at least it was still indicated on aerial navigation maps. In 2003, the Federal Aviation Agency determined that the town no longer existed and served no useful purpose on their charts. It would be excluded from any future maps. Prairie City, according to the 2010 census, had a population of 23.

Today, the wind blows the dust over the grassy landscape that once was the town of Strool, South Dakota. The prairie has reclaimed its own.

Special thanks to Janet Dunlap Rathbun, whose meticulous research led to a paper presented at the Dakota History Conference in 2003. *ALL ROADS LED TO STROOL: A Short History of a Small Town in Perkins County,* South Dakota © By Janet Dunlap Rathbun

BOBER

Sam H. Bober
Farmer, Seedsman
Newell

INSPIRED BY A SEED

BOBER, SAM HENRY
Farmer and Seedsman
b Borzova Ukraine Nov 14 1891; s of Benjamin and Hannah (Sonenschein); m Rose Stolar of St Louis Mo Apr 13 1916; ch, Louis M, Jack, Mira Lee (Mrs Henry Goldstein); educ, pub schs St Louis, att Woodbine NJ Agr Sch 1911-12, spec stud Mich St Coll 1913 and SD St Coll 1916, econ Harvard Coll summer 1937; animal husbandryman US Expt Farm Newell SD 1915-24; farmer, grower and distr fld seeds and Aberdeen Angus cattle 1924—; owner, Sam H Bober & Sons, Bober Seed House Rapid City SD 1945—; city commr Newell SD 1932-42; chm Butte Co Counc of Agr 1937; pres SD Seed Trade Assn 1939; chm Dist and Nat Farm Loan Assns Adv Coms 1950-54; mem, Fed Farm Cr Bd Wash DC 1955-56 and reapptd by Pres Eisenhower 1956-62, Seed Certif Com SD St Coll 1930-56; hon by SD St Coll for contr to agr 1950; mem Counc Nat Plng Assn; chm Fld Crops Com SDFB Fed 1948-49; chm Butte Co ARC War Fund drs 1941-45; mast Masonic Lodge Newell 1927; worthy patron OES Newell 1943; featured in Readers Digest story of Americanization of Sam Bober "From Russian Peasant to Amer Pioneer" Jul 1949; contr ed to Dak Farmer 1918-23; hobbies, bridge, books, travel; home, Newell.

Photo and article courtesy
Who's Who in South Dakota 1956

Northwestern South Dakota's prairies held more stories of Jewish pioneers than I'd anticipated, and now I was determined to pursue every one I could find. I'd heard about a farmer named Sam Bober, a Russian Jew who specialized in grain seeds, the mainstay of dinner tables everywhere. His story was celebrated in a museum in the little town of Newell, population less than 500, in Butte County.

All life stories begin with a seed. The stories of western South Dakota's Jewish pioneers provide abundant opportunity for inspiration. The life of Sam Henry Bober stands out as one of the most inspiring. Among his many accomplishments and claims to celebrity, Sam Bober's induction into the South Dakota Hall of Fame places him among the most outstanding of South Dakota citizens. Only three other Jewish individuals: Sylvia Henkin, the lone Jewish woman; Abe Blumenthal, descendant of the pioneering Blumenthals of Deadwood; and most recently Stanford Adelstein, also of Jewish pioneering stock, share this special place of honor. Sam Bober understood the power of a seed and turned the seed into a lifetime full of opportunities to make a difference.

The life journey of this son of Benjamin Bober and Hannah Sonenschein Bober begins in a *shtetl*, the little Ukrainian village of Borzova, on Nov. 14, 1891. Father Benjamin was a farmer, a man who barely managed to feed his wife and four children from his small plot of land. Life under the czar was a struggle. Sam, the only surviving boy and the oldest of the children, had three sisters, Anna, Bertha, and Eva. A brother, Louis, died in 1918.

When Sam was 12 a remarkable thing happened. A former neighbor returned to visit Borzova, telling of the marvels of life in America. The gentleman's appearance had improved noticeably- clearly he had prospered.

He spoke of houses with indoor bathrooms, and hot and cold running water. There were free schools in America. Most amazing of all was that he had been able to stand in line to shake the hand of the President of the United States. The neighbor was obviously telling such lies that he was arrested by the authorities for inflaming the czar's subjects. All this made an indelible impression on the boy.

Although the family was very poor and public education was not available, the Bobers managed to find the 25 rubles a year necessary to have Sam, their oldest boy, tutored in the Bible and Hebrew. As a result, Sam became a teacher at a young age, able to instruct others in reading and writing. He would walk three miles to a neighboring village in order to tutor other children.

Pogroms, vicious state-sanctioned assaults upon Jews and their *shtetls* were all too common in czarist Russia at the time. One such pogrom took place when Sam was a young teenager. The family was awakened in the night and told to flee to the synagogue for safety, while their house, and many others in the *shtetl*, were being destroyed. The youngster could see that his family must leave, and he convinced his parents that it was time to look for a new life in that magical place, America. Father went first, making his way to St. Louis in 1904, where he got a job cleaning Pullman cars. Within two years he had saved enough of his $40-a-month pay to send for Hannah and the children.

Leaving Russia was no easy matter. As much as the czar denied the Jews the right to live in peace, he also wanted whatever taxes he could extract from them. Hannah managed to scrape together enough money to bribe an official into taking them across the Rumanian border. Traveling the 30 miles by night, hiding during the day, they finally arrived at the safety of a Jewish family's farmhouse. It was there that Sam met Rose Lee Stolar, the girl who would someday become his bride.

As the Bobers' trip continued, at the Prut River Hannah once again had to offer a bribe, this time to the guards on either bank to take them across in order to reach the seaport to get to their ship. The stifling 9-day Atlantic crossing, with only herring, stale bread, and prunes to eat, finally brought the grateful family to the Statue of Liberty. From New York City they could take a train to St. Louis, where father had prepared a third-floor flat on Biddle Street. The air on Biddle Street was thick with smoke from local factories, but they were finally living in America.

Sam got a job in a biscuit factory, earning $3 a week. Overjoyed at finding the school actually wanted him, he enrolled in night school. This was not exactly the paradise they had envisioned. A Saturday night scrub-down required renting a towel at the local public bathhouse. Gradually, they became accustomed to their new surroundings, and Sam started making friends at a city park. At first the other kids teased him because of his short, stubby legs and his thick accent with broken English, but the boy had a talent for management, and he organized the Biddle Street boys into a club where they could play ball and run races.

ROSE STOLAR BOBER

Meanwhile, Sam had never lost touch with Rose Stolar, whose family had immigrated to America, where they had also made their home in St. Louis.

His next job at a printing office paid a little better than his previous subsistence earnings at the biscuit factory. Within four years he had saved enough to take a 10-day vacation to the hills of Missouri, which marked the next watershed event of Sam Bober's life. In school he had read Jefferson's quotation, *"He who can double his food deserves to rank next after his Creator."* Stirred by the beauty of the American landscape, his attachment to the land was kindled, and he returned to St. Louis where he headed for the public library's collection of agricultural college catalogs. The only school available to him with his limited means was the Baron de Hirsch agricultural school in Woodbine, New Jersey, and he proceeded to work his way east to enroll for one year. This was an amazing piece of luck; the Baron de Hirsch school was a perfect fit for a young Jewish man seeking a means of applying himself to agriculture.

JEWISH AGRICULTURAL MOVEMENT

The school Sam attended was founded by Baron Maurice de Hirsch, a French financier-philanthropist, who was convinced that the Jews were fundamentally an agrarian people and that agriculture would be their salvation. The motive underlying this agrarian movement lay in the relentless waves of pogroms, discriminatory laws and violent persecution that swept over Europe between 1880 and 1914, especially directed toward Russian, Polish, and Romanian Jews. In 1881 Czar Alexander II of Russia was assassinated by revolutionaries, and the Jews were made the scapegoats. Laws were passed in 1882 which expelled Jews from all hamlets and villages, and prohibited Jews from renting or buying land for agricultural purposes.

In London, England, on September 11, 1891, de Hirsch donated 2 million pounds and incorporated the Jewish Colonization Association. Such notable names as Rothschild appear as shareholders in the association. The objective of the Jewish Colonization Association was to rescue Jews from the murderous pogroms and the political, professional, and social persecution of Russia and Eastern Europe. They would accomplish this by promoting emigration and resettlement in agricultural areas of countries around the world, particularly the Americas. While some in the Jewish community saw the land of Israel as their only hope, Baron de Hirsch regarded the creation of the Jewish state as a fantasy. The association proposed to direct the Jews' attention to farming and to provide the indigent among them with an opportunity to find independence on the land through cooperative efforts and with minimal expense. Colonies were to be established throughout the New World from Canada to Argentina. The munificence of Baron de Hirsch benefited the Jewish Colonization Association by millions of dollars.

In the middle of the 19th century, back-to-the-soil movements were already stirring in Russia and being proposed for immigrant Jews in the United States. Nineteenth-century America looked upon the independent farmer as the quintessential American, the backbone of the nation. According to some leaders, for Jewish immigrants to remain dwellers in self-created ghettos in northeast metropolises was not in the best interests of America, the Jewish community, or the immigrant himself.

In the first issue of the Philadelphia publication, The Occident, April 1843, Julius Stern proposed establishment of a Jewish colony in one of the northwestern territories where Jews might devote themselves to "agriculture and the breeding of cattle, which occupations are the best props of every state." Stern actually hoped the colony might eventually develop into a Jewish state within the United States. The first Jewish agricultural colony of record in the United States was a settlement named Sholom, founded in 1837 by 13 Jewish families in Ulster

County, New York. These Jews had left New York City to engage in agriculture on farms they had purchased. They had tried to make farming pay for five years, but found it impossible to support themselves by farming alone, and were compelled to add to their earnings by small-scale manufacturing and trading. By 1842 they had sold their holdings and moved away.

In July of 1882 a group of 20 Russian families settled on farms in the southeastern part of Dakota Territory, in Davison County, and named the colony Cremieux, or Crimea. Located 50 miles from the nearest railroad station at Mount Vernon, and 26 miles from the county seat at Mitchell, distance compounded their many problems. Most of the colonists had quarter-section farms of 160 acres each, although some of the farms covered as much as a square mile. Under the leadership of Herman Rosenthal, a Russian from Kiev, formerly president of the Louisiana colony, they met with a fair amount of success the first year. Oats, wheat, rye, barley and flax were sown, and yielded good crops, especially the flax. In the second year wheat was more extensively cultivated, but the wheat bug destroyed a large part of the crop. Additionally, a prolonged period of drought caused the death of many cattle. In the third year, thunderstorms were so destructive to standing crops that the colonists were compelled to mortgage their farms. The rate of interest demanded on loans was so high, however, that most of the settlers sold out and moved away. A few remained a year or two longer, but excessive interest on their mortgages and a scarcity of water proved too powerful an adversary, and in the latter part of 1885 they also left the settlement.

Another attempt was made at a South Dakota colony soon thereafter. Twenty-five unmarried young men settled as farmers on a tract near Cremieux, at a place they called Bethlehem-Yehuda. Despite outside support, the experiment proved unsuccessful and after a year and a half, during which there was much strife and discontent, that settlement was also abandoned.

Of particular interest to Western South Dakotans is the fact that a de Hirsch colony was envisioned east of Rapid City in the fertile Rapid Valley area, but that colony never materialized.

Other colonies of Russian Jews settled in Connecticut, New Jersey, Virginia, Michigan, Kansas, Louisiana, Oregon, Colorado, and the Dakotas. The most successful among these were the ones founded in southern New Jersey, and as of 1900 four still remained.

With Jefferson's philosophy in mind and with the support of the de Hirsch foundation, Sam Bober pursued his education in agriculture. During his year at the de Hirsch school in New Jersey, he worked for eight hours in the fields and farms and then spent two hours in classes at night. When he had completed the year, he took a job fattening hogs with a livestock-feeding operation in Indiana. The farm's foreman had one method of fattening hogs, but Sam had his own ideas. Sam's method netted $300 more than the foreman's, which caught the owner's attention. He invited Sam to move from the bunkhouse into the big farm house, which pleased Sam immensely and added to his confidence. The next winter found Sam at Michigan Agricultural College where he studied pastures and feeding.

Now he was prepared to apply for a job in Montana managing a stock ranch. The owner was a big Irishman by the name of Joseph Riley. Riley could see that Sam, short (only 5 feet tall) as he was, would be at the mercy of the hired hands, who routinely spent Saturday nights getting drunk. Reluctant to hire Sam, but finding Sam quick-witted and determined, he handed

Sam a revolver with a warning to look out for "the Bohunks on Saturday night." Sam never needed a gun. Recognizing that all these ranch hands originated in various parts of Europe, and that they all enjoyed their native music, Sam bought a Victrola and played their favorite native music for them. German marches, Italian street songs, and Bohemian polkas resounded through the bunkhouse, as his comrades recalled their lives in their native lands. He bought books about America to read to the men, and the bunkhouse became a classroom in American citizenship. Two years later Joseph Riley died, and the ranch was sold.

HOMESTEADERS

Sam was free to strike out on his own, to become a homesteader, and he joined the rush for free government land. In 1915 he filed a claim on the prairie at Newell, South Dakota, where he put up a tarpaper shack and dug a well.

In order to support himself and make the necessary improvements on his claim, he took a job with the United States experimental farm at Newell. By 1916 he had accumulated enough savings to travel to St. Louis to propose to Rose Lee Stolar. In a trip familiar to many a young bride of that era, the newlyweds set out in Sam's new buggy for their life together on the homestead. A tarpaper shack on the windy prairie in the middle of nowhere was to be Rose's new home. Fortunately, there were kind neighbors who came to visit and share their provisions and encouragement. Rose made it through the winds of a sub-zero prairie winter by looking forward to spring.

Typical homestead shack
Retrieved from rootsweb.com

Land meant freedom to Sam Bober. In time, he filed a claim for an additional 160 acres, and when the deed for the land, signed by President Woodrow Wilson, arrived at the post office, Sam felt like "a stockholder in the most wonderful corporation on earth." The main requirement was to live on the land and develop it for 5 consecutive years. Sam's willingness to work hard and his ingenuity led to more opportunity.

By now the country was involved in World War I, and Sam, deeply patriotic, tried to enlist, but because of his stubby legs he was rejected. Instead, he applied himself vigorously to Jefferson's maxim, working toward building up food production. He believed it was his duty as a citizen to put his talents for agricultural management to use. He rode the prairies in Butte County and organized the first Farm Bureau group.

Bober recognized the importance of communication. He organized the first rural co-operative telephone line in Western South Dakota. It was, to be sure, primitive. Each rancher had to cut his own telephone poles and build his own line, but they elected Sam their secretary-treasurer. Telephone service cost the subscribers 25 cents a month.

SEEDSMAN

The government experimental farm offered Sam the opportunity to continually learn improved farming practices. He shared his knowledge throughout Butte County, showing his neighbor farmers how better methods could earn them higher yields. In later years he would study agriculture and agricultural economics at South Dakota State University.

Drought was always the South Dakota farmer's foe, and Sam showed his neighbors how they could overcome the lack of moisture, producing alfalfa on dry lands, and doubling or even tripling the amount of forage for their cattle compared to native grasses. He showed them how to produce better grain and destroy the sagebrush and cactus that obstinately tried to invade their pastures, by use of a new system of crop rotation. His experiments were not always successful, and he spent more than $30,000 on crops that failed, but he also introduced new grains and grasses that had been successful for other plant breeders. While his neighbor across the road was getting seven bushels to the acre of old varieties of wheat, Sam found a Russian variety called Kubanka that was not only rust-resistant, but produced 40 bushels to the acre. His business blossomed, having acquired customers in all 48 states and even abroad.

By now the couple was raising more than plants— they had three children, Louis, Mira Lee, and Jack. The family bought more land and started a company which they called the Bober Seed House. The Bober Seed House eventually accumulated 10,000 acres of land, setting aside 3,000 of those acres for experimental crops. Sam developed an early-maturing variety of seed corn and helped to introduce better grasses and hardy alfalfa into western South Dakota.

In Chicago in 1927 Sam took first prize at the International Livestock and Grain Show competition, beating out 400 other world growers with his Cossack alfalfa seed. He was becoming well known internationally, and in 1939 he was invited to the University of Kiev to advise the Russian government on raising seed. He brought a spoonful of the Russian variety of alfalfa seeds back to South Dakota where he planted and developed them. During World War I, as chairman of the Relief to Russia committee, Sam shipped a train carload of those Russian alfalfa seeds back to Russia.

During the Depression in the 1930s Newell fell on hard times. Sam Bober organized the Relief Society for those in need of help, and he persuaded merchants and ranchers to employ those who needed jobs. Sam was called, "Joseph, the Provider" by his neighbors.

Sam Bober had become one of the most decorated American agriculturalists. Now Sam's childhood American dream was about to come true; his expertise was sought by no less than President Calvin Coolidge who was vacationing in the Black Hills. He was called to the summer White House in Custer State Park where he got to shake hands with the American President.

In 1937, Bober took a "vacation" to Harvard University in order to study agricultural economics. There he met President Franklin Delano Roosevelt who invited him to view the excellent Bober Alfalfa Seed on his Hyde Park estate in New York. FDR gave Sam a personal tour of the estate.

He advised another president, Dwight D. Eisenhower, on agricultural issues, and Eisenhower was so impressed that he appointed Sam to the Board of Governors of the Federal Farm Land Bank. The Board then elected him chairman.

Bober participated in one of the most important developments in agricultural history in 1953. As chairman of the National Farm Loan Advisory Board, Sam helped author the Farm Credit Act which decentralized the handling of loans to farmers by putting the decision into the hands of the local stockholders. He was also a leader of the Crop Improvement Association. In 1964 he was appointed to the Agricultural Hall of Fame.

Sam's life was dedicated to serving his community. He was made president of the Community Club, was county chairman for the Red Cross, and helped several needy Protestant and Catholic children through school.

In 1957 Bober was featured in the B'nai B'rith national television special, "A Tribute to Freedom." Sam and Rose were intensely patriotic, proud Americans, ready to face the challenges and to help others achieve the American dream. Deeply appreciative of the opportunities this country had offered them, Sam often made speeches at 4th of July celebrations, but the Bobers' real day of celebration was September 26, the day Sam reached Ellis Island and the month in which they both achieved citizenship.

In 1966, joined by their family and friends in Newell, the Bobers celebrated their golden wedding anniversary. Among their gifts was the American flag under which Sam had taken the oath of office as chairman of the Federal Land Bank. Sam expressed his gratitude, saying, "This will be one of our most treasured possessions. The American flag has always stood out as a symbol of freedom, and it will always remind me of our priceless heritage." That same year, Sam Bober received an honorary Doctor of Science degree from South Dakota State University for his service to agriculture.

Sam died in Tucson, Arizona, on January 7, 1972. His death and that of his wife, Rose, marked the end of an era for Jewish homesteaders in northwest South Dakota.

The South Dakota Hall of Fame said of him, "The story of Sam Bober is a true manifestation of the American dream. Along with countless other episodes from the history of this country, his life serves to remind us that the promise of America is always open to those with the vision and the courage to pursue it."

Bober Day in Brookings
Courtesy of Newell Museum

SINYKIN AND KOZBERG

LITTLE SHTETL ON THE PRAIRIE

The prairie has reclaimed the land, but the night sky remembers one special shooting star- a settlement known as Jew Flats in far eastern Pennington County. Here the Northern Lights prevail, and the sparsity of population and remoteness from city lights renders Quinn, South Dakota, the nearest town, the ideal setting for a fine little astronomical observatory. This once was home to a small group of Russian Jews who just needed a safe and peaceful place to live, raise their families, and practice their religion. It was unique in its faithful adherence to Orthodox Judaism.

The land they claimed was just north of Peno (sometimes spelled Poeno) Basin, a few miles from Quinn. The name Peno derived from the Frenchman, Balboa Pynaux, a fur trapper and buffalo hunter married to an Indian woman. The Pynauxs lived in a dugout at Peno Springs, a common habitation for early fur trappers. An 1830 journal of an exploratory expedition up the Missouri River mentions Balboa Pynaux, also calling him "Pynaux the Yanktonais," a good hunter who brought in a plentiful supply of deer and buffalo. The good water of Peno Springs made the area popular with the Indians. Peno Springs may have been visited by the Gordon Party on its way to the Black Hills in 1874, and was likely the earliest inhabited spot between Fort Pierre and Deadwood.

Once the Deadwood Trail was established, guiding people, animals, and freight wagons from the landing at the Missouri River in Fort Pierre to the epicenter of the gold fields at Deadwood, Peno Springs became a favored stopping place for travelers. Following an old buffalo trail used by Indians and fur traders, thousands of tons of freight and hundreds of people passed this way between 1874 and 1908. For 15 years, the free range, good water, and bountiful grass also made the area perfect for the U Cross cattle outfit, an operation that ended in 1906 with the coming of the railroad and homesteading.

The first of the Sinykins, known by the name of Sinaikin in Russia, to arrive on America's shores was Sam, Harry David Sinykin's older brother, who started as a horse-and-wagon peddler in Sioux City and Dell Rapids, Iowa. Sam's thrifty habits prompted the local banker in Dell Rapids to encourage him to start a dry goods store. The store was successful, and Sam in turn encouraged his brother Harry to come to America and help him in the dry goods store.

HARRY DAVID SINYKIN AND ETTA FANNY KOVAL SINYKIN

The story of the Sinykins and the Jew Flats settlement begins with Harry David and Etta Fanny. They had married in in 1883 in Minske Kapulye (Kopyl), a province of Russia. In Minsk, Harry was a tin artisan and Etta Fanny managed the financial side of their business when Harry was away. Minsk was within the Pale, a limited area that confined Russian Jews to harsh conditions and a bitter life. Harry was ready to leave, but Etta Fanny had six children, and she was reluctant to pull up stakes. In 1892 Harry traveled alone to explore and find out what the New World held for them.

Harry went to the midwest looking for a place to settle in the United States, and he found work in the meat-packing industry in Iowa. He wrote many letters back to Etta in Minsk, telling her of the opportunities that America had to offer. After three trips between Russia and America in the 1890s, Harry became an American citizen in 1897. The promise of free land in South Dakota offered the kind of opportunity he wanted for his family, and Harry filed his homestead claim around 1901. His two oldest children came to join him in 1902, the third in 1904. In 1906 Etta was finally convinced of the need to leave Russia, and left, arriving in the United States with the three youngest children. Etta's mother had been a midwife in Russia, and as a girl Etta accompanied her mother, gaining knowledge about childbirth which would be valuable in her future in Jew Flats. The four oldest of the six siblings, Jack, Ted, Louis, Fanny, Rose, and Ruth, became homesteaders as well.

Harry David and Etta Fanny Koval Sinykin, 1915
Photo courtesy collection of Ruth Sinykin Kozberg by Diane Sinykin Small and Etta Fay Kozberg Orkin

Harry's first cousin, 17-year-old Jacob Paul Kozberg, and another cousin, an older girl, crossed the ocean in 1906, also bound for the American city of Sioux City. Sioux City, Iowa, was a Midwestern hub for many Jewish immigrants. Jake joined Harry and Etta Fanny at Jew Flats, where a small group of homesteading Russian Jews had established an agricultural colony. In time, there were probably 35 families and 16 single men including Jake, homesteading at Jew Flats, about half of whom were related. There were also many marriages within the community. In the case of the married couples, sometimes each spouse claimed their own homestead, and the colony was acquiring multiple acreages. These people preferred smaller communities to big cities, and the desolate grasslands of South Dakota may have reminded them of their old home in Russia. The difference was that here in America they might actually own a piece of it.

The land here was free! The United States government was encouraging settlement of the west. There was no czar telling you where you must or must not live. There were no special taxes levied on Jews. Your men could not be drafted into the czar's army for long years at a time— a dreaded fate. And most of all, there were no pogroms, the murderous, state-sanctioned rampages through your little *shtetl*.

Russian existence had been harsh, but neither was this was going to be easy. Trying to break ground, build a dwelling, improve the land, deal with the merciless elements, and still maintain *kashrut (kosher lifestyle),* were just the beginning of their challenges. For a filing fee of $10 each individual or family here was given a section, 160 acres, theirs to keep, provided they remained on the land for five years and "proved up" on it. These homesteading hopefuls were a gritty people.

Although many of them started in humble shacks and sod dwellings, the trademark prairie sod-buster's home, they made an honest effort to turn this settlement into a truly livable Jewish community.

KOZBERG

Jake Kozberg, second from right; Ted Kozberg, third from left.
Photo courtesy collection of Ruth Sinykin Kozberg, by Diane Sinykin Small and Etta Fay Kozberg Orkin

The values of religion and education were important to these people who had brought a Torah from Sioux City. Hyman H. Kozberg was a rabbi, a learned teacher and *shochet* (kosher slaughterer), skilled in the ritual slaughter of animals according to the laws of *Kashrut.* The religious men and boys rose at dawn to pray with prayer phylacteries, *tefillin,* strapped around their arms. The settlers of Jew Flats soon built a school and a synagogue.

Grindstone School in 1909.
Louis Sinykin in overalls. Ruth Sinykin is tall girl with white bib in the back row.
Photo courtesy collection of Ruth Sinykin Kozberg, by Diane Sinykin Small and Etta Fay Kozberg Orkin

They also had a *mikveh*, the special bath needed for ritual purification. If the nearby clear-running stream was all they had to start with, that would have to suffice. If that meant breaking through the ice in a Dakota winter in order to achieve ritual purity through complete immersion following a menstrual period, the women did what they must do, but Etta Fanny insisted that Harry build her a real *mikveh*, with walls and a roof.

They needed a school, and neighboring Grindstone was a lively little pioneering community with a school, ball team, dances, and Fourth of July celebrations. There was even a band of musicians and a male quartet.

Neighbors at Grindstone in 1910
Photo courtesy collection of Ruth Sinykin Kozberg by Diane Sinykin Small and Etta Fay Kozberg Orkin

It was an agrarian life. They broke ground, planted gardens and crops. They raised cattle, which at first were sheltered in dugouts when they weren't grazing in their pastures. All went well with the Jew Flats colony until 1911 when the region was stricken with drought. Unable to cope with the severe situation, most of the colony disbanded, but two families remained behind, Harry and Etta Fanny Sinykin, and their daughter Rose and her husband Isadore Moskovitch (Marsh). Their families stayed to tough out the worst that South Dakota had to offer.

Photo courtesy collection of Ruth Sinykin Kozberg by Diane Sinykin Small and Etta Fay Kozberg Orkin

Etta Sinykin and her daughter Fanny look on as Ben, Louie, and Cecelia, feed calves. Rose peeking in on left.
Photo courtesy collection of Ruth Sinykin Kozberg by Diane Sinykin Small and Etta Fay Kozberg Orkin

The nearest rabbi was in St. Paul, Minnesota. Etta Fanny and Harry David traveled to St. Paul to attend the weddings of their daughters. Rose Sinykin married Isadore Moskovitch on July 25, 1915, and Ruth Sinykin married Jake Kozberg three weeks later on August 15, both weddings performed by a rabbi, according to Jewish tradition, in St. Paul. Their sister Fanny's first marriage to Harry Steinberg produced two children, Benny and Cecelia, but that marriage ended in divorce in 1916. Fanny's second marriage was to Abe Cohne.

Rose and Isadore each claimed homesteads, settled down with their four children, three of whom were born at Jew Flats. Their living conditions improved, their homes became actual houses, and now they bought some of their necessities through the Sears and Roebuck catalog. They remained at their homestead at Jew Flats into the 1930s. In time, these families bought up land vacated by departing homesteaders by paying the back taxes, until bit by bit the family homestead grew to 5400 acres.

There was also opportunity for those who left the settlement and ventured into the Black Hills to start businesses. In the hard-drinking mining region, alcohol was bound to produce success. Brother Ted Sinykin already had a liquor store in Lead, and around 1911 or 1912 Jake moved to Lead where he bought out Ted's liquor store. The store did so well that he opened a saloon in Lead, followed by a second saloon in Deadwood. Jake and Ruth Kozberg moved to Lead for their business, where Ruth kept a *kosher* home, no mean achievement. Then, in 1916, Prohibition, which affected South Dakota a few years before the rest of the country, dried up the legitimate liquor industry, and the saloon became unlawful. Jake and Ruth left the Black Hills for St. Paul.

By now the Kozbergs owned a large tract of land at Jew Flats. This land remained in the family until 1965, when it was finally sold to the Willoweit family.

Jake Kozberg's saloon in Deadwood.
Photo courtesy the collection of Ruth Sinykin Kozberg by Diane Sinykin Small and Etta Fay Kozberg Orkin

The families of Jew Flats interacted, and some also married with other Jewish families of Lead and Deadwood. Henry Margolin, another of the original settlers, got his passport and left Russia in 1890, and as was customary, later brought his family over. Young Sam Margolin came to America with his mother, brothers, and sisters to join their father, and they also homesteaded at Jew Flats. Sam married Sarah Blumenthal of Deadwood, and the couple bought Salinsky's clothing store which they re-named the New York Store. The family later moved to Sioux City and then Hawarden, Iowa, where they operated a family store.

LOUIS SINYKIN

Louis, youngest of the children of Harry David and Etta Fanny, was raised at Jew Flats from early childhood. Diane Sinykin Small, Louis Sinykin's daughter, wrote of her father in a memoir, and tells of 4-year-old Abraham Louis Sinykin, son of a Russian tinsmith, awed at the sight of the Statue of Liberty and the masses of people in New York City. He told her of the train ride westward, the long journey to South Dakota, and of how the homestead in Jew Flats seemed like a paradise to him. In Jew Flats Lou discovered what would become a lifelong passion for horses. He rode the rodeo circuit for a while under the name of Bronco Lou, and in 1919 he competed for the world championship at Interior, South Dakota.

Bronco Lou, Trick Rider
Photo courtesy Diane Sinykin Small

Lou's first wife, Florence Mairowitz, who died quite young, and second wife, Florence Adams, raised their children on their land, which they named the Flying Triangle Ranch. Lou was a vivacious person who taught his children, Larry, Bill, Diane, and Vivian, about the land and the cattle, and endowed them with his love of horses. He also proved that it was possible to raise a traditional Jewish family while 80 miles away from Rapid City, the nearest Jewish community, and 300 miles from the nearest synagogue in Aberdeen. Both his sons became *Bar Mitzvah*, and his daughters were educated in Jewish tradition. They were among the last of the families to live at Jew Flats.

Although the Jew Flats population had dwindled in size, there were still Jewish families at Jew Flats until the 1950s. As of 2008 the one-room Grindstone schoolhouse still stood, but the last of the Jewish students were long gone. Diane Sinykin Small and Etta Fay Kozberg Orkin, cousins and both descendants of the homesteading pioneers of Jew Flats, to their credit, have been faithful keepers of this unique history.

Site of the former Jew Flats settlement
Photo by Ann Haber Stanton

BAILEY COHEN MARTINSKY

BADLANDS HOMESTEADER

Never would have I expected to find homesteading Jews in the far-off Badlands of Jackson County, South Dakota. This is an arid land of eroded, stratified, varicolored peaks and spires, a dizzying maze of canyons, the result of millions of years of deposition and erosion, from the late Cretaceous through the late Eocene and Oligocene epochs. The ancient sea, tropics, and woodland with meandering rivers all deposited an accumulation of sediments of silt, sand, and clay, each leaving its own discrete formations and its distinctive fossilized life forms. Time, wind, and water, have contrived to sculpt this region into an awe-inspiring moonscape. And somehow this became home to a kosher-keeping Jewish mother with a fierce determination to carve out a new life for herself and her family.

Jews were among those who grasped at the opportunity to take advantage of the Homestead Act of 1862, sometimes called one of the most important pieces of legislation in the history of the United States. Signed into law by President Abraham Lincoln after secession of the southern states, the Homestead Act turned over 270 millions acres, or 10% of the total area of the United States, to private citizens. Vast amounts of public domain were claimed and settled under this act. Eligibility for a homesteader required only being a citizen or intended citizen of the United States, someone who had never borne arms against this country, was the head of a household and at least 21 years of age. Although most homesteaders were newly arrived immigrants or landless eastern farmers, the definition was broad enough to include single women and even former slaves. The homesteader could claim a 160-acre parcel of land, but would have to "prove up" on a claim by living on the land, building a dwelling, making improvements, and farming for 5 years. For a filing fee of $10, the hopeful settler had a chance to own a very small, but priceless, piece of America.

Homesteader's sod shanty
Retrieved from rootsweb.com

Among the many American Jewish pioneering stories of Western South Dakota, that of the Adelstein family remains one of the more exceptional and enduring. With a heritage that traces its roots back to that homesteading era of 1910, and holds claim to many remarkable achievements, four generations of descendants of Bertha (Bailey) Cohen Martinsky remain closely tied to the fortunes of South Dakota. The Adelsteins continue to demonstrate that limitless energy and spirit that brought Bailey to South Dakota, attached her to the land, and allowed her to prosper.

Bailey Cohen Martinsky surveyed the dry prairie grass around them, the barren South Dakota Badlands landscape, and wondered if she'd made the right decision. The land company had promised "hundreds of quarters that will make fine homes... will make you independent and rich, at very low cost now... fine tracts of good agricultural land." Was this dusty, drought-ridden scene the same place she'd seen advertised back in Iowa?

Bailey Cohen's life had been no bed of roses. Born in a *shtetl* on the Polish-Lithuanian border under the rule of Czar Alexander II, her family and the other Jews within the Pale of Settlement, the area to which the Jews were confined, suffered from violent pogroms, enforced military conscription, restrictions from various professions and trades, as well as limits on educational opportunities. This czar had been comparatively tolerant, but upon his death in 1881 new waves of devastating rampages against Jews swept across the Pale. Hundreds of people became thousands, as emigrants emptied out of the small towns. At least one-third of Russia's Jewish population left Eastern Europe behind with dreams of a better life somewhere else; many headed for the United States of America.

Bailey's father had gone on ahead, and was already in America, working and saving up for passage for his family. After receiving the news in 1891 of Bailey's brother Joseph's orders to report to the Russian army, the Cohens knew the time had come for the rest of the family to leave— immediately. Bailey, 19 and pregnant, her husband Meyer Edelstein, her mother and several brothers, became part of the exodus, splitting up into two groups in order to more safely cross the treacherous Russian border. After reuniting in Austria, the family found passage on a ship sailing to New York City. Unlike many American Jewish immigrant families, the Cohens did not settle among the teeming masses on New York's fabled Lower East Side, but continued their journey on into the American heartland, to Des Moines, Iowa. With a Jewish population of about 500, friends and relatives already established there were ready to lend a hand. Settling down among Polish and Lithuanian Jews in the packing-house district on the east side of Des Moines, they found themselves in a community where at least their Yiddish was understood. The German Jews had their own community on the west side, and each group had their own synagogue.

The Cohens and the Edelsteins shared an apartment and Meyer went to work as a peddler, the most common and minimal of Jewish occupations. Here their first daughter, Anne, was born. Meyer soon managed to move his family into their own place. In 1894 a second child, son Moishe, was born, followed in 1896 by a third child, daughter Sarah. Meyer's work kept him on the road, often leaving Bailey alone with the children. When Meyer left for Chicago and never returned, Bailey knew that it would be up to her to take care of these children. In 1899 she married Louis Martinsky in hopes that he would make a good provider and father. Louis was a family friend from Europe who had roomed at the Cohen residence, and was quite a bit older than Bailey. He worked intermittently as a day laborer in a warehouse. The couple was soon expecting their first child, and before daughter Lillian was born they took an apartment next door to a grocery store which they operated together.

By the time their second child was born it was clear that Louis was never going to be of much help with either the children or with family support, and providing for the family again fell primarily to Bailey, the more energetic and ambitious of the two. The incompatible couple eventually went their separate ways.

Bailey bought some chickens and cows and set up a small dairy on the outskirts of town in order to support the family. Unable to afford hired help, much of the physical work of the dairy fell to young Moishe Edelstein.

Their family name by now had been changed to Adelstein, having been misspelled by a teacher when Anne started school. It was not until 1918 that Moishe learned the error, when he was notified of his father's death in Chicago. His name was changed to Morris by a teacher who told the boy he would need to change his Yiddish name to a real American one.

Having to awaken early in the morning to deliver milk, and later work the street corners selling newspapers after school, it was impossible for the growing boy to stay awake in class. When he was told that he would never learn mathematics or anything else, since he kept falling asleep, Morris reluctantly dropped out of high school to help support the family. This gave Bailey cause for concern. She knew she had to do more to improve her family's circumstances.

The Dawes Act of 1887 allotted parcels of land to individual Indians, and whatever surplus was left over was made available to non-Indians. The Sioux Agreement of 1889 had divided the Great Sioux reservation of Western South Dakota into six smaller reservations. Leftover land was now open to homesteading, and there began a great land boom in Western South Dakota. The land companies, in conjunction with the railroads, advertised at home and abroad. Posters appeared in the cities of America and Europe, shamelessly exaggerating the virtues of the land they were promoting. Lotteries were held for thousands of homesteads. With half a lifetime of hard work, strong faith, and stubborn self-reliance behind her, Bailey considered taking up the challenge of homesteading in South Dakota, this land of "golden opportunity."

In 1910 Bailey sent to Washington, D.C., for information about homesteading, and what she learned convinced her that this was the answer, her escape from poverty. Alone, she traveled to the end of the railroad where a land agent sent her to her new home. Home was 160 acres to the west of Interior, a remote, arid little settlement in the heart of western South Dakota's Badlands, on the edge of the Pine Ridge Indian Reservation. There she was met by representatives of the land companies, eager to show off their prizes to prospective buyers. Although many previous fortune seekers had long since relinquished their claims to this purportedly "good agricultural land," which was, in truth, of marginal value, valiant and desperate, Bailey saw possibilities.

On November 27, 1911, Bailey filed a homesteader's claim for that 160 acres in the Badlands, about seven miles northwest of the town of Interior, in an area later described by her son Morris as "fit only for rattlesnakes and prairie dogs, and so dry that it would take 50 acres to pasture one cow." Following that initial exploratory tour of her land, Bailey returned to Des Moines for the winter, arranged for Morris and the two oldest girls to stay with her family in Des Moines, and with the two youngest girls, Lillian and Esther, boarded the train for the railroad stop at Kadoka, South Dakota. They would need time to rest and adjust to this new environment before continuing on to Bailey's homestead claim.

She hired a wagon, and with her daughters and possessions, a supply of *kosher* food, and boards and tarpaper for building a lean-to, the indomitable Jewish mother set out across country. Near the town of Interior, Bailey would settle in to "prove up" on her stake, build a shack, farm the requisite acreage, and live on her claim for five years, thereby fulfilling her homesteading requirements.

Women Homesteaders in the Badlands
Retrieved from rootsweb.com

Bailey learned to do it all. With her nearest neighbors three to four miles away, she built a shanty which she heated with an old cast-iron stove. She hauled water. She learned to harness a team of horses, the gift of family in Des Moines. She milked two cows, also a gift, and cultivated, as she later wrote, "about 5 acres on my original homestead…"

In 1911 the region was stricken with drought. By then she had proven up on her claim and it was hers for the keeping. She took the girls back to Des Moines, but in 1916, she returned to South Dakota and filed for an additional stock-raising homestead claim. In her application she explained that she had "about 10 acres on my additional homestead and have planted alfalfa and small grains thereon for a few years, but the crops have been almost a total failure by reason of drouth (sic)." At the end of the application for the additional homestead extension, under the signature line was the instruction "sign full Christian name." Bailey wrote her name in cursive Hebrew characters. Despite Dakota blizzards, drought, rattlesnakes, crop failures, and untold hardship, Bailey remained determined to make this venture a success. She needed money, so she moved a shack she owned to the tiny Badlands town of Interior where she baked bread and doughnuts to sell to her Indian neighbors. She had grown up speaking almost nothing but Yiddish, but she learned the Lakota language, just as she had learned English. She had a rickety old wagon from which she sold beads and trinkets at pow-wows, 10 cents a bag, and she and her Indian friends developed mutual trust.

Kadoka was growing into a lively young town, with social organizations, general stores, implement dealers, lumberyards, banks, livery stables, two doctors and a dentist, grocery stores, a bakery, a drugstore and clothing stores, and essentially almost everything a family needed. There was even a baseball team and an opera house. This would be a good place to start a business and educate her children, and in 1917 Bailey left the homestead and started a general store in Kadoka, 25 miles northeast of Interior, along the route of the Chicago, Milwaukee, St. Paul, and Pacific Railroad line. Here in Kadoka, seat of Jackson County, trade center for the area and major cattle-shipping hub, her children stood a better chance of getting an education, where the independent school district offered classes through grade 10.

Martinsky's General Merchandise Store, sometimes locally called the "Jew Store," carried the slogan, "If it's to eat or to wear or to use, get it at Martinsky's." The Lakota Sioux were among her best customers. She extended credit to her patrons, including the Indians, whom she sometimes hired when she needed help. These Indian customers quickly learned that "the Jew lady" would not charge them a commission to take their $25 federal government allotment check. In the town of Martin they were charged 10% to use the check for purchases. To save the money, they would rather face a Dakota winter in an open wagon to make their few purchases.

With her thick Russian-Yiddish accent, despite her stern appearance, Bailey treated her customers fairly and with compassion. The family lived frugally in the back of the store, which patrons remembered as smelling of vinegar, dried apricots, and dry goods.

Main St., Kadoka, South Dakota
Photo courtesy Senator Stanford Adelstein

Despite strong competition, Bailey's store prospered. Meanwhile she continued to acquire income-producing property, purchasing one building that she leased to a creamery company, several rental houses and Main Street buildings. With Kadoka located midpoint between Chamberlain and Rapid City, as the tourist trade and cross-state business grew, she opened a rather rudimentary tourist court along the road for which, according to Morris, she had to haul water in barrels.

Now in her 50s, Bailey sold the Martinsky General Merchandise Store to two Jewish sisters-in-law from Sioux Falls, Nettie and Etta Margulies, and turned her attention to her other properties in Kadoka. In 1932, Bailey and her daughter, Sarah Adelstein Hoffman, by now a widow, repurchased the store and operated it until 1940, when Bailey's health began to fail.

As dedicated as Bailey Martinsky was to the success of her business, her devotion to her Jewish faith and the obligations of her Orthodox background were stronger yet. She kept the Sabbath, the busiest trade day of the week, by hiring non-Jewish employees to run the store, and she observed the holidays by closing her store altogether. On one occasion, lacking a calendar, she was devastated to learn that she had missed one of the Jewish holidays, observing Yom Kippur on the wrong date, an error which never ceased to trouble her.

As unimaginable as it seems, even on the prairie homestead Bailey Martinsky kept a *kosher* home. Except for the occasional *kosher* chicken and canned beef sent to her by her sister in Des Moines, Bailey was on her own. She followed the laws of *kashrut*, separating meat from milk, separating utensils and avoiding non-*kosher* foods. Her kitchen in Kadoka became known as the only place between Rapid City and Mitchell where a Jew could get a *kosher* meal. She was careful to follow the precept of giving *tzedakah*, charity. Above all, she was mindful of religious instruction for her children, hiring a *melamed*, a Jewish tutor, whenever she could. She was always concerned with their finding Jewish spouses, a seemingly impossible undertaking.

Morris Adelstein, who had grown up and changed his life by earning a battlefield commission in France during World War I, adopted a more liberal form of Jewish practice. Being forced to drop out of school as a young man did not impede Morris' talents or skills. In Des Moines, he was allowed to matriculate in Morningside College in Sioux City, graduating as a teacher.

He volunteered for the United States Army in 1916, quickly rising to sergeant in combat as one of the few educated members of an otherwise all Black combat engineer company. Returning from the war, he earned a civil engineering degree in Iowa City, Iowa, and then returned to Kadoka to join his mother. There he was encouraged by Chet Leedom, Republican political power of the area, to run for County Engineer in four counties as a Republican. As one of the few graduate engineers in the area, he had no competition and he won. Thus began the tradition of the Adelsteins voting Republican. In 1925, the banker L.A. Pier from Belvidere became Morris' business partner and they went on to found the extraordinarily successful Northwestern Engineering Company in Rapid City, a company that was responsible for paving the Pennsylvania Turnpike, building many major buildings in Rapid City, as well as building the original Rapid City Army Air Base, which is now Ellsworth Air Base.

In 1940, Bailey died in a nursing home in Mitchell, South Dakota, but her strong faith and adherence to Judaism was passed down to her children. Morris organized High Holiday services in western South Dakota, a role his youngest son, Stanford Adelstein, continued to fill upon his father's death.

Stan assumed management of the engineering firm in 1967, the year before Morris' death, and Northwestern Engineering Company (NWE) continued to prosper and expand. A subsidiary firm, Hills Materials, was his main business focus. Eventually, other interests demanded his attention and Hills Materials was sold. NWE now deals primarily in commercial real estate.

Like Morris, Stan married a Jewish woman. Ita was a member of a family of Polish Jews who fled from Lodz just as the doors were slamming shut in WWII, and barely escaped being swept up in the Holocaust. Stan and Ita raised three sons. Like his father, Stan also continues the tradition of Jewish leadership, serving as lay leader and Chairman of the Board of the Synagogue of the Hills. His leadership extends to involvement with Israel and much philanthropy. His military background and service to the Republican Party have added to his experience, and both went a long way toward helping him serve the community in his capacity as South Dakota State Senator. After Sol Star, Stan was only the second Jew to hold that position in over 120 years of South Dakota's history.

Like their parents, the Adelstein descendants are highly educated and hold positions of influence in their respective fields. The sons, like their parents, grandparents and great-grandparents before them, continue the tradition of marriage to Jewish spouses and of perpetuating the Jewish faith. Bailey, their extraordinary homesteading South Dakota pioneering great-grandmother, would have been very proud.

POZNANSKY

Benjamin, Marcus, Joseph, and Julia Poznansky
Photo courtesy Minnilusa Historical Association

FELIX POZNANSKY

Many Jewish families bear names based on place of origin or residence. Poznan, or Posen in German, is a city in Poland that held large, and in some cases very wealthy Jewish populations, possibly from as early as the 11th century. Documentary evidence of a Jewish presence in Poznan dates from the 13th century. Poznansky, Poznanski, Posner, or other variants, are all fairly common Jewish surnames. The "-sky" ending simply means "of" or "connected to."

Even for those who can trace their ancestry back to the Mayflower, unless you were an American Indian, the United States of America was, and always has been, populated with immigrants. Throughout the ages, sadly, Jews have needed safe harbors. Jewish immigration came in waves, and one of those waves was recognized in Dakota Territory of 1879. Refugees from Czarist Russia, Poland, Rumania, and Austria, whose primary language was Yiddish, were being assisted by the Baron Maurice de Hirsch Institute and the Jewish Colonization Association with headquarters in Cincinnati. The agricultural colonists were strongly motivated to escape religious persecution and social discrimination. They wanted the right to own and farm their own land, while freely practicing their faith. Baron de Hirsch was establishing agricultural colonies throughout the Americas, from Argentina to Saskatchewan. Felix Poznansky and the Morrises were inspired to provide such a haven in Rapid City. As early as 1879 Poznansky and the Morrises were members of a civic group whose purpose it was to encourage Jewish refugees to form an agricultural settlement in Rapid Valley, the fertile area east of Rapid City. Their proposal was ultimately rejected, and settlement failed to materialize.

Rapid City Journal, Jul 26, 1879

"The immigration meeting at Lewis Hall last Saturday night was well attended. Messrs. Morris and Poznansky were appointed a corresponding committee, and Judge Maguire may personally visit Cincinnati soon in furtherance of the main object— the inducing of a Jewish agricultural colony to settle in the Rapid valley."

Map of the western U.S. in Yiddish
Source Union Theological Seminary Library, Cincinnati, Ohio

Felix Poznansky's first stop in the Black Hills was Deadwood, where his name was associated with his interests in mining.

Rapid City Journal, May 18, 1889
Silver City and its prospects. Felix Poznansky and other Rapid City parties are interested... Galena ore in considerable quantities and undoubted good quality... The Sunnyside was of such quality that Mr Poznansky advocated sinking upon it. Samples of ore brought to town for assay yield as high as 79 ounces in silver and $70 in gold.

That interest in mining never waned, but in 1879 he moved to Rapid City, where he opened a clothing and tailoring shop, settled in, and with his wife, Bertha, raised a family.

Black Hills Daily Times Jul 6, 1884
Our tin resources. First discovery May 1883 on Etta mica lode. Developments are small, consisting of a number of open cuts and drifts.

Black Hills Daily Times, Aug 3, 1884
Negotiations finalized for consolidation at Central of Deadwood and Terra 80 stamp mills; Father DeSmet extracted 2,145 tons ore; mining news.

Black Hills Daily Times, Aug 13, 1884
Felix Poznansky, one of Rapid's solid business men and good citizens, is at the Merchants (hotel).

He also carried on business in several locations at once. It was quite common for Deadwood's merchants to develop business interests in neighboring towns. In September of 1885, Felix purchased a building in Chadron, Nebraska, from Deadwood's Ben Lowenthal, where Ben had started a branch of his Montana Store, and stocked it with a large supply of merchandise. Another well-known Jewish businessman, Meyer (Mike) Gottstein, Deadwood merchant and partner of Harris Franklin, was also preparing to start a business in Chadron.

Black Hills Daily Times, Sep 15, 1885
Deadwood merchants in Chadron. Chadron Journal reports Felix Poznansky in with large stock of goods to take immediate possession of new building purchased of Ben Lowenthal. Gottstein and Owens will soon be ready for business.

Black Hills Daily Times, Oct 10, 1885
Arrivals and departures via Northwestern Stagelines. Max Cohen, Max Fishel, Felix Poznansky. Felix Poznansky returns to Rapid by this morning's coach.

Although Felix would pursue his interests in mining throughout his life in the Black Hills, his primary support would depend on his talents as a tailor and purveyor of clothing. One unique photograph dated May 25, 1886, catches Felix and employees in the doorway of the Montana Store in Rapid City. The image finds his establishment in the process of being moved, propped up on blocks, out in the middle of dusty, unpaved Main Street, doing business as usual to make room for new construction. A dress blowing in the breeze shows that his business catered to ladies as well as gentlemen. This photo captures the stubborn grit of the pioneer merchant.

Felix Poznansky's Montana Store in the middle of Sixth St. in Rapid City, 1880
Photo courtesy David Strain

The false cornice, a popular architectural ruse of the day, was calculated to give the tiny box of a structure the appearance of a much larger building while it also functioned as a place for signage.

The Montana Store was moved to Fifth and Kansas City Streets and in 1887 it found a new home in Felix's new two-story brick building. Evidence of Felix's talent as a tailor can be found in this letter from Joseph Gossage to his future bride, Alice Bower, as noted by Laura Bower Van Nuys in her history of the South Dakota Bower family, "The Family Band". Joe Gossage, the well-liked publisher of the Rapid City Journal, the city's first newspaper, wrote to his fiancée: "I will next week leave my order for my wedding suit with our clothier Felix Poznansky... Dear Alice. I will be dressed so that you will not be ashamed of me— plain and neat and not gaudy."

Felix came to be a prominent civic leader. Among his many contributions, he served on Rapid City's City Council, the school board, and for jury duty. Some sources credit Felix with helping to establish Rapid City's first water company. He and his family were members of the prestigious Masonic Lodge. His daughter, Julia, was an active member of the Masonic women's auxiliary, the Order of the Eastern Star, organized for the betterment of their community.

Black Hills Daily Times, Jun 3, 1887
At the Merchants: Felix Poznansky and wife.

Black Hills Daily Times, Jul 8, 1890
Grand and petit jurors for September term of U.S. courts drawn yesterday. Felix Poznansky.

Felix was a learned layman, skilled in the Jewish ritual of circumcision. He traveled to distant parts of western South Dakota when called upon to perform the *mitzvah* (sacred duty) of *brit milah* (the covenant of circumcision). Interested newspaper reporters referred to Felix as rabbi; however, there is no evidence that he was ordained. "Rabbi" was most likely a convenient and respectful designation, and "frontier Judaism" requires community participation.

Black Hills Daily Times, Aug 19, 1888
Jewish rite of circumcision today. Felix Poznansky of Rapid is in the city and today will celebrate the Jewish rite of circumcision on the infants of Nathan Colman, Wolff Fink and Barney Franklin.

Black Hills Daily Times, Feb 9, 1892
Felix Poznansky, rabbi, was in Lead and circumcised the infant son of Mr. and Mrs. Joe Chamison.

When Felix died on July 3, 1907, at the age of 77, the Black Hills Weekly Journal published a lengthy, detailed obituary. He was buried in the family plot in the original Jewish section of Rapid City's Mountain View Cemetery. Mrs.

Bertha Poznansky died March 29, 1922, and is buried beside her husband.

Black Hills Weekly Journal, Jul 5, 1907

With the passing of Felix Poznansky closes a long and eventful life. Born in Wloclawek, Russia-Poland on April 21, 1830, he entered upon what would now be called a strenuous life, but which he pursued with an earnestness that was so natural to him that he did not recognize anything unusual. When 14 years he left his home and walked to Paris, France where he remained for two years. He then had a fever for the newer country of America, and he took a stowaway passage for New York. When found, he was almost thrown overboard, so angry was the ship's crew to find him there. From New York he went to Titusville, Pennsylvania, and later to Ohio. From place to place he traveled, making his expense with a peddler's pack upon his back. He remained some time at Ottumwa, Iowa, and then went to Nebraska, spending some time in Nemaha County. The Colorado gold fever then caught him, and a few years were spent at Breckenridge. The excitement in Montana next attracted his attention, and he went to Butte where he developed some of the best mines in that section. It was then that he went back to New York to claim his bride, Miss Bertha Abrams, whose home was in Newburgh of that state. Mr. and Mrs. Poznansky were married March 14, 1866, and returned to Montana, later going to Denver. Leaving his family in Denver, he came to the Black Hills in 1878, spending a few months in Deadwood, Rochford and Rockerville. In 1879 the family settled in Rapid City on Main St. where Chase's store now stands, in a log house built by the late J.A.C Smith.

This all sounds very commonplace, but when one remembers the years that have passed and the changes that have taken place in the modes of traveling and living, one can understand what he must have passed through. The experiences of his life would make a very interesting book, and many have listened with pleasure to the recital of some of them. Of his life in Rapid City there is little need to say much for it is well known. He early went into the dry goods and clothing business, but for the past several years has been interested in promoting the mining interests of the Black Hills. He has filled several positions of trust in the city, among which were a member of the school board and city alderman and at the time of his death was a member of the city council.

Having always kept his Jewish faith, he was known as "Rabbi" throughout the Hills, and was often sent for to officiate at important ceremonies.

Six children came into the family, one of whom, a little daughter, died in Helena, and another, also a girl, died in childhood in Rapid City. The others are well-known here, Marcus and Julia, having always remained here, while Joseph has made his home in Deadwood, and was with his father at the time of his death. Ben has for the past fourteen years spent much of his time in Philadelphia, but was here on a visit to his parents a couple of months ago. He was reached yesterday by telegraph at Des Moines, Iowa, and will be in on this morning's train so that all the family will be present for the last services a devoted family can pay to a beloved husband and father. Mr. Poznansky was for many years a member of the Masonic Lodge, and by his wish the services will be conducted by that body under the leadership of Hon. J.R. Schrader. The services will be at home...

JOSEPH POZNANSKY

Joseph was born in Helena, Montana, but raised and educated in Rapid City. The first known reference to Joseph appears at his 13th birthday in December of 1879, the age of *Bar Mitzvah*. This was celebrated with a grand party. To achieve *bar mitzvah* Joe would have been schooled in Hebrew as well as the basics of Judaism, which his father could provide. Clearly, the young scholar had impressed the reporter of the Rapid City Journal.

Rapid City Journal, Dec 27, 1879

"We were one of a party of friends of Master Joseph Poznansky who met at his parents' residence to celebrate his 13th birthday. A banquet was spread, the bill of fare of which embraced as great a variety of the edibles and wines as are usually displayed in the cities of the East. The guests all enjoyed themselves in the highest degree. Our young friend in whose honor of the entertainment was given will, if we are as good a judge of human nature as we think we are, make his mark in the world—make a record worthy of the first male birth of the driving, enterprising city of Helena, Montana. In school he is the aptest and most decorous of scholars, and in business—in which, as young as he is, he has had considerable experience—he is smart, honest, and obliging. And now, since the Israelites have wisely concluded to take a new departure and give special attention to diversified industry, we would suggest Joseph undoubtedly possesses all the natural elements of successful journalism, and we would recommend him to throw the yardstick aside and try a type case."

Joseph Poznansky
Photo courtesy Minnilusa Historical Assn.

Joseph Poznansky
Photo courtesy Adams Museum and House

Among Joseph's jobs was employment as a bookkeeper at Harris Franklin's First National Bank in Deadwood. The American National Bank, owned by Ben Baer and Harris

Franklin—already men of wealth— had merged with the First National Bank by consolidation, making the First National Bank extraordinarily strong. In the roll call of stockholders and directors of the First National Bank appear the names of some of Deadwood's leading Jewish pioneers, including Baer, Franklin, and Jacob Goldberg.

Black Hills Daily Times, Feb 15, 1893
Poznansky back at First National bank. Joe Poznansky is again connected with the First National Bank as bookkeeper.

Joe Poznansky was present at the scene of a bank robbery in Deadwood. Joe happened to be busy at his usual duties on Nov. 17, 1910, when the bank became the scene of an attempted robbery. The story, as reported by the Deadwood Daily Pioneer-Times on Nov. 18, 1910, tells that a stocky, 30-year-old man entered the bank at about 11 a.m., and approached the teller's window, asking nervously, "have you any money here?" The assistant cashier, Joe Poznansky, answered, "We have a little." The robber then said, "Hand it over and get it out quick," as he reached for the gun in his pocket. Then without waiting for Joe to either comply or refuse, he thrust the gun through the grating and pulled the trigger. When the gun discharged, Joe dodged beneath the counter, and the bullet which glanced off the counter struck the chandelier, was reflected from the ceiling and lodged in the brick partition between the banking room and the director's room. A woman customer who was in the bank at the time was so frightened that she rushed into the director's room, crashing through the window, taking the glass plate with her. The holdup man turned toward several customers who happened to be in the bank at that moment, and waving his gun in the air, ordered them to throw up their hands.

Some did as he ordered, but the man paid no further attention to them. Neither did he make any attempt to reach in through the window, to retrieve any money, or leave the building. Then he must have decided to change his plan, because he turned to the teller's window and threw the gun on the counter saying, "What the hell's the use."

Bank President, Harris E. Franklin, who had been seated at his desk, reportedly rushed to the director's room where a shotgun was usually kept, but found it had been moved because of some remodeling which was going on at the time. Franklin then returned to the teller's cage where the gun which the holdup man had thrown down, had been moved from in front of the window to the end of the counter by Cashier D.A. McPherson. McPherson was remarkably cool in approaching the window while the gun was still within the reach of the bank robber. Franklin grabbed the gun and passed around to the outside, held it to the man's face and ordered him to throw up his hands. The bandit was arrested, charged with assault and intent to commit a felony, and was sentenced to 8 years and 9 months in state prison. The would-be robber, identified as Tom Dare, managed to escape two days later, only to be recaptured on Yellow Creek.

Joseph later settled into a less exciting life, opening a dry goods store in Sturgis and marrying Lucille Leslie in August of 1917.

BENJAMIN POZNANSKY

Class of 1890 – Benjamin Poznansky and classmates
Photo courtesy South Dakota School of Mines and Technology

Benjamin Poznansky had the distinction of being the only male of three members of the first graduating class of the School of Mines in Rapid City. The women were Carrie Feigel and Eva Robinson.

Black Hills Weekly Journal, May 30, 1890
The graduating exercises of the School of Mines will be held this evening at Library Hall. Three students will graduate with the degree of Bachelor of Science. Mr. Benjamin Poznansky, Miss Carrie Feigel, and Miss Eva Robinson.

After graduation Ben left Rapid City to work for the Mennen Company in Colorado. A Mennen advertisement from 1898 speaks of "borated talcum toilet powder" to be used "after bathing and shaving." Ben died in Pueblo, Colorado, in December of 1918, still quite young. He is buried beside his family in the original Jewish section of Mountain View Cemetery in Rapid City.

MARCUS (MOX) POZNANSKY

Mox Poznansky
Photo courtesy Minnilusa Historical Association

Marcus, more familiarly known as Mox, was the youngest Poznansky son. Like his older brothers Mox was born in Helena, Montana. As a young boy Marcus had a job as the Rapid City cattle herder. As a young man he worked at the Bee Hive, a retail store. Later on he and Ed Schleuning operated a meat market, which they eventually sold to Algernon Holcomb.

Described as a short man, quite proper, extremely kind, Mox went into the insurance business. His offices were in the Harney Hotel, on the corner of Main and Eighth Street.

Mox Poznansky
Photo courtesy Minnilusa Historical Association

Mox Poznansky
Photo courtesy Minnilusa Historical Association

Harney Hotel, Main St., Rapid City.
Photo courtesy Minnilusa Historical Association

Mox remained single all his life. He died in an automobile accident on March 14, 1947, and was buried in the family plot in Mountain View Cemetery.

JULIA POZNANSKY

Julia, the last of the Rapid City Poznanskys, was remembered as being distinguished, ladylike, displaying "good manners and upbringing." A bright young woman, Julia also graduated from the South Dakota School of Mines.

Julia (center) clowning with girlfriends
Photo courtesy Minnilusa Historical Association

She never married, and worked alongside her brother Mox in their insurance agency in the Harney Hotel. She participated in some of the earliest activities of the Jewish community as it developed in Rapid City. She was a member of Rapid City's branch of Hadassah, which indicates that there were enough Jewish women to form such an organization. Julia was a member of the Eastern Star, the women's adjunct of the Masons. She was an early member of the Synagogue of the Hills, and a generous contributor to the synagogue.

Rapid City Journal, Sep 7, 1963

Julia Poznansky, 79, died in a local hospital Friday night. Miss Poznansky for more than a quarter century had operated the M. Poznansky insurance agency in the Harney Hotel... Miss Poznansky was the daughter of pioneer businessman Felix Poznansky, and had remained in the home constructed by her father at 509 Kansas City St. in 1880. She was a member and past Matron of the Order of the Eastern Star. Her parents and three brothers preceded her in death. Miss Poznansky attended Rapid City High School and the School of Mines.

Julia passed away in 1963, and was buried with her family in Mountain View Cemetery. The Poznansky family had been touched by the tragedy that confronted so many families of that time with the death of Rosa, a 6-year-old, born in March of 1881 and died in June of 1887. Rosa was initially buried in the first Jewish cemetery in Rapid City, making a total of 3 graves in that cemetery. When Mountain View Cemetery came into being, those 3 graves were exhumed and moved to a special Jewish section of the new burial grounds on the west side of Rapid City. The site of Rapid City's first Jewish cemetery, at the top of Eighth Street, renamed Mount Rushmore Road, is now embedded in a heavily trafficked, commercially zoned route leading to Mount Rushmore.

Although they left no offspring in the Black Hills, the Poznansky name is not forgotten. Julia's signature appears on a scroll commemorating the donation of a *Torah* presented to the Synagogue of the Hills shortly before she died. Julia's name is recited in remembrance at *yizkor*, the memorial list read on Yom Kippur at the Synagogue of the Hills. When she died, two generations of living Jewish pioneer history in the Black Hills passed with her.

MORRIS

JACOB AND LOUIS MORRIS

Brothers Jacob and Louis Morris were born in Russia/Poland in the mid-1800s. When their father died, their mother decided to emigrate to New York City with her children. Like so many youngsters of the day, the older children had to work in order to help support the family. Jacob worked in New York and then had a dry goods store in Washington, D.C. In 1882 Jacob married Hannah Isaacs in New York City and they had five children: Sadie; Miriam Rose; Bertha; Milton; and Julian. Jacob and his family traveled to Cheyenne, Custer, Deadwood, and finally Rapid City, Dakota Territory, where brother Louis had already established a dry goods and clothing business.

Advertisement for Louis Morris store
Photo courtesy Minnilusa Historical Association

commercial world, and would continue operating for over 30 years. After Louis retired, Jacob continued running the store.

Jacob Morris's first Rapid City store
Photo courtesy Minnilusa Historical Association

The wooden building formerly occupied by Felix Poznansky's Montana Store at the corner of Main and Sixth St. would be replaced in 1886 by a brick building with spaces for retail and offices, erected for Jacob and Louis Morris. The dealers in dry goods and clothing established themselves firmly in Rapid City's fast-growing

The sturdy brick J.&L. Morris building would withstand the test of time. The beautiful Victorian, now the result of a major historic preservation project, currently houses the elegant Prairie Edge Trading Company and Galleries. It has held many businesses throughout the years, including a notorious saloon owned by "Big Jack" Clower which occupied the first floor, from which the secondary name of "Clower Building" derives.

RCC Clothing, owned by Nathan and Ruth Horwitz, western clothing outfitters, originally set up shop near the Virginia Café in 1948. In 1963 they moved to the Morris Building, eventually expanding to have other RCC stores in South Dakota, Nebraska, Wyoming, and Colorado.

Jacob and Louis Morris Store
Photo courtesy Minnilusa Historical Association

Hot Springs, whose warm mineral waters once offered relief for Sol Star and other sufferers of rheumatism, is now a resort and retirement retreat. The Morrises left a Star of David engraved in the cornerstone of their branch store in Hot Springs.

PART THREE

WHAT REMAINS

My journey had come full circle. I was back in Rapid City where there were historical footprints of other Jewish families and imprints of their lives. There had been continuous commercial, cultural, and social interaction between the towns of the Hills and throughout western South Dakota. Harris Franklin, Ben Baer, and Jacob Goldberg had all established branches of their Deadwood businesses here. Joseph Levinson, son of Deadwood jeweler, Sol Levinson, had opened a branch of his jewelry store in Rapid City. Jews from Rapid City and Sturgis and Spearfish attended weddings and *brit milahs* (circumcisions) in Deadwood.

Patriarch Felix Poznansky, tailor and clothier, was also *mohel* (ritual circumcisor) for the entire region. The Poznansky family, respected and well thought of, made their lives here, contributing to the town's welfare and development.

Little remained physically of the Jewish presence in Rapid City, but those remnants were striking. One vestige was the imposing brick structure with Victorian embellishments now known as the Clower Building, on the corner of Main and Sixth Streets, showing its age, but aging gracefully. That building was erected by Louis Morris for his dry goods business. This was a decaying doyenne, a grand old lady with origins reaching back to the earliest days of settlement. Someday, someone with vision would surely have to restore this treasure to her former glory. She was too elegant, too full of history to simply be allowed to crumble.

And there was still the lovely stained glass sign that hung in the doorway of what had once been Levinson's jewelry store on 7th Street.

I learned that Joseph Poznansky, one of Felix and Bertha's three sons, was an accomplished artist who painted landscapes in oil. There had to be evidence of his paintings somewhere in the Black Hills. I later heard that an oil painting of a local landscape by Joseph Poznansky was included in an exhibit at The Journey Museum in Rapid City.

THE JEW PEDDLER TRAIL

In the 1870s and 1880s, the period surrounding the great Black Hills Gold Rush, there was hardly an untrodden square foot of terrain in the higher Hills. The prospectors needed supplies delivered to their camps, and it was the practice of pack-peddlers, many of them Jewish, to travel out into the countryside to fill those needs. Jewish peddlers would originate from businesses in Rapid City and Deadwood carrying 100-plus-pound backpacks loaded with overalls, socks, needles, eyeglasses, and other small necessities, with their stores on their backs.

The fundamental requirement for anyone relating history is to demand nothing less than an accurate and unvarnished account. Names such as Jew Peddler were applied without consideration of the offense they may have caused. One small section of their route became commonly known as the Jew Peddler Trail. The Jew Peddler Trail was an effective, if strenuous, shortcut created to eliminate 3 miles of difficult travel along curving streams between the towns of Mystic and Canyon City. Part of the trail is reasonably level and easily hiked, but part of it slopes downward toward Slate Creek at a precipitous angle, making for difficult footing. None of this was easy.

Peddling was a difficult life, with the peddler hoping for a friendly welcome and perhaps a safe night's lodging. George Frink of Mystic permitted Harry Hyman (H.H.) Marks, known as a Jew Peddler, to stay overnight at the Frink home. The Frinks' son, Russel, remembers being gifted with a pair of overalls by H.H.

George Frink standing on the right. President and Mrs. Calvin Coolidge visiting the Black Hills in 1927
Photo courtesy Minnilusa Historical Association

Many of our pioneer businessmen in the early censuses report their employment as "traveling salesman". Most of the peddlers were immigrants, many of whom spoke Yiddish as their first language. There are frightful stories arising in farm country of dogs being set on the peddler, but more often he was welcomed, and occasionally offered a lesson in English. Perhaps the wandering life of the peddler led to a farmer's deeper appreciation of a safe roof over his own head and the reassurance of a reliable meal. Peddling was a way for a determined and ambitious a young man to gain a foothold in the business world. The more successful among the peddlers went on to open their own brick-and-mortar stores. H.H. Marks, who lived from 1863 through 1953, was one of the best known and successful of the Black Hills peddlers. Whereas some others used horse and wagon, H.H. carried out his trade on foot, and went on to open a clothing store in Rapid City. He married, and they had a daughter named Elizabeth, a child with long golden curls, over whom the parents obviously doted. After his wife passed away in the late 1920s, H.H. moved to Keystone, where he opened a tailor shop. He died there in 1953 and is buried in the Keystone cemetery. Among those attending his funeral was a small contingent of Jewish people from Rapid City. H.H. was remembered as one of Keystone's more picturesque characters.

Hyman Harry Marks
Photo courtesy Robert Hayes

Another store in Rapid City that was headquarters for Jewish peddlers was Harry Brussels' menswear store. Such fundamentals as were needed for those times as Headlight overalls, similar to those worn by young Russel Frink, were sold at Brussels' establishment, whose store window sported a metal Oshkosh B'Gosh sign. Brussels, a former wagon peddler from eastern South Dakota, either went himself, or sent representatives out into the Hills with packs of goods for sale. Brussels' store was eventually bought by Nathan Horwitz, who brought his wife Ruth and their young family from Duluth to join him in Rapid City in 1948. Horwitz completely remodeled the store, incorporating an adjoining bath house which increased the total floor space, and brought in a Western motif. Other Jewish merchants of Rapid City during the years surrounding the Gold Rush included Jacob and Louis Morris, Hyman Levy, and Felix Poznansky.

Marks Building on Main St., Rapid City
Photo courtesy Minnilusa Historical Association

The Jew Peddler Trail is only a memory. The land on which it sits is privately owned, unmarked, and does not accommodate hikers, but the history of the Jewish peddlers and their trials and trails can never be erased.

One of the ways in which Deadwood recognizes the significance of its pioneers and their descendants is through the Society of Black Hills Pioneers. Among the original Jewish members of this ongoing organization were Ben Baer, Sol Bloom, Benjamin Blumenthal, Paul Rewman, Harris and Nathan Franklin, Jacob Goldberg, David Goldbloom, Paul Rewman, Sam Schwarzwald, Solomon Star, and Charles Zoellner. They are a source of pride to all who appreciate their challenges and contributions.

Charlie Zoellner with the Society of Black Hills Pioneers
Courtesy Centennial Archives, Deadwood Public Library

DEADWOOD'S SYNAGOGUE

The Hebrew Congregation of Deadwood formed early on during the opening days of the Gold Rush. The Hebrew Benevolent Society was organized on April 17, 1879, and although there was congregational worship and Jewish life was open and active, there was never a brick-and-mortar synagogue building in Deadwood. The Vienna Bakery offered matzos for the Passover celebration. Newspaper announcements in the early days of Lead and Deadwood show that there was observance of the high holidays with closing of business establishments. Religious services and holiday observances were held primarily at the Masonic Temple but occasionally at City Hall or the Elks Lodge.

JEWISH CEMETERIES

Mount Moriah Cemetery was established in 1878 and is the resting place of such figures as Calamity Jane, Wild Bill Hickok, and Seth Bullock. Death is the great equalizer. Here madams and murderers lie alongside pillars of society. Sadly, there are many children. Every grave has a story to tell.

Mount Zion, the discrete Jewish section high atop Mount Moriah Cemetery, was a well-kept secret for many years, known primarily to the local population. A visit now always reveals some small stones placed on the gravestones as a token of remembrance left by a visitor or a tourist. Wolff Fink rests in Mount Zion beneath a tombstone engraved in ornate Hebrew. The Colman family plot is simple, with markers for 8 family members, and tells a tragic story of childhood loss. The Wertheimer gravestone is among the oldest, and so badly eroded that it's close to illegible. There are Franklins, Jacobses and Schwarzwalds, Levinsons and Finks, and many more. The official list says there were

86 burials, but in actuality that is a modest number and does not reflect the true numbers of burials, much less the extent of the Jewish population. Most of the Jews of the Gold Rush are buried elsewhere.

One tombstone in Mount Zion, that of Lt. Lester L. Dansky, is particularly intriguing for its comparatively contemporary inscription. The monument, which sits beside that of Mrs. Elizabeth Kiemer, is artistically engraved with the image of an airplane, and indicates that this man was a fighter pilot in WWII. His story is well worth relating. Lester was born in Fallon, Montana, August 6, 1916, second son of 7 children born to immigrants Joseph and Edith Dansky. Joseph had emigrated from Eastern Europe through the port of Galveston, Texas, and arrived in September of 1900, shortly after a disastrous hurricane had wreaked havoc upon the port city, leaving an estimated 8,000 dead in its wake. Following the promise of free homesteading land, Joseph traveled north to Montana, where he met Edith Kristol and they were married in Bowman County in 1911.

In 1932, at the age of 16, Lester left his home in Montana for Deadwood, where he earned a living by applying his love of cars to servicing, selling, and generally working around cars. Through this interest he developed a close friendship with Mrs. Kiemer, a Jewish woman whom he called "Aunt Betty." Elizabeth and Henry Keimer owned Keimer Hall, an establishment for dancing and legitimate entertainment. Lester joined Elks Lodge #508, was a sociable young man who enjoyed skiing, made friends easily, and settled into Deadwood. In 1939 Lester joined the Black Hills Flying Club as Member #13, and took lessons from famed pilot and flight instructor Clyde Ice, a pioneer in aviation. Ice had taught himself aviation by purchasing a surplus WWI tri-wing, repairing it, and flying it. Flying airplanes would also direct Lester's life and his fate.

Lester decided to join the Royal Canadian Air Force in 1941. He wrote home to his sister Irene (Renie) from his training base in Manitoba, inquiring about the family, and telling her that he had joined the RCAF. His training was broken up by a month's-long hospital stay when he was stricken with pleurisy. This was followed 3-1/2 months later by an attack of measles, all of which seriously interrupted his training time. In 1942 he wrote to Renie telling her of a 5-day vacation he took to visit Aunt Betty in Deadwood. He wrote, "I love the Air Force" and said that he would finish his training, become commissioned as an officer, and receive his Wings in May, following which he expected to be shipped overseas to do some "scrapping." He also wrote of his brother Leonard coming to join the RCAF, this organization that he thought so highly of, and saying that he would be home to visit his family before leaving for Europe.

In May of 1942, for reasons unexplained, Lester transitioned from the RCAF to the U.S. Army Air Corps. He received his Wings as a pursuit pilot and was commissioned as a 2nd Lieutenant at Napier Field in Dothan, Alabama. His sister Myrtle traveled there to pin the silver wings on her brother's uniform. Lester's brothers Harold and Leonard also served as Lieutenants in the U.S. Army Air Corps. Renie, served as a volunteer in the Navy WAVES (Women Accepted for Volunteer Emergency Service). This was truly a patriotically dedicated family.

In November of 1942 Lester was stationed in New York at Mitchell Field in central Long Island. The naval base was only 8 miles from Republic Aviation, manufacturers of the P47D Thunderbolt, the plane that he would fly in Europe. In a letter to his mother he said he had transferred from pursuit aircraft to twin-engine bombers, and that Mitchell Field was to be the permanent station for his service squadron.

On June 12, 1943, Lester wrote to Renie from England, speaking of the friendliness of the English people, their "undaunted faith and hope" in the face of the terrific beating they were taking. He remarked about how green the countryside was, something a young man from Montana and South Dakota was sure to notice. In one last letter to his mother written on August 22, 1943, Lester reassures her that the food is good, and not to worry, that he is OK and can take care of himself. A few weeks later, the family received word that Lester was missing in action. On November 24, a telegram arrived informing his family that he had, in fact, been killed in action over England. Military records held at the American Air Museum in Britain say that his plane collided with another fighter plane on August 31. "The Secretary of War extends his deep sympathy." No further explanation was given. Lester was 27 years old. The location of his remains is unknown, but Elizabeth Keimer, or Aunt Betty as he called her, so loved this young man, that she had a monument engraved with a fighter airplane erected next to the plot that she would occupy in Mount Moriah.

Rapid City had two original Jewish burial grounds. The earliest burials from the cemetery high on 8th St., an area that is now highly commercial, were removed to Mountain View Cemetery when that was developed. The historic Jewish burial area in Mountain View Cemetery is now closed to further burials, having been replaced by burial spaces on the western perimeter, close to Sheridan Lake Road.

SYNAGOGUE OF THE HILLS

The Deadwood Torah of the Synagogue of the Hills has an inspiring heritage. Seven generations now trace their connection to the Jewish people who established and perpetuated Jewish life in the days when Dakota was still a Territory and through the infancy years of statehood. To the Jewish pioneers and those that followed, the Torah, inheritance and guidepost, was the center of religious life.

Initially the Torah was kept in the Deadwood home of the Blumenthals. In the years following 1934, it was kept in the home of Sam and Sarah Margolin on Van Buren Street in Deadwood. As the years passed, the population of Deadwood declined, with the younger generation moving on. As Deadwood's need for a Torah gradually diminished, Rapid City was replacing Deadwood as the residential and commercial hub of the Black Hills, and a congregation was formed by the growing Jewish community of Rapid City and nearby Ellsworth Air Force Base. In the 1950s the Deadwood Torah was delivered by the Margolins to the Rapid City home of Morris and Bertha Adelstein. The Adelsteins carried the Torah to Ellsworth Air Force Base, where it would remain in the Base's chapel for 30 years, for use by the Synagogue of the Hills.

In 1996 the congregation decided to leave the Base and relocate to a more convenient location, one closer to Rapid City. The Torah was moved temporarily to the Hills Materials Quarry Room on Sturgis Road owned by Stanford Adelstein. In 1997 Stan, long-time synagogue President and lay leader, donated a permanent residence at 417 North 40th Street in Rapid City and the Deadwood Torah was installed in the present ark alongside a companion, the Shalom Torah from Ellsworth Air Base. The ark, the cabinet in which the ark was installed, was especially built by Joshua Benjamin Stanton.

In 1998 the Deadwood Torah appeared to be in need of koshering, and Ritual Committee Chairman, Steven Benn, sent the Torah to Rabbi Honan in Texas who was asked to perform this *mitzvah*. Rabbi Honan koshered the Torah, replaced the original wooden rollers with new rollers, and wrote, "It is written in a 42 line/column format which dates back 100 years... It is written in an Ashkenazic form, consistent with the alleged German origin... The Torah would not have been handled by a woman, although it is possible that a woman was contracted to act as a carrier since she would be less apt to be the target of vandalism... It is possible that it could have arrived as a dowry... Synagogues were established once *Sefer Torahs* were physically in place".

Rabbi Honan's opinions as to the origins of the Deadwood Torah are consistent with the available historical evidence. This was supported by the analysis of *Sofer* (scribe) Neil Yerman in 2010, when it was decided to have both Torahs re-examined. Torahs can develop irremediable problems such as blurring of their ink over time, rendering them unkosher. Sofer Yerman determined that the Deadwood Torah is written on calfskin in a style that is common to Ashkenzi scribes in Eastern Europe. The ink applied to the lettering is also a product commonly used in the writing of Torahs in Eastern Europe, especially Germany.

Its counterpart in the synagogue, the Shalom Torah, is written on goatskin in a Sephardic style, probably from Spain. Both Torahs are about 150 years old now. The Shalom Torah was found to be the more suitable for repair, but the Deadwood Torah was left as it was, and is considered a treasured historical relic. The original rollers remain in a cabinet at the Synagogue of the Hills, and may someday be replaced, restoring the Deadwood Torah's historical integrity.

WHERE DID ALL THE JEWS GO?

There remained the eternal question of where all the Jewish pioneers went. The same question might be applied to many remote communities of that era around the country. The answer was all too simple.

A few of Deadwood's Jewish pioneers, like Jacob Wertheimer, rest in Mount Zion. They may have left the old towns, mining camps, and homesteads for greener pastures. Some just made their fortunes and were gone, but many more left with empty pockets.

As the Gold Rush subsided, the allure of warmer climes or bigger cities was a great temptation. Goldberg left for California, the Franklins for New York, Baer for St. Paul. After high school, most of their children reached for higher education and for a wider pool of potential spouses.

The youngsters, like their parents and grandparents, wanted newer, broader opportunities. Also, I was assured that Dakota winters can be cruel. That alone, no doubt, factored into many a decision to leave.

SOME BLACK HILLS JEWISH PIONEERS

Each year on Yom Kippur, the names of the deceased are memorialized on a Yizkor Memorial List, kept at Rapid City's Synagogue of the Hills, where the Deadwood Torah also resides. The oldest list contains the names of some of the Jewish pioneering ancestors. This list contains about 300 names, but it is far from complete. There were many wives and children whose names never were mentioned, and many people who took part in this epoch who will forever remain anonymous.

Abrams, Max

Agrant family

Aldrich, Theresa Nathan

Aldrich, Leo

Appel, Morris

Baer, Ben (Banker, Silent partner of Harris Franklin; Organized first stock exchange)

Baer, Ida Flarsheim, (Mrs. Ben)

Baer, Ira

Baer, Helen

Baer. Jerome

Baer, Fernand

Baer, Edwin

Baker, Louis (Jew Flats homesteader)

Baum, Meyer (Buried in Mt. Zion)

Berg, I. (Lead jeweler)

Behrman, Jacob

Bernard, Albert (Buried in Mt. Zion)

Bloom, Bertha

Bloom, Sol (Clothing merchant, Deadwood and Lead)

Blumenson, Gertrude

Blumenthal, Abe (Clothing merchant, father of 7 in Blumenthal Family Band)

Blumenthal, Benjamin (Arranged to bring Torah from Germany, Bnai Brith)

Blumenthal, Frieda Lowenthal (Came to Deadwood with Torah)

Blumenthal, Saul

Blumenthal, Sarah

Blumenthal, Dorothy

Blumenthal, Minnie

Bober, Mrs. Sam

Bober, Sam (Seed expert from Russia)

Borst, William (Jew Flats homesteader)

Brown, William (Member of first Chevreh Kaddishe)

Burstin, Bertha (Buried in Mt. Zion)

Cahn, Gus

Chamison, J. (Buried in Mt. Zion)

Chamison, Mrs J. (Buried in Mt. Zion)

Chamison, Paul

Chasen, Aaron (Jew Flats homesteader)

Chesen, Ezek (Jew Flats homesteader)

Cohen (Partner in gold-mining firm of Lewis, Cohen & Johnson)

Cohen, Alexander (Buried in Mt. Zion)

Cohen, H.

Cohen, Israel

Cohen, L.

Cohen, Maurice

Cohen, Robert

Cohen, Pincus

Cohen, Mrs. Frankie B.(Buried in Mt. Zion)

Cohen, Sol

Cohn, Ed

Cohn, Isaac

Cohn, P.

Cohne, Abraham ("Abe", Jew Flats)

Cohne, Fanny Sinykin Steinberg (Mrs. Abe, Jew Flats)

Colman, Amalia (Arrived in Deadwood with infant Anne. Buried in Mt. Zion alongside Nathan and 6 of her 7 children)

Colman, Anne (First Jewish child to arrive in Deadwood; Married by father Nathan in Franklin Hotel; Buried in Chicago)

Colman, Blanche (First Jewish child born in Deadwood; First woman attorney in Black Hills; Buried in Mt. Zion)

Colman, Nathan (First Jewish Lay Leader in Deadwood; Judge; Merchant, Buried in Mt. Zion)

Colman, Theresa (Daughter of Nathan and Amalia; Lawrence County Auditor, Buried in Mt. Zion)

Cowan, Israel (Bnai Brith)

Dansky, Lt. Lester L. (Buried in Mt. Zion)

Deutsch, Louis

Ehrman, Sol

Epstein, Lewis

Fantle, Charles

Fantle, Sam

Feenburg, Infant (Buried in Mt. Zion)

Feiler, Celia (Buried in Mt. Zion)

Fink, Anna (Buried in Mt. Zion)

Fink, Herman

Fink, Joseph (Deadwood pawnbroker, Buried in Mt. Zion)

Fink, Louis

Fink, Wolff (Wolf) (Jeweler, owner of jewelry manufacturing business, Lead, Buried in Mt. Zion)

Fishel, Adolph (newsdealer)

Fishel, Mrs. Adolph

Fishel, Clara L.

Fishel, Gus

Fishel, Hazel

Fishel, Louis (newsdealer)

Fishel, Max (Deadwood merchant)

Fist, Emanuel

Flarsheim, S.

Fox, Burt (Jew Flats homesteader)

Frank, Fannie (Buried in Mt. Zion)

Frank, Child of Moses (Buried in Mt. Zion)

Frankenberg, Alex (Prospector for gold)

Franklin, Bernard (Barney) (Brother of Harris, large family in Central City)

Franklin, Barney's child (Buried in Mt. Zion)

Franklin, Barney's infant (Buried in Mt. Zion)

Franklin, Harris (Deadwood liquor merchant, City Council, County Commissioner; Organized first stock exchange)

Franklin, Anna (Wife of Harris, Buried Mt. Zion)

Franklin, Mildred (Daughter of Nathan, raised in Franklin mansion)

Franklin, Nathan (Son of Harris, Pharmacist; Deadwood's Mayor for 4 years; Franklin Hotel)

Friedlander, M.

Friedlander, Miss

Friedwald, Max (Lead)

Friedwald, Mrs M.

Gavenman, Peggy

Gavenman, Lawrence

Goldberg, D. (Clothier, Deadwood)

Goldberg, F.

Goldberg, J. (Clothier, Deadwood)

Goldberg, Jacob (Grocer, Board member first public library, Deadwood)

Goldberg, Joseph (Deadwood Grocer, Son of Jacob)

Goldberg, Julia (Daughter of Jacob)

Goldberg, Mrs. Jacob

Goldberg, Ralph

Goldberg, Sam (Son of Jacob, Deadwood Grocer)

Goldbloom, Bonnie

Goldbloom, David (Buried in Mt. Zion)

Goldbloom, Dorothy

Goldbloom, Bertha

Goldbloom, Jennie (Wife of David, Buried in Mt. Zion)

Goldbloom, M.

Goldstone, David (Peddler)

Gottstein, Dora

Gottstein, Infant of Dora, Buried in Mt. Zion)

Gottstein, J.

Gottstein, Samuel H. (Nephew of Meyer, Buried in Mt. Zion)

Gottstein, Meyer (Mike) (Partner of Harris Franklin and Max Idelman), Liquor merchant, Deadwood)

Grantz Mrs. O. P.

Grantz, O. P.

Gross, L.V.

Grossfeld, Ed (Spearfish)

Gumbiner (Merchant)

Haas, Ed

Halle, Nathan (Buried in Mt. Zion)(rooms w/ Sol Rosenberg & Co)

Halstine, Abraham (Buried in Mt. Zion)

Hammitt, George (Jew Flats homesteader)

Hattenbach, Aaron (Grocer; Supervisor at U.S. Grant Mining Co.)

Hattenbach, Adelia (Adele)

Hattenbach, David

Hattenbach, Dena

Hattenbach, Joseph

Hattenbach, Jennie (Wife of Joseph)

Hattenbach, Nathan

Hattenbach, Arthur

Hattenbach, Flora

Hattenbach, Maurice

Hattenbach, Leah

Hattenbach, Zetta

Hattenbach, Laurence

Hess, Sam (Cattleman)

Heyme, Charles

Himmelman, Sam

Hoffman, Abraham

Holstein, Louis

Holstein, Belle

Holstein, Nettie

Holzman, David (Clothing merchant; Married Rebecca Reubens, first Jewish bridegroom in Deadwood)

Holzman, child (Buried in Mt. Zion)

Hutter, H. (Buried in Mt. Zion)

Hyman, Charles H. (salesman w/ Sol Bloom)

Idelman, Max (Partner of Myer Gottstein)

Israel, Mrs. (mother of Ida Levinson)

Jacobs, Berthald (Clothing merchant, Deadwood, Buried in Mt. Zion)

Jacobs, Ruth (Clothing merchant, Wife of Berthald, Buried in Mt. Zion)

Jacobs, Dora (Wife of Simon, accompanied Torah from Germany to Deadwood)

Jacobs, D.J. (confectionery)

Jacobs, L.D. (Jacobs' Bazaar, Lead)

Jacobs Mrs. L.D.

Jacobs, Louis

Jacobs, Morris

Jacobs, Nathan

Jacobs, Henry

Jacobs, Sidney (Clothing merchant New York Store; Deadwood's second Lay Rabbi)

Jacobs, Simon (Merchant; carried Torah from Germany to Deadwood)

Jacobs, Sheldon

Jacobs, Doran

Kaufman, -

Keimer, Elizabeth (Owner of Keimer Hall; Buried Mt. Zion)

Keimer, Carl

Keimer, Henry H.

Kessler (Dry goods store in Carbonate)

Kiehlbauch, Henry (Jew Flats homesteader)

Klein, Charles (Owner Deadwood's first movie theater)

Klein, Hilda (Mrs. Charles)

Koenigsberger, S.

Koenigsberger,

Kohen, Mrs. Thomas

Kohn, Child

Kohorn, B.H.

Kohorn, Sidney (Buried in Mt. Zion)

Kohorn, Infant of Sidney (Buried in Mt. Zion)

Kozberg, Hyman (Rabbi, Jew Flats)

Kozberg, Jacob Paul (Jew Flats; Saloon owner Lead & Deadwood)

Kozberg, Ruth Rachel Sinykin (Jew Flats, Mrs. Jacob Paul)

Krainson, Isaac. J. (Lead tailor) (Buried Mt. Zion)

Krainson, Charlotte, Wife of Isaac, Buried Mt. Zion)

Kronick, Lewis (Jew Flats)

Kuh, Julius

Levinson, Bernard

Levinson, Rebecca Marx

Levinson, Sol (Deadwood jeweler, Buried in Mt. Zion)

Levinson, Joseph (Lead, Deadwood, Rapid City jeweler; Buried in Mt. Zion)

Levinson, Ida

Levy, Charles M.

Levy, Hyman (Rapid City tailor)

Liebmann, L.

Liebmann, Morris

Liebmann, Mrs. Morris

Lilienthal (Merchant; Officer first Jewish Benevolent Society)

Liverman, Moses

Livingston, Joseph

Lowe, W.E.

Lowenthal, Ben

Lowenthal, David

Lowenthal, Esther

Lowenthal, Augusta (Gussie)

Loewenthal, Max

Lowenthal, Pauline

Magee, David

Mandel Brothers (Clothing merchants, Deadwood)

Margolin, Sam (Clothing merchant, New York Store, Deadwood; Jew Flats)

Margolin, Sarah

Margolin, Faye Jean

Margolin, Henry (Jew Flats)

Margolin, Hugh

Margolin, Peggy

Marks, Harry Hyman (Merchant, Keystone and Rapid City, Buried Keystone Cemetery)

Marks, Elizabeth (Daughter of Harry Hyman)

Martinsky, Bertha (Homesteader, Kadoka merchant, Buried in Des Moines)

May, Aaron

Mayer, Simon

Meyer, Elmer (Jew Flats homesteader)

Meyer, Louis (Jew Flats homesteader)

Minzer, Louis (Buried in Mt. Zion)

Minzer, Gus L.

Morris, Jacob (Dry goods merchant, Rapid City)

Morris, Julian

Morris, Lewis (Dry goods merchant, Rapid City)

Moskovitch, Isadore ("Issie" Marsh, Jew Flats)

Moskovitch, Rose Sinykin (Mrs. Isadore Marsh, Jew Flats)

Moskovitch, Cecelia

Munter, William (Merchant; Officer first Jewish Benevolent Society)

Nathan, Charles

Nathan, Leo

Nathan, Louis

Nathan, Tessie

Niederman, Maurice (Liquor merchant, Deadwood; married Anne Colman, moved to Chicago)

Oppenheimer, Ben

Pincus, L.

Posner, Charles

Poznansky, A.J.

Poznansky, Blanche

Poznansky, Benjamin (First male graduate South Dakota School of Mines, Rapid City)

Poznansky, Felix (Deadwood, then Montana Store Rapid City, tailor. First mohel in Black Hills)

Poznansky, Joseph

Poznansky, Julia (Member original Synagogue of the Hills, Rapid City)

Poznansky, Marcus (Mox) (youth was Rapid City herder; Insurance business as adult)

Poznansky, Bertha (Mrs. Felix)

Poznansky, Rosa

Poznansky, Sol

Rabinovich, Lorence (Jew Flats homesteader)

Rabinovich, Zelda (Jew Flats homesteader)

Reuben, J.

Reuben, Leah

Reubens, Louis (Conducted first Jewish wedding, Deadwood)

Reubens, Mrs. Louis (Home held first Jewish wedding, Deadwood)

Reubens, Rebecca (First Jewish bride, Deadwood)

Reubenstein, Julius

Rewman, Paul (English Jew, President first telephone company, President first light and power company) Society of Black Hills Pioneers, Buried in St. Ambrose Cemetery, Deadwood)

Rivin, Isaac (Jew Flats homesteader)

Robbins, Joseph L (Jew Flats homesteader)

Roet, Isaac (Blacksmith, farmer, Camp Crook)

Roet, Jenny (Wife of Isaac)

Rosenbaum, L.

Rosenbaum, J.

Rosengarden, M.

Rosenthal, James

Rosenthal, Jennie

Rosenthal, Leo

Rosenthal, Miss Laura

Rosenthal, Solomon (Clothing merchant, Rosenthal's Palace, Deadwood)

Rosenkranz, Fred

Rosenkranz, Henry

Roth, Moses B (Jew Flats homesteader)

Rubin, Daughter of Ida L. (Buried in Mt. Zion)

Safken, August (Jew Flats homesteader)

Safken, George (Jew Flats homesteader)

Salinsky (Clothing merchant, New York Store, Deadwood)

Schelesky, Jacob (Jew Flats homesteader)

Schiller, J.A.

Schwartz, J

Schwarzwald, Sam (Furniture merchant, Deadwood)

Schwarzwald, Gussie (Furniture merchant, Deadwood)

Selig, Joe W (Jew Flats homesteader)

Shane, Dora

Shane, Frances

Shane, I.

Shane, Mrs I.

Shane, Samuel

Shapiro, Joseph (Jew Flats homesteader)

Snider, Goldie P. (Jew Flats homesteader)

Shneerer, Frederick Benjamin

Shulkin, Solomon (Jew Flats homesteader)

Siegel, Henry

Siegel, Joseph

Siegel, Solomon

Silver, Oscar (Clothing merchant, Deadwood and Lead)

Silver, Mrs. Oscar

Silverberg, Henry

Silverberg, Joseph

Sinykin, Etta Fanny Koval (Mrs. Harry) (Mother of Fanny, Ted, Jack, Rose, Ruth & Louis, Jew Flats)

Sinykin, Harry D. (Father of Fanny, Ted, Jack, Rose, Ruth & Louis, Jew Flats)

Sinykin, Abraham Louis A. ("Bronco Lou", Jew Flats)

Sinykin, Fanny (Jew Flats)

Sinykin, Florence Mairowitz (first wife of Louis A., Jew Flats)

Sinykin, Florence Adams (second wife of Louis A., Jew Flats)

Sinykin, Arthur Theodore. ("Ted", Jew Flats)

Sinykin, Betty Juster (Mrs. Arthur Theodore, Jew Flats)

Sinykin, John L. ("Jack", Jew Flats)

Sinykin, Genevieve Bloom (Mrs. John L., Jew Flats)

Star, Solomon (Deadwood's first Jewish mayor for 14 years; Hardware merchant; Deadwood Flouring Mill; Postmaster; Partner of Seth Bullock; Organized first stock exchange; Owner S&B Ranch, Belle Fourche; Mason; Society of Black Hills Pioneers; Unmarried; Buried St. Louis)

Stein, -Steinberg, Harry (first husband of Rose Sinykin, Jew Flats)

Steinberg, Benjamin (son of Fanny and Harry Steinberg, Jew Flats)

Steinberg, Cecelia (daughter of Fanny and Harry Steinberg, Jew Flats)

Stern, M. (salesman, Bloom's Clothing Store)

Strass, Rosa

Strool, Benjamin

Strool, Reizel

Usdansky, Isaac (Jew Flats homesteader)

Waxman, Reuben (Jew Flats homesteader)

Weidenfeld, A.

Welf, Art (Merchant, Black Hills Mercantile)

Welf, Benjamin

Welf, Infant of B. Welf (Buried in Mt. Zion)

Werner, -

Wertheimer, Henriette/Henrietta (Owner Merchant's Hotel, Deadwood; Buried in Mt. Zion)

Wertheimer, Jacob (City Councilman, Owner Merchant's Hotel, Deadwood; Buried in Mt. Zion)

Wertheimer, Henry

Wertheimer, M.J. (Max)

Wertheimer, Louis

Whitehead, Judge Ed (Officer first Hebrew Benevolent Society)

Whitehead, Mrs. Ed

Wilfing, Albert (Buried in Mt. Zion)

Wolf, Frieda

Zoeckler brothers

Zoellner, Arthur (son of Charles and Charlotte)

Zoellner, Charles I.

Zoellner, Charlotte (Mrs. Charles)

Zoellner, Jonas

Darling, you asked me if any of their stories in particular resonated with me from among this remarkable collection of Jewish pioneers. Where can I even start?

One episode in the later years of the lives of Blanche and Tess Colman touched me to the core and reminded me of how their lives spanned such important historical happenings, from the opening of the Black Hills Gold Rush, to the first air mail flight, through two world wars, and into the catastrophic years of the Holocaust.

In a letter which her great-nephew Al Alschuler, dated February 6, 1976, shared with me, Blanche wrote of the Homestake Mine, her employer, reaching a depth of 8,000 feet in its quest for gold ore. It's hard to imagine the determination, the equipment and the manpower involved in such an undertaking in a day with only the basic tools of the Industrial Revolution available to them. Today, having since been sold off by the Homestake Mining Company, that complex cavern yields a very different treasure. It has been converted into an underground science laboratory for studying neutrinos, tiny particles from space that reveal the Earth's origins, and where other scientific experiments in physics and biology are taking place. Now, millions of dollars are being dedicated to these experiments, not only by the U.S., but by science laboratories around the world. Thanks to all that digging in the ground, someday a Nobel Prize may come of one or more of these experiments. Remember, Darling, your Grandma made this prediction.

I recently received a wonderful message from a gentleman named Carl Stern sent to Al Alschuler, referring to the heroic actions of his great-aunts Blanche and Tess Colman during the World War II.

"A few days ago, I received a copy of your well written essay about Blanche Colman. You make mention that Blanche issued an affidavit to me which enabled me to emigrate to U.S. I would like you to know that Blanche in 1937, issued papers to my entire family including my parents and sister. By early 1938, when Blanche and Tess felt that our family was comfortably settled in New York City, they issued affidavits to my mother's sister and family including two young daughters. I would estimate that in total Blanche and her sister were directly responsible for bringing 5 families totaling at least 20 individuals to U.S. and saving them from the perils of the Holocaust. I recall that both of these ladies frequently expressed regret that they were unable to save my mother's youngest sister and family with 3 young children who unfortunately perished in the Holocaust. The papers they issued arrived too late.

In my opinion no collection about Blanche would be complete without mentioning the people they helped to get out of Germany... After my parents and wife, Blanche and her sister Tess rank as the most important people in my life and without their kind help it is most likely that I too would have perished in the Holocaust.

Best regards,
Carl Stern"

But what about Felix Poznansky and his fellow Jews in 1879 Rapid City, who tried to rescue Jews from the misery being inflicted upon them in anti-Semitic Eastern Europe? Had their plan to open up Rapid Valley as an agricultural colony succeeded, just think of how that might have changed Rapid City.

How did this experience change me, you ask? The search was enthralling, and it became an inspiring journey into our past. It gave me a much deeper appreciation for what it means to be Jewish, and strong, and adventurous in a young America, where just getting from here to there was a monumental, dangerous, time-consuming effort. And we complain about the inconvenience of travel on jet airplanes?

Now, a time when women have come into their own, it's hard to imagine fighting for the right to vote or to manage our own finances, or to have a say in deciding how many children we will bear. We take these for granted now. With only a few exceptions, women of the 1880s were expected to remain in the shadows of their husbands. There was little recognition of women's names, much less their accomplishments, in the newspapers of the late 1800s and early 1900s. Society notices relegated ladies' activities to card parties and teas. There were some outstanding professionals, businesswomen, activists, and volunteers, but for the most part, women took a back seat.

Darling, did you know that my mother, who lived in a tenement on the Lower East Side of New York when she first came to America, had seven little babies to take care of? Can you imagine her carrying bundles of wet wash that she'd just scrubbed on a washboard, up to the roof so that she could dry the laundry in the sun? And we complain if our washing machine breaks down and we have to drive to the laundromat?

As of 1959, the length of time since the Black Hills Gold Rush took place, only a little over 80 years, precious little had been researched or written about the Jews who contributed to that landmark era. From the 1876 Gold Rush stampede into the Black Hills, to the passing of Blanche Colman, who at age 94 was the last of Deadwood's originals, the Jewish pioneers were more than a footnote to Black Hills history; they were influential, active participants in the main story. Their history must not be allowed to vanish into the ether. Until the Jewish chapter of western South Dakota's place in America's story has been included, the account remains incomplete. Rapid City's Synagogue of the Hills, keeper of the Deadwood Torah, carries on the legacy the Jewish pioneers of the Black Hills Gold Rush laid down in 1876. They did more than pass through—they mattered.

Rapid City Journal, Sep 7, 1963
Synagogue of the Hills Sunday school will begin classes for children 5 years and up Sunday at 10 a.m. at the Auto Bankers Building, Seventh and St. Joe. The Sisterhood of the Synagogue is in charge. Anyone wishing information on the course of study may call Mrs. M.A. Rivkin at FI2-1669.

So darling, now you know the story, at least the part that I was able to find. There was so much more—more people, more incidents, but I'm sorry to say those will remain untold. So many lives with stories to tell. There were Jewish stories everywhere. There still are.

The editors of the New York Lantern loved it, you know, but it had an unsatisfying ending: the magazine fell on hard times, went into bankruptcy, was forced to shutter its doors. The story never got printed. Perhaps their story will find its way into print someday, and maybe you'll be the one to write it. Here are my notes, take them, they're yours now. Find more stories.

**Red Rockers on porch of Franklin Hotel, 1999
Diana Haber Hirsch, Rabbi Howard Berman,
Ann Haber Stanton**
Photo by Daniel Stanton

BIBLIOGRAPHY
BOOKS:

Estelline Bennett, **Old Deadwood Days**
    Lincoln and London: University of Nebraska Press, 1928.

Laura Bower VanNuys, **The Family Band, from the Missouri to the Black Hills 1881-1900**
    Lincoln and London: University of Nebraska Press, 1961

John O. Bye, **Back Trailing in the Heart of Short Grass Country**
    Everett Alexander Printing Company, 1956

Directory of Sioux City Jewry, December 1969

Eastern Pennington County Memories,
    Wall, SD: American Legion Auxiliary, Carrol McDonald Unit, 1965

Mildred Fielder, **Carbonate Camp, SD Historical Collections**, undated

Mildred Fielder, **Silver Is the Fortune**
    Pierre: SD State Historical Society, undated

William J. Fishman, **East End Jewish Radicals. 1875-1914**
    London: Gerald Duckworth and Co., 1975

Orlando Goehring, **Keeping the Faith: Bertha Martinsky in West River Dakota,**
    South Dakota History Bulletin

Ernest Grafe and Paul Horsted, **Exploring with Custer**
    Custer: Golden Valley Press, 2002

Paul Haivala, **Short History of Black Hills State University**
    Black Hills State University

Alvin M. Josephy Jr., **Black Hills, White Sky**
    Times Books, 1978

George Kingsbury, **History of Dakota Territory**
    1915

Irma Klock, **Central Black Hills**
    Pierre: SD State Historical Society 1986

Irma H. Klock, **All Roads Lead to Deadwood**
    Pierre: State Publishing Co., 1978

Mary Kopco, **Adams House Revealed.** Deadwood: Adams Museum and House, 2006.

Lawrence County Historical Society, **Some History of Lawrence County**, Deadwood, 1981.

Bob Lee, **Gold, Gals, Guns, Guts**
Pierre: South Dakota State Historical Society Press, 1976

Kenneth Libo, **We Lived There Too: In Their Own Words and Pictures - Pioneer Jews and the Westward Movement of America, 1630-1930**
New York: St. Martin's-Griffin, 1984

Thomas Loomis, **A Holy Terror, the Uncle Sam and the Golden Reward: in Shadows of the Homestake**
(2000-2003) MATRIX Vol. 10, No. 3, Keystone Area Historical Society, 1991

John McClintock, **Pioneer Days in the Black Hills**
Norman: University of Oklahoma Press, 193.

James McLaird, **Hard Knocks, A Life Story of the Vanishing West, by Harry (Sam) Young**
Pierre: South Dakota Historical Society Press, 2005

Rick Mills, **Railroading in the Land of Infinite Variety**
Hermosa: Battle Creek Publishing Co., 1990

George Moses, **Those Good Old Days in the Black Hills**
Rapid City: Rapid City Journal, 1981

Allan N. Niederman, **Colmans of Deadwood & Niedermans of Chicago, Family Album, Chicago**

Watson Parker, **Black Hills Ghost Towns**
Athens: Swallow Press, 1974

Watson Parker, **Gold in the Black Hills**
Lincoln and London: University of Nebraska Press, 1966

Watson Parker, **Deadwood, the Golden Years**
Lincoln and London: University of Nebraska Press, 1981

Eka Parkison, **Rapid City Pioneers of the 19th Century, Volume 2**
Rapid City: Rapid City Society for Genealogical Research, 1997

Beverly Pechan, **Deadwood, 1876-1976**
Charleston: Arcadia Publishing, 2005

Beverly Pechan, **Keystone and its Colorful Characters**
Keystone: Permelia Publishing, undated.

Bernard Postal, **A Jewish Tourist's Guide to the U.S.**, undated.

Rachel Calof, et al, **Rachel Calof's Story, Jewish Homesteader on the Northern Plains,**
Bloomington and Indianapolis: Indiana University Press, 1995

Helen Rezzato. **Mount Moriah, Kill a Man- Start a Cemetery**
Rapid City: Fenwyn Press, 1989

Doane Robinson. **Encyclopedia of South Dakota**
    Pierre, 1925

Harriet Rochlin, **Pioneer Jews, A New Life in the Far West**
    Wilmington: Houghton-Mifflin, 2000

Linda Mack Schloff, **And Prairie Dogs Weren't Kosher**
    St. Paul: Minnesota Historical Society Press, 1996

Howard Shaff, **Paving the Way: The Life of Morris E. Adelstein**
    Keystone: Permelia Press, undated

Bernard Shuman, **A History of the Sioux City Jewish Community, 1869-1969**
    1969, Bolstein Creative Printers, Inc. Sioux City

David Strain, **Black Hills Hay Camp: Images and Perspectives of Early Rapid City**
    Dakota West Books & Fenske Printing, 1989

Donald Toms, **Flavor of Lead, an Ethnic History**
    Lead: Lead Historic Preservation Commission, 1992

Sophie Trupin, **Dakota Diaspora, Memoirs of a Jewish Homesteader**
    Lincoln and London: University of Nebraska Press, 1984

Laura Bower Van Nuys, **The Family Band, From the Missouri to the Black Hills, 1881 to 1900**
    University of Nebraska Press, Lincoln, 1961

Sally Roesch Wagner, **Daughters of Dakota, Schooled in Privation**
    Yankton: Self-published, 1991

Mark S. Wolfe, **Boots on Bricks, Walking Tour of Historic Downtown Deadwood**
    Deadwood: Deadwood Historic Preservation Commission, 1996

David A. Wolff, **Seth Bullock: Black Hills Lawman**
    South Dakota State Historical Society Press, 2009

ESSAYS & ARTICLES:

Al Alschuler, **Colmans and Others of Deadwood.**
    Western States Jewish Historical Quarterly, Judah Magnes Museum, Berkeley, July 1977

Blanche Colman, **Early Jewish History of the Black Hills of South Dakota,**
    Deadwood, 1953

George Moses, **Those Good Old Days in the Black Hills.**
    Rapid City Journal, 1991

Janet Dunlap Rathbun, **All Roads Lead to Strool: A Short History of a Small Town in Perkins County, South Dakota**, Presented at the Dakota History Conference, 2003

WEBSITES:

www.deadwood.searchroots.com, Deadwood "South Dakota Revealed"
   Webmaster: Jerry Brown, 2004

www.realsouthdakota.com,
   Webmaster: Daniel J. Stanton

www.oldstonehouse.com,
   Webmaster: Diana Hayes

www.rcfoundersparkplaza2.blogspot.com
   Webmaster: Richard Dunwiddie

PERIODICALS:

Adams Banner, editors, Jerry L. Bryant and Mary Kopco.

Black Hills Daily Times

Deadwood Magazine

Deadwood Pioneer

Deadwood Public Library Index of Historical Newspaper Archives. Newsprint content

New York Times

Rapid City Journal, George Moses' weekly columns

South Dakota Magazine

South Dakota Dept. of History, Report and Historical Collections,
   compiled by the SD Historical Society, Pierre, Vol XXXI, copyright 1962. pp.333-334

South Dakota History Bulletin, Winter 2006 edition

HISTORICAL ORGANIZATIONS:

Adams Museum - Deadwood History, Inc.

Homestake Adams Research and Cultural Center

Minnilusa Historical Society

Journey Museum and Learning Center

Westerners, Black Hills Corral

Jewish American Society for Historic Preservation

CONTRIBUTORS:

David Akrop
Marc Aldrich
Al Alschuler
Marion Bernstein
Ellen Bishop
Emily Buckhannon
Richard Dunwiddie
Russel Frink
Rose Mary Goodson
Faye Gitter
Arlette Hanson
Linda M. Hasselstrom
Florence Hawki
Robert Hayes
Chris Hills
Diana Haber Hirsch
John Hirsch
Lise King
Jerry Klinger
Mary Kopco
Rick Mills
George Moses
Joyce Niederman
Michael Niederman
James Watson Parker
Watson Parker
Olga Parker
Beverly Pechan
Charles Rambow
Sihaya Reed
David Stanton
Daniel Stanton
Joshua Stanton
David Strain

INTERVIEWS:

Stanford M. Adelstein
Marc Aldrich
Sarah Niederman Alschuler
Rabbi Howard Berman
Jerry L. Bryant
Russel Frink
David Gradwohl
Ruth and Nathan Horwitz
Etta Fay Orkin
Dr. Watson Parker
Eka Parkison
Steve Norquist
Charles Rambow
Janet Dunlap Rathbun
Reid Riner
Diane Sinykin Small
William E. Walsh

ABOUT THE AUTHOR

Ann Haber Stanton at Black Hills Ghost Town of Tinton

Ann Haber Stanton moved to South Dakota from New York City in 1959 and loves living in the green Black Hills. Rapid City was a great place to raise her three sons, David, Joshua, and Daniel.

In 2001, she participated in Leadership Rapid City, a program designed to groom community leaders. LRC was the springboard for designing Founders Park Plaza, an outdoor history lesson about the birth of her adopted hometown.

Ann is a longtime member of the Synagogue of the Hills, the only synagogue serving the Jewish community for 350 miles in any direction. She began to research the history of the Black Hills' Jewish population in 1991. Impressed at how profoundly Jewish pioneers had been involved in settling and developing the Black Hills and surrounding communities, she was disappointed to learn how little was written about that unique Jewish experience. She has been researching, writing, and giving talks on this subject since 1992.

www.ingramcontent.com/pod-product-compliance
Lightning Source LLC
Chambersburg PA
CBHW081227080526
44587CB00022B/3849